STRATEGIC MANAGEMENT
PRINCIPLES AND PRACTICE

Barry J. Witcher & Vinh Sum Chau

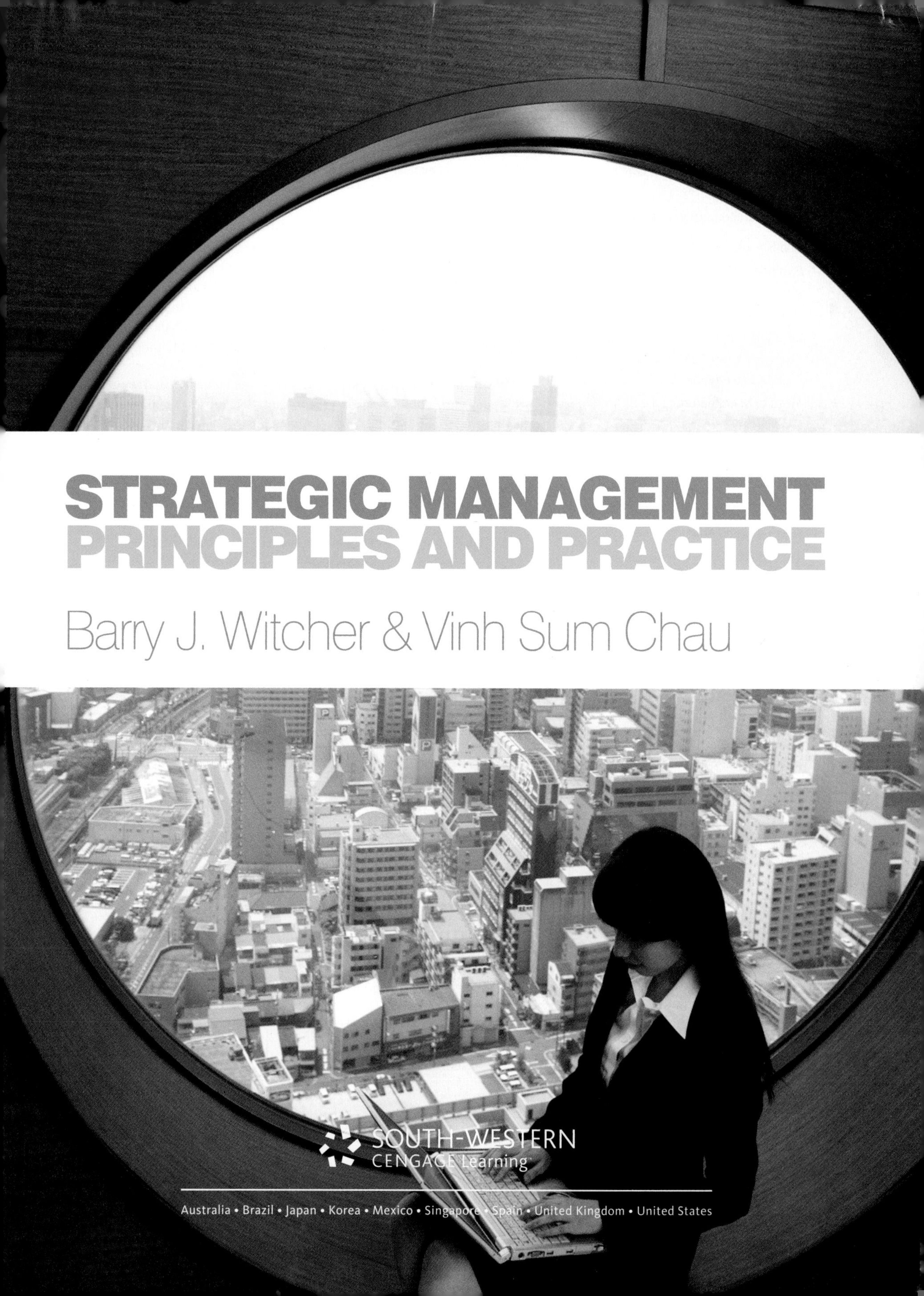

STRATEGIC MANAGEMENT
PRINCIPLES AND PRACTICE

Barry J. Witcher & Vinh Sum Chau

SOUTH-WESTERN
CENGAGE Learning

Australia • Brazil • Japan • Korea • Mexico • Singapore • Spain • United Kingdom • United States

Strategic Management: Principles and Practice

Barry Witcher and Vinh Chau

Publishing Director: Linden Harris

Publisher: Thomas Rennie

Development Editor: Charlotte Loveridge and Jennifer Seth

Editorial Assistant: Charlotte Green

Content Project Editor: Oliver Jones and Adam Paddon

Head of Manufacturing: Jane Glendening

Senior Production Controller: Paul Herbert

Typesetter: Knowledgeworks Global Ltd.

Cover design: Adam Renvoize

Text design: Design Deluxe

For product information and technology assistance, contact **emea.info@cengage.com**.

For permission to use material from this text or product, and for permission queries, email **clsuk.permissions@cengage.com.**

British Library Cataloguing-in-Publication Data
A catalogue record for this book is available from the British Library.

ISBN: 978-1-84480-993-6

Cengage Learning EMEA
Cheriton House, North Way, Andover,
Hampshire, SP10 5BE, United Kingdom

Cengage Learning products are represented in Canada by Nelson Education Ltd.

For your lifelong learning solutions, visit **www.cengage.co.uk**

Purchase your next print book, e-book or e-chapter at **www.CengageBrain.com**

Printed in China
1 2 3 4 5 6 7 8 9 10 – 12 11 10

Dedications

Per Kate, mia moglie, che è la mia vita. Also for my daughters, Che, Rosamund and Ashley.
– B. J. Witcher.

In loving memory of my dearest grandmother, who in life strived to be educated, through whose living virtues this book strives to educate. Thank you for 30 years of upbringing, and an eternity of fulfilment.
– V. S. Chau.

Brief contents

What is strategy? 3

Determinants of strategy 57

Strategy 153

Strategy development 237

Contents

List of cases

Preface and acknowledgements

As we write these words hard rain is falling on the world's economies. The economic boom of the opening years of the twenty-first century has ended. This will have profound consequences for organizations and their strategic management. Most of all the change is likely to have a profound impact upon how people think about how organizations should be managed. This is due, at least in part, because some believe that it is the strategic mismanagement of organizations that has brought the economic troubles upon us.

Certainly the *management* part of strategic management is every bit as important as the 'strategic' or 'strategy' part. We have written this book in a way that we hope we have been true to our belief that management matters. In other words, we think strategic management should be a managed organization-wide process or activity. The final responsibility for strategic management belongs to an organization's top and senior managers.

Everybody in some way is a part of strategic management and has to some degree responsibility, but the primary aim of strategic management is to manage an organization in its entirety so that it will achieve its overall and longer-term purpose. This can only be the responsibility of the top.

The purpose of this book is to help you understand how organizations can be managed as a whole and in a changing world. It introduces theory in ways that engage readers who have little or no business and management experience. Thus it is suitable for first degree-level courses in business and management. It is likewise suitable for people who may already have a first degree or equivalent qualification in a non-management subject, but who are now taking a first business and management qualification such as a certificate, diploma, or masters.

The conceptual essentials of strategic management are presented in ways that help the reader to understand concisely, and easily, the prescriptive and emergent perspectives that are current in the subject. The practical importance of organizational context is emphasised in the light of current international issues and debates. Included with the standard models and approaches is an emphasis upon seeing clearly how the strategic context is different from functional management.

Organization of the Text

The structure of the parts and sequence of the book's chapters are shown in the Figure. The different colours correspond to four broad areas of strategic management: strategic purpose (green), strategic analysis (red), level of strategy (yellow), and implementation (blue).

The first part of the book covers strategic purpose. It provides an overview of the (often competing) perspectives of the subject (chapter 1), and explains the central importance of purpose, which is the necessary starting point for understanding the strategic management of any organization (chapter 2).

The second part concerns strategic analysis. It includes the use of strategic objectives to provide a balanced framework (chapter 3) for the analysis of external influences and the opportunities and threats facing an organization (chapter 4), and the internal resources and the strengths and weaknesses of an organization (chapter 5).

The third part of the book considers strategy at a single organization level (chapter 6), the corporate level, which takes into account strategy for managing several organizations (chapter 7), and strategy for global (internationally-focused) organization (chapter 8).

The final part covers implementation. It takes into account organizing (chapter 9), managing implementation to enable performance (chapter 10), and strategic leadership (chapter 11).

While the book's structure (see the figure) would seem to offer a managed and planned sequence for strategic management, a word of warning is necessary. This order of things does not mean that strategic management is a compartmentalised process of

FIGURE: The order of chapters

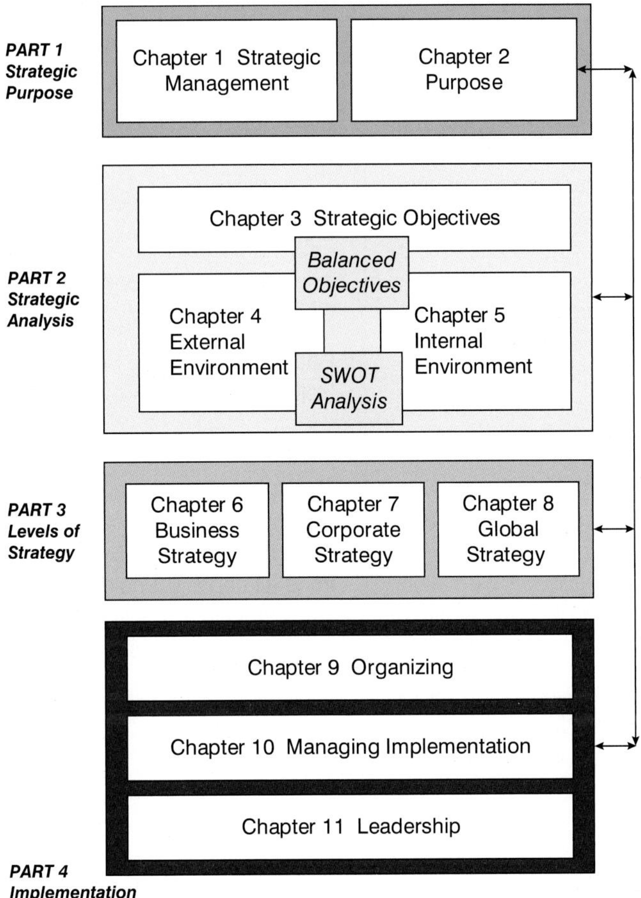

activity. Quite the reverse is true. Strategic management is a holistic and integrated business function. Purpose, strategic objectives, and the strategy to achieve these objectives, must always be considered together.

This is also true of implementation: this is the translation of longer-term purpose, objectives and strategy, into organizational structures, management systems, and daily management. While practically, the management of the long and shorter-term components of strategic management may be the responsibility of different people, they inform each other at all times (see the directions of the arrows in the figure).

Strategic management is a relatively new business and management subject, which has advanced substantially from its corporate strategy roots.[1] It is probably the most alive of all those subjects that comprise business management and help make the discipline a coherent field of study and research. Strategic management has its fair share of paradigmatic, theoretical and methodological wars. Current issues and interpretations of what constitutes success and failure are changing all the time. Almost as soon as they are written, case studies are out-of-date and theories fly out of fashion, typically to reappear later in another guise.

So, be warned! Be on your guard. Read textbooks and articles in a discerning way and always keep an open mind. Be clear about where you think ideas come from and be conscious of the perspectives, context and the complexity that produce them. Consider pros and cons, and think about how a particular theory may (or may not) be appropriate to a particular instance of practice.

Businesses and organizations have a wide variety of management approaches and techniques available to them. There is often no 'one answer' for solving an issue. Nonetheless managers must still make their particular choices. So, be clear about the logic of any decision for any particular instance. You should decide, as any manager must, and reach a definite conclusion for the particular case under consideration. In so doing, always disentangle your views and ideas from those of others.

1 See Howard Thomas, 'Forward: theoretical pluralism and multi-disciplinary traditions', in Jenkins M. & Ambrosini V. (2007), *Advanced Strategic Management: A Multi-Perspective Approach,* London: Palgrave Macmillan.

The publisher thanks the following academics who supplied feedback on the original proposal or during the writing process:

Dermot Breslin, Management School, University of Sheffield

Peter Considine, Staffordshire University Business School, Staffordshire University

Sheena Davies, Portsmouth Business School, University of Portsmouth

Jonathan Gander, Faculty of Business and Law, Kingston University

Mairi Gudim, Business School, University of the West of Scotland

Ken Russell, Aberdeen Business School, The **Robert Gordon University**

Andy Sharp, Caledonian Business School, Glasgow Caledonian University

Catherine L. Wang, School of Management, Royal Holloway University of London

Tjeerd Zandberg, Stenden University

The publisher also thanks the various copyright holders for granting permission to reproduce material throughout the text. Every effort has been made to trace all copyright holders, but if anything has been inadvertently overlooked the publisher will be pleased to make the necessary arrangements at the first opportunity. Please contact the publisher directly.

About the authors

Dr. Barry J. Witcher

Dr Barry J. Witcher is Reader in Strategic and General Management at the Norwich Business School, University of East Anglia (UEA) where he teaches strategic, general and change management and is Principal Director of the MSc courses. He holds a BSc in economics and a PhD in advanced econometrics. Barry has attracted major ESRC grants for conducting research in strategic planning and performance management frameworks for strategy deployment and implementation after starting his career in the City of London's banking and financial sector. Over the years, he has supervised over 30 PhD students to completion and held a number of esteemed visiting positions at overseas universities. He is also Chair of the UK Hoshin Kanri Practitioner's Network (established under ESRC funding) – details can be found at: www.hoshin-kanri.co.uk. Publications include articles in the *Journal of Marketing, Journal of Management Studies, British Journal of Management* and *International Journal of Operations and Production Management.*

Dr. Vinh Sum Chau

Dr Vinh Sum Chau is Lecturer in Strategy and Strategic Management at the University of East Anglia's Norwich Business School and faculty member of the UK ESRC Centre for Competition Policy (CCP). He holds a BSc with honours in economics and law, an MSc with distinction in business management and a PhD in strategic management. At UEA, Vinh currently teaches strategic management to bachelor and masters students and business research methods to masters and doctoral students where he is also convener of the Business School's distinguished scholars research seminar series and annual doctoral colloquium. He is also Chair of the School's Research Ethics Committee and Deputy Director of the postgraduate research programme. Vinh holds the Chair of the British Academy of Management's special interest group and annual conference track in Performance Management and he has hosted a number of national seminars funded by the ESRC and published widely in the areas of performance management, strategy implementation, service quality, and customer satisfaction. Publications include articles in the *British Journal of Management, International Journal of Operations and Production Management* and *Journal of Services Marketing.*

Walk through tour

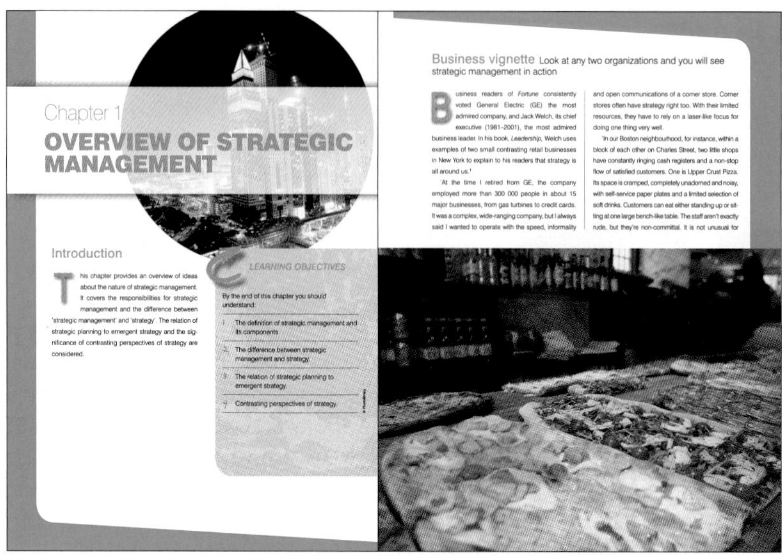

Chapter 1

OVERVIEW OF STRATEGIC MANAGEMENT

Introduction

This chapter provides an overview of ideas about the nature of strategic management. It covers the responsibilities for strategic management and the difference between 'strategic management' and 'strategy'. The relation of strategic planning to emergent strategy and the significance of contrasting perspectives of strategy are considered.

LEARNING OBJECTIVES

By the end of this chapter you should understand:

1. The definition of strategic management and its components.
2. The difference between strategic management and strategy.
3. The relation of strategic planning to emergent strategy.
4. Contrasting perspectives of strategy.

Business vignette Look at any two organizations and you will see strategic management in action

Business readers of *Fortune* consistently voted General Electric (GE) the most admired company, and Jack Welch, its chief executive (1981–2001), the most admired business leader. In his book, *Leadership*, Welch uses examples of two small contrasting retail businesses in New York to explain to his readers that strategy is all around us.[1]

'At the time I retired from GE, the company employed more than 300 000 people in about 15 major businesses, from gas turbines to credit cards. It was a complex, wide-ranging company, but I always said I wanted to operate with the speed, informality and open communications of a corner store. Corner stores often have strategy right too. With their limited resources, they have to rely on a laser-like focus for doing one thing very well.

'In our Boston neighbourhood, for instance, within a block of each other on Charles Street, two little shops have constantly ringing cash registers and a non-stop flow of satisfied customers. One is Upper Crust Pizza. Its space is cramped, completely unadorned and noisy, with self-service paper plates and a limited selection of soft drinks. Customers can eat either standing up or sitting at one large bench-like table. The staff aren't exactly rude, but they're non-committal. It is not unusual for

Learning Objectives Appear at the start of every chapter to help you monitor your understanding and progress.

Chapter 6

BUSINESS-LEVEL STRATEGY

Introduction

Chapters 4 and 5 were about the external and internal environments; once an organization understands these, it must manage its overall strategy for achieving its purpose. This chapter is about business-level, or single business, strategy. A **business level strategy** can be defined as the organization's fundamental strategic choice of what approach to adopt to achieve its competitive advantage from the given options at the business unit level. Corporate-level, or multi-business, strategy is discussed in the following chapter. This chapter considers competitive advantage and generic strategy; the role of the value chain for managing these; the concept of the business model; and strategy activity mapping.

LEARNING OBJECTIVES

By the end of this chapter you should understand:

1. The meaning of a business-level strategy.
2. Generic strategies as a basis for competitive advantage.
3. The value chain as a vehicle for managing generic strategy and strategic activities.
4. Business models and strategy activity maps.

Business vignette Strategies involve inter-connecting and tailoring activities ...

In an interview in 2004, Henry Mintzberg tells how much he admires strategy at IKEA, the Swedish home furnishings retailer: 'An organization that I think has a wonderfully integrated strategy is IKEA. Think about all the intricate interconnections and how that strategy has worked out piece by piece in all kinds of intricate, fascinating ways by people living every aspect of it.'[1]

Similarly Michael Porter writes about how effectively the company manages its activities: 'IKEA targets young furniture buyers who want style at low cost. What turns this marketing concept into a strategic position is the tailored set of activities that make it work ... to perform activities different from its rivals.'[2]

Anders Dahlvig, the IKEA chief executive, explains his organization's competitive advantage as a totality of many things: 'Many competitors could try to copy ... The difficulty is when you try to create the totality of what we have. You might be able to copy our low prices, but you need our volumes and global sourcing presence. You have to be able to copy our Scandinavian design, which is not easy without a Scandinavian heritage. You have to be able to copy our distribution concept with the flat-pack. And you have to be able to copy our interior competence – the way we set out our stores and catalogues.'[3]

Business Vignette Appear at the start of each chapter to show how issues are applied in real-life business situations.

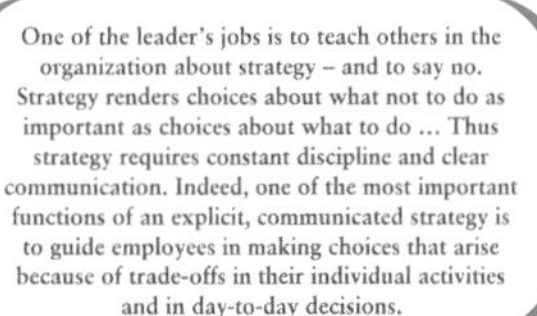
One of the leader's jobs is to teach others in the organization about strategy – and to say no. Strategy renders choices about what not to do as important as choices about what to do ... Thus strategy requires constant discipline and clear communication. Indeed, one of the most important functions of an explicit, communicated strategy is to guide employees in making choices that arise because of trade-offs in their individual activities and in day-to-day decisions.

Quotes Quotes are used throughout the text to illustrate a spectrum of opinions; these are ideal for provoking class discussion and examination questions.

Principles in Practice Examples of key principles in real-life scenarios.

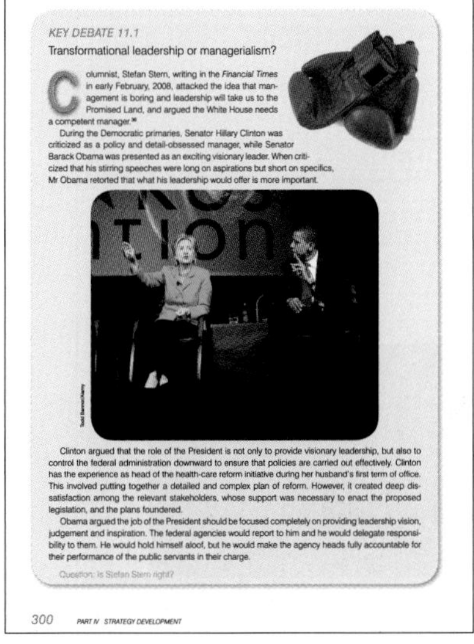

Key Debates Discussions of different perspectives on key issues.

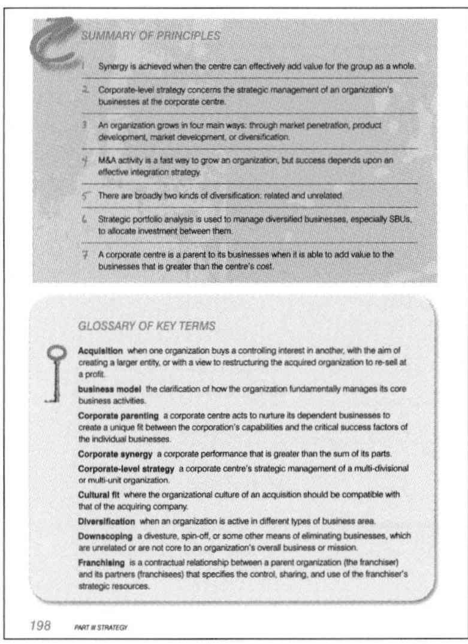

Summary Each chapter ends with a comprehensive summary that provides a thorough re-cap of the key issues, helping you to assess your understanding and revise key conent.

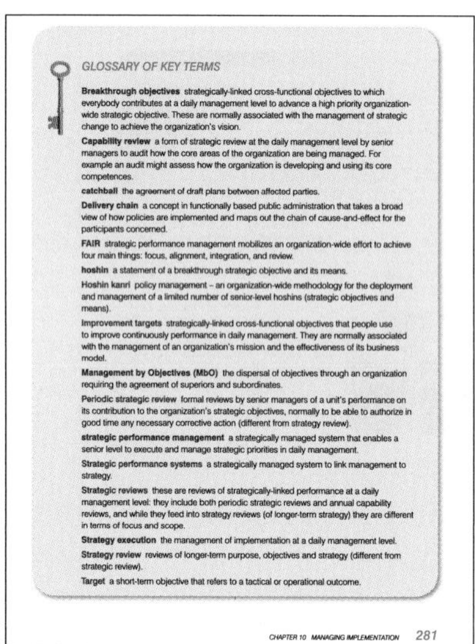

GLOSSARY OF KEY TERMS

Breakthrough objectives strategically-linked cross-functional objectives to which everybody contributes at a daily management level to advance a high priority organization-wide strategic objective. These are normally associated with the management of strategic change to achieve the organization's vision.

Capability review a form of strategic review at the daily management level by senior managers to audit how the core areas of the organization are being managed. For example an audit might assess how the organization is developing and using its core competences.

catchball the agreement of draft plans between affected parties.

Delivery chain a concept in functionally based public administration that takes a broad view of how policies are implemented and maps out the chain of cause-and-effect for the participants concerned.

FAIR strategic performance management mobilizes an organization-wide effort to achieve four main things: focus, alignment, integration, and review.

hoshin a statement of a breakthrough strategic objective and its means.

Hoshin kanri policy management – an organization-wide methodology for the deployment and management of a limited number of senior-level hoshins (strategic objectives and means).

Improvement targets strategically-linked cross-functional objectives that people use to improve continuously performance in daily management. They are normally associated with the management of an organization's mission and the effectiveness of its business model.

Management by Objectives (MbO) the dispersal of objectives through an organization requiring the agreement of superiors and subordinates.

Periodic strategic review formal reviews by senior managers of a unit's performance on its contribution to the organization's strategic objectives, normally to be able to authorize in good time any necessary corrective action (different from strategy review).

strategic performance management a strategically managed system that enables a senior level to execute and manage strategic priorities in daily management.

Strategic performance systems a strategically managed system to link management to strategy.

Strategic reviews these are reviews of strategically-linked performance at a daily management level: they include both periodic strategic reviews and annual capability reviews, and while they feed into strategy reviews (of longer-term strategy) they are different in terms of focus and scope.

Strategy execution the management of implementation at a daily management level.

Strategy review reviews of longer-term purpose, objectives and strategy (different from strategic review).

Target a short-term objective that refers to a tactical or operational outcome.

CHAPTER 10 MANAGING IMPLEMENTATION 281

Glossary and Key Terms Key terms are highlighted in colour throughout and explained in full at the end of each chapter, enabling you to find explanations of key terms quickly.

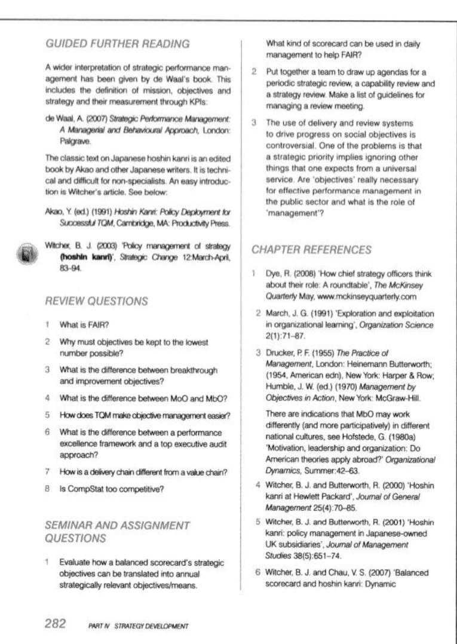

GUIDED FURTHER READING

A wider interpretation of strategic performance management has been given by de Waal's book. This includes the definition of mission, objectives and strategy and their measurement through KPIs:

de Waal, A. (2007) *Strategic Performance Management: A Managerial and Behavioural Approach*, London: Palgrave.

The classic text on Japanese hoshin kanri is an edited book by Akao and other Japanese writers. It is technical and difficult for non-specialists. An easy introduction is Witcher's article. See below:

Akao, Y. (ed.) (1991) *Hoshin Kanri: Policy Deployment for Successful TQM*, Cambridge, MA: Productivity Press.

Witcher, B. J. (2003) 'Policy management of strategy **(hoshin kanri)**', *Strategic Change* 12:March-April, 83-94.

REVIEW QUESTIONS

1 What is FAIR?
2 Why must objectives be kept to the lowest number possible?
3 What is the difference between breakthrough and improvement objectives?
4 What is the difference between MoO and MbO?
5 How does TQM make objective management easier?
6 What is the difference between a performance excellence framework and a top executive audit approach?
7 How is a delivery chain different from a value chain?
8 Is CompStat too competitive?

SEMINAR AND ASSIGNMENT QUESTIONS

1 Evaluate how a balanced scorecard's strategic objectives can be translated into annual strategically relevant objectives/means. What kind of scorecard can be used in daily management to help FAIR?
2 Put together a team to draw up agendas for a periodic strategic review, a capability review and a strategy review. Make a list of guidelines for managing a review meeting.
3 The use of delivery and review systems to drive progress on social objectives is controversial. One of the problems is that a strategic priority implies ignoring other things that one expects from a universal service. Are 'objectives' really necessary for effective performance management in the public sector and what is the role of 'management'?

CHAPTER REFERENCES

1 Dye, R. (2008) 'How chief strategy officers think about their role: A roundtable', *The McKinsey Quarterly* May, www.mckinseyquarterly.com
2 March, J. G. (1991) 'Exploration and exploitation in organizational learning', *Organization Science* 2(1):71–87.
3 Drucker, P. F. (1955) *The Practice of Management*, London: Heinemann Butterworth; (1954, American edn), New York: Harper & Row; Humble, J. W. (ed.) (1970) *Management by Objectives in Action*, New York: McGraw-Hill.
There are indications that MbO may work differently (and more participatively) in different national cultures, see Hofstede, G. (1980a) 'Motivation, leadership and organization: Do American theories apply abroad?' *Organizational Dynamics*, Summer:42–63.
4 Witcher, B. J. and Butterworth, R. (2000) 'Hoshin kanri at Hewlett Packard', *Journal of General Management* 25(4):70–85.
5 Witcher, B. J. and Butterworth, R. (2001) 'Hoshin kanri: policy management in Japanese-owned UK subsidiaries', *Journal of Management Studies* 38(5):651–74.
6 Witcher, B. J. and Chau, V. S. (2007) 'Balanced scorecard and hoshin kanri: Dynamic

282 PART IV STRATEGY DEVELOPMENT

Online Encyclopaedia Icons These appear throughout the text to link concepts being discussed in the main text with more detailed explanations available in the online encyclopaedia provided on the companion website.

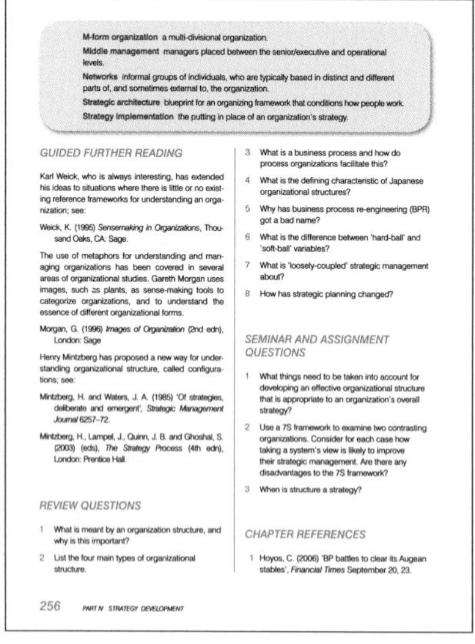

M-form organization a multi-divisional organization.

Middle management managers placed between the senior/executive and operational levels.

Networks informal groups of individuals, who are typically based in distinct and different parts of, and sometimes external to, the organization.

Strategic architecture blueprint for an organizing framework that conditions how people work.

Strategy implementation the putting in place of an organization's strategy.

GUIDED FURTHER READING

Karl Weick, who is always interesting, has extended his ideas to situations where there is little or no existing reference frameworks for understanding an organization; see:

Weick, K. (1995) *Sensemaking in Organizations*, Thousand Oaks, CA: Sage.

The use of metaphors for understanding and managing organizations has been covered in several areas of organizational studies. Gareth Morgan uses images, such as plants, as sense-making tools to categorize organizations, and to understand the essence of different organizational forms.

Morgan, G. (1996) *Images of Organization* (2nd edn), London: Sage

Henry Mintzberg has proposed a new way for understanding organizational structure, called configurations; see:

Mintzberg, H. and Waters, J. A. (1985) 'Of strategies, deliberate and emergent', *Strategic Management Journal* 6257–72.

Mintzberg, H., Lampel, J., Quinn, J. B. and Ghoshal, S. (2003) (eds), *The Strategy Process* (4th edn), London: Prentice Hall.

REVIEW QUESTIONS

1 What is meant by an organization structure, and why is this important?
2 List the four main types of organizational structure.
3 What is a business process and how do process organizations facilitate this?
4 What is the defining characteristic of Japanese organizational structures?
5 Why has business process re-engineering (BPR) got a bad name?
6 What is the difference between 'hard-ball' and 'soft-ball' variables?
7 What is 'loosely-coupled' strategic management about?
8 How has strategic planning changed?

SEMINAR AND ASSIGNMENT QUESTIONS

1 What things need to be taken into account for developing an effective organizational structure that is appropriate to an organization's overall strategy?
2 Use a 7S framework to examine two contrasting organizations. Consider for each case how taking a system's view is likely to improve their strategic management. Are there any disadvantages to the 7S framework?
3 When is structure a strategy?

CHAPTER REFERENCES

1 Hoyos, C. (2006) 'BP battles to clear its Augean stables', *Financial Times* September 20, 23.

256 PART IV STRATEGY DEVELOPMENT

Further Reading At the end of each chapter allows you to explore the subject further, and acts as a starting point for projects and assignments.

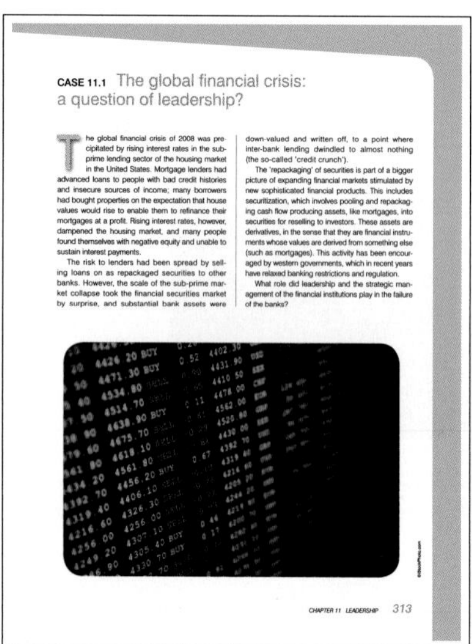

CASE 11.1 The global financial crisis: a question of leadership?

The global financial crisis of 2008 was precipitated by rising interest rates in the sub-prime lending sector of the housing market in the United States. Mortgage lenders had advanced loans to people with bad credit histories and insecure sources of income; many borrowers had bought properties on the expectation that house values would rise to enable them to refinance their mortgages at a profit. Rising interest rates, however, dampened the housing market, and many people found themselves with negative equity and unable to sustain interest payments.

The risk to lenders had been spread by selling loans on as repackaged securities to other banks. However, the scale of the sub-prime market collapse took the financial securities market by surprise, and substantial bank assets were down-valued and written off, to a point where inter-bank lending dwindled to almost nothing (the so-called 'credit crunch').

The 'repackaging' of securities is part of a bigger picture of expanding financial markets stimulated by new sophisticated financial products. This includes securitization, which involves pooling and repackaging cash flow producing assets, like mortgages, into securities for reselling to investors. These assets are derivatives, in the sense that they are financial instruments whose values are derived from something else (such as mortgages). This activity has been encouraged by western governments, which in recent years have relaxed banking restrictions and regulation.

What role did leadership and the strategic management of the financial institutions play in the failure of the banks?

CHAPTER 11 LEADERSHIP 313

End of Chapter Cases Long cases discuss in depth the issues and principles encountered during the chapter.

About the website

Visit the Strategic Management: Principles & Practice companion website at www.cengage.co.uk/witcher or www.cengage.co.uk to find valuable teaching and learning material including:

For students

- Online encyclopaedia providing supplementary information and linked throughout the text using the online encyclopaedia icons
- Web links to relevant companies and other resources
- Review questions and answers to test and develop understanding

For lecturers

- Instructor's manual with teaching notes containing helpful hints and tips for answering questions that appear in the text
- PowerPoint slides of the key ideas and illustrations from the textbook.
- Additional case studies
- ExamView test bank

These resources can also be uploaded to any major virtual learning environments, such as Blackboard/WebCT and Moodle, and please contact your local Cengage Learning representative (see: http://edu.cengage.co.uk/contactus/) should you wish to pursue this.

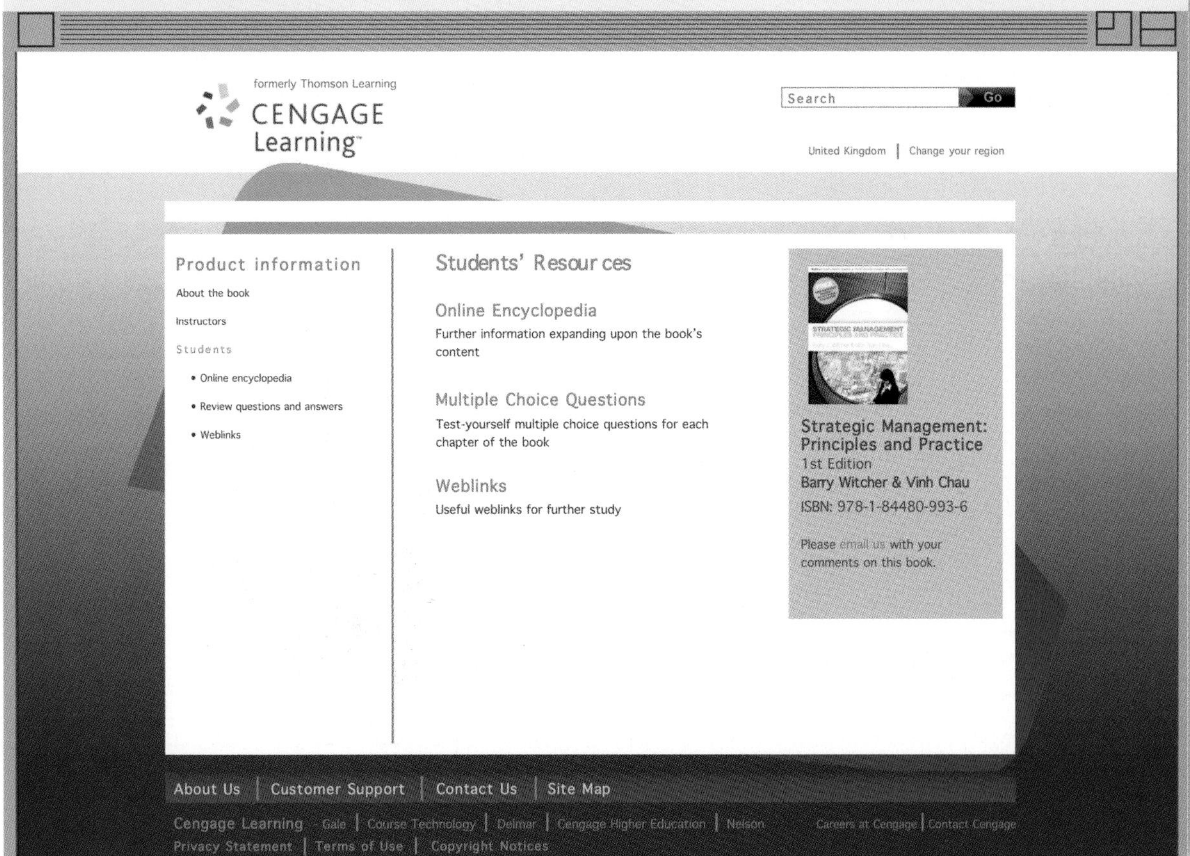

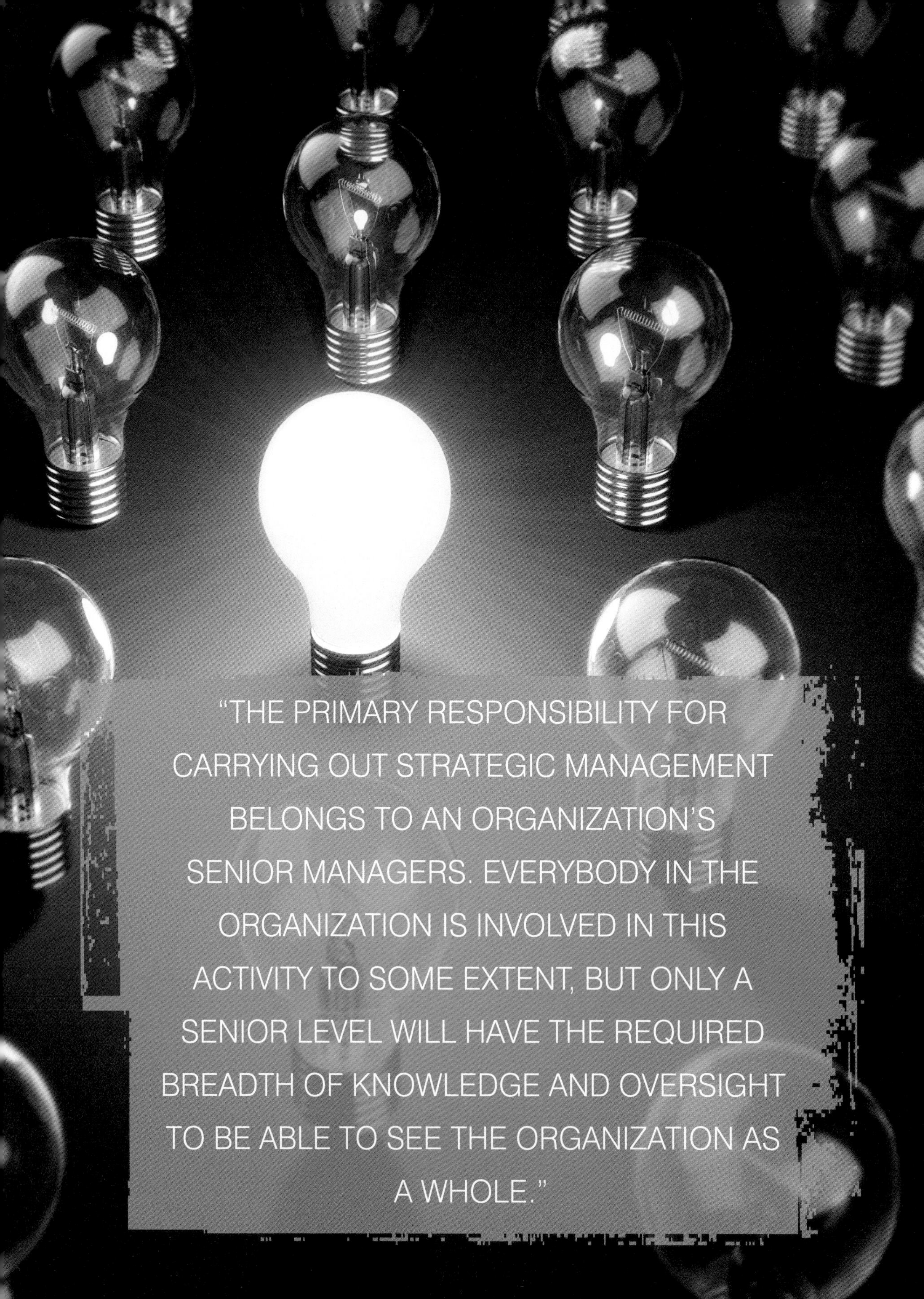
"THE PRIMARY RESPONSIBILITY FOR
CARRYING OUT STRATEGIC MANAGEMENT
BELONGS TO AN ORGANIZATION'S
SENIOR MANAGERS. EVERYBODY IN THE
ORGANIZATION IS INVOLVED IN THIS
ACTIVITY TO SOME EXTENT, BUT ONLY A
SENIOR LEVEL WILL HAVE THE REQUIRED
BREADTH OF KNOWLEDGE AND OVERSIGHT
TO BE ABLE TO SEE THE ORGANIZATION AS
A WHOLE."

What is strategy?

PART I WHAT IS STRATEGY?

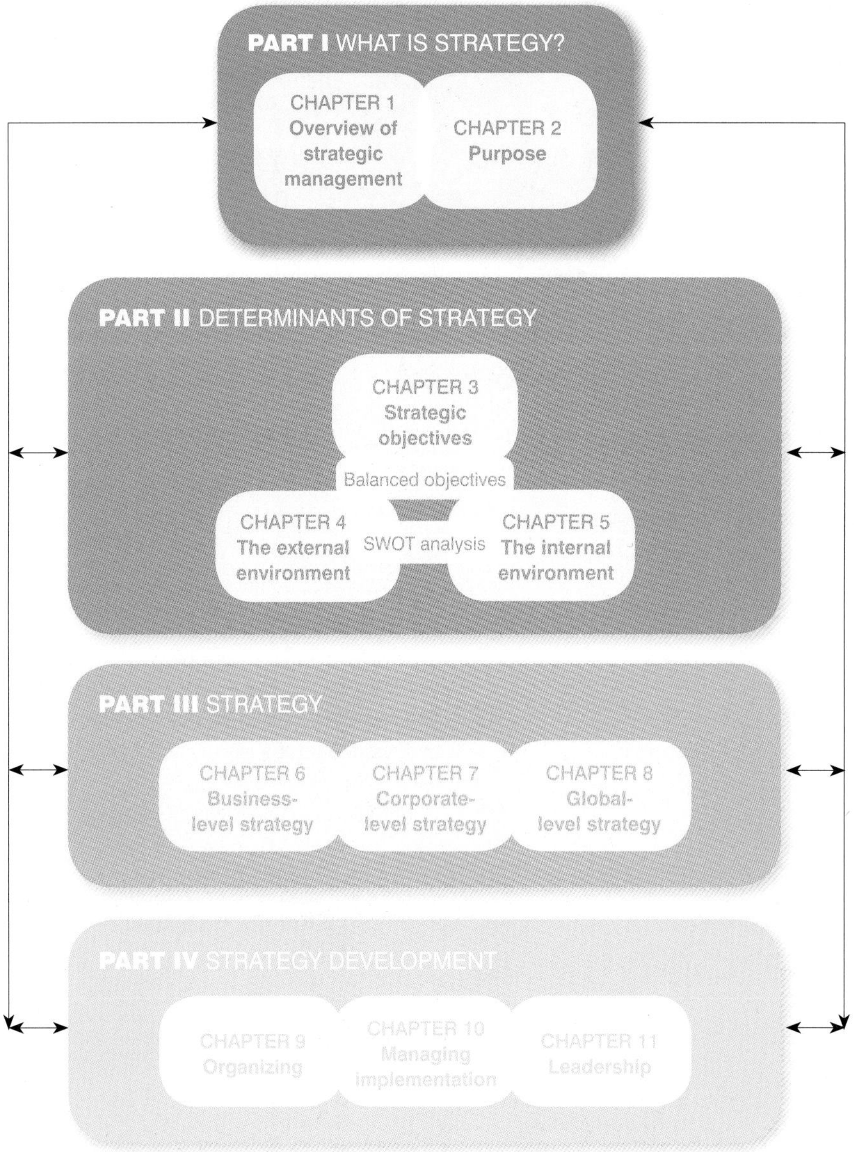

CHAPTER 1 **Overview of strategic management**

CHAPTER 2 **Purpose**

PART II DETERMINANTS OF STRATEGY

CHAPTER 3 **Strategic objectives**

Balanced objectives

CHAPTER 4 **The external environment**

SWOT analysis

CHAPTER 5 **The internal environment**

PART III STRATEGY

CHAPTER 6 **Business-level strategy**

CHAPTER 7 **Corporate-level strategy**

CHAPTER 8 **Global-level strategy**

PART IV STRATEGY DEVELOPMENT

CHAPTER 9 **Organizing**

CHAPTER 10 **Managing implementation**

CHAPTER 11 **Leadership**

Chapter 1

OVERVIEW OF STRATEGIC MANAGEMENT

Introduction

This chapter provides an overview of ideas about the nature of strategic management. It covers the responsibilities for strategic management and the difference between 'strategic management' and 'strategy'. The relation of strategic planning to emergent strategy and the significance of contrasting perspectives of strategy are considered.

LEARNING OBJECTIVES

By the end of this chapter you should understand:

1. The definition of strategic management and its components.
2. The difference between strategic management and strategy.
3. The relation of strategic planning to emergent strategy.
4. Contrasting perspectives of strategy.

Business vignette Look at any two organizations and you will see strategic management in action

Business readers of *Fortune* consistently voted General Electric (GE) the most admired company, and Jack Welch, its chief executive (1981–2001), the most admired business leader. In his book, *Leadership,* Welch uses examples of two small contrasting retail businesses in New York to explain to his readers that strategy is all around us.[1]

'At the time I retired from GE, the company employed more than 300 000 people in about 15 major businesses, from gas turbines to credit cards. It was a complex, wide-ranging company, but I always said I wanted to operate with the speed, informality and open communications of a corner store. Corner stores often have strategy right too. With their limited resources, they have to rely on a laser-like focus for doing one thing very well.

'In our Boston neighbourhood, for instance, within a block of each other on Charles Street, two little shops have constantly ringing cash registers and a non-stop flow of satisfied customers. One is Upper Crust Pizza. Its space is cramped, completely unadorned and noisy, with self-service paper plates and a limited selection of soft drinks. Customers can eat either standing up or sitting at one large bench-like table. The staff aren't exactly rude, but they're non-committal. It is not unusual for

your order – given at the cash register – to be greeted with a bland 'Whatever'. But the pizza is to die for; you could faint just describing the flavour of the sauce, and the crust puts you over the edge. Investment bankers, artists and cops start lining up at eleven in the morning to see the "Slice of the Day" posted on the door, and around lunch and dinner, the line can run twenty deep. A fleet of delivery people work non-stop until closing. At Upper Crust, strategy is all about product.

'Then there's Gary Drug, about half the size of a New York subway car. A large, newly renovated, twenty-four-hour pharmacy is a short walk away. No matter. Gary Drug, with its sinister, narrow aisle and shelves packed to the ceiling, is always busy. Its selection ranges from cold remedies to alarm clocks, with tweezers and pencil sharpeners mixed in. There is a personable pharmacist tucked in back, and a wide selection of European fashion magazines in a comer up front. Everything the store sells matches the mix of the neighbourhood's quirky residents. Salespeople greet customers by name when they walk in and happily give advice on everything from vitamins to foot massages. The store offers instant home delivery and a house charge account that bills you once a month. At Gary Drug, strategy is all about service.'

Strategic management

Strategic management is the management of an organization's overall purpose, to ensure that the needs and enablers of the present are balanced with those of the future. (Purpose is defined and discussed in Chapter 2.) The subject's perspective takes an overall and holistic view of organizational management. The different parts of strategic management (as outlined on page 309) should work together in harmony to deliver to the organization's **stakeholders** the value they expect over time. Thus, while every business management subject covers strategic issues, their perspective is partial and typically about functional strategy.

While strategic management is applicable to every type and size of organization, an important role for many is to achieve and sustain competitive advantage. This requires not only that an organization should be fit for purpose, but that it should have a strategy to create value that will enable it to compete effectively with rivals.

Responsibilities for strategic management

The primary responsibility for carrying out strategic management belongs to an organization's senior managers. Everybody in the organization is involved in this activity to some extent, but only a senior level will have the required breadth of knowledge and oversight to be able to see the organization as a whole. In a large and complex organization it is likely that the time senior managers spend on strategic management will take most of their time and for other levels it will be much less.

Strategic management is the management of an organization's overall purpose, to ensure that the needs and enablers of the present are balanced with those of the future.

KEY DEBATE 1.1

What is strategic management?

Paul Robinson, a speech writer for President Reagan, wrote a book about his time as a student at Stanford University in California,[28] in which he said he thought strategic management '... gives a sense of a subject that didn't know what it was. One article, entitled Crafting Strategy, argued executives should develop their business strategy the way potters crafted clay, abandoning conscious, analytical thought in favour of feel and intuition ... This Mintzberg was the author who had compared running big companies to making clay pots.'

In fact, the titles of textbooks and college programmes display a bewildering variety of names, such as 'business policy', 'corporate strategy', 'competitive strategy', or just 'strategy'. On the whole, these texts emphasize strategic thinking and leadership, rather than management.

These differences stem, at least in part, from the variety that exists in the range of different social science and business management perspectives. Mintzberg and others[29] compare strategy to an elephant and suggest there are ten different schools of strategy, which are different from each other because they only look at a part of the strategy elephant.

This is ironic, because if strategy is about anything, it is about seeing the whole picture, even if it is as big as an elephant.

Question: If you were a business person how would you want to see strategy?

Figure 1.1 shows how the amounts of time spent by different participants in strategic and daily management are likely to differ. **Daily management** is work carried out in those parts of the organization that are primarily about shorter-term operational and functional activity.

In the sense that daily management must be consistent with the overall needs of the organization, strategic management is sometimes considered to be a top-down management process. Strategic management should guide an organization's personnel in how they develop their own objectives and plans to support a senior level's strategy. It is also bottom-up in that everybody should have some role in developing and feeding back reports on progress in whichever part of the organization they are working. While strategic planning is likely to be sequenced within a pre-determined planning cycle, or calendar, strategic management is a broader, flexible, and continuous activity. This also applies to an organization's overall strategy, which is a subset of strategic management.

FIGURE 1.1 Involvement in strategic management

Strategy and strategic management

In the context of an overall strategic management process, an organization's **strategy** is an overall approach, or a general pattern of behaviour, for achieving an organization's purpose, including its strategic objectives. A strategy is necessary if an organization is to take both a long and broad view to managing its activities over time: the long view is important for setting the overall direction of the enterprise and is fundamentally about strategic change, while the broad view is important for managing synergy and is fundamentally about strategic control.

Strategy developed as a business management concept in the 1960s, in the work of Alfred Chandler, a business historian, who used strategy as a concept for understanding the structures used by large organizations to manage growth,[2] and Igor Ansoff who had been a vice-president at Lockheed Electronics.[3] Chandler understood strategy as a pattern of objectives, which includes purposes or goals, and the major policies and plans for achieving these. Ansoff, however, argued that objectives and strategy (which might include policies and plans) were different since they act upon each other: a strategy is used to achieve an objective, and if a strategy cannot be found, then the objective has to be changed to make it more realistic. The idea that strategy is the means to achieve an objective is the narrow concept of strategy. The view that strategy concerns both objectives and means is the broad concept of strategy, which is more associated with textbooks and courses on 'strategy', rather than 'strategic management' where the narrow concept is more useful.[4]

The strategy hierarchy

Strategy is defined above in an overall sense for the organization as a whole but, of course, strategy occurs at different levels. This is illustrated in the case of a corporation with several businesses in Figure 1.2. This illustrates a hierarchy in organizational strategy: corporate strategy influences business strategy, which influences departmental strategy, and so on, through operational levels and the strategies of teams and individuals. The ways in which different levels of strategy interact varies in different organizations. So, for example, a corporate strategy may be broken down into sub-strategies that are passed down to develop strategy at lower levels; or the direction of influence may work through a looser alignment of strategies, when corporate strategy serves as a point of reference to guide the development of local strategy. There may also be cross-functional strategy, or inter-departmental policies, to encourage effort in those concerns that require collaborative attention.

So be warned, 'strategy' can apply anywhere in an organization. It is context that actually defines how,

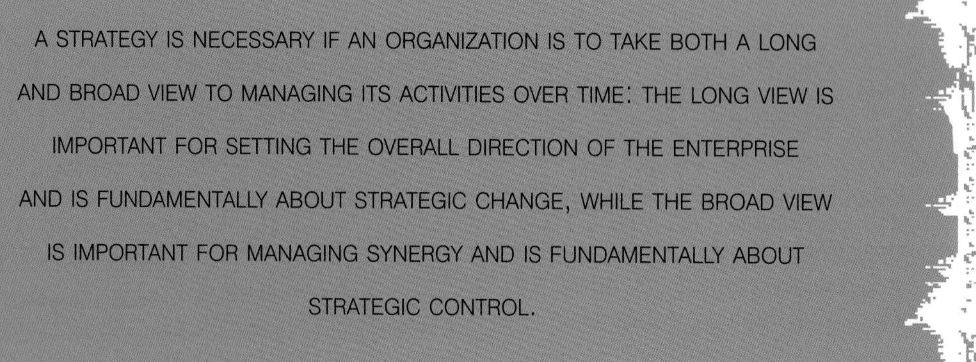

PRINCIPLES IN PRACTICE 1.1

Strategy in China

Beijing State-owned Assets Management Co., Ltd (BSAM) was established in April 2001 by the Chinese government. It is a wholly-owned state enterprise funded by the Beijing Municipal Government. Its purpose is to manage the operations of state-owned assets and to grow financial capital through: (1) the disposal of non-core assets; (2) attracting financial and industrial investors; and (3) the expansion into profitable and high-tech areas. China is going through fundamental economic change, and many state-owned enterprises need financial restructuring, a clean-up of their non-performing loans, and improvement of the overall quality of their assets.

In the words of BSAM's Chairman, Li Qiqing, the role of the company is: 'As a company, we are dedicated to hastening the pace of modernization in accordance with the highest international standards. To achieve our targets, we will further expand our highly qualified staff and seek technological and financial co-operation with reputed international companies to expand and diversify our business ventures. We will pay attention to corporate governance and we are confident that our new management system, coupled with a company culture dedicated to the spirit of creativity, loyalty, hard work and team spirit, will be a model to be emulated overall in China. With the co-operation of all we are convinced that BSAM is a key link to a better future for Beijing, our business partners and our staff, and that we can jointly face the challenges of tomorrow with confidence.'[23]

There are five strategies, which are to:

1. Develop as a large scale holding company through equity management in diverse financial institutions, to be able to act quickly to provide investment capital through one-to-one financial services.
2. Strengthen international co-operation and establish strategic alliances with foreign companies, to act as investors, or be able to provide advanced technology, management expertise or international networking.
3. Engage in state-owned capital operations of large-scale enterprises, to obtain the best advantages for investment.
4. Employ international and professional competences.
5. Develop corporate values and culture generally, in terms of corporate governance to emphasize the accountability and conduct of board members and managers, which enhance internal control reforms and transparency.

Question: How will the five strategies help the company achieve its role?

where and who uses it. The most important use for strategic management, however, is the organization's overall strategy as this influences all other strategy. The influence of overall strategy on lower level strategy is typically organized by senior managers through strategic planning.

Strategic planning

Strategic planning is about how senior managers sequence decision-making as a programme to achieve the organization's longer-term purpose, stra-

FIGURE 1.2 Strategy hierarchy

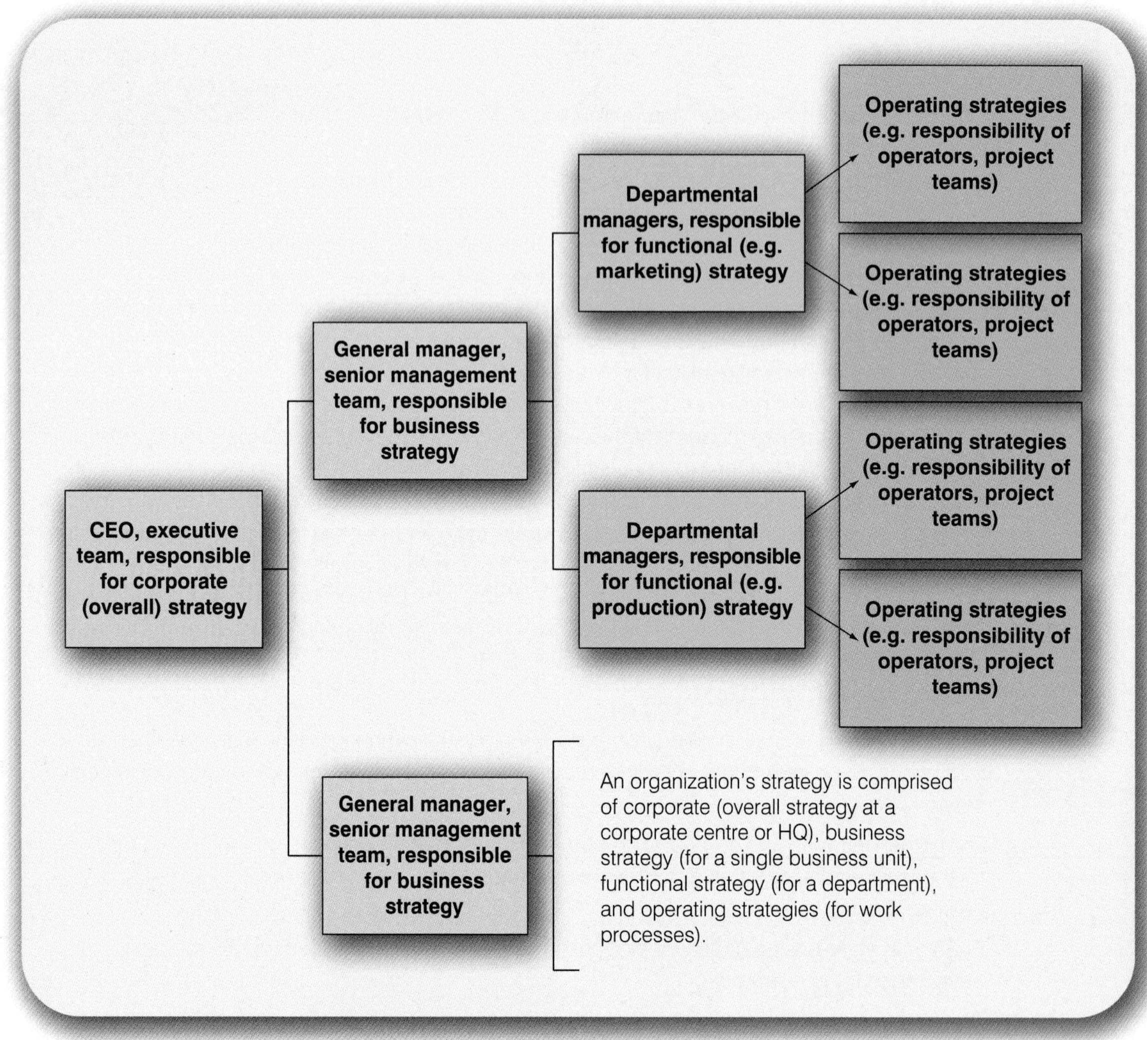

tegic objectives and overall strategy, and the implementation process for cascading responsibilities and resources logically to lower levels. The idea behind most strategic planning is simple. Chronologically it follows POST: Purpose, Objectives, Strategies and Tactics. An example that is fairly typical of the sequence is a process carried out at a business level for Honeywell[5]:

1 Review the business fundementals to question basic assumptions to see if the vision, values, mission and core competencies of the organization continue to remain appropriate, and check behaviour against values.
2 Conduct an external situation analysis.
3 Conduct an internal current condition analysis.
4 Develop issues to identify the critical areas to derive action statements.
5 Create strategic initiatives from the action statements, order them according to priority and examine these against the business fundementals, situation, and current conditions.

© iStockPhoto.com

The basic reason for strategic planning is to provide a capacity to manage change. Peter Lorange's classic work, *Corporate Planning* describes strategic planning as a strategic decision-making tool designed to motivate and support strategic change.[6] He identified four roles:

- To allocate a company's scarce resources, such as funds available for discretionary use, critical management talent that can be transferred from one use to another and sustainable technological knowledge.
- To help adapt to environment opportunities and threats, to identify relevant options and to provide an effective strategic fit with the environment.
- To co-ordinate strategic activities to reflect internal strengths and weaknesses to achieve efficient internal operations.
- To instil systematic management development by building an organization that is learning from the outcomes of its strategic decisions so it can improve on its strategic direction.

Long range planning

Strategic planning has changed over the years from a high point sometime around the mid-twentieth century. Writing in the 1960s Ansoff gives a major role to strategic planners in large organizations.

PRINCIPLES IN PRACTICE 1.2

Strategic planning according to Baldrige

The influential Malcolm Baldrige Performance Excellence Framework[24] defines best practice strategic planning.

It emphasizes the following principles: (1) all tasks should be planned properly; (2) plans should be effectively implemented so that people are working to these plans; (3) work is monitored and progress is reviewed; (4) necessary action is taken effectively to account for any deviation from plan.

Organizations should have in place structures and management systems to ensure these principles actually work in practice, and which fully involve everybody.

Good strategic planning has the following: (1) a defined strategy; (2) action plans derived from strategy; (3) a recognition and understanding of the differences between short- and longer-term plans; (4) an approach for developing company strategy that takes into account the external environment and internal strategic resources; (5) an approach for implementing action plans that considers key processes and performance measures; (6) an approach for monitoring company performance relative to the strategic plan; and (7) an approach for evaluating organizational performance in relation to strategy-related changes.

Question: Do you think these criteria for best practice strategic planning omit anything?

These analyse the elements of strategy and detail planning's sequence of tasks. Specialists examine strategic trends and undertake competitor analyses. An emphasis is placed on an examination of past trends in order to predict, or forecast events, sometimes far into the future. The use of planning specialists is often associated with long-range planning. This is a systematic procedure for long-term goal-setting, programming and budgeting, based on an extrapolative forecast that is typically a set of predictions made on the basis of the historical growth of the organization.[7]

Its weakness is that strategic objectives degenerate into little more than a mechanically fixed set of percentage improvements that are based on the previous years. The process is typically optimistic and fails to adjust easily when unforeseen change arises. Futurology is difficult though. McKinsey, the consultants, were retained by AT&T, America's major telephone operator, in 1984 to report on the future of wireless communications; it predicted that there would be fewer than one million mobile (cellular) phones by the year 2000, but when the new century dawned there were actually 741 million.

However, planning is necessary for the longer-term, say over five or even more years, if the organization is building physical plants or developing new markets, as these things can take years. The technical difficulties of producing a long-term plan are great. There is also the possibility, if planning is not managed effectively, that it will be influenced by political factors that serve vested interests rather than the collective needs of the wider organization. For example, powerful individuals can use them to reinforce their status or the autonomy of their group. If this happens then they are unlikely to be taken seriously as guides to action, and feelings of 'going-through-the-motions' or a 'tick-the-boxes' mentality will take over the planning process. The result is that a strategic plan turns out very differently from a senior management's expectations.

Emergent strategy

Taking the idea that an organization's intended strategy is changed during its implementation, Mintzberg and Waters argue that new strategy emerges to modify and change the planned strategy, so that over time the realized strategy is different from the one originally intended by senior managers.[8] Thus, strategy is a mixture of a senior management's **deliberate strategy**, which is a planned strategy designed by senior managers for implementation at other organizational levels, and **emergent strategy**, which is strategy not foreseen by senior management that arises during the implementation of deliberate strategy (see Figure 1.3).

The idea that strategy should be planned as two stages, first involving senior managers in its formulation, and then as a second stage, implemented top-down by the rest of the organization, has been associated in the strategy literature with a 'classical or design school' of strategy. This contrasts with a 'processual or learning' school, comprised of scholars who believe strategy forms a concurrent intertwining of both formulation and implementation together over time. The process of strategy formation has been likened to the act of walking, when one foot follows the other, until a destination is reached. Mintzberg compares strategy to making pots: the activity is more a craft than a science.[10]

In his book, *The Rise and Fall of Strategic Planning,* Mintzberg argues that there are three fundamental fallacies about strategic planning[11]:

1 Predetermination – planners believe they can predict accurately, but this only leads to a false sense of security.

2 Detachment – planners believe they are professionals, which encourages them to think they are objective and can offer a valuable expertise, but this only distances planners from the customer and creates an indifference to products.

FIGURE 1.3 Intended strategy becomes realized strategy[9]

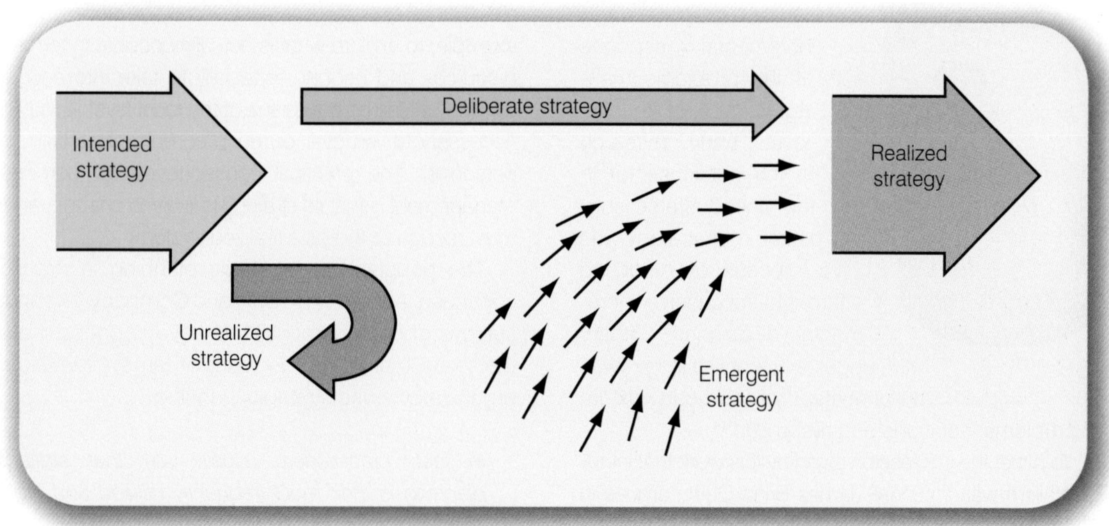

3 Fallacy of formalization – planners believe innovation and difference are generated by analysis and structure, but this only squeezes out passion and intuition.

There are also questions about how deliberate, and rational, managers can be in making their strategic decisions. In an attempt to bring a more realistic perspective to the notion of rationality in economic decision-making, Herbert Simon suggests managers are subject to **bounded rationality**.[12] The extent to which they can make a fully rational decision is limited by the complexity of problems, the time constraints they are under and because the necessary information is often unavailable. Thus the decision-making cannot be perfect, but a manager instead should be satisfied a decision is sufficient to give a good enough result. Simon called this form of decision-making **satisficing** (a combination of 'satisfied' and 'sufficient'). Given the three evil sisters of administrative science (complexity, ignorance and uncertainty), strategic planning should take account of the limited cognitive capacity of managers, which requires that strategic plans should be implemented incrementally rather than quickly as a pre-determined top-down master plan.

Logical incrementalism

For many organizations the implementation of a strategy can happen by default and accident. This may

be because of bad strategic management, but it may be a pragmatic and incremental response to the problems managers face at a local level. Early research in the public sector in the United States suggested that strategy was a process of muddling through successive incremental decisions.[13] Others suggested that strategy was an unrelated garbage can mixture of problems, solutions and resources.[14]

To offset the impression given by this work that incrementalism was irrational, James Brian Quinn argues in his book, *Strategies for Change,* that incrementalism is a logical response by business divisional management to their local circumstances.[15] He called this **logical incrementalism**. A corporate level deploys its intended strategy through its business divisions (see Figure 1.4), where managers, responding to their local circumstances and conditions, implement the corporate strategy incrementally as opportunities arise. It may be necessary, for example, to explore what is actually possible in terms of resources and people, especially to take into account existing strategies and plans at the local level. It may be necessary to win over or reach compromises with key personnel. The practical consequence for corporate management is that its strategy is likely to change, and it must recognize this as a realized strategy.

The popularity of strategic planning in practice continues. According to Bain and Company, its annual surveys of management tools have suggested over the years that 80–90 per cent of large international organizations use strategic planning:

> *In fact, practitioners usually say that strategic planning is their most frequently utilized and highly satisfying management technique. One of our survey participants commented, 'it's so easy to get absorbed in daily operating urgencies that we need the strategy process to challenge traditional thinking and redirect where we spend our time and money'.*[16]

FIGURE 1.4 The deployment of strategy and its incremental modification

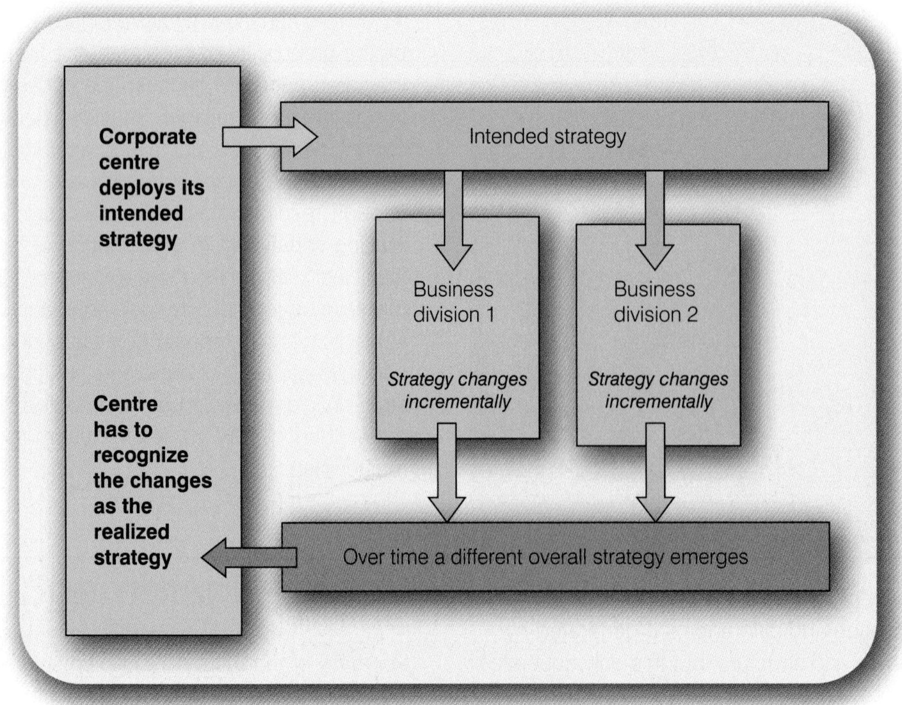

Practitioners say that strategic planning is their most frequently utilized and highly satisfying management technique. One of Bain & Co's survey participants commented, 'it's so easy to get absorbed in daily operating urgencies that we need the strategy process to challenge traditional thinking and redirect where we spend our time and money'.

Strategic planning may have changed from what it was in the early 1990s when Henry Mintzberg made his original observations. This is certainly so for individual organizations.[17] The important thing, in whatever form planning takes, is for senior managers not to become disconnected from the reality of their organizations. If this happens, the senior level can, in the words of Henry Mintzberg, 'shout down all the strategies they like; they will never work'.[18]

Managers should manage so they understand both ends of strategy in the organization at once. A deliberate and top-down strategic plan produced by a senior management team has to mesh with those strategic priorities which are drawn up and managed on the ground. In other words, there should be scope for initiative and creative action on the part of the individuals and units who are responsible for making strategy happen. This calls for a managed reconciliation between those influences on strategy from outside-in, and those that derive from inside-out. Strategic management is as much about strategically planning the organization to be dynamically capable, as it is about designing an externally sustainable position. Both are important, but they require different frameworks or models for thinking about strategy.

Outside-in thinking

The most influential strategy scholar since the beginning of the 1980s is Michael Porter of the Harvard Business School.[19] His ideas about how strategy should sustain an organization's competitive position in its chosen industry, classically define strategic management as the management of competitive difference. Porter's thinking belongs to a well-established industrial organization tradition, which dates back at least to the 1960s, and places an importance on the external environment as a determining influence for successful strategy. The direction of this influence is **outside-in** (see Figure 1.5).

The principal areas examined include the external environment, the analysis of an industry, the selection of a strategy designed to achieve above-average returns in the industry, and finally, the

STRATEGIC MANAGEMENT IS AS MUCH ABOUT STRATEGICALLY PLANNING THE ORGANIZATION TO BE DYNAMICALLY CAPABLE, AS IT IS ABOUT DESIGNING AN EXTERNALLY SUSTAINABLE POSITION. BOTH ARE IMPORTANT, BUT THEY REQUIRE DIFFERENT FRAMEWORKS OR MODELS FOR THINKING ABOUT STRATEGY.

FIGURE 1.5 Outside-in and Inside-out influences on strategy

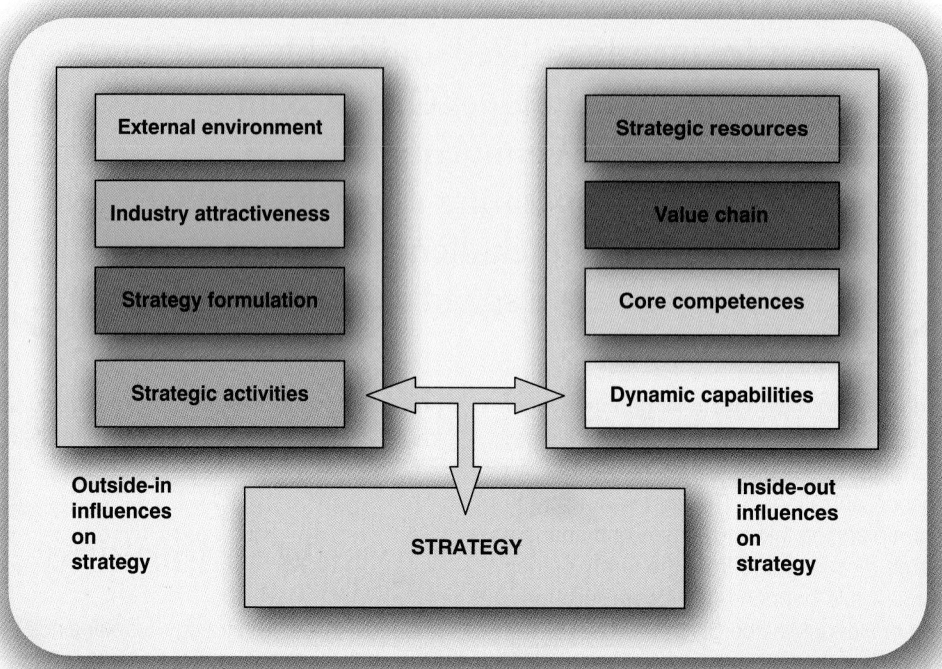

PRINCIPLES IN PRACTICE 1.3

In the head and programmed planning

In his book, *The Rise and Fall of Strategic Planning,* Henry Mintzberg writes that organizations 'engage in formal planning, not to create strategies but to programme the strategies they already have, that is, to elaborate and operationalize their consequences formally.'[25]

Elsewhere he gives an example of a supermarket chain: '... planning did not give this company an intended strategy. It already had one, in the head of its entrepreneur, as his vision of its future... Rather, planning was the articulation, justification, and elaboration of the intended strategy the company already had. Planning for it was not deciding to expand into shopping centres, but what schedule, etc. In other words, planning was programming: it was used not to conceive an intended strategy, but to elaborate the consequences of an intended strategy already conceived.'[26]

More recently he has said: 'I believe strategy is simply putting things in one's head, making sense of things in a meaningful way. When we reify strategy it suddenly becomes this Big Thing, and strategy is a sense of where you are going, what direction you and your organization are taking. Strategy in a sense is to move an organization forward, it is not this mysterious thing removed from practice ... you can do all the analysis you want; [*but*] life remains rich and complicated. That is what strategy has to be about – not the neat abstractions of the executive suite, but the messy patterns of daily life and how to make sense of them.'[27]

Question: What does Mintzberg mean by 'in the head' and a 'programme'?

KEY DEBATE 1.2

How do the Japanese do it?

One of the most influential debates about whether planning really works is centred on an article in the *California Management Review* by Richard Pascale, called the Honda Effect. Pascale interviewed Honda executives about how they had entered the American motorcycle market. They told him their success was a story of miscalculation, mistakes and unforeseen events. It was how they had learnt about and reacted to these things that accounted for their eventual success and which Pascale called the Honda effect.

The North American story contrasted with one written by the Boston Consulting Group to explain the success of the Japanese in the British motorcycle market.[30] This presented success as an outcome from good strategic planning. The *California Management Review* re-published Pascale's original article with added commentary and articles from both sides of the debate; it was edited by Mintzberg as a special edition of the journal.[31]

Pascale contrasted the reasons for Honda's success with motorcycles in the American market with the Boston Consulting Group conclusions that the Japanese success was based on a rationally directed and deliberately planned process to grow market share in order to reap economies of scale. The Honda managers involved in the American success reported how they had given up their original strategy to sell large motorbikes when the bikes proved unreliable. They saw instead a new market entirely for a small bike (they had been using such bikes to get around Los Angeles). Their success with this product enabled them to use this as a foundation to expand into the existing large bike market. Pascale argues the Japanese are swift to adapt to threats and are flexible enough to see opportunities on the periphery of markets.

Michael Goold, one of the authors of the original BCG report, writing in the special edition, claims that both planning and opportunism were necessary. It is also possible that Honda's longer-term success would have happened regardless. Its capability to raise quality while lowering costs came close to bankrupting Harley Davidson, which only survived because it adopted Japanese business methodologies and management philosophies.

Richard Rumelt, also writing in the special edition, observes that the UK motorcycle factories had been producing only 14 cycles per worker per year, against a Honda equivalent of about 200 cycles! His view is that the 'process/emergent' school is right about having the capabilities to react quickly and intelligently to new knowledge. At the same time, though, the 'design' school is right about the reality of forces like scale economies, accumulated experience and the cumulative development of core competencies over time.

The debate may be too simple. In writing a review of studies that used Honda as an example of strategic success, Andrew Mair points out that they use tendentious and dualist accounts, which fail to show that what really happened was complex.[32]

Question: How can the emergent and design approaches complement each other?

KEY DEBATE 1.3

Is business good for business?

The global financial crisis has shaken up ideas about strategic management, especially the roles of leadership and management (see Chapter 11). However, disquiet about prevailing management theories has been around for some time. In his last article, the late Sumantra Ghoshal argues that a single ideology has colonized all the management-related disciplines over the last 50 years. This has happened even though there are many different disciplines within management, many of which are grounded in quite different assumptions and traditions.

The present ideology 'is essentially grounded in a set of pessimistic assumptions about both individuals and institutions ... [*and*] views the primary purpose of social theory as one of solving the 'negative problem' of restricting the social costs arising from human imperfections ... [*it has*] led management research increasingly in making excessive truth-claims based in partial analysis and both unrealistic and biased assumptions ... Unlike theories in the physical sciences, theories in the social sciences tend to be self-fulfilling ... a management theory – if it gains sufficient currency – changes the behaviour of managers who start acting in accordance with the theory ... we have adopted the 'scientific' approach of trying to discover patterns and laws, and have replaced all notions of human intentionality with a firm belief in causal determinism for explaining all aspects of corporate performance.'[33]

Most management research is concerned with existing management issues and change rather than social change. Gibson Burrell and Gareth Morgan argue that business management, including strategic management, is either interpretivist (subjective) or functionalist (objective), and is concerned with the present view of organizational reality so that it is oriented towards maintaining the status quo.[34]

Question: How can strategic management accommodate the views of Sumantra Ghoshal?

management of strategically-linked activities to sustain the chosen strategy. The purpose of outside-in is to identify and address the opportunities and threats in the external environment; classically, the aim is to fit the organization strategically within its environment so that it will be able to sustain above-average returns over time.

Inside-out thinking

An alternative view to the industrial organization tradition is the resource-based view. This is an **inside-out** approach to strategy thinking. Its origins go back in economics at least to Edith Penrose,[20] and many scholars now claim it is 'arguably the dominant theoretical foundation in strategic management today'.[21] At its heart is the idea that strategic resources can be characterized as firm-specific, which makes it difficult for rivals to emulate or buy them, and as such they constitute an organization's competitive advantage.

Inside-out influences concern the identification and management of strategic resources, the value chain, core competences and dynamic capabilities. The purpose of inside-out thinking is essentially to build a framework for marshalling the learning abilities of an organization around the core processes of its business model. The aim is to achieve an internal fit of strategic resources so that they sustain above average returns.[22]

SUMMARY OF PRINCIPLES

1 Strategic management should be a managed process.

2 The components of strategic management broadly comprise purpose, analysis, strategy, and implementation.

3 The prime responsibility for strategic management rests with senior managers.

4 Everybody participates in strategic management.

5 There are organizational strategy hierarchies, but overall strategy is the most important.

6 Strategic planning is a sequence of stages.

7 Strategic planning should accommodate emergent strategy.

8 There are two directions of influences on thinking about strategy, outside-in and inside-out.

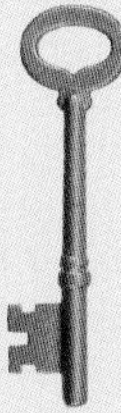

GLOSSARY OF KEY TERMS

Bounded rationality the extent to which making a fully rational decision is limited by complexity, lack of time and absent information.

Daily management is work carried out in those parts of the organization that are primarily about short-term operational and functional activity.

Deliberate strategy a planned strategy that is designed by senior managers for implementation at other organizational levels.

Emergent strategy strategy that is not foreseen by senior management and which arises during the implementation of, and changes, deliberate strategy.

Inside-out these are influences on thinking about strategy that are primarily driven by internal conditions that are specific to the organization concerned.

logical incrementalism the implementation of a deliberate strategy in small and logical steps.

Outside-in these are influences on thinking about strategy that are primarily driven by conditions in the external environment.

Satisficing the process of making a satisfactory decision that is sufficient to give a good enough result.

Stakeholders individuals and groups who receive value from an organization.

Strategic management the management of an organization's overall purpose, in ways that ensure that the needs and enablers of the present are balanced with those of the future.

Strategic planning the sequencing of strategic management decisions in advance by an executive or senior management.

Strategy an overall approach, or a general pattern of behaviour, for achieving an organization's purpose, including its strategic objectives.

GUIDED FURTHER READING

This chapter has covered the important debate about the design and emergent schools of strategy, but the range of scholarship, and views, are greater than this. For an easily read summary of 'ten schools', see:

Mintzberg, H., Lampel, J. and Ahlstrand, B. (2005) *Strategy Safari: A Guided Tour through the Wilds of Strategic Management* (2nd edn), London: Prentice Hall.

For a good oversight of the history and the ideas of the major contributors, see:

Moore, J. I. (2001) *Writers on Strategy and Strategic Management* (2nd edn), London: Penguin Business.

Over the last few years, some European scholars have proposed a new school, 'strategy-as-practice', which takes a micro-view of what people do at an everyday level of practice; see Paula Jarzabkowski's book. A good critical review and summary of this is available (see below):

Jarzabkowski, P. (2005) *Strategy as Practice: An Activity-Based Approach,* London: Sage.

Kaplan, S. (2007) Paula Jarzabkowski 'Strategy as practice' [a review], *Academy of Management Review* 32(3):986–98.

For a general critique of the approach, see:

Carter, C., Clegg, S. R. and Kornberger, M. (2008) 'Strategy as practice?', *Strategic Organization* 6(1):83–99.

REVIEW QUESTIONS

1 What is strategic management for?

2 Distinguish the components of strategic management.

3 If strategic management is a managed process who does the managing and why?

4 Distinguish between strategy and strategic management.

5 Why is it important to differentiate between levels of strategy?

6 What is strategic planning?

7 How is intended strategy changed by emergent strategy?

8 Why is incremental strategy logical?

9 Why are the outside-in and the inside-out ways of thinking about strategy complementary?

SEMINAR AND ASSIGNMENT QUESTIONS

1 Discuss with anyone known to you who works in an organization what strategy means to them. Ask them how 'strategy' helps them do their work. What are your conclusions?

2 Consider strategic planning and how useful it is to organizations. Explain why Henry Mintzberg thinks it does not work. Compare these two things and reach a definite conclusion for the strategic management of two contrasting organizations.

3 If strategy really is all in a senior manager's head, how is it possible to get it out and share it with others?

CHAPTER REFERENCES

1 Welch, J. (with Welch, S.) (2005) *Winning,* New York: Collins.

2 Chandler, A. D., Jr. (1962) *Strategy and Structure: Chapters in the History of the Industrial Enterprise*, Cambridge, MA: MIT Press, p. 13.

3 Ansoff, H. I. (1965) *Corporate Strategy: An Analytic Approach to Business Policy for Growth and Expansion*, London: Pelican edition (pub. 1968), chapter 6.

4 This distinction between the two concepts was made in Hofer, C. W. and Schendel, D. (1978) *Strategy Formulation: Analytical Concepts*, St. Paul, MN: West Publishing.

5 Jones, R. D. (1998) The new management accounting system at Honeywell's Micro Switch Division. In Christopher, W. F. (ed.) (1998) *New*

Management Accounting, Crisp Publications, pp. 1–17.

6 Lorange, P. (1980) *Corporate Planning: An Executive Viewpoint,* Englewood Cliffs, NJ: Prentice Hall.

7 Ansoff *op cit.*

8 Mintzberg, H. and Waters, J. A. (1985) 'Of strategies, deliberate and emergent', *Strategic Management Journal* 6:257–72.

9 Adapted from Mintzberg and Waters (1985), *op cit*. Figure 1.1.

10 Mintzberg, H. (1987) 'Crafting strategy', *Harvard Business Review* July–August, 66–71.

11 Mintzberg, H. (1994) *The Rise and Fall of Strategic Planning,* London: Prentice Hall.

12 Simon, H. A. (1947) (1997, 4th edn), *Administrative Behaviour: A Study of Decision-Making Processes in Administrative Organizations,* New York: Free Press, p. 67.

13 Lindblom, C. E. (1959) 'The science of muddling through', *Public Administration Review* 19 (Spring):79–88.

14 Cohen, M. D., March, J. G. and Olsen, J. P. (1972) 'A garbage can model of organizational choice', *Administrative Science Quarterly* 17(1):1–26.

15 Quinn, J. B. (1980) *Strategies for Change – Logical Incrementalism*, Homewood, IL: Irwin.

16 Rigby, D. and Bilodeau, B. (2007) 'Selecting management tools wisely', *Harvard Business Review* (December):20–2.

17 Ocasio, W. and Joseph J. (2008) 'Rise and fall – or transformation? The evolution of strategic planning at the General Electric Company, 1940–2006', *Long Range Planning* 41:248–72.

18 de Holan, P. M. and Mintzberg, H. (2004) 'Management as life's essence: 30 years of the "Nature of Managerial Work"', *Strategic Organization* 2(2):205–12.

19 Porter, M. E. (1980) *Competitive Strategy: Techniques for Analysing Industries and Competitors*, New York: Free Press.

20 Penrose, E. T. (1959) *The Theory of the Growth of the Firm,* Oxford: Basil Blackwell.

21 Stieglitz, N. and Heine, K. (2007) Innovations and the role of complementarities in a strategic theory of the firm, *Strategic Management Journal* 28:1–15, p. 1.

22 Helfat, C. E., Finkelstein, S., Mitchell, W., Peteraf, M. A., Singh, H., Teece, D. J. and Winter, S. G. (2007) *Dynamic Capabilities: Understanding Strategic Change in Organizations,* Oxford: Blackwell Publishers.

23 Corporate Presentation of BSAM, *Beijing State-Owned Management Company*, corporate presentation of BSAM, edited April 29, www.Strategy4choice.com/SAMintro.pdf.

24 NIST (National Institute of Science and Technology) (2008) *Malcolm Baldrige National Quality Program*. http://www.quality.nist.gov

25 Mintzberg, H. (1994) *op cit.* p. 333.

26 Mintzberg, H. (1981) 'What is planning anyway?' *Strategic Management Journal* 11:319–24.

27 de Holan, P. M. and Mintzberg, H. (2004) *op cit.*

28 Robinson, P. (1994) *Snapshots from Hell: The Making of an MBA,* London: Nicholas Brearley.

29 Mintzberg, H. Ahlstrand, B. and Lampel, J. (1998) *Strategy Safari*, London: Prentice Hall.

30 Boston Consulting Group (1975) *Strategy Alternatives for the British Motorcycle Industry,* London: HMSO.

31 Mintzberg, H., Pascale, R. T., Goold, M. and Rumelt, R. P. (1996) *op cit.*

32 Mair, A. (1999) 'Learning from Honda', *Journal of Management Studies* 36(1):25–44.

33 Ghoshal, S. (2005) 'Bad management theories are destroying good management practices', *Academy of Management Learning and Education* 4(1):75–91, p. 77.

34 Burrell, G. and Morgan, G. (1979) *Sociological Paradigms and Organizational Analysis,* Glover: London.

CASE 1.1 Strategic management at Tata Steel

The Tata group of companies is a large multi-national conglomerate that employs around 350 000 people and has revenues approaching £15 billion. The group consists of nearly 100 companies and is India's largest private sector group. Its businesses range across seven industrial sectors: information systems and communications, engineering, materials, energy, consumer products and chemicals. Tata was founded in the mid-nineteenth century, and since that time its declared purpose has been to explore and develop business opportunities, and to assist in the development of India.

When the Indian economy was liberalized in the 1990s Tata rethought its strategic management. A view emerged that the group was too loosely connected to manage itself for globalization.[1] The group moved to reduce its exposure to the Indian economy, by internationalizing its activities, which saw the acquisition of established overseas companies with global brands, and the adoption of global business methodologies and management philosophies. These changes have required the Tata group to restructure its traditional shape.

At the group's core is a holding company, Tata Sons, which is owned by three philanthropic charitable trusts and the Tata family; the chairman acts as the chief executive for the Tata group. Tata Sons owns the Tata name and trademark, and has minority stakes in the other companies. The Tata companies cross-hold stakes in each other, which gives considerable freedom to the individual companies (they also operate as autonomous legal entities, with their own independent boards of directors and executives).

Ratan Tata, Tata's chief executive, has overseen the number of Tata companies reduced from around 300 to 90 (28 are publicly listed). These changes are intended to make the group more cohesive and competitive. The group's strategic objectives are that each company should (1) deliver returns greater than the cost of capital; (2) be in the top three of its industry; and (3) achieve high growth in global markets.

According to R. K. Krishna Kumar, a director of Tata Sons, global branding is a natural evolutionary course for the group: 'The Japanese started this way, so did the Koreans, and there's really no reason to ask whether the trajectory is the right one – it's a strategic necessity for companies and countries as they evolve.'[2] The advantages of brands are twofold: they add additional value to products, and by controlling the brand, the corporate group is able to increase its influence on the managements of the individual companies.

During the mid-1990s Tata Sons introduced a Brand Equity and Business Promotion Agreement, which requires the group's companies to pay a percentage of their annual revenues for using the Tata name and brand. The companies must also apply the group's code of conduct, which documents Tata's general principles and ethics and its Tata Business Excellence Model (TBEM). The model is based on the Baldrige Excellence Framework and it is used to 'deliver strategic direction and drive business improvement. It has elements that enable companies following its directives to capture the best of global business processes and practices.'[3]

The group's strategic management remains primarily collaborative and emergent rather than controlling and prescriptive.[4] However, it may prove difficult to maintain the distinctiveness of the Tata Brand if the companies are free to pursue their own strategy. For example, in different regions of the world the group seems to be following different approaches: in developing economies Tata companies seem to be diversifying into unrelated businesses, while the opposite is true for more developed economies (conglomerates may have advantages in a developing context, but not in an industrial one).[5]

Vision 2007 at Tata Steel

The originally-named Tata Iron and Steel Company was established in 1907, and is now the world's third largest steel company, with an annual crude steel

EXHIBIT 1.1 Vision, 2002–2007[6]

Vision 2007

To seize the opportunities of tomorrow and create a future that will make us an EVA positive company.

To continue to improve the quality of life of our employees and the communities we serve

Revitalize the core Business for a sustainable future

Uphold the spirit & values of TATAs towards nation building

Venture into New Businesses that will own a share of our future

Strategic Goals

Move from commodities to Brands

EVA Positive Core Business

Continue to be Lowest Cost Producer of Steel

Value creating Partnerships with Customers & Suppliers

Enthused & Happy employees

Sustainable growth

Strategy

Manage Knowledge

Outsource Strategically

Encourage Innovation and Allow the Freedom to Fail

Excel at TBEM

Unleash people's potential and create leaders who will build the future

Invest in attractive new Businesses

Ensure Safety & Environmental Sustainability

Divest, Merge, Acquire

TATA

TATA STEEL

output of around 28 million tonnes. It employs around 83 000 people across 24 countries. In 2002 the company introduced a five-year strategic plan called Vision 2007. This is represented as a pillared house (see Exhibit 1.1), with Tata Steel's purpose placed at its top, supported by values, strategic goals and strategy.

The purpose of Vision 2007 was two-fold: to make Tata Steel's economic value added (EVA) positive, and to improve the quality of life for employees and the communities the company serves. The company had become the lowest cost supplier of steel in the world, but the EVA was problematic.

Ratan Tata, in July 2001, said: 'We recognized that, regrettably, the steel industry does not cover the cost of capital ... If you have to invest ... as we did in the modernization of the plant, and if it doesn't give us a return that is equal to the cost of capital, then we have destroyed shareholder value ... we have to do much more in steel to make it an investor-attractive area of business'.[7]

Six strategic goals were listed: (1) to move from a commodity-based business to brands; (2) to achieve positive EVA in core businesses; (3) to continue as the lowest cost producer of steel; (4) to achieve value creating partnerships with customers and suppliers; (5) to have enthused and happy employees; and (6) to achieve sustainable growth.

To achieve these, the following strategies were identified: (1) manage knowledge; (2) outsource those business areas that do not effect the company's sources of competitive advantage; (3) encourage innovation and a culture of calculated risks; (4) excel at TBEM; (5) unleash people's potential and create leaders who will build the future; (6) invest in attractive new business that will complement steel; (7) ensure safety and environmental sustainability; and (8) divest chronically under-performing non-core businesses, while merge and acquire those that add synergy and accelerated growth and that can be organized as profit centres.

Several initiatives were introduced, which included new brands, such as Tata Steeium (cold rolled steel), Tata Shaktee (galvanized corrugated sheets), Tata Pipes, and so on, and which were organized as profit centres. Other initiatives included changes to improve the integration of the supply chain. In 2007 the Anglo-Dutch company, Corus, was acquired for £6.7 billion to improve Tata's access to European Union markets and expand operations at the high-value end of steel products. In 2005 the company acquired Singapore's NatSteel and Thailand's Millennium Steel, to strengthen its industry position in higher-value finished products in the growing Asian markets.[8]

The strategic management process

The TBEM is managed as an annual process; this includes checking and assessing the core values of the Tata group, including business methodologies and management philosophies, such as customer-driven processes, a long-range view of the future and a systems perspective. A key part is the strategic planning process: how the company develops strategy, including its strategic objectives, action plans and related human resource plans, and how plans are deployed and performance-tracked (the process is shown in Exhibit 1.2).

Seven strategic tasks are involved, which from left to right in Exhibit 1.2 are purpose statements (vision, mission, values), through to performance and progress review. The Exhibit shows beneath these the processes involved in carrying out these tasks, moving through time from left to right. Strategy is developed through a consideration of purpose, an analysis of the environment and opportunities, objectives and targets, and the determination of the key strategic initiatives and functional excellence plans (thus strategy is developed with operational effectiveness).

Balanced scorecards are used to derive the key strategic imperatives from the strategic objectives, which are linked to the needs of key stakeholders. The voice of the customer and the importance of critical success factors are shown carried forward across the departments, and the management of performance and its review. Rewards and recognition refer to the alignment of human resource plans, and the internal communication forums are used to provide company-wide feedback for strategy development and deployment.

The TBEM provides a framework for the group to understand how strategy is being applied and how it works at an operational level. Executives from other Tata companies participate in the annual audit activity and play a part in assessing the extent to which Tata

EXHIBIT 1.2 The strategic management process[9]

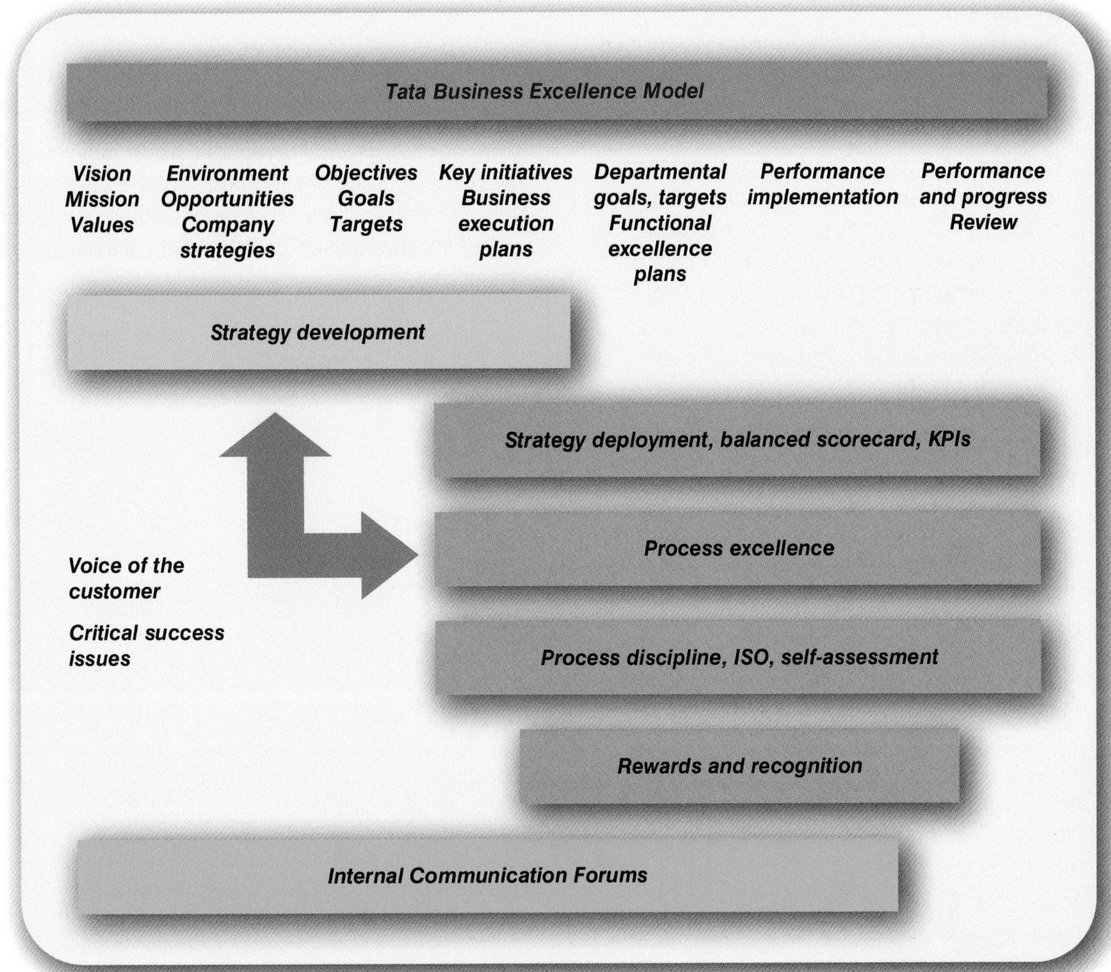

Steel conforms to the criteria laid down in the group's Brand Equity and Promotion Agreement. The feedback is used to promote best practice in the wider group through its regional forums.

Discussion questions

1 What is the role played by the group's Tata Business Excellence Model?

2 Are the elements of Vision 2007 consistent and how are they likely to promote joined-up management?

3 Work out how Tata Steel conforms to this book's strategic management model: consider the model's four components. What are the strengths and weaknesses of the group's strategic management in relation to Tata Steel?

Case references

1 Kakani, R. K. and Joshi, T. (2006) 'Cross holding strategy to increase control: case of the Tata Group', *Working Paper* 06–03, School of Management, XLRI, Jamshedpur.

2 Krishna Kumar, R. K. reported in Leahy, J. (2008) 'The burning ambition of the Tata group, India and globalization', *Financial Times,* January 25, p. 5.

3 Tata (2008) Our commitment, TBEM and TQMS, at: www.tata.com.

4 Tata (2008), *op cit.*

5 Goldstein, A. (2007) 'The internationalization of Indian companies: the case of Tata', conference paper, *Thrust and Parry in the Global Game: Emerging Asian Corporate Giants and the World Economy,* Tokyo Club Foundation for Global Studies, Tokyo, 13–14 November.

6 Tata Steel (2002) 'Vision 2007', Annual Report 2002–2003.

7 Kanavi, S. (2001) 'Given the right incentives, India can be a steel supplier to the world', *Business India,* July 23.

8 Goldstein, A. (2007) *op cit.*

9 Tata Chemicals (2008), www.tatachemicals.com

This case study was prepared using only publicly available sources of information for the purposes of classroom discussion; it does not intend to illustrate either effective or ineffective handling of a managerial situation.

Chapter 2

PURPOSE

Introduction

This chapter covers purpose, and the three dimensions that define its role for strategic management: vision, mission and values. The importance of the primacy of the customer and other stakeholders is considered, along with the importance of organizational culture, business ethics and governance.

LEARNING OBJECTIVES

By the end of this chapter you should understand:

1. The importance of strategic purpose.
2. The difference between vision, mission and value for strategic management.
3. The concept of stakeholders.
4. Organizational culture and purpose.
5. The significance of business ethics and governance for purpose.

Business vignette Using purpose sorts out the things that matter

Rudy Giuliani, ex-mayor of New York City, points out in his book, *Leadership*, that purpose is fundamental to how a leader manages an organization.

He commented, when 'consider[ing] an agency I tried to look at its core purpose and direct every decision based on how well it helped advance that purpose ... aligning the resources and focus along with that purpose ... finding the right organizational structure starts with a mission. Then you have to identify your aims, and what you should do to achieve them; find the right people for the job; and constantly follow up to make sure everyone is sticking to the original purpose, that no one's taken over your team and sidetracked them. My interest in avoiding the pitfalls of organizational confusion began years ago, when I was the US Attorney for the Southern District of New York. That's when I began to develop an approach to managing based on organizational structure. The first question is always, "What's the mission?" Ask yourself what you'd like to achieve – not day-to-day, but your overarching goal. Then assess and analyze your resources ... think about the job thematically ... means not just making use of my own resources, but thinking how best to integrate them with outside resources. Consider organized crime.

Rudy Giuliani

Checking it against our mission statement reveals that prosecuting its leaders was obviously worthwhile. The goal was not to tot up a number of arrests and score convictions, but to eliminate some of the [crime] organizations – a far broader purpose ... Any complex system will inevitably evolve in ways that no longer make sense when circumstances change ... A leader has to be aware of mismatches ... The organization of systems was a top priority for me ... Anyone leading a large organization risks losing a feel for the forest while managing the trees. I deliberated on the purpose not only of individual agencies, but of government itself. I'd go through the questions: What are we here for? What are the available resources? ... The reality is that there's only so much a city government can do – or should do ... One of my immediate goals was to streamline the government to allow us to focus on our major priorities ... The organization chart is not simply a cold management contrivance. It's a living, evolving tool a leader uses to send a message – to those that work for him, and even to remind himself – regarding the organization's goals and priorities ... I always strive to determine the purpose of an organization, then to set it up so that everything else flows from there.'[1]

Purpose

There is no sensible management at any level of any organization without **purpose**. This is especially important if everybody is to work effectively together. Thus senior managers spend considerable time clarifying and making it meaningful to the rest of the organization. Not only should purpose inspire and motivate everybody, it should also be used strategically to help everybody in the organization to develop their priorities and roles, and to understand the priorities and roles of others they work with.

there are three dimensions that are important to how the organization manages itself as a collective entity: (1) **vision** – a view of some desired future state or ideal for the organization; (2) **mission** – a statement of the organization's present main activities; and (3) **values** – the expected collective norms and behaviour of everybody in the organization. Each of these is relevant to a basic area of strategic management (see Figure 2.1).

Visionary purpose concerns **strategic change**, or **transformational change**, which is focused on an overall strategy for changing an existing business

> **There is no sensible management at any level of any organization without purpose.**

An organization's purpose is the primary and basic reason for its existence. Ultimately, a basic purpose for being in existence is founded on belief. People have to believe that the organization serves a useful purpose. This requires some sort of belief system to make sense of what an organization does, and in everyday work, much has to go unquestioned. The conventional view is that organizations are purely instrumental in the sense that they exist to serve their stakeholders; particularly their customers. In this, model. Missionary purpose is associated with **improvement change**, which is focused on sustaining an existing business model.[2] Strategic change defined in this way is primarily associated with the outside-in (industrial organization) perspective, while the inside-out (resource-based) view is primarily about incremental improvement. The management of change within these perspectives requires different approaches to organizational learning. Learning associated with vision is explorative in that it is

FIGURE 2.1 Three roles for purpose in strategic management

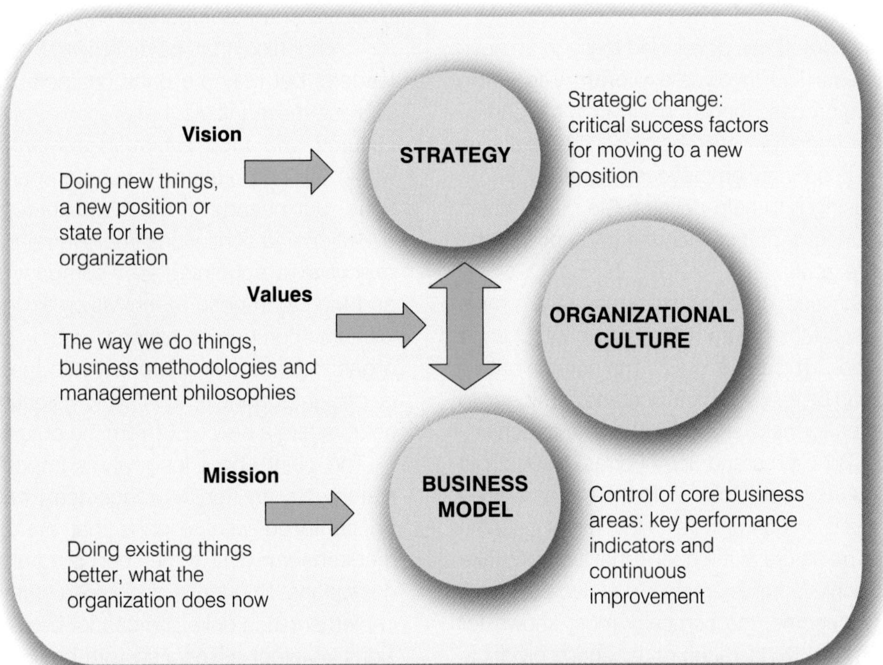

primarily outside sources of information that are important for deciding strategy. Learning associated with mission primarily exploits an organization's existing experience with its existing business model.[3]

Values as purpose concerns the appropriate organizational culture for vision and mission (see Figure 2.1). In other words, values should be managed to take into account the required business methodologies and management philosophies, or core competences, that an organization's people need to achieve vision, while effectively managing the key business areas, or the **core capabilities**, of its business model.

© iStockPhoto.com

Vision statements

An organization's **vision** is a statement of its aspiration and view of its future. It represents a statement of intent to move to an improved condition or towards a desired state of being. Thus it provides everybody with a sense of purpose in terms of the direction it is going in, and making things better.

A vision statement is typically short and to the point. It should be memorably different from the ordinary, and for a competitive organization, the difference should be relatively outstanding – ambitious but not overblown. Because a vision provides the basic rationale for change, the reasons for change and the broad implications for action should be made obvious to the organization as a whole. The introduction of a new or modified vision usually requires an organization-wide communications programme to explain the reasons for change. Vision should adequately excite and motivate to encourage people to rethink their work and to stretch them. It should appear to everybody as realistic, but senior managers need to walk a narrow line between distant ambition and the possibilities of getting there carefully.

A vision is sometimes developed through an envisioning process. This involves **exploratory learning** and a thinking process that should involve the participation of the important stakeholders. This dialogue should include ordinary employees since they will be involved in using it to help develop the plans which will help to close gaps between the present and the desired future goals.

A particular kind of vision statement is a simple 'big idea' – something very different that will change the organization. This is used as a memorable catchphrase that can be easily communicated as a slogan to spur people on to make exceptional efforts to achieve an ambition. Bill Collins and Jerry Porras[4] write about a 'Big Hairy Audacious Goal' or 'BHAG', pronounced 'bee-hag': this is so daring in its ambition that it seems impossible. The nature of the goal is that it should take decades to achieve: for example, Sony had a 25 year old vision to become 'the company most known for changing the worldwide image of Japanese products as poor quality'.[5] In the 1960s Japanese products were poor, this changed dramatically but, of course, other Japanese companies also played their part. Many had similar slogans: such as Komatsu's declared intent to 'encircle Caterpillar', and Canon's to 'beat Xerox' (see 'strategic intent', Chapter 3).

Collins and Porras argue that organizations should not change their core values and purpose.

In writing about visionary companies, they emphasize the importance of building an organization over time. Visionary companies should not be mistaken for companies that have grown through visionary leaders, but they are ones characterized by having in place mechanisms that preserve core values, tight cultures, and a top level management that has risen within the corporation. These companies are ambitious, but change is managed through purposeful evolution and continuous improvement. If a new chief executive is appointed to a company from outside, and tries to impose a new vision that is not aligned with the company's historic core values, then the organization is unlikely to buy into the change. That is one important reason why visionary companies seldom hire a new CEO from the outside.

The point about longevity is important. Purpose statements are for the longer-term and should not be confused with slogans that are used to drive medium-term (say, three-year) programmes or business plans. Shorter-term purpose statements are for implementation only, and cannot be used as expressions of intent associated with basic purpose, strategic objectives and the overall strategy to achieve these. These things should be stable over time.

Mission statements

A **mission** statement explains why an organization exists. This is normally short and concise and should only consist of a few sentences. However, it is generally longer than a vision statement, since it should explain the scope of what the organization does now, with a rationale that explains how it adds value for its main stakeholders. The style and form of statements vary considerably in practice since organizations use them in different ways.

Not every organization uses a mission statement (or a vision statement) for strategic management, and it can be used differently in different parts of the organization.[6] It may be used for public relations to influence important publics, or for marketing to include claims, or aspirations, to provide a quality service that is distinctive, and sets what the organization does uniquely apart from its competitors. Care is necessary to ensure that the organization is able to live up to its claims. The statement may claim 'excellence' and 'quality' but if it

© iStockPhoto.com

actually fails to deliver these, then reputation will suffer. Platitudes like 'we make your life better' can leave both customers and employees feeling cynical.

The use of mission as part of strategic management is about how an organization identifies those areas of the business that are core to what the organization is trying to do, and outlines how these areas fit together strategically to deliver value to its stakeholders.

Stakeholders

Stakeholders are individuals and groups who benefit directly by receiving value from what an organization does and provides. The relationship with stakeholders is typically reciprocal since the organization will to some extent depend on the support of its stakeholders. These include the groups shown in Figure 2.2. Some will be more important than others, such as owners who can remove senior managers from the organization and change the strategic management of their organization.

FIGURE 2.2 Stakeholders in an organization

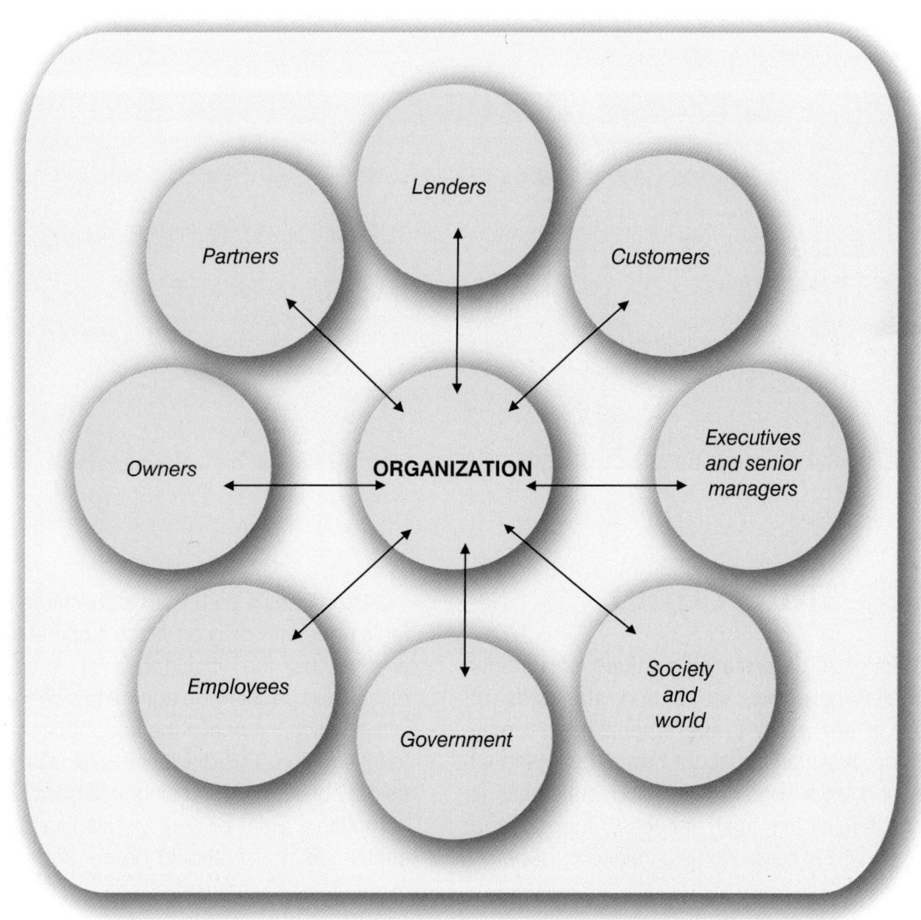

Peter Drucker, in an often quoted piece from his classic book, *The Practice of Management*, puts the customer first:

> *If we want to know what a business is we have to start with its purpose. And its purpose must lie outside of the business itself. In fact, it must lie in society since a business enterprise is an organ of society. There is only one valid definition of business purpose: to create a customer.*[7]

The primacy of the customer for commercial organizations should be obvious in everything they do. However, for some forms of enterprise, such as a co-operative, employees and customers may participate in the ownership of the organization. In the case of public service organizations, political purpose is important. Philip Joyce in his book, *Strategic Management for the Public Services,* identifies professionals and other employees, service users and citizens, and other providers, as stakeholders.[8] The type and range of stakeholder are an important influence on an organization's values.

Values statements have become more important with the rise in global organizations and a requirement to integrate corporate management philosophies and business methodologies across global workforces that are comprised of contrasting national cultures. More specifically, large organizations have to harmonize cross-functional activity with functional ones; this needs a general context in which individuals can work consistently in relation to each other, so that they are able to develop and sustain organization-wide competences.

An organization's general context for working must be stable over a long period. Jim Collins in his book, *Good to Great*, argues that the best companies sustain their position by preserving their core values and purpose, while their business strategies and operating practices continuously adapt to a change.[9] It does not matter what these core values are so much that to be successful, companies must have them, and senior managers are aware of them and are able to build them explicitly into the organization, and preserve them over time.

IF WE WANT TO KNOW WHAT A BUSINESS IS WE HAVE TO START WITH ITS PURPOSE. AND ITS PURPOSE MUST LIE OUTSIDE OF THE BUSINESS ITSELF. IN FACT, IT MUST LIE IN SOCIETY SINCE A BUSINESS ENTERPRISE IS AN ORGAN OF SOCIETY. THERE IS ONLY ONE VALID DEFINITION OF BUSINESS PURPOSE: TO CREATE A CUSTOMER.

Values statements

A statement of an organization's **values** documents the expected collective norms and standards of behaviour of everybody in the organization; it may also include expectations about how people should manage and work together. A good statement is designed to reinforce trust, fairness, support and honesty, on which most working relations depend.

A company's core values constitute its basic strategic understanding on which it operates, and Collins emphasizes the importance of a culture of self-disciplined people who adhere to a consistent system, within which they have the freedom and responsibility to take action. This discipline is felt as much intuitively as it is consciously. It may not be possible to lay down completely a set of core values exactly 'in so many sentences', but it should be communicated through

PRINCIPLES IN PRACTICE 2.1

Defining stakeholder value at Honeywell

Honeywell defines value for four primary stakeholders as follows.

1 Customers: Customer value means instant access to highly reliable, defect-free products and services that enhance their competitiveness.

2 Employees: Personal value is personal growth, recombination and rewards, and quality of work life for all.

3 Shareholders: Shareholder value is generating ever-increasing returns for all investors with the proper balance between short-term results and long-term growth.

4 Community members: Community value means sharing our capabilities and resources for the betterment of the communities in which we live and work.

Honeywell depicts its value creation process as a four part cycle: world class workforce, best practice, customer delight and robust business performance. Stakeholder value changes as the organization and its environment change, so the cycle is never ending.

The cycle is driven by leadership (training and workshop experience in leadership is required for all managers, supervisors and individual team leaders).

For Honeywell: '... the value creation process is the foundation around which we communicate and align our strategic initiatives. It is understood by all employees and provides them with a fundamental template to organize and communicate local action plans that support organizational strategies'.[27]

a common organizational culture which is shared by key managers and, to some extent, by employees.[10]

Organizational culture

The anthropologist, Clifford Geertz, explained culture as a historically transmitted pattern of meanings, which is embodied in symbolic forms that people use to communicate, perpetuate, and develop their knowledge and attitudes about life.[11] In the context of business organizations, Edgar Schein, in his influential book, *Organizational Culture and Leadership,* explains **organizational culture** in a similar way**,** as the shared basic assumptions and beliefs learned from experience.[12] These operate unconsciously to determine the taken-for-granted perceptions everybody in an organization has of the environment. Assumptions and beliefs are forged over time as people learn from dealing with the organization's problems, and they become embedded in behaviour, which reliably and repeatedly proves itself over time.

It is important not to think of organizational culture superficially as artefacts and espoused values, which are really only manifestations of something deeper. Schein explains that there are three levels of culture (see Figure 2.3); these should be understood for how they influence each other.

Artefacts are visible as work places and processes and constitute how people appear and visibly interact with each other. Espoused values are the conscious reasons for the organization and its action, such as documented purpose statements but also slogans and commentary published in communication media, such as newsletters, emails and so on. The

PRINCIPLES IN PRACTICE 2.2

Examples of purpose statements

Bank of China (Hong Kong)

Our Vision, Mission and Values (VMV)

We believe that a strong corporate culture inspires passion among employees in what they do. In order to reach a higher level of business performance, new vibrancy has to be injected into our corporate culture. After careful formulation and thorough discussion, the Board approved the Group's Vision, Mission and Core Values (VMV), the bedrock of our corporate culture, in 2004. With this initiative, we have embarked on building a coherent and bank-wide corporate culture and spirit that will motivate us and move us forward in the twenty-first century.

Our Vision is: To be our customer's premier bank

Our Mission is to:
Build customer satisfaction and provide quality and professional service
Offer rewarding career opportunities and cultivate staff commitment
Create values and deliver superior returns to shareholders

Our Core Values are:
Social responsibility – We care for and contribute to our communities
Performance – We measure results and reward achievement
Integrity – We uphold trustworthiness and business ethics
Respect – We cherish every individual
Innovation – We encourage creativity
Teamwork – We work together to succeed
The first letters of the initial words of mission, form 'BOC', and of vision, form 'SPIRIT', and taken as a whole, our Mission and Core Values form the acronym 'BOC SPIRIT' – a simple yet powerful message that all our employees can identify with and work together as a team towards corporate goals.[28]

Bank Islam (Malaysia)

Our Vision: To be the global leader in Islamic banking
'Global leader' is defined as being the ultimate guidance and source of reference for innovative Shariah-based products and services

Our Core Values
Leader – Our Islamic products are the benchmark
Reputed as the pioneer in Islamic banking, we helped to build the Islamic banking industry
Dynamic – Progressive and innovative
We are constantly moving ahead as we offer new and technologically advanced products and services
Professional – Fast, efficient and responsive service
We are knowledgeable and equipped to handle global business challenges

(*Continued*)

Caring – Approachable and supportive partner
We help to fulfil every customer's financial needs
Trustworthy – Dependable and reliable
Fully Shariah-compliant products, services and corporate values

Our Mission Statement
To continually develop and innovate universally accepted financial solutions in line with Shariah principles
To provide a reasonable and sustainable return to shareholders
To provide for a conducive working environment and to become an Employer of Choice for top talents in the market
To deliver comprehensive financial solutions of global standards using state-of-the-art technology
To be a responsible and prudent corporate citizen
In the performance of this corporate mission, Bank Islam shall be guided by its corporate brand values of being: A LEADER; DYNAMIC; PROFESSIONAL; CARING AND TRUSTWORTHY[29]

Question: Compare these two sets of statements. What are the organizations trying to achieve?

The Bank of China building in Hong Kong

FIGURE 2.3 Three levels of culture

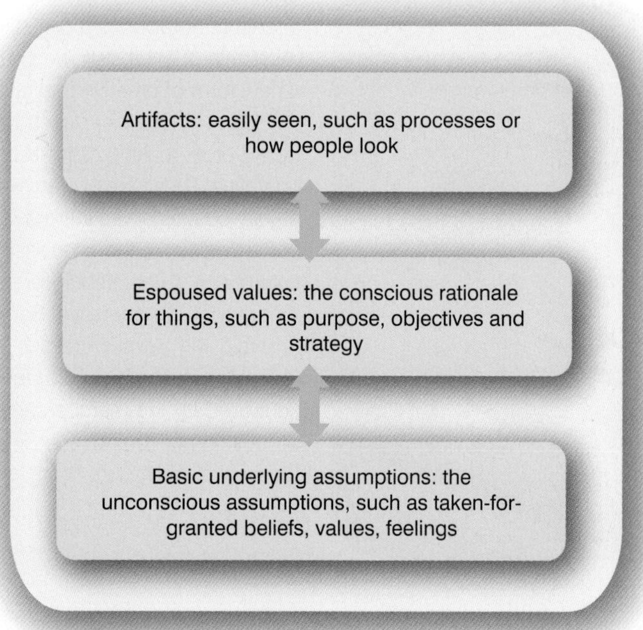

PRINCIPLES IN PRACTICE 2.3

A mission not just for profit

A social business is a profit-making company driven by a larger mission. Like a conventional company it has to recover its full costs and make as much money as possible, subject to its mission, which is driven by a cause, rather than profit. The phrase, 'make as much money as possible' is the thing that differentiates the social business from a non-profit organization. Investors typically receive an annual dividend, but the social mission takes priority and most of the profits are returned to build the business.

The Grameen Bank was founded in Bangladesh by Muhammad Yunus in 1976. Ten years later Yunus received the Nobel Peace Prize for his bank's work in helping to alleviate poverty. This was achieved through the provision of very small (micro) loans to community entrepreneurs, and work involving joint ventures with large western companies, such as the Norwegian telecoms business, Telenor, and Groupe Danone, the French yogurt maker.

The banking industry had believed it impossible to make money through the provision of micro-loans to the poor. In 2006, when Yunus received his Nobel Prize, Grameen reported $725 million in disbursed loans, and $20 million profits. The bank's example has been followed in other countries, notably in Mexico, where the Compartamos Banco has reported returns on investment as high as 40 per cent.

The idea for the yogurt began in 2005, when Franck Riboud, the chief executive of Groupe Danone, told Yunus the company wished to find ways to help the poor. The result was Grameen Danone Foods; its mission is to bring affordable food nutrition to malnourished children in Bangladesh with a fortified yogurt. The brand name is Shokti Doi, which in Bengali means 'yogurt for power'.

Muhammad Yunus

The idea of a hybrid enterprise with longer-term aims, rather than a purely shorter-term profit-driven company, has been attracting wider attention, notably from Bill Gates, the former chief executive of Microsoft, who has been advocating a new form of creative capitalism.

However, there are already good examples of hybrid profit-making organizations, notably the co-operative. These are of many kinds, including community co-operatives in Ireland, which involve rural communities in the management of small local enterprises, to household brands, such as United Kingdom's Co-operative Bank, which managed to avoid the worst excesses associated with the global financial crisis. A co-operative is owned and controlled by the members they serve; these may be customers, producers, employees, or another group of stakeholders.[30]

Question: Consider how a social business might differentiate its vision, mission and values.

KEY DEBATE 2.1

Was Enron a bad case of disconnected values?

Organizations do not always use purpose statements accurately. Perhaps the most notorious instance is Enron, a company that failed amid scandal in 2002, which led to suicide and jail sentences for some of its executives.

At the turn of the century Enron was the world's largest energy company and it aspired to become the blue-chip electricity and gas company of the twenty-first century. The company won praise and was used as an illustrative example of a 'uniquely entrepreneurial culture' by Gary Hamel,[31] and in a leading strategic management textbook it was given as 'a good example of how a company's values, beliefs and philosophy connect closely to its strategy'.

According to Enron's website and its annual report (1998), the company believed (among other good things) in 'integrity: We work with customers and prospects openly, honestly, and sincerely. When we say we will do something, we will do it; when we say we cannot do something, then we won't do it'.

In his book about leadership, Jack Welch, suggests Enron's problems came about because its organizational culture became disconnected from its original core values.

'In its prior life, Enron was a simple, rather mundane pipeline and energy company. Everyone was focused on getting gas from point A to point B cheaply and quickly, a mission they accomplished very well by hiring expertise in energy sourcing and distribution. Then ... the company changed missions. Someone got the idea to turn Enron into a trading company. ... the goal was faster growth ... figuratively speaking – the guys in overalls were suddenly riding the elevator with MBAs in suspenders. Enron's new mission meant it focused first on trading energy and then on trading anything and everything. That change was probably pretty exciting at the time, but obviously no one stopped to figure out and explicitly broadcast what values corresponding behaviours would support such a heady goal. The trading desk was the place to be, and the pipeline and energy generation businesses got shoved to the background. Unfortunately, there were no processes to provide checks and balances for the suspenders crowd. And it was in that context – of no context – that Enron's collapse occurred.'[32]

Question: What really disconnected at Enron?

basic underlying assumptions are felt consciously and determine how people carry out their work.

Senior managers should be conscious of culture, or they are likely to find that culture manages them. Culture is expressed in an everyday sense, as 'the way we do things', and because individuals find it practical to work 'with the system' rather than change it, it is likely that in the end everybody becomes part of the culture. This happens without managers fully realizing the strength of its influence. To an outsider it is sometimes called 'going native'. This is especially so if managers are trying to effect change in large and complex organizations, where there are subcultures, or, as Schein called them, 'clans'. These are likely to involve specialists and professionals, or groups that are based within well-defined business areas such as physically removed departments and units. Schein suggests that managers find it difficult to change something as fundamental as an organizational culture, but they should be aware of how it influences the effectiveness of decisions and their implementation.

> **Senior managers should be conscious of culture, or they are likely to find that culture manages them.**

If Collins is right about core values, change is not necessarily a good thing. The 'way we do things' is often a firm-specific quality that gives an organization its unique competitive advantage: it provides the reason why customers prefer a particular organization (see Chapter 5). Core values should be understood, especially by anyone who comes from another organization and who is appointed to a senior management team to take responsibility for strategic management.

Johnson and others consider the United Kingdom's National Health Service (NHS).[13] This is a large and complex organization with a multiplicity of subcultures, as well as an extensive multiplicity of stakeholders. To help managers think systematically about organizational culture, they offer a framework called a **cultural web** (see Figure 2.4).

This specifies six categories, which are stories, symbols, power, organizational structures, controls,

FIGURE 2.4 The cultural web[13]

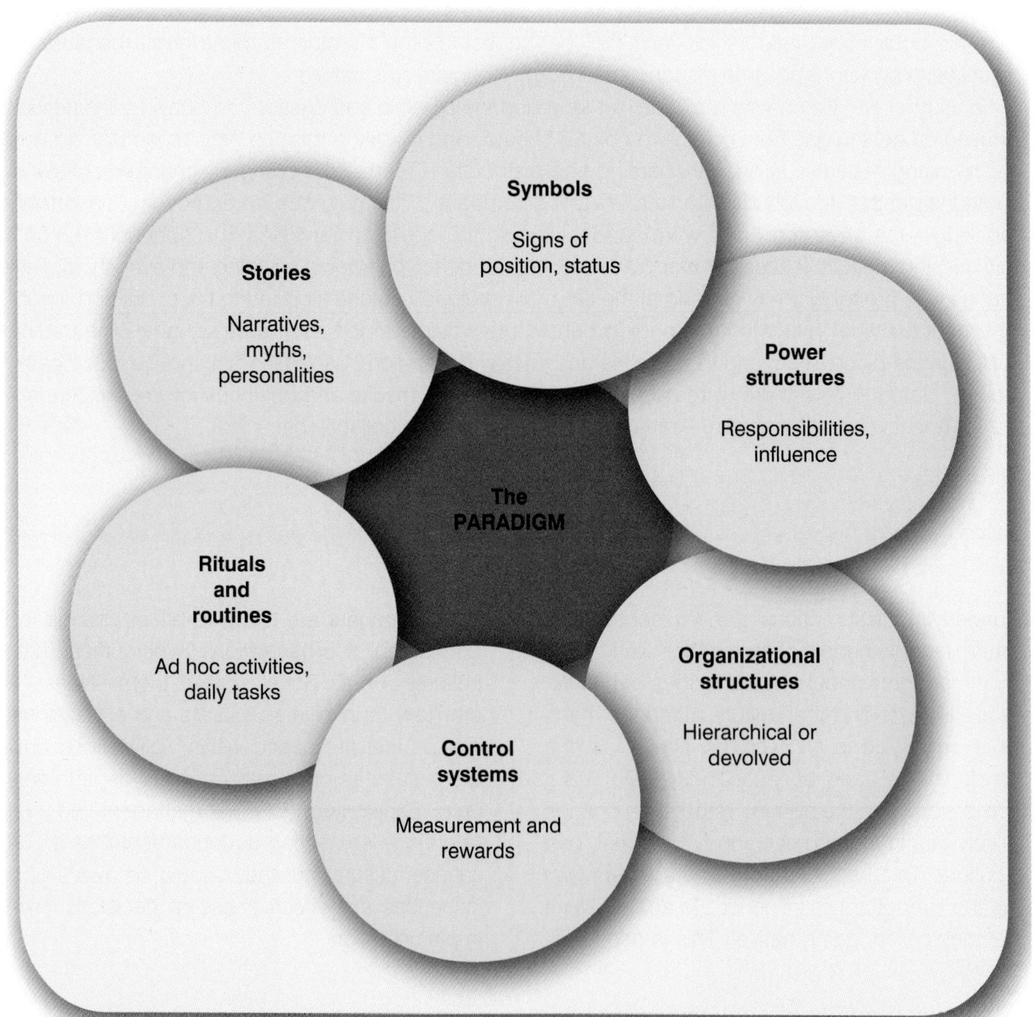

Johnson, G., Scholes, K. and Whittington, R. (2008) *Exploring Corporate Strategy*, Harlow: Pearson Education. Used with permission.

routines and rituals. These combine and inter-relate but can be used to indicate the underlying collectively held taken-for-granted assumptions, or 'paradigms'.[14] Stories are important since this is an area that managers can influence. These refer to narratives that people within the organization use to talk to each other, and which get reflected in company newsletters and so on. The nature of stories typically reflects collective views about desired leadership styles and behaviours, and may feature as important ingredients of the first impressions of new recruits and outsiders. Stories may be apocryphal and recognized as such, but if they 'tell a good story' they serve to unite people in a collective unconsciousness of what the organization is all about.

At Starbucks, senior managers have influenced and built an organizational culture that is summed up by the Starbuck's phrase, the 'Third Place' – the place where customers would think of spending time after home and work: where the coffee is good, the staff do not hassle and there is a friendly ambience conducive to getting out the laptop. An important reason for Starbuck's global growth is its distinctive service. The culture has been imposed and has not allowed much adaptation at a country level. This has drawbacks, of course: for example, the associated Americanisms with Starbucks are unlikely to have a universal appeal, and perhaps played a part in the reasons for the closure of shops in Australia in 2008.[15] (National culture and globalization are considered in Chapter 8.)

In general, though, people want to feel they belong and work in an organization that has a clear common purpose which is recognized beyond the organization. This is a powerful altruistic force that helps to reinforce a positive corporate image held of the organization by stakeholders, such as customers and investors. An involving culture, and the sense of identity it brings, helps to make people feel good about themselves and what they do. When, for example, an employee says they work for Apple, and the response is, 'Oh, that's an exciting company', they feel they belong to something worthwhile, so that next time they will go a little bit further in pleasing an Apple customer.

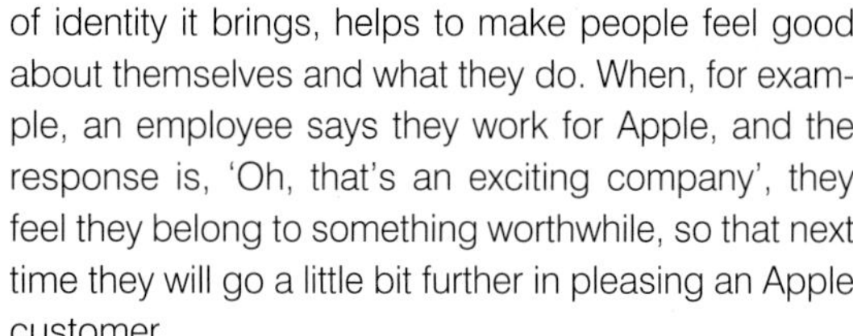

Corporate image and identity

The **corporate image** of an organization lies in the eye of the receiver, particularly in the eye of an external stakeholder. A **corporate identity**, on the other hand, is the organization's self-image, held collectively by its employees. If corporate identity is understood as a communicable (and visual) expression of an organization's purpose, then it can be strategically managed to influence corporate image, and ultimately to determine long-term corporate reputation.[16] Public relations (PR) is often used to explain purpose to influence how stakeholders see and think about the organization and the value it offers. However, the strategic management of identity primarily concerns internal marketing to create positive feelings among employees, involving communication strategies that convey purpose and meaning, define success and offer valuable lessons from experience. Managers should be willing to come out from behind their desks to create a feeling of trust and to show that employees are cared about. Tom Peters called this 'walking the talk', a form of management by walking about.[17]

Internal marketing is prone to the dangers of faddism. It should be strategic rather than short-lived, and be seen to involve senior managers for the long-term, not just as another flavour of the month. However, employees need to be kept interested and feeling involved. Ray Kroc, ex-chief executive of McDonald's, said a 'thousand communication techniques [*are needed*] to keep morale high and instil an atmosphere of trust and co-operation. These [*include*] Hamburger University and the "All-American Hamburger Maker" competition among employees.'.[18]

KEY DEBATE 2.2

Are purpose statements fit for purpose?

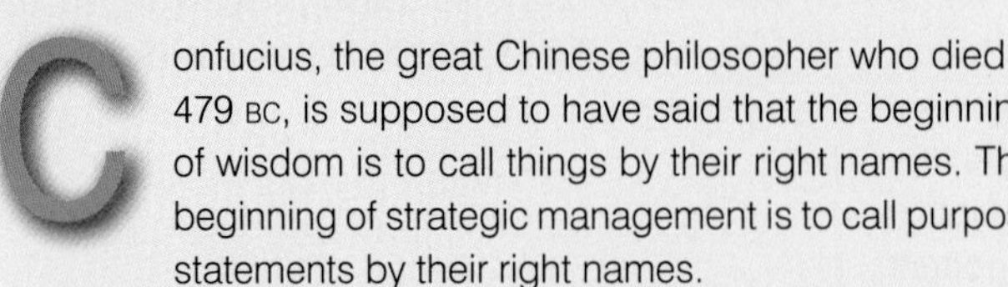

Confucius, the great Chinese philosopher who died in 479 BC, is supposed to have said that the beginning of wisdom is to call things by their right names. The beginning of strategic management is to call purpose statements by their right names.

Most organizations use purpose statements,[33] but the words, vision and mission, are commonly confused. The idea that they should perform distinct roles does not meet with universal acceptance.

Campbell and Yeung propose a broad view for mission, which incorporates purpose, strategy, behaviour standards and values.[34]

Bartlett and Ghoshal, on the other hand, argue that purpose itself should replace overall strategy: while senior managers decide purpose, it should be the job of the rest of the organization to find the means to achieve it.[35]

A purpose in this sense can be a vision that acts as a strategy, which serves as an overall point of reference for sensing opportunities.[36] This view is consistent with the emergent view (see Chapter 1).

Question: Are purpose statements really necessary?

Business ethics

Recent corporate scandals and (safety) disasters have highlighted many issues about how organizations conduct their business and scope their activities. A key influence is how the increasing demand for natural resources has put a strain on the environment as economic growth accelerates, particularly in emerging markets. Water, oil and the atmosphere are all under pressure, making it necessary to innovate to find new ways to make environmentally-friendly products, which must comply with changes in regulatory standards.

Business ethics concern the universal morals that an organization adopts and abides by.[19] Organizations may document these formally as codes to give an explicit set of guidelines for everybody to follow; or they may be written as a values statement and articulated for key stakeholders, such as employees, a community or society. An industry's, or a profession's, ethics are understood as those commercial practices and behaviours that are generally accepted by participants as essential to trust and stable business relationships.

Ethics are obviously important to many non-profit organizations, which involve serving the wider community. However, commercial organizations may use ethics to drive corporate strategy, and one of the best known is The Body Shop:

> *Activism has been part of the DNA of The Body Shop. The company's campaigns against human rights abuses, in favour of animal and environmental protection and its commitment to challenge the stereotypes of beauty perpetuated by the cosmetics industry, have won the support of generations of consumers. The unique blend of product, passion and partnership that characterizes the story of The Body Shop will continue to evolve. It is a shared vision. The company continues to lead the way for businesses to use their voice for social and environmental change.*[20]

The Body Shop was founded by Anita Roddick, an activist and campaigner for environmental and social issues, and the shops closely reflected her concerns. She died in 2007, and the year before Body Shop was taken over by the large French fashion company, L'Oreal. The Body Shop is against using animal testing for cosmetics, but L'Oreal has pursued different aims. In recent years other multinationals have shown an interest in smaller ethically-driven companies.

Ben and Jerry's Holdings, a company which has a social mission and makes 'natural homemade' ice-cream, was taken over by Unilever in 2000. In 2009 Coca-Cola bought a financial stake in Innocent, the maker of 'real fruit' smoothies. While these big companies are simply diversifying, as they have always done, into new and growing markets, it is questionable if the smaller companies will be able to hold to the values that were originally a major part of their success. Ben Cohen, co-founder of Ben and Jerry's, now thinks this is not possible and has regrets about his sale.[21]

The nature of ethics and a sense of what is right vary from country to country. These differences are reflected in the norms and behaviours of their business cultures. A good example is a practice used in Chinese communities called guanxi; *guan* and *xi* approximate to 'a door' or 'to close up' and 'a joined-up chain' respectively.[22] This is the practice of building a network of inter-personal relationships and connections through a process of reciprocal manners or, as it seems sometimes through suspicious western eyes, favours.[23] There are similar practices in Russia (*blat*) and in Arab countries (*wasta*).

Corporate social responsibility

Corporate social responsibility (CSR) is the view that large (especially international) organizations should fulfil a corporate (and world) citizen role. This involves how they should pursue profits hand-in-hand with good citizenship, such as how they affect the environment. They should also set a good example by achieving high standards of business morality, especially in relation to their practices in the developing world. Good practice, however, does not necessarily lead to enhanced value for stakeholders.[24] However, in corporate image terms, especially for a global brand, CSR is more important than ever. For example, Wal-Mart is known for its single-minded insistence that its suppliers produce the lowest prices. In 2008 it publicized how it was moving to create a greener supply chain, when it introduced a scorecard for its Chinese suppliers. This is written in simplified Chinese and evaluates suppliers for how they reduce packaging waste. Wal-Mart will no doubt ask for lower prices if this does lead to lower supplier costs.

Governance

Organizational **governance** is a non-executive function that ultimately decides purpose, critically appraises and approves a senior management's strategic management, its progress and results. These things are the

KEY DEBATE 2.3

Do boards control their executives?

In their book, *The Puritan Gift*, Kenneth and William Hopper argue that present-day corporate boards are composed of financially-oriented directors, who identify with the shareholders rather than with the organization and its employees[37]. This is made worse by the cult of the professional manager and the belief that leaders can manage any kind of business without the domain knowledge that would give them an understanding of how the organization they are running works. The rot set in during the 1970s, when the large corporations began to finance growth through borrowing rather than reinvested revenue. The focus of boards changed from the long-term to a shorter-term one focused on satisfying shareholders.

John Kay suggests that sometimes boards and executives lose control of the basic purpose of the business. General Electric Company (GEC) was a successful United Kingdom-based conglomerate, which employed around 40 000 people in 1995, when it came under new management. The company had successfully fought off competition from the Japanese and had accumulated a 'cash mountain', which its chief executive refused to spend on new businesses, and was often times criticized by investors as too conservative.

The company's new management changed its name to Marconi and sold off most of the old core businesses, such as those in heavy engineering and domestic electronics. The proceeds were reinvested in telecommunication companies. This was done at the height of the dot.com boom, and by 2005 Marconi was bankrupted and reduced to a rump of about 4500 employees.

In Kay's view, it was not a case simply of the Marconi board doing its job badly, but that the job itself was wrong: 'senior executives [*should*] understand that managing companies is not about mergers, acquisitions and disposals but about running operations businesses well; and that corporate strategy is about matching the capabilities of the business to the needs of its customers'.[38]

Question: Could the global financial crisis, as the Hopper brothers suggest, be another story of boards not understanding the businesses they are supposed to oversee and manage?

primary responsibility of a group of governing directors, such as a board of directors, or a committee of trustees. A board is comprised of non-executive members, who are representatives of the owners, those who have a substantial financial involvement, and perhaps other stakeholders. These do not take part in the actual management of the organization. There are also executive members who include the chief executive and the senior officers, who are charged with the management of the organization. There is a chairman, who may be different from the chief executive. In European countries it is considered good practice to separate the role of chairman from that of the chief executive. An important role for the board is to appoint and (sometimes) remove the executives.

The role of governance is essentially one of oversight, to make sure that the business of the organizations is being conducted properly and effectively to achieve overall purpose. In this it should consider the following:

- To provide overall direction in terms of purpose, including direction (vision), the form and boundaries of the businesses conducted (mission), and how the organization should conduct itself ethically and appropriately (values) on behalf of its key stakeholders.
- To oversee the formulation and implementation of the organization's strategic objectives and its strategy.
- To agree and facilitate policies and guidelines to promote the organization's key priorities.
- To understand how the organization works.
- To be aware of conditions and developments external to the organization that have a bearing on the organization's purpose and conduct of that purpose.

The extent to which a board influences or makes strategy seems to vary. A McKinsey survey[25] suggests that a board is often active in challenging strategy during its formulation and will be involved in approving its final form, but only a minority of boards are active in developing the content of a strategy.

The role of the non-executive is potentially important as a questioning presence. For example, in a publicly listed company there is likely to be short-term (typically investor) pressure on executives to deliver results. This could encourage executives to give too little attention in their strategic management to the longer-term investment needs of the organization. Non-executives should be able and willing to overturn the strategic implications of executive decisions, since they have access and the opportunity to deliberate the detail of these choices.

© iStockPhoto.com

For example, the **non-executive directors** at Ford questioned and eventually removed Jac Nasser from his position as chief executive. Nasser's strength as a chief executive had been based on a visionary view of the future. He saw little prospect of growth from assembling cars and selling them in showrooms. Ford's future was in developing services, from finance to recycling, to give Ford revenues over the entire life of the vehicle it sold. It included the purchase of Kwikfit in the United Kingdom, a tyre and exhaust service company. However, Ford's non-executives thought the purpose of Ford was to make cars and his departure was a back-to-basics move. (Kwikfit was in the end sold back to its original owner at a loss – the global financial crisis has been unkind to the car industry: it could turn out that Nasser was right.)

The sorry tale of corporate scandals and failures over the last few years, down to the unfortunate strategies of the banks, has raised questions about how effectively boards, and in particular the non-executives, do their job. However, it is likely that, while corporate leaders are successful they are unlikely to be asked unsettling questions by their boards (strategic leadership is covered more fully in Chapter 11).[26]

THE SORRY TALE OF CORPORATE SCANDALS AND FAILURES OVER THE LAST FEW YEARS, DOWN TO THE UNFORTUNATE STRATEGIES OF THE BANKS, HAS RAISED QUESTIONS ABOUT HOW EFFECTIVELY BOARDS, AND IN PARTICULAR THE NON-EXECUTIVES, DO THEIR JOB.

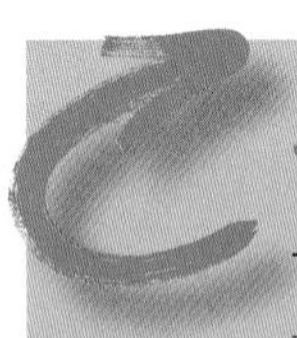

SUMMARY OF PRINCIPLES

This chapter has made the following important points:

1. To be effective, strategic management must, before all else, clarify the organization's purpose.
2. Vision, mission and values statements have different roles in strategic management and should be managed as an integrated set.
3. Organizations create value for their stakeholders; the primacy of the customer is central.
4. Strategic management should take account of organizational culture.
5. Business ethics are important to purpose.
6. Organizational governance is a function that oversees an executive's strategic management.

GLOSSARY OF KEY TERMS

Business ethics the universal morals that an organization works to.

Core capabilities distinctive organizational capabilities that are difficult for a rival to copy.

Corporate identity a communicable expression of an organization's purpose.

Corporate image an image of an organization held by its stakeholders.

Corporate social responsibility the view that large (especially international) organizations should fulfil a corporate (and world) citizen role.

Cultural web shows the manifestations of an underlying culture (or paradigm).

Exploratory/exploitative learning terms used by March (1991) for the kinds of learning (based on feedback) an organization requires for different modes of change.

Governance a non-executive function that ultimately decides purpose, critically appraises and approves a senior management's strategic management, its progress and results.

Improvement change is focused on sustaining an existing business model.

Mission a statement of the organization's present main activities.

Non-executive directors directors of a board with no involvement in the daily management.

Organizational culture basic assumptions and beliefs shared by organizational members.

Purpose the primary and basic reason for the existence of the organization.

Strategic change transformational change that is focused on changing an existing business model.

Tranformational change fundamental change to an organization's business model.

Values the expected collective norms and behaviour of everybody in the organization; this may also include expectations about how people should manage and work together.

Vision a view of some desired future state or ideal for the organization.

GUIDED FURTHER READING

This chapter has focused on organizational purpose from the viewpoint of strategic management, and has only brushed the surface of corporate governance, which is a subject in its own right, especially from the perspective of principal-agent theory.

Robert Freeman presents a stakeholder map that he uses to classify stakeholders according to two dimensions: the nature of the stake they have in the organization, and the power they are able to exert, see:

Freeman, R. E. (1984) *Strategic Management: A Stakeholder Approach*, Boston: Pitman, p. 63.

A good comprehensive review of stakeholder theory is:

Donaldson, T. and Preston, L. E. (1995) 'The stakeholder theory of the corporation: concepts, evidence, and implications', *Academy of Management Review* 20(1):65–91.

Corporate image and identity form another important specialist subject. A special issue was devoted to organizational identity in the *Academy of Management Review*. This includes a view of identity from the perspective of stakeholder theory; see:

Scott, S. G. and Lane, V. B. (2000) 'A stakeholder approach to organizational identity', *Academy of Management Review* 25(1):43–62.

REVIEW QUESTIONS

1 What is the purpose of a purpose?

2 Explain the difference between vision, mission and values.

3 Why are some values core?

4 What do different types of stakeholders get from the organization?

5 How does the organizational culture of an organization affect the way it is managed?

6 From its purpose statements, work out an organization's corporate image and identity.

7 What are business ethics and corporate social responsibilities?

8 What is the role of corporate governance for strategic management?

SEMINAR AND ASSIGNMENT QUESTIONS

1 Find examples of purpose statements from company home pages on the web, and sort them into vision, mission and values statements: pick out and explain how the best ones work and why the worst ones do not. Do organizations seem to know the difference?

2 Think of an organization in which you would like to work and list all the important stakeholders involved. Rank these in descending order of importance and explain why.

3 Consider how an organization's culture might be changed to improve a company's business ethics. Can a commercially-oriented organization that has to deliver short-terms results really afford a strategic long-term view?

CHAPTER REFERENCES

1 Giuliani, R. W. with Kurson, K. (2002) *Leadership,* London: Little, Brown, pp. 317–19.

2 Stieglitz, N. and Heine, K. (2007) 'Innovations and the role of complementarities in a strategic theory of the firm', *Strategic Management Journal* 28:1–15.

3 March, J. G. (1991) 'Exploration and exploitation in organizational learning', *Organization Science* 2(1):71–87.

4 Collins, J. C. and Porras, J. I. (1994) *Built To Last: Successful Habits of Visionary Companies*, New York: Harper Business.

5 Collins, J. C. (2001) *Good to Great: Why Some Companies Make the Leap … and Others Don't,* London: HarperCollins.

6 Campbell, A., Devine, M. and Young, D. (1990) *A Sense of Mission*, London: Economist Publication.

7 Drucker, P. F. (1955) *The Practice of Management*, London: Heinemann Butterworth. (1954, American edn), New York: Harper & Row, pp. 34–5.

8 Joyce, P. (1999) *Strategic Management for the Public Services,* Buckingham: Open University Press.

9 Collins (2001) *op cit*. p. 195.

10 Ouchi, W. G. (1981) *Theory Z: How the American Business Can Meet the Japanese Challenge*, London: Addison-Wesley.

11 Geertz, C. (1973) *The Interpretation of Cultures,* New York: Basic Books.

12 Schein, E. H. (1985) *Organizational Culture and Leadership,* London: Jossey-Bass.

13 Johnson, G., Scholes, K. and Whittington, R. (2008) *Exploring Corporate Strategy,* Harlow: Pearson Education, exhibit 5.8.

14 *Ibid.* There are several definitions for 'paradigm', but in the way it is used here it is an unconscious collectivity or consensus about what are legitimate organizational practices and ideas; its nature is such that the underlying fundamental assumptions are rarely questioned or explicitly understood.

15 Smith, P. (2008) 'Starbucks tastes Australian defeat with 61 store closures', *Financial Times,* July, 30 20.

16 Gray, E. R. and Balmer, J. M. T. (1998) 'Managing corporate image and corporate reputation', *Long Range Planning* 31(5): 695–702.

17 Peters, T. J. and Waterman, R. H. (1982) *In Search of Excellence*, London: Harper & Row.

18 Miller, G. J. (1990) 'Managerial dilemmas: political leadership in hierarchies'. In Cook, K. S. and Levi, M. (eds) *The Limits of Rationality,* London: The University of Chicago Press, 324–48, p. 344.

19 European Foundation for Quality Management (EFQM) (1999) *The EFQM excellence model,* Brussels: EFQM. http://www.efqm.org

20 Body Shop (2003). www.thebodyshop.com

21 Ben Cohen (2009) interviewed on BBC Radio 4, April 7.

22 Al, J. (2006) 'Guanxi networks in China: its importance and future trends', *China and the World Economy* 14(5):105–18.

23 Tian, X. (2007) *Managing International Business in China,* Cambridge: Cambridge University Press.

24 Vogel, D. (2005) *The Market for Virtue: The Potential and Limits of Corporate Social Responsibility,* Washington, DC: Brookings Institution Press.

25 McKinsey and Company (2006) 'Improving strategic planning: a McKinsey survey', *The McKinsey Quarterly* www.mckinseyquarterly.com

26 Stiles, P. and Taylor, B. (2001) *Boards at Work: How Directors View Their Roles and Responsibilities,* Oxford: Oxford University Press.

27 Jones, R. D. (1998) 'The new management accounting system at Honeywell's Micro Switch Division'. In Christopher, W. F. (ed.) (1998), *New Management Accounting,* Crisp Publications, pp. 1–17.

28 Bank of China (2008) www.bochk.com

29 Bank Islam (2008) www.bankislam.com

30 Seelos, C. (2009) 'New models for the future', *Financial Times,* February 12, and Kelly, M. (2009) Not just for profit, *strategy+business, www.strategy-business.com,* February.

31 Hamel, G. (2008) 'Quest for innovation, motivation inspires the gurus', interview by Erin White, *The Wall Street Journal,* May 5.

32 Welch, J. and Welch, S. (2005) *Winning,* New York: HarperCollins, pp. 22–23.

33 Rigby, D. and Bilodeau, B. (2007) 'Selecting management tools wisely', *Harvard Business Review,* December:20–2.

34 Campbell, A. and Yeung, S. (1991) 'Creating a sense of mission', *Long Range Planning* 24(4):10–20.

35 Bartlett, C. A. and Ghoshal, S. (1994), 'Changing role of senior management: beyond strategy to purpose', *Harvard Business Review*, November–December:79–88.

36 Waterman, R. H., Peters, T. and Phillips, J. R. (1980) Structure is not organization' *Business Horizons* June:14–26; Hamel, G. and Prahalad, C. K. (1994) *Competing for the Future*, Boston, MA: Harvard Business School Press; and Christensen, C. M. (1997) *The Innovator's Dilemma: When New Technologies Cause Great Firms to Fail,* Boston, MA: Harvard Business School Press.

37 Hopper, K. and Hopper, W. (2009) *The Puritan Gift: Reclaiming the American Dream Amidst Global Financial Chaos,* New York: I. B..

38 Kay, J. (2002) 'A vital item is missing', *Financial Times* January 29,13.

CASE 2.1 HP's core values under fire

Hewlett-Packard (HP)'s core values are based on the 'sort of people we are, like working with'; this is the HP Way. It reflects a set of deeply-held beliefs, which have been at the heart of the company's purpose and activities since it was established. According to one of its founders, David Packard, the HP Way distinguishes the company more than its products have done[1] (see Exhibit 2.1).

Things changed in 2005, when the HP Way was withdrawn and replaced with a 'vision and strategy' that emphasized diversity and inclusion:

> *At HP, we believe diversity is a key driver of our success. Putting all our differences to work across the world is a continuous journey fuelled by personal leadership from everyone in our company. Our aspiration is that the behaviours and actions that support diversity and inclusion will come from the conviction of every HP employee – making diversity and inclusion a conscious part of how we run our business throughout the world. Diversity and inclusion are woven into the fabric of our company. They are an intrinsic part of our nature and key to fulfilling our vision for HP: to be 'a winning e-company with a shining soul'.*[3]

This statement was supported by a list of 'policies and practices that support diversity'. There is now no longer a HP Way statement. It had outlived its usefulness. It was felt by the HP board that despite its (mainly) organic growth and relatively high rates of return on investment, the company had grown conservative and complacent.

In 1999 Carly Fiorina became the first chief executive to be appointed from outside the company and she had no experience of the HP Way. Her background had been in sales at AT&T, where she worked her way up to become a vice-president. Fiorina took a

EXHIBIT 2.1 The HP way[2]

HP's organizational values (The HP Way)

'I feel that in general terms it is the policies and actions that flow from belief that men and women want to do a good job, a creative job, and if they are provided the proper environment they will do so.'

Bill Hewlett

HP's organisational values and our commitment to meeting our corporate objectives shape our strategies and policies.

- We have trust and respect for individuals.
- We focus on a high level of achievement and contribution.
- We conduct our business with uncompromising integrity.
- We achieve our common objectives through teamwork.
- We encourage flexibility and innovation.

Traditional practices as management by wandering around, hoshin planning and the open door policy, are supported by others, including a ten-step business planning process, and total quality control.

© MTP/Alamy

leading part in divesting the group's telephone equipment business, Lucent Technologies, in 1995.

At HP she masterminded its friendly merger with the struggling computer giant, Compaq, in 2002. The merger was designed to enlarge the new company to challenge IBM as an end-to-end solutions provider for HP customers.

The leading shareholders, Walter Hewlett, son of the founder, and the Packard family, were opposed to the merger. One of the questions was how the new company could compete in the personal computer (PC) market with the successful Dell. Walter Hewlett thought that HP should reduce its emphasis on PCs and increase investment in areas such as digital photography and commercial printing equipment. He felt HP should restructure to improve shareholder value rather than attempt to grow market share. As one observer put it, here was a 'potential culture clash between hard-driving Compaq and egalitarian HP'.[4]

The merger was approved by a bare 51 per cent of HP shareholders, and Carly Fiorina was appointed chairman and chief executive of the enlarged company, which retained the HP name. Michael Capellas, Compaq's chief executive, who had helped Fiorina mastermind the merger, stepped down after six months. The loss of such a senior executive seemed bad news, but the new company started to do better than expected. HP continued to rely heavily on its very profitable and growing printer business, and the losses on personal computers were cut dramatically. The new company seemed to be sorting out its product range and sales forces, which had overlapped significantly.[5]

Carly Fiorina and the HP way

Interviewed by the *Financial Times* in 2003, a successful Fiorina offered insights into her leadership style. In her time at Lucent she had gone on stage to address an audience of salespeople with three socks stuffed down the front of her trousers.

'You have to speak to people in the language they understand,' she said. '... these were guys who, to be direct, thought a lot about the size of their balls. They were sales guys. It was a very macho culture. They thought they had been taken over by a bunch of wimps and that they were going to run the place, and I needed to tell them who was in charge. ... I tell people inside HP that leadership requires a strong internal compass ... So you have to learn to ignore a lot of conventional wisdom and a lot of talk that isn't core to the purpose of what you're doing ... No change programme is unanimously supported. ... HP was such a great company, but it was almost frozen in time ... some ways [*it had*] lost its ambition. Its rate of innovation had declined rapidly. It was growing in single digits in the middle of the biggest technology boom in history ... But this was a company that had not ever brought in an outsider at the top ... 50 per cent of our employees had been there less than five years, but not in the senior ranks, which were genuinely built from within ... Because I was an outsider I couldn't dictate, knowing this was a strong and deep culture and I was only one person. I know that big companies can thwart a CEO. The organization had to decide its own vision, its goal and its willingness to change. Then I could lead ...

'If you looked at our company values today, you would find they are the exact same values that have guided HP for 60 years, except we have added "speed and agility". We don't want to change the fact that trust and respect are part of our value system, that contribution is important and that passion for customers is important ... Those basic values originally were referred to as "the HP Way". Over time, the phrase came to mean any defence against any change. I would go into meetings where somebody would bring up a new idea and someone would say: "We don't do it that way, that's not the HP way".

'Especially for a technology company, it is death if you stop trying new things. HP tended to be very process intensive, which is really important when you're dealing with big complex systems and problems. The downside is that sometimes HP processed endlessly and never decided. Compaq tended to be fast and aggressive, which is good in a fast-moving market. The downside was sometimes Compaq lacked judgement. Sometimes they had to do things over and over because they hadn't thought it through ... We said: "The goal is to be fast and thorough".'[6]

Subsequent problems

Carly Fiorina was fired in February 2005 after HP shares had fallen to around 15 per cent of what they been over the previous year largely due to concerns about HP's ability to execute its strategy profitably. Waters and London (2005) summarized the reasons in the *Financial Times*.

'Dell is fast becoming to technology what Wal-Mart is to retailing: an operator that by virtue of its scale and business model is impossible to beat on price ... The PC market is structurally unattractive if you aren't a Dell. A lot of well-managed companies, well-resourced companies have tried and failed ... As companies such as HP and Sun have abandoned parts of their high-tech bastions to compete more directly with Dell, their earnings have come under pressure and market share has fallen ... Standardization and commoditization are sucking profits out of the business. Standardization is bad for profits for two related reasons.

'First, it makes it harder for companies to differentiate their products and demand premium prices. Second, it makes it easier for customers to shop around, freeing them from the lock-in that comes with being dependent upon on the single supplier of a proprietary technology.

'When this process began in the late 1990s, its impact was masked by booming demand for technology. Over-capacity following the end of the boom, however, changed the rules. Now customers have the upper hand. They are pushing computer companies to make their products interchangeable, giving them greater freedom to change supplier ... it is an industry of standard building blocks ... The big computer systems companies – IBM, HP, Sun – have responded by offering cheaper, more flexible, products. Failure to do so would leave the market open to new low-cost competitors. Thus HP's purchase of Compaq was partly designed to make it the leader in low-cost servers – products that are replacing the corporate computers that used to account for much of its profits. The company has been left with little choice but to cannibalize its own business.

'... Mike Winkler, HP's head of marketing, conceded late last year that the company was selling low-price servers using its traditional sales techniques. One response was to adjust the compensation system for HP salespeople to reward them for the profitability of their sales rather than simply the revenue generated. But five years into Ms Fiorina's tenure, this proved to be too little, too late ... IBM ... chooses to remain a technology conglomerate but has shuffled its portfolio of businesses to focus more on the more profitable parts of the industry. Thus PCs and computer disk drives are out: management consulting and software are in ... Apple ... has hit on a different formula: better products command higher prices. Hence the iPod ... this echoes the turnaround at Motorola ... HP has the R&D investment and engineering culture to bring out dynamic innovations. The trouble is that new hit products have been in short supply ...

'HP's decision to sell a rebranded version of the iPod [failed] ... [*in 2004*] Ms Fiorina proudly trumpeted 200 new consumer technology products from HP, yet none of those has caught the consumer imagination ... perhaps HP should sell its PC operation, which requires a business approach rather than one of technology innovation. Michael Porter ... wrote that there are only two basic types of strategy: high value and low cost. Success for any business starts with a decision about which path to follow. Arguably, Ms Fiorina lost her job this week because her "high-tech, low cost" notion ignored that stricture'.[7]

The abandonment of the HP Way may have been important: 'new practices have been nothing short of trampling of company's heart and soul'.[8] Fiorina had said 'we didn't involve middle and first-line supervisors in the process enough ... I had underestimated in many ways the people of the company, their appetite for change and their ability to do hard things. And I learned that sometimes you have to go slow to go fast'.[9]

Back to basics?

HP has overtaken IBM in revenue, and Dell has stumbled in the PC market. Mark Hurd, a new chief executive, is 'squeezing more out of HP's existing portfolio of businesses by pushing tighter management disciplines deeper into the organization ... he found glaring weaknesses in the organization and processes he inherited ... [*He has handed*] back clearer responsibility to divisional managers for operations. But to become "great", he says, companies eventually have to accept the organization they have and turn to the hard task of honing their processes to perfection. "The way you get good at this stuff is you do it for years". He pauses for emphasis. "You do it for years. And at the end of the day, when you've done it for years, this stuff rolls off people's tongues" '.[10]

It seems that 'processes' are back in favour at HP. Hurd has not changed the strategic logic that drove the Compaq merger, but he has reorganized HP back to a more decentralized model, which is more consistent with HP's original culture, and which refocuses HP on its strengths as a technology and product company, with services in more of a supporting role.[11] In 2007 HP overtook Dell as the world's largest PC maker by sales, and its operating margins have risen from 3.9 to 5.8 per cent.

'Asked whether the turnaround in HP's business vindicates the decision by Carly Fiorina ... to pursue the acquisition of Compaq, Mr Bradley [*who heads the PC division*] declines to be drawn ... "You can't affect the past; you can just focus on how you drive profitable growth in the future, and that's what we spend our time on"'.[12]

Discussion questions

1 Collins and Porras use HP as an example of a visionary company with core values; they argue that organizations should not change their core values. Does HP prove them right?

2 Fiorina may well have been right all along, but after her departure some things were put into reverse. If you had been Carly Fiorina, would you have done things differently?

3 Search for information on the web about how Dell and HP compare; for example, how do Dell's purpose statements compare with those for HP? Do they differ and, if so, what does this suggest for their different approaches to strategic management?

Case references

1 Packard, D. (1995) *The HP Way: How Bill Hewlett and I Built the Company,* New York: Harper Business School Press.

2 Hewlett-Packard (2002) home page http://www.hp.com, December 12.

3 Hewlett-Packard (2005) Our vision and strategy, http://www.hp.com February.

4 Morrison, S. (2002) 'Investors weigh up merger outcomes', *Financial Times,* March 15, p. 26.

5 Waters, R. and London, S. (2002) 'Resilient HP rebounds from Capellas exit', *Financial Times,* November 22, p. 32.

6 Maitland, A. (2003) 'I have learnt from my mistakes', *Financial Times*, November 20, p. 14.

7 Waters, R. and London, S. (2005) 'A struggle over strategy: HP counts the cost of "playing the other guy's game" ', *Financial Times,* February 11, p. 15.

8 Dong, J. (2002) 'The rise and fall of the HP Way', *Palo Alto Weekly,* online edit, www.paloaltoonline.com, April 10.

9 Maitland, A. (2003) *op cit*.

10 Allison, K. and Waters, R. (2007) 'Hewlett-Packard comes back fighting', *Financial Times,* April 30, p. 27.

11 Burgelman, R. A. and McKinney, W. (2006) 'Managing the strategic dynamics of acquisition integration: lessons from HP and Compaq', *California Management Review* 48(3):6–27.

12 Allison, K. (2008) 'HP hits the right note with celebrities and piano-black case', *Financial Times,* January 11.

This case study was prepared using only publicly available sources of information for the purposes of classroom discussion; it does not intend to illustrate either effective or ineffective handling of a managerial situation.

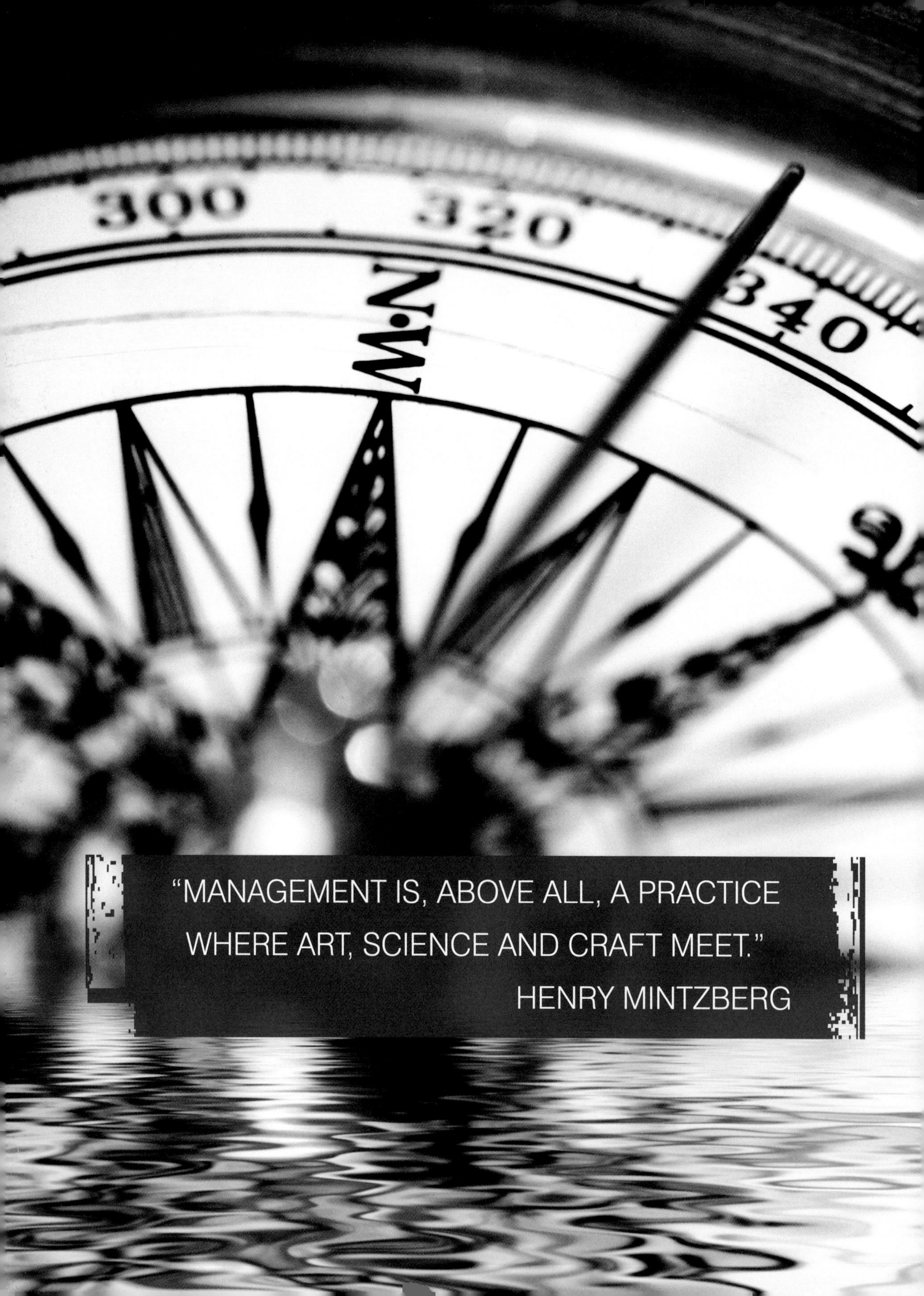
300
320
N.W
340
"MANAGEMENT IS, ABOVE ALL, A PRACTICE
WHERE ART, SCIENCE AND CRAFT MEET."
HENRY MINTZBERG

Determinants of strategy

II

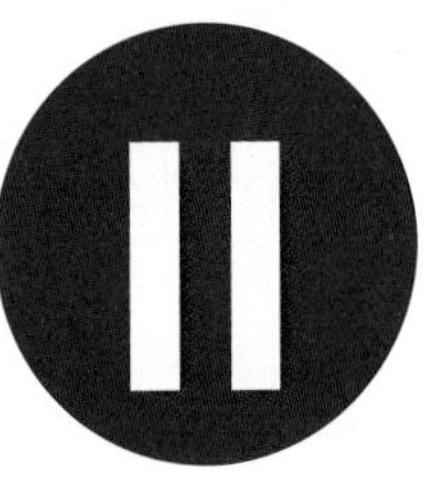

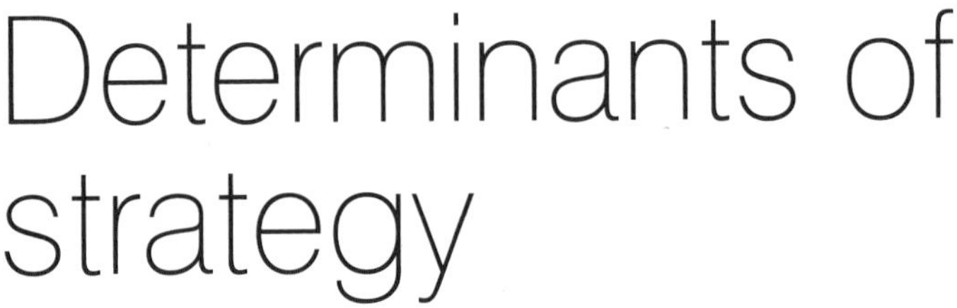

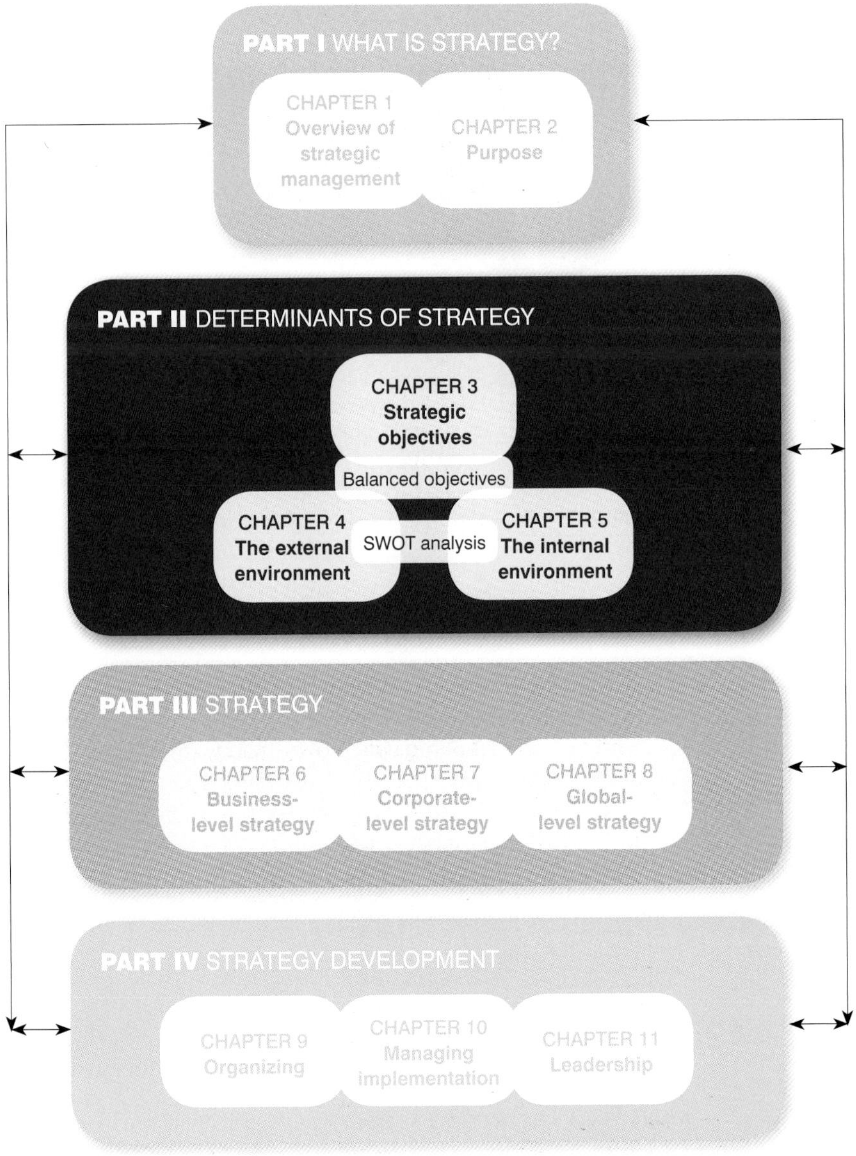
PART I WHAT IS STRATEGY?
CHAPTER 1 Overview of strategic management
CHAPTER 2 Purpose
PART II DETERMINANTS OF STRATEGY
CHAPTER 3 Strategic objectives
Balanced objectives
CHAPTER 4 The external environment
SWOT analysis
CHAPTER 5 The internal environment
PART III STRATEGY
CHAPTER 6 Business-level strategy
CHAPTER 7 Corporate-level strategy
CHAPTER 8 Global-level strategy
PART IV STRATEGY DEVELOPMENT
CHAPTER 9 Organizing
CHAPTER 10 Managing implementation
CHAPTER 11 Leadership

Chapter 3
STRATEGIC OBJECTIVES

Introduction

This chapter considers the general management of objectives, the importance of balance and critical success factors. The importance of the concept of the *strategic* balanced scorecard and its associated tool, the strategy map, is also discussed.

LEARNING OBJECTIVES

By the end of this chapter you should understand:

- The nature and use of objectives.
- The importance of balance in managing objectives.
- The strategic balanced scorecard.
- The nature of a strategy map.
- The management of a balanced scorecard.

Business vignette Working to priorities is working to objectives

'By simply choosing a particular set of criteria for judging business success or failure, you are immediately defining a set of values and a particular way of working', says Mark Bromley, Director of Business Objectives and Performance at EDF Energy. 'Conversely, as soon as you exclude particular business factors from the measurement process, you will almost certainly find that those factors have little or no bearing on the directions you set for yourself and those around you. It's necessary to make the choice between what is really strategic and important, and other performance management objectives and measures.'

The French-owned EDF Energy Group provides over one-fifth of the European Union's electricity. In 2007 it employed more than 150 000 people and achieved a turnover of over £50 billion. The Group's corporate senior managers use a balanced scorecard approach to link overall objectives to continuous improvement. By so doing, EDF aims to instil a strategy-linked driven culture throughout all of its divisions.

The Group's strategic vision is expressed in the form of five ambitions, each with a group-level measure; see Figure 3.1 (the star symbol signifies good progress, diamonds indicate satisfactory

FIGURE 3.1 EDF Energy Group balanced scorecard

Ambition to:	Measures:	status	forecast
Meet shareholders' expectations	Net income	★	◆
	Capital expenditure	★	◆
	Working capital (free cash flow)	■	◆
Care for our customers	Mass market customers	●	◆
	Major business customers	●	◆
Be a positive point of reference (corporate image)	Corporate responsibility index	●	◆
Be safe and responsible	Health, Safety and Environment management index	★	◆
Maximize employee satisfaction	Employee opinion survey	●	◆

performance, circles mean that performance is below expectations and squares suggest that performance is well below expectations).

The ambitions are used across the Group to create a working knowledge of performance and a cultural alignment around its corporate purpose.[1]

The nature of objectives

An **objective** is a statement of a specific outcome that is to be achieved. Objectives must be meaningful and clear to the people who devise and use them, including the people who must manage the objectives. Thus, objectives have to be linked to realistic measures of progress and achievement so that those managing the objectives will know in enough time if it is necessary to intervene and make appropriate changes. Objectives form the basis of a common language for

> Objectives form the basis of a common language for understanding the wider context for any part of work, particularly for identifying the inevitable knock-on effects of change, since agreement with others is usually needed to implement change successfully.

understanding the wider context for any part of work, particularly for identifying the inevitable knock-on effects of change, since agreement with others is usually needed to implement change successfully. This requires common ways of working that are based on dialogue and consensus, and the determination and management of objectives, in ways that are transparent and can be clearly understood by all.

Peter Drucker, who has deservedly been called the 'father of modern management' and who wrote extensively about the use of objectives, argues persuasively that their role is to liberate managers by making things clearer about what has to be done and that this makes work easier. 'Each manager, from the "big boss" down to the production foreman, or the chief clerk, needs clearly spelled-out objectives. These objectives should lay out what contribution they and their unit are expected to make to help other units obtain their objectives. Finally, they should spell out what contribution the manager can expect from other units towards the attainment of their own objectives. Right from the start, in other words, emphasis should be on team-work and team results.'[2]

It is generally observed in the management literature that objectives should be practical and therefore **SMART**:

- **S**pecific
- **M**easurable
- **A**ction oriented (some might use 'agreed upon')
- **R**ealistic
- **T**ime-bound

In practice, strategic objectives *can* be usefully open, general and intangible. These objectives are often ambitious, perhaps to a degree that can seem unrealistic. This happens when the objective is used as a spur to creative thinking about having to do things differently, and to encourage a diversity of solutions for open-ended problems.

It is our view that these kinds of objectives must be grounded if they are to be managed strategically. So, for example, Gary Hamel and C. K. Prahalad argue that the competitive success of the Japanese during the 1980s was due to the simplicity of their long-term vision statements, which Hamel and Prahalad call statements of **strategic intent**.[3] Examples are Komatsu's declared intent to 'Encircle Caterpillar', and Canon's to 'Beat Xerox'. The aim of these was to create an organization-wide obsession with a level of achievement that was at the time out of all proportion to a firm's existing resources and capabilities. This type of strategic objective is an open objective, but the nature of its translation into mid-term objectives for implementation is SMART.

'Strategic intent is like a marathon run in 400-metre sprints. No-one knows what mile 26 will look like, so the role of top management is to focus the organization on the ground to be covered in the near 400 metres, and it does this by setting corporate challenges that specify the next 400 metres ... top management is specific about the ends (reducing product development times by 75 per cent, for example) but less prescriptive about the means'.[4]

The 'challenges' are medium-term plans, and the 'ends' are the targets associated with the plan's objectives: for example, the objective is 'reducing development times' and its associated target is 75 per cent. The 'means' are the actions that have to be developed to achieve the plan's objectives. The principle is that the closer strategically related objectives come to execution at an operational level, the more detailed and specific they must become. The development of medium-term plans and the deployment of strategically related objectives in daily management are discussed in Chapters 9 and 10.

It was Nobel Prize winner, Herbert Simon, who first wrote that organizational goals should be set by senior management and then broken down into sub-goals for use at each level of the organization.[5] In this way each lower-order goal becomes a means to a higher-order goal. In this sense there is a hierarchy

© iStockPhoto.com

> STRATEGIC INTENT IS LIKE A MARATHON RUN IN 400-METRE SPRINTS. NO ONE KNOWS WHAT MILE 26 WILL LOOK LIKE, SO THE ROLE OF TOP MANAGEMENT IS TO FOCUS THE ORGANIZATION ON THE GROUND TO BE COVERED IN THE NEAR 400 METRES ...

of objectives (which is analogous to the strategy hierarchy; see Figure 1.2). The organization's overall objectives, such as corporate objectives, are translated and used to deploy lower-level sub-objectives (typically this is a form of management by objectives, discussed in Chapter 10). At an operational level objectives are often referred to as targets, and corporate objectives are sometimes called goals. However, there is no clear consensus, and goals, targets, aims, objectives, are words that may be used interchangeably. So in understanding what they mean, like the everyday use of 'strategy', you should note how a particular context in which they are being used defines what they exactly mean.

PRINCIPLES IN PRACTICE 3.1

Grounding objectives, bottom-up at Toyota

'In my experience, agreeing objectives for new programmes was accomplished by employees, engineers and staff, bringing proposals to their supervisors for approval. This is how all new initiatives got started. Through it all, the superiors avoided ever telling anyone exactly what to do. As my first manager and mentor at Toyota told me, "Never tell your staff what to do. Whenever you do that, you take the responsibility away from them." So, the Toyota managers, the good ones anyway, would rarely tell their people what to do; they would lay out a problem, ask for analysis or a proposal, but always stop short of saying: "Do this". The employee, upon getting the problem to work on (actually, finding the problem to work on was usually his job too), would develop solution options to take to the manager. The manager's first answer was, invariably, "No". The employee would return to his desk and rework his proposal – three times, five times, ten times if necessary. The manager was the "judge and jury" while the employee was the attorney with whom rested the "burden of proof" to justify his proposal by presenting and analysing all the viable options. It took me a good three years to figure out how this worked.

This was the famous Japanese "bottom-up decision-making" in action. My initial reaction was a level of disillusionment, declaring bottom-up decision-making a huge lie. Wasn't "bottom-up" supposed to be some kind of enlightened form of democratic self-management whereby people essentially do what they want? It took a while for me to see that this wasn't a lie so much as it was objective management, but it was powerful nonetheless: no one was telling anyone else what to do. What a beautiful answer to the control-flexibility dilemma that dogs all large organizations: the company gets basic adherence to the desired corporate objectives, and the workers are free to explore best possible real solutions to problems that they themselves know best.'[25]

Question: What is the difference between objectives and means?

The general management of objectives

Whatever the context for objectives, the woes that beset objective management are numerous. We summarize some of the worst deadly sins in Table 3.1: any of these can kill or maim progress. Senior managers should actively manage organization-wide review to ensure that there are owners for objectives who take responsibility for their progress (see Chapters 10 and 11). This should involve an open and transparent approach that makes sure owners and others are not too cautious because they fear failure, or too optimistic because of unrealistic assumptions and estimates of outcomes and progress. Objectives are central to both organizational learning and motivation; so objective owners should be involved in setting their own objectives.

Realism and practicality are important. Objectives should clarify what has to be done, but it has to be recognized they are often subjective and rely on personal judgement. They should not just be plucked from out of the air as a nice thing to have. If a desired outcome is essential for management success, then whatever it takes should be used to produce it, and this may mean changing the nature of an objective as work progresses. Although if this is a higher level objective and because

TABLE 3.1 The ten deadly sins of objective management

In general the following should be avoided in the management of objectives:

1	Too many objectives: Sub-objectives can breed like rabbits and mushroom out of control at lower levels.
2	Meaningless objectives for those who must manage them: Without relevance there is no motivation.
3	Useless objectives: It must be possible to review objectives and learn from the experience of using them.
4	Old objectives: Objectives should not be based on tradition ('we have always had this objective'), convention, or anything else that is distant from the real issues that require resolution.
5	Myopic objectives: Objectives should never lose sight of how they fit into the broader reasons for having them; there should be a clear view both ways – backwards to the overall strategic objectives, and forwards to the value received by the customer.
6	Insular objectives: Objectives should be managed during their implementation to take account of the objectives and plans of everybody affected by them (especially if they are cross-functional).
7	Inconsistent objectives: Objectives should work synergistically and not against each other; this may mean that some people must achieve less of something (perhaps spend more of their budget) if others are to be more effective (perhaps to save far more on their budgets).
8	Pet objectives: Based on vested interest, individual (career) favoured projects, or on only partial functional and sectional needs.
9	Non-agreed objectives: In developing objectives the potential contributions of third parties, and the possible effects on others of the plans should be agreed in principle before implementation.
10	Complex objectives: Objectives should be kept as simple as possible; for example, any attempt to plan for everything, builds too many layers of contingency into objectives, which only distorts the overall picture of why the objectives exist in the first place.

it is likely to affect many people, changes should be very rare; the focus should instead be placed on finding alternative means. As a working principle, higher level objectives should be managed by senior managers in ways to keep them relatively stable.

There is no reliable method for setting objectives, but their management should be flexible and based upon an open understanding of the organization's current way of doing things. In other words, how things are done now is the starting point for doing things differently. It is important to manage objectives actively so that different things can be attempted as necessary to achieve a desired result.

Objectives and strategic management

Purpose must be is translated into a set of primary objectives, which are called '**strategic objectives**'. These serve as the indicators and measures of a firm's or an organization's long-term effectiveness in managing purpose. These cover the most important areas of the enterprise and are used to help determine the priorities for the implementation and execution of objectives. There is a natural tendency for managers to react more positively to short-term, rather than longer-term, objectives; and as Drucker powerfully points out: 'There are few things that distinguish competent from incompetent management quite as sharply as the performance in balancing objectives [*to*] "obtain balanced efforts, the objectives of all managers on all levels and in all areas should be keyed to both short-range and long-range considerations... Anything else is short-sighted and impractical."'[6] This is basic for effective strategic management (see Figure 3.2).

FIGURE 3.2 Striking a balance in strategic objectives

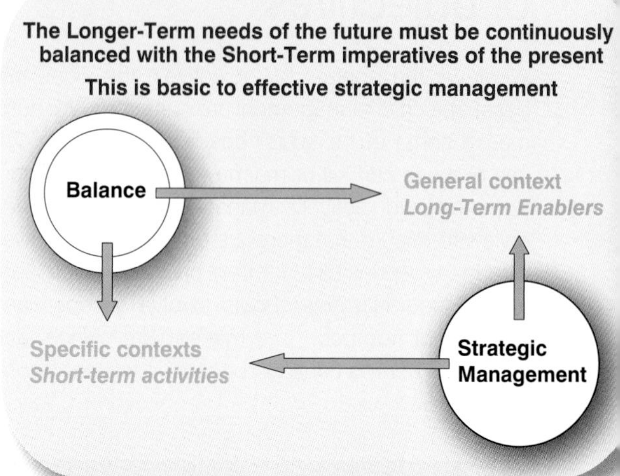

Determining the balance is not easy; this is clear from remarks of senior managers who have had responsibility for strategy. Consider the respective remarks from EdArditte, a senior vice-president of strategy and investor relations at Tyco International, and Stuart Grief, vice president of strategy and business development at Textron:

> *'The responsibility is both in the short and long-term results. There has to be a balance, but there's never a perfect answer for how you balance them. You need a dialogue that aligns resource allocation, people and money with both the short and long-term.'*[7]
>
> *'Balancing the short versus long-term is the biggest challenge we have. How do you balance the trade-off between the short-term compensation lift from near-term performance and the investments – and therefore the depressed economics, shorter-term – that make the long-term strategies pay off?'*[8]

KEY DEBATE 3.1

Can objectives really be used to manage organizations strategically?

Much of the early work in economics assumed that firms would have to follow profit-maximizing objectives. Dissident economists, notably Cyert and March, saw firms as satisficing collections of coalitions which are motivated by their own objectives.[28] As Simon observed, 'The goals that actually underlie the decisions made in an organization do not coincide with the goals of the owners or of top management but have been modified by managers and employees at all echelons'.[29]

The early pioneers of management theory pointed to the inadequacy of a single profit objective. Drucker identified eight core business areas where objectives should be set: these included market standing, innovation, productivity, physical and financial resources, profitability, manager performance and development, worker performance and attitude, and public responsibility.[30] The problem is that this is a loosely-related, or even unrelated, group of lagged and lead objectives. At least with financial objectives a manager could be certain the objective means something. Also if the objectives are wrong it may be better to have no objectives at all (although the very act of managing objectives can make managers aware that they ought to be doing something else).

The answer for Ansoff is to distinguish clearly between financial and strategic objectives[31]. The strategic objectives are those organizational characteristics that enable a successful longer-term performance. This is very similar to Rockart's critical success factors, but it is probably difficult to be sure what an organization's CSFs are. The answer would seem to be to make a constant review of the basic assumptions that underlie an organization's purpose and its strategic objectives.

Question: According to Kaplan and Norton the strategy map is the answer – how?

Critical success factors

In pioneering work that addressed the importance of balance, John Rockart popularized the concept of **critical success factors (CSFs)**. These are the factors that primarily account for an organization's success in achieving its strategic purpose. He based his ideas on research at the Massachusetts Institute of Technology.[9] Ronald Daniel had earlier observed that critical success factors were likely to be different in different industries: for example, in the automobile industry, styling, an efficient dealer network and the tight control of manufacturing costs are paramount; in food processing, new product development, good distribution and effective advertising are major success factors.[10]

Rockart went further and argued that CSFs are a function of four things:

1. the structure of a particular industry (following Daniel)
2. competitive strategy, industry position and geography
3. environmental factors (Rockart gives the example of the abrupt rise in world oil prices in the 1970s)
4. temporal factors (internal concerns that at different times require special attention)

Rockart suggests CSFs can be applied to monitor current results, and to build for the future. CSFs make an organization's key activities explicit and offer up strategic insights that go beyond a mere shared

The Massachusetts Institute of Technology – home of CSFs

understanding of purpose. He uses an example of CSFs and the associated measures for a communications company active in the development of microwave technology. These are:

- Image in financial markets: measure is P/E ratio.
- Technological reputation with customers: measures are order/bid ratio, customer perception interviews.
- Market success: measure is the change in market share (all products).
- Risk recognition in major bids/contracts: measures are company experience with similar new or old customers, prior customer relationship.
- Profit margin on jobs: measure is profit margin as ratio on profit on similar jobs in this product line.
- Company morale: measures are employee turnover, absenteeism etc., informal feedback.
- Performance to budget on job: measures are job cost budgets/activities.

CSFs are often confused with **key performance indicators (KPIs)**. However, there is an explicit distinction between them. KPIs are those strategically-related incremental targets used at lower levels in the organization, such as in daily management. They are derived from or aligned with the overall strategic objectives but are not longer-term in the sense that they are directly associated with CSF objectives and measures (discussed in chapter 10). In the way that Rockart drew a distinction between a CSF and its measures, he heralded the balanced scorecard's important distinction between a strategic objective and its measures.

The balanced scorecard

Robert Kaplan and David Norton introduced the **balanced scorecard** in a *Harvard Business Review* article in 1992.[11] It is perhaps the most widely adopted management methodology of recent times and is used by every kind of organization.[12] Its role is to help organizations take a fuller account not only of their essential financial objectives, but also of the strategic objectives that identify and measure those core activities that enable and lead to desired financial and other outcome objectives.

Lagged and lead measures

Kaplan and Norton distinguish between outcome **measures**, which they call **lagged measures** of past progress, and process measures of performance that are leading to future outcomes, which they call **lead measures**. Lagged measures include taking account of present financial performance and productivity, while

By permission of Harvard Business Press. Jacket design by Diane Levy.

lead measures include taking account of changing perceptions such as customer satisfaction and retention, and the development and management of employees. The present woes of General Motors are put down to the corporation's focus in the United States on the financial (and market) attractiveness of large, rather than small, cars. The organization did not want, or was unable, to foresee the implications of changing consumer preferences from gas guzzlers to economy cars.

Objectives *and* measures

A balanced scorecard is comprised of a limited number of strategic objectives and measures. Each objective has its own set of measures. These are formulated to enable senior management to move an organization strategically towards the achievement of an overall vision. The objectives and measures are decided in terms of four different **perspectives**. These are shown in Figure 3.3 and some examples of an objective for each of the four perspectives, along with examples of possible measures, are given in Table 3.2 (for simplicity only one objective per perspective is shown; an ideal number is three or less, see below). Kaplan and Norton argue that the chosen objectives and measures should answer four fundamental questions (see Figure 3.3).

The perspectives cover important areas of concern to different stakeholders. The financial perspective will matter more to people who have a financial stake in the organization, such as owners and lenders to the business. The customer perspective is a more direct concern with the buyers and users of the organization's products and services. The other two perspectives are more directly relevant to the employees of the organization. It is important in the design of the scorecard that the questions shown in Figure 3.3 should as far as possible reflect the perspectives (or the voice of) the relevant stakeholder.

For example, if it is important to an important shareholder that a given rate-of-return to investment is thought necessary, then senior managers should reflect this in a financial objective.

> The role of the balanced scorecard ... is to help organizations take a fuller account not only of their essential financial objectives, but also of the strategic objectives that identify and measure those core activities that enable and lead to desired financial and other outcome objectives.

FIGURE 3.3 The four perspectives of the balanced scorecard[13]

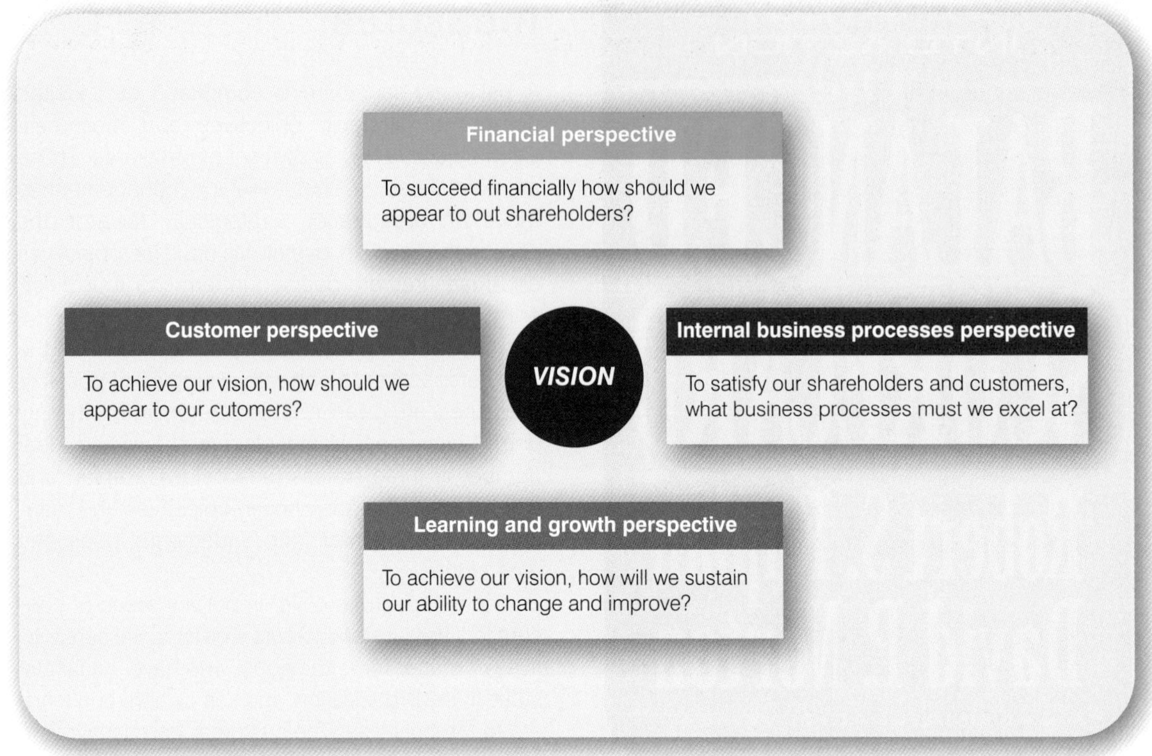

The number of perspectives can be customized to add new ones, but the number of perspectives should be restricted to around four or it is likely that the scorecard will lose its focus. It is better to broaden the interpretation of the original four perspectives than to increase the number and lose the value of the scorecard's compactness. The four perspectives are not meant to be prescriptive, although they should be robust enough for most circumstances.

The original Kaplan and Norton article used different names for the internal business processes, and the learning and growth perspectives. These were respectively called the 'internal business' and the 'innovation and learning' perspectives. These early names did not fully reflect the strategic significance of core business processes, and the importance of core competences to vision. These changes reflected broader changes to Kaplan and Norton's thinking, which was evident in new work published in 1996, which provided a central role for vision, and introduced the strategy map.[14]

Kaplan and Norton had originally thought of the balanced scorecard as a **performance measurement (or performance management)** tool, rather than as a strategic approach for managing objectives. They adapted their ideas when some of their client firms began to apply the scorecard to progress vision in strategic management.[15] This difference is important because in practice some organizations take a performance measurement view of the scorecard, while others follow a more strategic approach. In this regard, the scorecard is understood to have two roles: one for the control of performance and the other for use in planning.

TABLE 3.2 Four perspectives as a framework for objectives and measures

Financial perspective
Objective: To maximize financial returns to the owners of an organization's capital
Measured by:

- Return on capital employed
- Payments (e.g. dividends) to owners
- Cash flow

Customer perspective
Objective: To sustain customer relationships
Measured by:

- Customer satisfaction and delight index
- Repeat purchase patterns
- Brand awareness in target segments

Internal processes perspective
Objective: To create and maximise value in the customer-vendor relationship
Measured by:

- Value stream analysis (to minimize non-value creation activities) index
- Value chain activities (co-ordination, optimization activities) index
- Continuous improvement (innovation, change) index

Learning and growth perspective
Objective: To motivate people and develop competences
Measured by:

- Recruitment and retention rate
- Skills and training index
- Employee conditions and satisfaction index

Strategy maps

A **strategy map** is a document used to think about a scorecard's perspectives, objectives and measures which explores possible cause-and-effect relationships and the associated CSFs. While the balanced scorecard is a powerful reference framework for objective representation, the strategy map is a methodology to examine the scorecard and evaluate the basic assumptions for choosing the objectives and measures. Kaplan and Norton write about 'cause-and-effect hypotheses', which sound scientific, if not deterministic, and perhaps operationally-focused. However the idea is not to think up definite answers to specific issues, but rather to think strategically about real and possible connections as an inter-related whole.

Kaplan and Norton had originally thought a consensus on the choice of objectives and measures would emerge among senior managers through a discussion based around the answers to the four questions (see Figure 3.3) and this would be enough to provide a reference framework for thinking about performance management. For strategic thinking, however, the map provides a broader canvas for senior managers to map out the CSFs for the achievement of their strategic vision. The strategy map is used to document the CSFs in terms of the possible cause-and-effect linkages between the perspectives and the objectives. The strategy map enables managers to explore the relationships

PRINCIPLES IN PRACTICE 3.2

Balanced scorecard at the University of Virginia Library

The University of Virginia Library adopted the balanced scorecard in 2001. The reason was to make the library accountable to purpose, and to identify and develop indicators of purpose, which could be used to manage strategically those CSFs that would actually produce a difference in performance. The balanced scorecard is shown below. This shows only objectives and not measures (the number of measures will be at least twice the number of objectives). The library has defined its purpose as a set of core values, shown in the centre of the figure.[26]

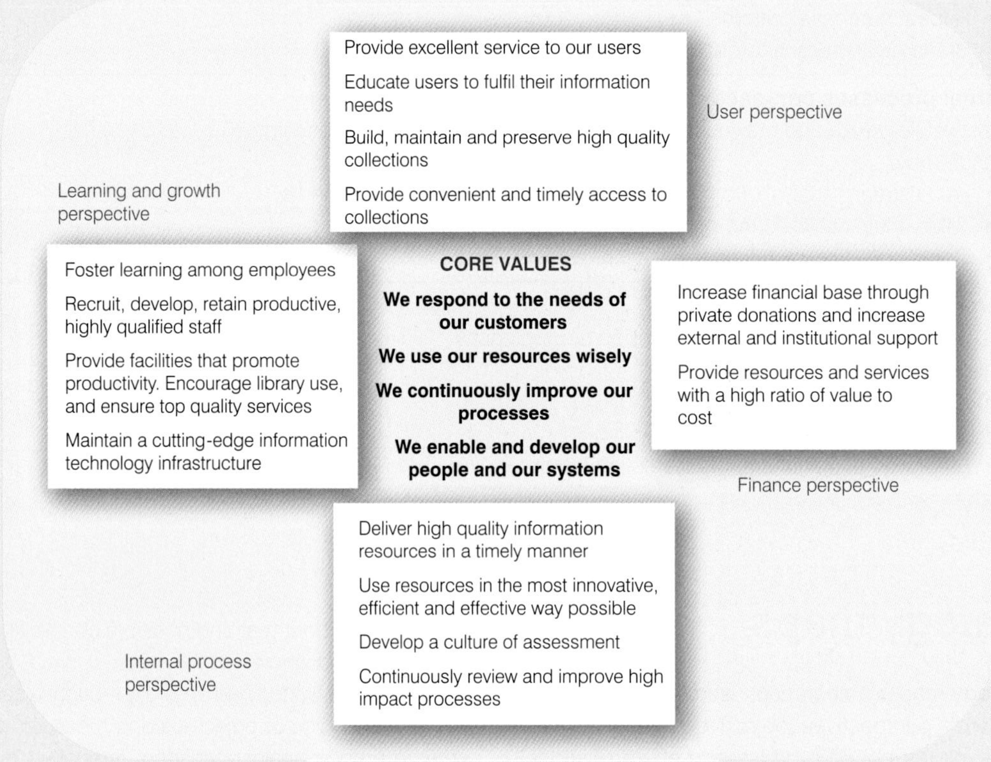

Question: Values are different from vision; is this scorecard about change?

systematically to understand how the scorecard objectives relate to both the vision and the mission of the organization and how to select and check the appropriate measures for the scorecard's objectives. Figure 3.4 illustrates this idea for a university: the arrows show directional links between areas of core activities that contribute to the two strategic themes of organizational growth and influence and knowledge contribution.

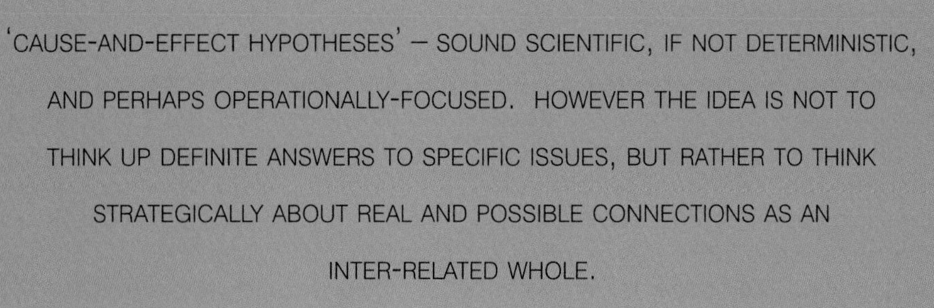

The strategy map retains a focus on financial results, but it also recognizes the importance of the enablers of those results. It is a principle of scorecard management that no perspectives are favoured to the detriment of the others. The position of the financial perspective at the top of the cause-and-effect hierarchy shown in Figure 3.4 does not imply an order of priority; rather, it only shows the direction of cause-and-effect influences. So, for example, the learning and growth perspective takes into account that growth and influence require

FIGURE 3.4 A strategy map for a university

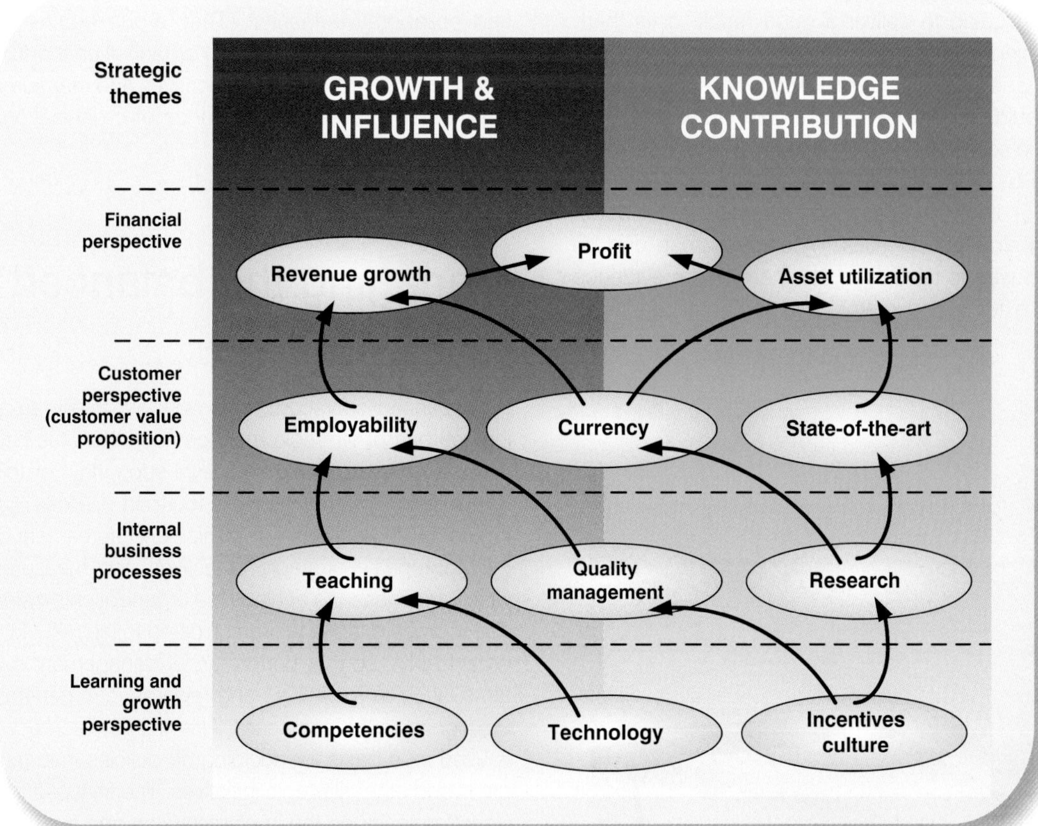

particular learning skills, which are necessary to manage the key processes that create the value to students and sponsors, who provide the necessary income to meet the financial objectives of the university.

There cannot be any known definitive and deterministic quantitative linkage between the non-financial and financial perspectives. The financial perspective is a dependent variable, but working out a definite causal link to the other perspectives, which may or may not be independent variables, is difficult as the influences generated by the external environment dominate over internal improvement. For example, when a prototype of the scorecard was used to improve non-financial performance at Analog Devices, an American semiconductor company, its stock prices fell due to the vagaries of the business cycle and lag effects.[16]

The important thing is for senior and other levels of management to use the strategy map continuously. As one senior manager has put it: 'It is important to use this as a strategic tool and ask, "why are we off on that particular measure? Are we measuring the right thing? Is it what we are doing is never going to deliver a good result, or is there something else going on here?" ... and using it to inform and have an informal discussion about where we should be putting resource going forwards'.[17]

If the scorecard is used with other analytical techniques used for crafting strategy choices (Chapters 4 and 5), it becomes a powerful framework for determining strategic priorities. A strategy map can be readily used to take account of, and order evidence about, external and internal environmental conditions (see Table 3.3). The left-hand column indicates the evidence of factors taken into account for strategic analysis (these can be used for a SWOT analysis: see Figure 5.7). The three columns to the right-hand side constitute the three levels of objective deployment: starting with the strategic objectives in the scorecard, followed by objectives in a medium-term plan (Chapter 9), and strategically-related objectives in daily management (Chapter 10).

There is nothing about the scorecard and its strategy map that necessarily determines what the content of the objectives and measures should be. Rather, they are frameworks for thinking about and monitoring decisions and for working out the assumptions about longer-term strategy. The balanced scorecard approach aims to encourage decision-takers to understand the importance of the different perspectives as related elements. Kaplan and Norton[18] argue that strategy maps also give employees generally a clear and visual understanding of how their jobs are linked to the overall objectives of the organization, and that this enables them to work in a co-ordinated and collaborative fashion. They argue against an exact and deterministic-based organizational understanding of corporate level objectives and measures, but instead stress the importance of organizational alignment and communication.

Managing the balanced scorecard

If a balanced scorecard is to work effectively as an integral part of strategic management, then it is necessary to have in place high level supports. For this, Kaplan and Norton propose a four-part process (see Figure 3.5). This starts with senior level agreement on the appropriate strategic objectives and measures, which are chosen to achieve the organization's vision. The scorecard is then communicated to the rest of the organization, so that performance management systems, such as incentives and rewards, can generally be aligned to the scorecard. After this, the scorecard is used as a basis for deciding on policies, mid-term plans and other strategic initiatives. The final part provides feedback on the implementation and execution of these, but in ways that enable senior managers to

TABLE 3.3 Strategy map as an organizing framework for strategic priorities

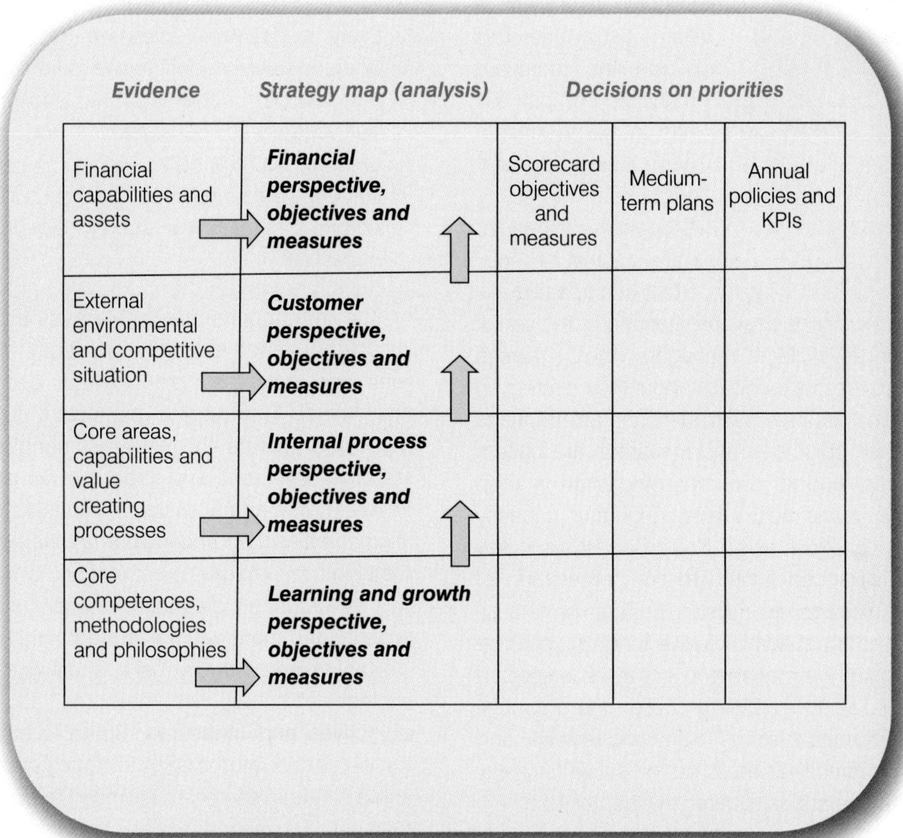

Evidence	Strategy map (analysis)	Decisions on priorities		
Financial capabilities and assets	***Financial perspective, objectives and measures***	Scorecard objectives and measures	Medium-term plans	Annual policies and KPIs
External environmental and competitive situation	***Customer perspective, objectives and measures***			
Core areas, capabilities and value creating processes	***Internal process perspective, objectives and measures***			
Core competences, methodologies and philosophies	***Learning and growth perspective, objectives and measures***			

evaluate and learn how the scorecard's objectives and measures are working, and to test the assumptions against the CSFs. Kaplan and Norton emphasize the importance of the senior management team taking full charge and responsibility for managing the scorecard. This requires the chief **executive** to take responsibility for the whole process, while each of the four parts should be the responsibility of an individual executive.

The non-financial variables on the scorecard are difficult to identify correctly and in principle the wider organization should be involved in their formation (the first part of the model). The objectives and measures should be based on knowledge of the means that will be used to achieve them. Yet the means are rarely known at the time when objectives and measures are set, with the result that if they are too low, the organization's potential will be unfulfilled; if they are too high, then the organization will seem to have under-performed to its expectations.

FIGURE 3.5 The process for managing the balanced scorecard[19]

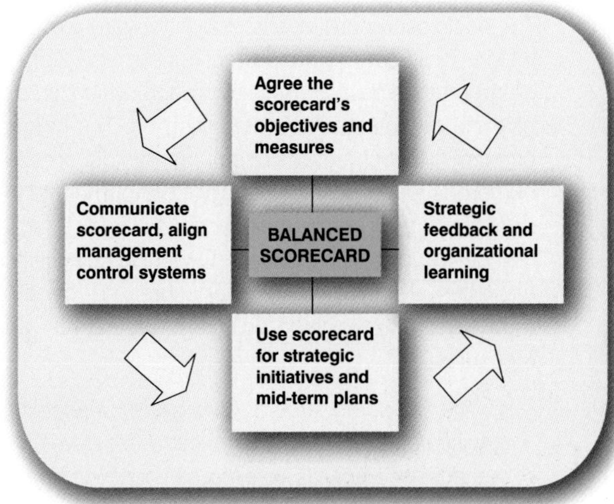

What is needed is to set rational objectives and measures as meaningful yardsticks of what is achievable. This is why the scorecard management process has to be a continuously managed learning cycle.

In general, organizations are poor at organizing an effective capability for organizational learning at the senior management level. Most managers do not have a procedure to receive feedback about their strategy in a way that enables them to examine the assumptions on which their objectives and measures are based. The scorecard and its accompanying strategy map should give to the senior level a greater capacity for strategic learning, which Kaplan and Norton say makes the balanced scorecard the cornerstone of a strategic management system.[20] They have suggested that a formal administrative function could be used to support the management of the scorecard.[21] Its role would be to oversee and align the organization's management systems, plans and reviews, and would report directly to the chief executive (strategy support systems are considered in Chapter 10.)

What makes a scorecard strategic?

The basic scorecard idea is straightforward, but confusion easily sets in when practitioners lose sight of its importance as a strategic approach, which aims to give the organization its overall priorities. The biggest problem is that objectives and measures become too numerous to manage, especially if newcomers to the approach try to create their measures from a larger number of existing measures. Owen Berkeley-Hill, a manager at Ford, found the scorecard became unwieldy if it involved too many objectives and measures:

> ... *The first scorecards at Ford* [were] *unrelated to any strategic planning,* [as] *these were developed because scorecards were the fashionable management accessory. The main driver appeared to be the now often-quoted Kaplan and Norton expression – 'If you can't measure it, you can't manage it'. Every conceivable measure for the particular operation was added to the card that was then reduced so it could fit a shirt pocket. What was not taken into consideration for this monthly exercise was the effort involved in collecting and verifying the measures before publication. To no-one's surprise the second edition was never published.*[22]

The over-abundance of objectives and measures is typically down to confusion about which objectives and measures are strategic and which are operational. This applies particularly to measures. Measures provide the essential handle for understanding and reviewing progress on an objective. However, it is often easier to measure known and alike activities than uncertain and different ones, and measures are typically more reliable for tracking specific indicators for diagnostic control, rather than for broader and more general strategic matters.

Kaplan and Norton make a distinction between strategic objectives and measures, and **diagnostic objectives and measures**. Strategic objectives and measures deal with the CSFs for an organization's vision and a strategic scorecard is limited to strategic objectives only. The diagnostic objectives monitor the health of the organization to ensure it remains fit for purpose; they indicate whether the organization remains in control and can signal up the unusual events that require attention. Senior managers are proactively involved with strategic objectives, and become involved with diagnostic objectives by exception, when their intervention is required. This is important because a scorecard's focus on vision keeps the number of scorecard objectives and measures to a manageable number.

There is no absolute rule about what this should be, but effective scorecards typically have no more than about 8 objectives and 24 measures. An organization's diagnostic objectives and measures, on the other hand, can run into many dozens. Some of these will be strategically-linked KPIs, which are in place to monitor and drive improvement in the key areas of the business; especially those that are particularly important to the organization's mission and business model (see Chapter 5). Of course, the needs of the scorecard's objectives may require adjustments to the diagnostic objectives, but diagnostic objectives should not be on a strategic balanced scorecard. According to Kaplan and Norton, the aim of vision-linked objectives and measures is to drive competitive breakthroughs. However, there is no reason why scorecard objectives and measures should only be used to achieve this type of breakthrough.

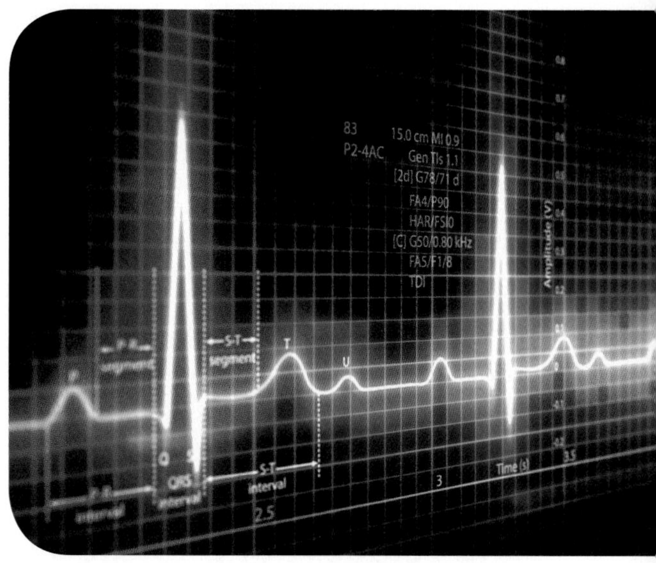

Non-profit and public sector balanced scorecards

A non-profit or a public sector organization is likely to have a very different vision to an organization active in a competitive environment. To some extent, of course,

PRINCIPLES IN PRACTICE 3.3

A strategic scorecard at Philips Electronics

Philips is a related diversified conglomerate, which employs a quarter of a million people across the world. Philips designed the scorecard to provide a shared understanding of the organization's strategic policies and vision of the future. Their operating principle in the design was to determine factors that were critical for achieving the company's strategic goals. Philips Electronics' management teams use it to guide the quarterly business reviews worldwide in order to promote organizational learning and continuous improvement.

The four perspectives are known as the four CSFs. These are: 'Competence' (knowledge, technology, leadership, and teamwork), 'Processes' (drivers for performance), 'Customers' (value propositions), and 'Financial' (value, growth and productivity).

The management team of each business unit reached a consensus on which CSFs distinguish the business unit from the competition. They used a value map to derive customer CSFs by analyzing customer survey data that reflected perceived performance relative to the price for competing products. Process CSFs were derived by determining how process improvements can deliver customer requirements. Competence CSFs were identified by determining what human resources and competences were required to deliver the other three perspectives of the card. Standard financial reporting metrics were used as financial CSFs.

The next step was for each business unit to determine key indicators at the business unit level that measure CSFs. Assumptions about relationships between processes and results were quantified and performance drivers determined. Targets were then set based on the gap between present performance and desired performance for the current year plus two and four years into the future. (Targets were SMART.)[27]

Question: In what way is this scorecard strategic?

there are always alternatives for an organization's products and services, and most organizations must manage financial, along with other enabler, objectives. However, organizations may change the content of the four perspectives, depending upon their strategic purpose, but the nature of the scorecard remains essentially the same (see Figure 3.6).

Figure 3.6 shows a suggested template for a public sector scorecard. The most important difference is a centrally placed 'strategic' box. This is similar to a commercial organization's vision, although the aim may not be about moving the organization to a future position, so much as about a policy requirement to achieve a public service priority.

The relation of a strategic balanced scorecard to other scorecards

The success of the scorecard has meant that many organizations, especially non-profit ones, call any list of objectives and measures a scorecard. It is important to distinguish these from the real strategic balanced scorecard. The translation of strategic objectives for implementation and daily management is discussed in Chapters 9 and 10. However, note at this point that a large and complex organization may have several levels of scorecards, just as they have a hierarchy of strategy (noted above). So, a strategic scorecard may be translated into scorecards for different parts of an organization. A business division may have its own scorecard, and at an operational level departments and units may document their KPIs and other daily management objectives in the style of a balanced scorecard. These may be derived from, or aligned with, a corporate level scorecard.

In their example of practice at Mobil Oil, Kaplan and Norton show how Mobil's division allowed their business units to develop their own scorecard in the light of local circumstances.[24] The objectives and measures they used did not have to add up a higher level divisional scorecard, but rather managers chose local measures that would influence the measures on the divisional scorecard. In other words, it was not a simple decomposition of the higher-level scorecard. Also at lower levels scorecards inter-related to some extent; for example, where a unit was an internal

FIGURE 3.6 The public sector scorecard[23]

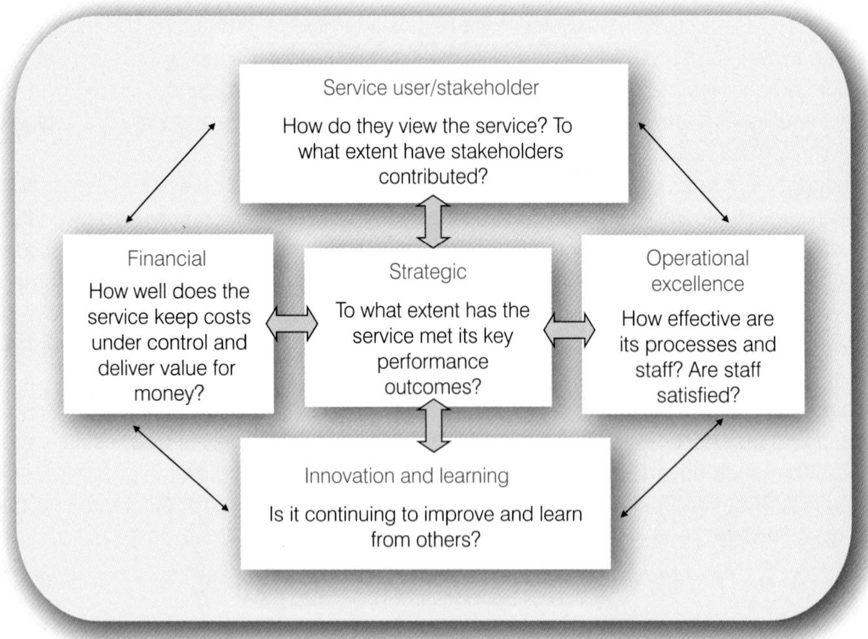

KEY DEBATE 3.2

How should the balanced scorecard be managed?

Kaplan and Norton, in their recent work, have emphasized the importance of administrative supports for the scorecard, such as a strategy office.[32] A lot of this looks like the old corporate planning office that used to administer and plan the strategic plan.

David Otley has made the point that effectiveness may depend upon how other management control systems are managed in relation to the scorecard.[33]

If the influence of the strategic objectives and measures are to reach down to operational levels, where the actual improvement activities reside, the organization's deployment system is important. Arthur Schneiderman, the inventor of the balanced scorecard prototype, used hoshin kanri[34] and argues that a state-of-the-art business methodology, such as PDCA-based continuous improvement (see Chapter 5), is necessary for the management of objectives.

It is important to measure the right things, improve analytical skills, and ensure that a disciplined focus is maintained (as an acronym it spells out MAD).[35]

Question: How would you as a senior manager manage MAD?

supplier to another, the customer perspective on its scorecard was likely to reflect the scorecard requirements of that internal customer.

Some organizations continue to use different versions of Kaplan and Norton's original performance measurement scorecard, which are strategic only in the sense that they may relate to an organization's strategy (such as Tesco's Steering Wheel, see Case 3.1). Many textbooks and journal articles about the balanced scorecard present the approach as a strategy implementation tool. This chapter is different as its purpose has been to explain the use of the *strategic* balanced scorecard and its use to develop overall strategic objectives.

> **The objectives and measures they used did not have to add up a higher level divisional scorecard, but rather managers chose local measures that would influence the measures on the divisional scorecard. In other words, it was not a simple decomposition of the higher-level scorecard.**

KEY DEBATE 3.3

Do balanced scorecards really work?

Many continue to question the underlying ideas of the balanced scorecard. Kaplan and Norton suggest that the strategy map should be used pragmatically. But observers, such as Ittner and Larcker, and Jensen, suggest the map is used superficially in practice; managers do not really question the underlying assumptions of the objectives and measures.[36]

There is also confusion about its role: whether it should be used for controlling performance, or more strategically for a planning and learning approach. Zingales et al. suggest it is used for control, while Mooraj et al. find that European-based organizations use it for planning – but Antarkar and Cobbold argue it is equally effective for both.[37]

The scorecard may be unsuitable for organizations that have a large number of stakeholders, and alternative approaches have been suggested, notably for performance management, see, for example, Neely, A., Adams, C. and Kennerly, M., who argue their own framework for linking stakeholder value to strategic objectives is superior.[38] However, as one study of German organizations points out, the balanced scorecard is not really a tool meant to integrate the needs of stakeholders into strategic objectives.[39]

At least one theorist thinks that Kaplan and Norton's work does not contribute any new and convincing theory, and it is rather only 'persuasive rhetoric'.[40]

Question: What do you think a balanced scorecard does, and does it do that well?

SUMMARY OF PRINCIPLES

1. The balance between the needs of today and those of the future are central to strategic management.

2. The closer strategically related objectives come to execution at an operational level, the more specific and detailed they become.

3. CSFs should be identified to account for factors that are primarily responsible for the strategic success of the organization, and should not be confused with KPIs, which are measures generally associated with the incremental targets at operational levels.

4. The balanced scorecard is comprised of four perspectives, which are used to group lagged and lead objectives, and it is important that every objective has measures to indicate performance; the perspectives should be managed as an integrated set.

Strategy mapping should be used creatively as a set of associated hypotheses, and not as a deterministic process.

The chief executive and the senior management team have responsibility for managing the balanced scorecard.

A strategic scorecard is based on vision which keeps the objectives and measures to a manageable number.

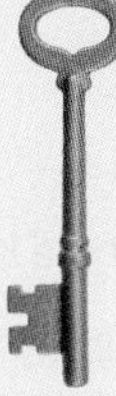

GLOSSARY OF KEY TERMS

Balanced scorecard (the) a documented set of objectives and measures expressed from the point of view of four key areas of organizational concern.

Critical success factors (CSFs) the factors that primarily account for an organization's success in achieving its strategic purpose.

Diagnostic objectives and measures these monitor the health of the organization to ensure it remains fit for purpose; they indicate whether the organization remains in control and can signal up the unusual events that require attention.

Executive the senior level of an organization's management.

Key performance indicator (KPI) a strategically related incremental objective.

Lagged measures (see measures).

Lead measures (see measures).

Measures a quantified indicator of an objective: lagged measures are indicators of past performance, and lead measures are indicators of the enablers of future performance.

Objective a statement of an outcome to be achieved.

Performance measurement (management) quantification of purpose, progress and results in work (traditionally a human resource concern).

Perspectives different points of view used in the balanced scorecard to specify objectives and measures.

SMART Specific, Measurable, Action-oriented, Realistic, Time-bound, used as criteria to evaluate the quality of objectives.

Strategic intent a very ambitious and seemingly unrealistic long-term organizational goal used by Japanese firms.

Strategic objective and measures objectives and measures used to progress an organizational long-term vision.

Strategy map a document used to think about a scorecard's perspectives, objectives and measures, which explores possible cause-and-effect relationships and the associated CSFs.

GUIDED FURTHER READING

This chapter follows mainly the Kaplan and Norton balanced scorecard canon. Despite a huge extant literature on the subject, the work of Kaplan and Norton remains paramount and they continue to publish widely. The most useful for further reading include their first two books on the subject, and a recent paper that puts the ideas in the broader context of management systems:

Kaplan, R. S. and Norton D. P. (2001) *The Strategy-Focused Organization: How Balanced Scorecard Companies Thrive in the New Business Environment*, Boston, MA: Harvard Business School Press.

Kaplan, R. S. and Norton, D. P. (1996) *The Balanced Scorecard: Translating Strategy into Action*, Boston, MA: Harvard Business School Press.

Kaplan, R. S. and Norton, D. P. (2008) 'Mastering the management system', *Harvard Business Review,* January:63–77.

Many of the ideas have antecedents in Japanese organizational management. The prototype balanced scorecard was developed as part of hoshin kanri (see Chapter 10) at Analog Devices (see Stata, 1989). To see how the balanced scorecard can fit alongside hoshin kanri as complementary approaches, see our paper below:

Stata, R. (1989) 'Organizational learning – the key to management innovation', *Sloan Management Review* Spring:63–74.

Witcher, B. J. and Chau, V. S. (2007) 'Balanced scorecard and hoshin kanri: dynamic capabilities for managing strategic fit', *Management Decision* 45(3):518–37.

There are also other approaches which seem similar. The most notable is the tableau de bord, which has been used in France for decades. It has more in common with a performance management system than a strategic scorecard; see:

Epstein, M. and Manazoni, J-F. (1998) 'Implementing corporate strategy: from tableaux de bord to balanced scorecards', *European Management Journal* 16(2):190–203.

REVIEW QUESTIONS

1 How do strategic objectives achieve purpose?
2 Should strategic objectives be SMART?
3 What does balance mean in the context of strategic management?
4 Why is balance important?
5 How are strategic objectives different from objectives used for implementation and execution?
6 What is the difference between strategic and diagnostic objectives?
7 How is strategic management different from performance management?
8 What is the nature of the link between the financial perspective and the other perspectives?
9 What is the difference between a CSF and a KPI?
10 How do senior managers take responsibility for a balanced scorecard?

SEMINAR AND ASSIGNMENT QUESTIONS

1 Design a balanced scorecard for your own (or group's) career aspirations.
2 With a group, draw a strategy map to show the main CSFs involved in achieving a successful career.
3 Discuss the strengths and weaknesses of Kaplan and Norton's original performance management system in relation to those of the later strategic balanced scorecard. In regard to particular organizations of your choice reach a definite conclusion about which is best for them.

CHAPTER REFERENCES

1 Witcher, B. J. and Chau, V. S. (2008) 'Contrasting uses of balanced scorecards: Case

studies at two UK companies', *Strategic Change* 17(3/4):101–14.

2 Drucker, P. F. (1955) *The Practice of Management*, London: Heinemann Butterworth. (1954, American edn, New York: Harper & Row.), p. 124.

3 Hamel, G. and Prahalad, C. K. (1989) 'Strategic intent', *Harvard Business Review* May–June:63–76.

4 Drucker (1955) *op cit.* p. 67.

5 Simon, H. A. (1947) *Administrative Behaviour: A Study of Decision-Making Processes in Administrative Organizations*, New York: Free Press.

6 Drucker (1955) *op cit.* p. 83.

7 Dye, R. (2008) 'How chief strategy officers think about their role: a roundtable', *The McKinsey Quarterly* May www.mckinseyquarterly.com

8 *ibid.*

9 Rockart, J. F. (1979) 'Chief executives define their own data needs', *Harvard Business Review* 57, March–April:81–93.

10 Daniel, D. R. (1961) 'Management information crisis', *Harvard Business Review,* September–October:111.

11 Kaplan, R. S. and Norton, D. P. (1992) 'The balanced scorecard – measures that drive performance' *Harvard Business Review,* January–February:71–9.

12 Rigby, D. and Bilodeau, B. (2007) 'Selecting management tools wisely', *Harvard Business Review,* December:20–2.

13 Adapted from Kaplan and Norton (1992) *op cit.* and Kaplan, R. S. and Norton, D. P. (1996) *The Balanced Scorecard: Translating Strategy into Action*, Boston, MA: Harvard Business School Press.

14 Kaplan, R. S. and Norton, D. P. (1996) *The Balanced Scorecard: Translating Strategy into Action*, Boston,MA: Harvard Business School Press.

15 Kaplan, R. S. and Norton, D. P. (2001) 'Transforming the balanced scorecard from performance measurement to strategic management: part 1', *Accounting Horizons* 15(1): 87–104.

16 Schneiderman, A. (1999) 'Why balanced scorecards fail', *Journal of Strategic Performance Management* January:6–11.

17 Mackay, A. (2005) *A Practitioner's Guide to the Balanced Scorecard* (research report) London:CIMA, p. 33.

18 Kaplan, R. and Norton, D. P. (2005) 'The office of strategy management', *Harvard Business Review,* October:72–80.

19 Adapted from Kaplan and Norton (1996) *op cit.*

20 Kaplan and Norton (1996) *op cit.* p. 269.

21 Kaplan, R. and Norton, D. P. (2005) *op cit.*

22 Berkeley-Hill, O. (2002) 'Is the balanced scorecard concept compatible with Policy Deployment?'. Unpublished paper in Lean Operations, Cardiff Business School, January 10.

23 Adapted from Moullin, M., Soady, J., Skinner, J., Cullen, J. and Gilligan, C. (2007) 'Using the public sector scorecard in public health', *International Journal of Health Care Quality Assurance* 20(4):281–289, Figure 1.

24 Kaplan, R. S. and Norton, D. P. (2001) *The Strategy-Focused Organization: How Balanced Scorecard Companies Thrive in the New Business Environment,* Boston, MA: Harvard Business School Press.

25 Shook, J. Y. (1998) 'Bringing the Toyota Production System to the United States: A personal perspective', in Liker, J. K. (ed.) *Becoming Lean: Inside Stories of US Manufacturers*, Portland, OR: Productivity Press, pp. 40–69.

26 University of Virginia Library (2009), www2.lib.virginia.edu/bsc

27 Gumbus, A. and Lyons, B. (2002) 'The balanced scorecard at Philips Electronics', *Strategic Finance* 84(5):45–49.

28 Cyert, R. M. and March, J. G. (1963) *A Behavioural Theory of the Firm,* Englewood Cliffs, NJ: Prentice Hall.

29 Simon, H. A. (1976) *Administrative Behaviour* (3rd edn), London: Free Press.

30 Drucker, P. F. (1955) *The Practice of Management*, London: Heinemann Butterworth. (1954, American edn, New York: Harper & Row.), p. 60.

31 Ansoff, H. I. (1965) *Corporate Strategy: An Analytic Approach to Business Policy for Growth and Expansion*, London (Pelican edition published 1968).

32 Kaplan and Norton (2005), *op cit.*; Kaplan, R. S. and Norton, D. P. (1996), *The Balanced Scorecard: Translating Strategy into Action*, Boston, MA: Harvard Business School Press.

33 Otley, D. (1999) 'Performance management: a framework for management control systems research', *Management Accounting Research* 10:363–82.

34 Schneiderman (1999), *op cit.* p. 9.

35 Scopes, J. (2006) Balanced scorecard in the UK, *PMA Forum*, email, February 23.

36 Ittner, C. D. and Larcker, D. E. (2003) 'Coming up short on non-financial performance measurement', *Harvard Business Review,* November:88–95; Jensen M. C. (2001) 'Value maximization, stakeholder theory, and the corporate objective function', *European Management Journal,* 7:3, 297–317.

37 Zingales, F., O'Rourke, A. and Hockerts, K. (2002) *Balanced Scorecard and Sustainability: State of the Art*, working paper 65, Centre for the Management of Environmental Resources, INSEAD; Mooraj, S., Oyon, D. and Hostettler, D. (1999), 'The balanced scorecard: a necessary good or an unnecessary evil?', *European Management Journal* 17:5, 481–491; Antarkar, N. and Cobbold, I. (2001) *Implementing the Balanced Scorecard – Lessons and Insights from a Multi-Divisional Oil Company,* working paper, Maidenhead: 2GC Limited. www.2gc.co.uk

38 Speckbacher, G., Bischof, J. and Pfeiffer, T. (2003) 'A descriptive analysis on the implementation of balanced scorecards in German-speaking countries', *Management Accounting Research* 14(4):361–88.

39 Neely, A., Adams, C., and Kennerley, M. (2002) *The Performance Prism: The Scorecard for Measuring and Managing Business Success*, London: Prentice Hall.

40 Norreklit, H. (2003) 'The balanced scorecard: what is the score? A rhetorical analysis of the balanced scorecard', *Accounting, Organizations and Society* 28:591–619.

CASE 3.1 Tesco's steering wheel[1]

Tesco is a UK-owned supermarket company with an annual revenue of £59.4 billion (year to end February, 2009). There is no strategic scorecard in the sense of one based upon a corporate level strategic vision. Instead there is Tesco's steering wheel, which is used by corporate executives to focus its stores on the delivery of Tesco's core purpose (shown in Exhibit 3.1).

This purpose is not visionary in that it is designed to take Tesco to a new position or state, but rather it is a statement of the values, which are fundamental to manage purpose in the stores. The primary aim of the steering wheel is to link every employee's personal objectives to corporate values and to help staff balance these values effectively in the daily management of work. The wheel has the four Kaplan and

EXHIBIT 3.1 *Tesco's core purpose*

Our core purpose is to create value for customers to earn their lifetime loyalty.

Our success depends on people: the people who shop with us and the people who work with us.
If our customers like what we offer, they are more likely to come back and shop with us again.
If the Tesco team find what we do rewarding, they are more likely to go that extra mile to help our customers.

This is expressed as two key values:

No-one tries harder for customers, and Treat people as we like to be treated.

We regularly ask our customers and our staff what we can do to make shopping with us and working with us that little bit better. This is our Every Little Helps strategy:

- Shopping trip
  Customers have told us they want – clear aisles, to be able to get what they want at a good price, no queues and great staff. We call this our Every Little Helps Shopping Trip for customers and use it every day to ensure we are always working hard to make Tesco a better place to shop, at home and abroad.
- A great place to work
  Our staff have told us what is important to them – to be treated with respect, having a manager who helps them, having an interesting job and an opportunity to get on. Helping achieve what is important to our staff will help us to deliver an Every Little Helps Shopping Trip for our customers.
- The way we work
  The way we work is how we deliver Every Little Helps to make Tesco a better place to shop and work in. We use simple processes so that shopping is Better for customers, Simpler for staff and Cheaper for Tesco.

EXHIBIT 3.2 The steering wheel

Norton perspectives, but also an additional perspective, which was added in 2006, as a 'community' perspective. Each segment of the wheel has its own set of objectives, as can be seen in Exhibit 3.2.

The operational performances of Tesco stores on the wheel's objectives are reported and reviewed quarterly at board level, and afterwards a summary report is prepared and sent to the top two thousand managers to cascade to staff in the stores. The remuneration of senior management is shaped by the wheel's objectives with bonuses varying according to the level of their overall achievement. Once a year the corporate group reviews how the wheel has worked, and the objectives may be changed and modified depending on prevailing circumstances, and to check that they remain consistent with the needs of Tesco's stakeholders. An important consideration is to make sure the objectives remain appropriate and robust measures of performance in the stores.

At store level every member of staff uses a 'plan and review' document to think about how their work relates to the five perspectives. This involves agreeing these with supervisors and other managers in staff appraisals, which are normally conducted on a twice-a-year basis. Every employee is asked to develop their own objectives and explain how they will carry these out in ways that are consistent with the needs of the steering wheel. They are asked to state what their work will look like when it is completed, to identify the main steps required to achieve their work objectives, such as the key dates, any support materials, and also who can help them achieve their contribution to the wheel's objectives.

The steering wheel is a people-based and performance management approach. It is not a strategic scorecard in the Kaplan and Norton sense of being based on a strategic vision. Rather, it includes objectives that are essentially diagnostic in nature.

© Photolibrary

However, it is still an important part of Tesco's strategic management in that it links activity in daily management to Tesco's long-term core purpose, but it is not designed to bring about the kind of fundamental strategic change that is associated with a strategic vision. Of course, Tesco takes into consideration vision and related strategy in its review of the wheel's performance, but there is no corporate level scorecard based on vision alone. In fact, Tesco has what it describes as four long-term strategies for growth:

1. To sustain growth in the core UK market: The UK is Tesco's biggest market and the core of its business. Tesco aims to provide all of its customers with excellent value and choice.
2. To expand by growing internationally: Tesco is an international retailer. Wherever the company operates it focuses on giving local customers what they want.
3. To be strong in non-food as well as in food: Tesco wants to be as successful at selling non-food products like clothes, books, DVDs and CDs as it is with food.
4. To follow its customers into new retailing services.

If Tesco were to have a strategic scorecard, these four strategies would be linked to its objectives and measures and designed to achieve a growth-based vision. This could also involve all five perspectives of the steering wheel, where the objectives and measures could be used to identify those CSFs necessary for the achievement of this vision. The number of the objectives and measures on this strategic scorecard would be fewer than the numerous KPIs of the steering wheel, and we should expect Tesco's executive to align the annual objectives of the steering wheel to be consistent with the longer-term needs of the strategic scorecard.

Discussion questions

1 How does the steering wheel compare to Kaplan and Norton's classical view of what a balanced scorecard should be, and how does it differ? Given your experience of shopping (or even working) at Tesco, or a similar supermarket, does the steering wheel seem a good idea and does it work?

2 The steering wheel is probably as much about organizational culture as it is about strategic management. Is this a case of an organization using culture as a strategy?

3 If you were a senior manager working for another organization that was not a retailer, how would you adopt this idea for your organization?

Case references

1 Adapted from Witcher, B. J. and Chau, V. S. (2008) 'Contrasting uses of balanced scorecards: Case studies at two UK companies', *Strategic Change* 17:101–114. The Tesco Exhibits can be seen at www.tescocorporate.com

2 Tesco (2007) *Tesco's Four Strategies*, Tesco Company website: www.tescocorporate.com

This case study was prepared using only publicly available sources of information for the purposes of classroom discussion; it does not intend to illustrate either effective or ineffective handling of a managerial situation.

Chapter 4
THE EXTERNAL ENVIRONMENT

Introduction

Organizations must identify and clarify the nature of strategic options facing them in order to be able to choose their **strategy.** The appropriate industry and competitive stances are critical components of long-term performance. This does not necessarily imply the need to take a conservative or static view, but rather that **strategizing** is an on-going activity that must be grounded in reality, and also must consider ideas for which there is not yet a market. Environmental analysis is relevant to both of these.

This chapter considers the factors that can be used to explore the possibilities of change, including the unexpected. Successful strategy takes advantage of an industry's growth opportunities, while also creating a strong competitive position.

LEARNING OBJECTIVES

By the end of this chapter you should understand:

1. The general external environment.
2. Industry life cycles.
3. The main competitive forces in an industry.
4. Strategic groups.
5. Blue ocean strategy.

Business vignette See the bigger whole picture ...

The most significant trend in the world economy is the rise of the BRIC economies. This is an acronym for the growing importance of the economies of Brazil, Russia, India and China.[1] By 2025 they could together account for over half of the size of the combined economies of today's richest countries: the United States, Japan, Germany, the United Kingdom, France and Italy. By 2050 their economies could be even larger.

The BRIC countries have important advantages in the supply of primary commodities (from Brazil and Russia), services (India), and manufactured produces (China). These advantages seem likely to continue, but how events will actually unfold is uncertain. It is likely that much depends on how the BRIC countries continue to manage their economies. The following seem important: (1) to pursue sound macro-economic policies and create a stable economic infrastructure; (2) to develop strong and stable political institutions; (3) to continue to open their economies to trade and foreign direct investment; and (4) to maintain high levels of secondary education.

Between 2002 and 2007, annual real growth averaged between 10.4 per cent in China, 7.9 per cent in India, 6.9 per cent in Russia and 3.7 per cent in Brazil. Rapid growth and large populations (around 42 per cent of the world's total in

2008) have given the **BRIC countries** some of the most promising markets and industries in the world.

These are long-term factors, but they provide the context that organizations, no matter where they are in the world, will have to use in the immediate term to inform strategy and make sure that everybody has identified the right issues. On this basis an organization can prioritize the opportunities and provide a strategic framework for that prioritization.

For example, the BRIC economies were immediately hit by the global financial crisis in 2008. However, the BRIC economies have built up a strong consumer demand, which could cushion the economic recession and provide early opportunities for a recovery in the world economy after 2009.

The external environment

An organization's **external environment** consists of conditions that influence the external changes in its industry, especially those that influence the intensity of competition. External conditions are constantly changing and organizations need to monitor and review strategy continually to effectively manage any emerging threats and to be able to exploit advantageous opportunities. Many changes are difficult to identify and their consequences are often uncertain and even unknowable. As a consequence there are broadly four different ways to think about the external environment (Figure 4.1).

Scanning involves making an overview of the whole and general external environment to derive an overall picture of what is happening to pick up events and signals which are relevant to the organization's vision, mission and strategic objectives. **Scenarios** are imagined possible events and their consequences; these help people consider what could occur unexpectedly in the future. Both involve thinking about the environment in ways that are primarily exploratory and open-ended.

Monitoring involves regularly checking for developing changes in the environment to identify opportunities and warn about threats. This is particularly useful for tracking consumer behaviour and the activities of competitors and potential rivals. **Forecasting** involves the prediction of possibilities based on calculations and estimates of existing data. Monitoring and

FIGURE 4.1 The aims of environmental analysis

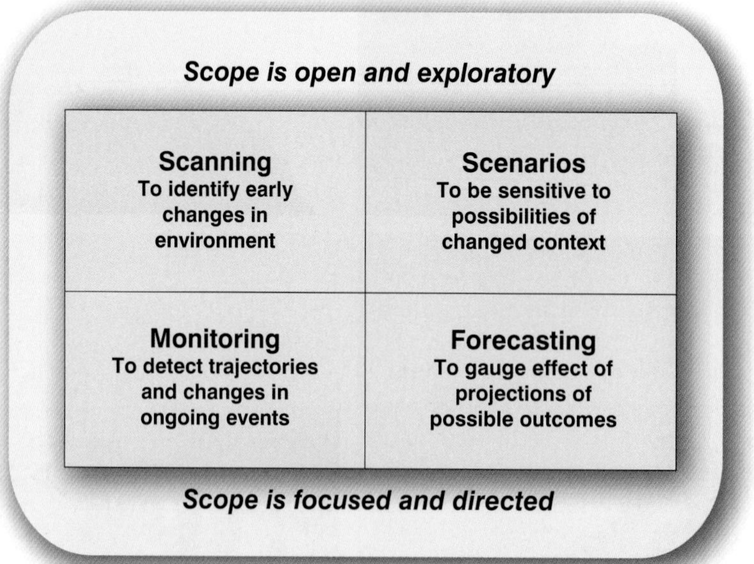

© iStockPhoto.com

forecasting are primarily based around pre-determined ends, so their scope is more focused and specific.

Not all thinking about influences on strategic decisions has the same process behind it: while some is based on objective information and statistics, other thinking may be more about using intuition. Information is always incomplete, so sensing what is actually happening is important. The sense of something important does not always have to be proven, but it is important to go on to check assumptions and the nature of any unfolding reality.

The PESTEL framework

The **PESTEL** framework is a mnemonic used in strategic management to group macro-environmental factors to help strategists look for sources of general opportunity and risk. These factors are fundamental and changes in them can lead to the transformation of industries, especially over the longer-term. PESTEL stands for political, economic, social, technological, environment and legal factors.[2]

Political

Political matters concern the influence that governments have on industries. One of the most important in western countries has been a trend to encourage healthy life styles and discourage alcohol consumption. The smoking ban in public places, combined with stricter drink-driving laws, has seen more people drinking in their homes, rather than out at pubs. More alcohol products are now sold through supermarkets and other retail outlets. This trend has still some distance to go, especially in such countries as Ireland, where the role of the local pub in a local community remains important: in 2001 pub sales accounted for around 70 per cent of the total of drinks sold. If Ireland follows its neighbour, the United Kingdom, where pub

© Peter Titmuss/Alamy

sales account for about 30 per cent, then the outlook for Ireland's brewing industry seems bleak.

More dramatic trends concern international security, the risk from terrorism and disruptions caused by international disputes. Some areas of the world are relatively more unstable, and organizations have to understand the political changes and emerging trends in those countries that account for important parts of their business.

Economic

Economic factors concern cost-related matters for the organization. During the last century the developed economies became consumer societies, when markets became the dominant economic systems for distributing resources and creating wealth. This is continuing as the emerging economies bring perhaps an extra billion consumers, as annual household incomes rise above $5000: a level when family spending seems to extend to discretionary buying. Consumer spending

© iStockPhoto.com

power in emerging economies is expected to increase from $4 trillion to more than $9 trillion in 2015, which is nearly the current spending power of Western Europe. This trend will be increasingly linked to the development of more sophisticated sources of information, and consumers are likely to have access to the same or similar products and brands.

The upward pressures on commodity prices, especially for oil, were beginning to look permanent until the onset of the global financial crisis in 2008. At the time of writing, there is no sign about when the world's economy will recover. However, while globalization must have slowed down (world output actually fell in 2008 for the first time since the 1940s), it is likely that globalization will continue, if only at a slower pace.

Social

Social factors relate to changes in society. One obvious impact is the way demographic structures are comprised. The post-world-war baby boom, from 1945 to around 1960 in developed economies, brought into existence a sizeable and distinct group of consumers. These are now aged between 50 to 65 years old; they are the largest and wealthiest over-50 group in history. Their spending is likely to take a disproportionate share of consumption in markets in industries that have not previously seen older customers as profitable areas. While baby boomers are likely to spend more on health and leisure as they become older, they will continue to influence consumer electronics, clothing and home-furnishings, which are areas that have not typically been associated with the older consumer.

Another important influence is the growth in tourism. The United Nations World Tourism Organization has forecasted that international visits will double from roughly 800 million (2008) to 1.6 billion (2020). There are always winners and losers in conditions of change. For example, the hotelier industry will benefit as a whole, but this is likely to make the industry more attractive to corporate organizations. The growth of budget hotel chains, such as Premier Inn, which offers a basic low-cost service, is likely to damage the traditional and more expensive guesthouses and family-run hotels.

Technology

Technological changes concern trends in the technical and material foundations of an industry. All industries undergo technological change. Some, however, are particularly dynamic, such as the computer hardware and software industries, where the knock-on effect for other industries is wide-ranging in terms of both production technology such as computer-based information systems, and the emergence of new markets, notably the opportunities and threats associated with the Internet. Some organizations have now moved significantly up the industry life cycle. For example, the prices of cell (mobile) phones have fallen substantially, so that manufacturers like Nokia are now investing heavily to incorporate wireless Internet services to add value and to get better prices for products.

Environmental

This concerns trends in environmental factors, such as the awareness of the damaging effects of industrialization on the limited space, beauty and health of the countryside. There are also global concerns about resources, and most important of all, how climate change brought about global warming. The Intergovernmental Panel on Climate Change has reported that global greenhouse gas emissions need to be reduced by 90 per cent by 2050, if global warming is to be held within a two degree centigrade increase. A general move to a low carbon economy is under way. This is beginning to influence organizational strategy;

© Photolibrary

for example, because of the global financial crisis, General Electric has cut investment, but it is increasing its spending on infrastructural **projects** such as turbines for wind farms, and reverse osmosis devices used to purify water.

Legal

Legal issues are those factors that relate to the changes in the law and **regulation**. National legal frameworks vary considerably and their consequences for individual industries are profound. One of the most significant trends has been the tightening of regulatory accounting standards following the large corporate failures, such as Enron, Tyco International, Peregrine Systems and WorldCom, and the bursting of the dot.com bubble. In July 2002, the Public Company Accounting Reform and Investor Protection Act (otherwise known as the Sarbanes-Oxley Act) became law in the United States. Similar regulatory measures were introduced throughout the world.

The important thing about PESTEL analysis is that the influences are pervasive and should always be thought about not as a simple list of unrelated bullet points, but as an inter-related set that should be used to scan continuously, or review constantly, the general environment as a whole. For example, one of the industries most adversely affected by the global financial crisis is the car industry, especially the Detroit car firms, General Motors, Ford and Chrysler.

In fact, these organizations have been experiencing adverse PESTEL problems for a long time. It seems likely that a mix of influences, such as criticism of gas-guzzling vehicles from environmentalists, new regulations to restrict fuel emissions, rising oil prices and changes in social attitudes, are forcing the American-owned car companies to produce smaller cars. They have produced small cars profitably in most overseas markets (including the BRIC economies), but the relative profitability of the larger vehicles in their domestic market has been too attractive to make them change. Toyota brought in a strategic

The important thing about PESTEL analysis is that the influences are pervasive and should always be thought about not as a simple list of unrelated bullet points, but as an inter-related set that should be used to scan continuously, or review constantly, the general environment as a whole.

objective to develop environmentally-friendly cars in the 1990s, while GM had produced an electronic car in the 1960s, the company, unlike Toyota, did not make it a strategic priority and it continued to focus production on large and conventionally-powered vehicles. GM's application for chapter 11 bankruptcy protection in 2009 may eventually bring about a fitter and leaner company, but it is probably too late now for it to compete effectively with Toyota.

Structural breaks and black swans

PESTEL analysis is primarily about monitoring and reviewing longer-term trends, but a global financial crisis is a **structural break** that subverts trends and changes existing behavioural patterns. It is a fundamental and unpredictable event in the general environment, which is likely to require organizations to rethink their purpose and strategy rather suddenly. Some unpredictable events are potentially so very catastrophic that a societal, or even a world response, is required. The World Health Organization's projected impact of an influenza A/H5N1 pandemic (avian flu) is 7 to 350 million deaths.

Nassim Nicholas Taleb is the author of *The Black Swan*.[3] In 1698, Dutch explorers discovered black swans in a river inlet in what later became known as Western Australia. Before then, Europeans had no reason to believe that swans were any colour but white. David Hume, the philosopher, used black swans to illustrate that no matter how many times something can be proved, it only takes a single event to prove it untrue. Taleb argues that black swan events have three properties: (1) based on previous knowledge its probability is low; (2) when it happens it has a massive impact, and (3) people do not see it coming, but afterwards everybody saw it coming.

According to Richard Rumelt a structural break is the best time to be a strategist because old sources of competitive advantage weaken and new ones appear. He argues that a break occurred in the 1980s because of changes in technology. The development of microprocessors led to cheaper computing, personal and desktop computers, and the rise of a new kind of software industry. These changes brought about the Internet and electronic commerce that enabled Silicon Valley's small team culture to overtake

Japan's advantages in structural engineering and organizational management. It 'changed the wealth of nations'.[4]

There seems to be no obvious and useful way to see structural breaks coming. Taleb writes about turning black swans into white ones. For example, downturns in the world economy occur in cycles: there have been four global recessions over the last 50 years. While the timing of a future downturn is uncertain, it is possible to learn something from these. Some industries, for instance, seem able to weather recessions better than others, such as utilities, telecommunication services, health care and consumer staples, but these are less likely to grow significantly during an upturn.[4]

Strategic risk management

Strategic risk management is a systematic and overall approach for managing those external events and trends that could seriously harm an organization's effectiveness for achieving its longer-term purpose. According to Richard Waterer, a senior vice-president at Marsh & McLennan Companies, risk management is a central part of any organization's strategic management.[5] It involves methodically addressing the risks attached to the management of an organization's core business areas, or, in other words, those that are important to the effective strategic management of an organization's purpose.

Sharman and Smith.[6] suggest it should have the following key aspects:

- Statement on the value proposition for risk management (specific to the organization in relation to business objectives and the risk environment).
- Definition of agreed risks; definition of the objectives for risk management based on the organizational objectives and supporting business strategy.
- Statements on the required corporate culture and behavioural expectations with regard to risk taking.
- Definition of organizational ownership of risk management strategy at all levels.
- Reference to the risk management framework or system being employed to deliver the above requirements.
- Definition of the performance criteria employed for reviewing the effectiveness of the risk management framework in delivering the risk management objectives.

Compliance requirements have helped to drive the documentation of strategic risks in organizations. The US Securities and Exchange Commission (SEC) now requires publicly-listed companies to document the key business areas and the underlying assumptions that are core to strategic success.[7]

Industry life cycles

The **industry life cycle** (similar to the product life cycle) is based on the premise that industries and products go through a life cycle of phases (see Figure 4.2). The phases are associated with the need for different strategies as the underpinning competitive conditions change in each of the phases.

The cycle begins with an introductory phase, which is followed by one of growth, the shakeout phase, then a phase of maturity and, finally, an aging phase. The competitive position of an organization will be different during each phase of the cycle. In the introduction phase, a new product or service is introduced to new consumers who are unfamiliar with it, and the pioneering organization has a dominant, or near monopoly, position in the newly established industry. For example, in the new era of UK household telecommunications (as a development from the original electric telegraphy connections), BT (British Telecommunications) in the early 1980s provided a dominant monopoly position of telephone connections, owning the physical infrastructure as well as the entire network of dialling numbers.

During the growth phase there are likely to be several rivals and incumbents and competition is likely to be strong and based on product functionality; there is likely to be no clear industry leader. So, in the mid-1990s, cable communications companies such as Cable & Wireless, were offering similar telecommunications services to those of BT, and a large number

PRINCIPLES IN PRACTICE 4.1

Choosing and reviewing strategy

The former chief executive of General Electric, Jack Welch, argues that the process of thinking about strategy should be as straightforward as possible:

More than a few times over the past three years, I have been on speaking programmes or at a business conference with one big strategy guru or another. And more than a few times, I have listened to their presentations in disbelief. It's not that I don't understand their theories about competitive advantage, core competencies, virtual commerce, supply chain economics, disruptive innovation, and so on, it's just that the way these experts tend to talk about strategy – as if it is some kind of high-brain scientific methodology – feels really off to me …

Forget the arduous, intellectual number crunching and data grinding that gurus say you have to go through to get strategy right. Forget the scenario planning, year-long studies, and hundred-plus page reports. They're time-consuming and expensive, and you just don't need them.

In real life, strategy is actually very straightforward. You pick a general direction and implement like hell … you just should not make strategy too complex. The more you think about it, and the more you grind down into the data and details, the more you tie yourself into knots about what to do … strategy is an approximate course of action that you frequently revisit and redefine, according to shifting market conditions. It is an iterative process and not nearly as theoretical or life-and-death as some would have you believe.[21]

Question: What could be the advantages and disadvantages of keeping things simple?

of BT customers switched to them for convenience and better pricing offers. In the shakeout phase, there is strong competition, and users are careful in their choice of products or companies. In the late 1990s the rise of mobile (cellular) telephone networks meant that BT had to recover a part of the market by entering into the mobile industry, with initially BT Cellnet, and later merged with O2 (now demerged).

During the maturity phase there are only a few dominant rivals with little difference in terms of product functionality and with stable prices, but competition is likely to be based on branding and promotion. So, at the start of the present millennium, a standard household telephone connection was only one of many communications media, and a wide range of products existed in the industry. In the aging phase (hence the conversational term, 'an aging industry'), there is evidence of a drop-off in the volume of usage, and organizations may consider rebranding themselves as producing alternative products or providing alternative services. For example, BT is currently presented with a number of very similar markets to enter into, and the focus of BT is not specifically *tele*communications *per se*, but rather communications in general; this means, the diversification into such wider ranging services as broadband connections, Internet security, email account subscriptions, and virtual storage space, in addition to the standard landline connections and sale of acces-

FIGURE 4.2 The industry life cycle

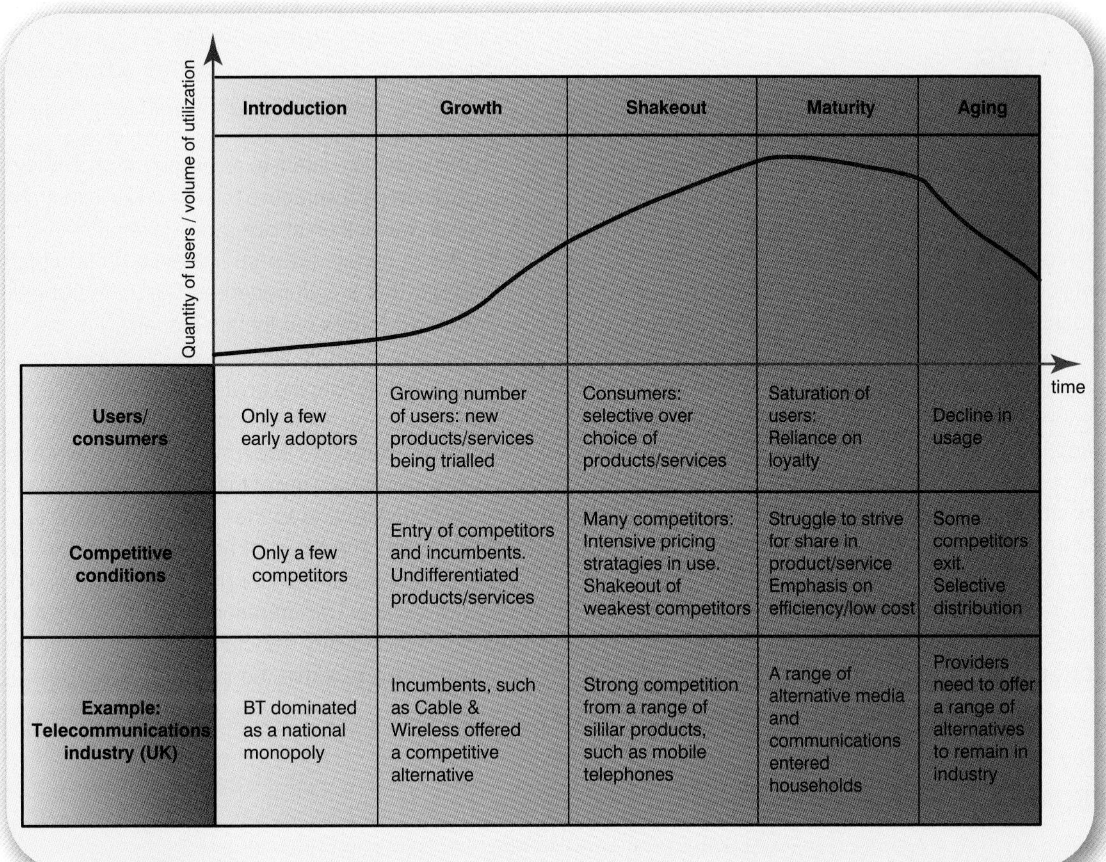

sories. For this reason, in the UK the regulator for the then telecommunications industry recently changed its name from Oftel (Office of Telecommunications) to Ofcom (Office of Communications) to provide a more accurate reflection of its work and the changing nature of the industry.

In practice an industry's phases are hard to identify precisely, and are even more difficult to forecast, since there is no universally recognized standard length of cycles, and competitors typically organize to influence the length of the cycle. However, the value of the concept lies in its use as a powerful tool for clarifying strategic options. Industries and markets seem to develop broadly along trajectories, from uncertain beginnings, through typically chaotic and intensely competitive growth, to afterwards reach more mature and relatively stable states.[8]

The attractiveness of an industry to a possible entrant should be considered against the industry's history, especially the reasons for any previous issues and crises, and how these have been resolved by industry incumbents. Existing industry competition and resources are likely to have developed along a trajectory or path of competencies, which will have built up the existing organizations to become increasingly dependent upon certain skills and other strategic resources; this tendency is conditioned by how an industry's technology is developing. Again, BT is a good example, as it was the UK's first and only household utility that monitored customer usage volume from its own base rather than the customer's home. Building on this technology and resource competency has enabled other organizations in the communications industry to become more advanced.

Industry profitability and the five competitive forces

Arguably the most influential contribution to thinking about **competitive strategy** has come from Michael Porter who introduced the industry profitability and five competitive forces framework (see Figure 4.3).[9] The forces determine an industry's intensity of competition and the longer-term profitability of all the organizations that make up an industry.

The central force is the intensity of the rivalry between existing competitors. This force is influenced by four other forces: the threat of new business, the bargaining power of customers, that of suppliers, and the threat of substitute products and services. The strength of these forces and the way they influence each other determine an industry's profitability and shape its structure.

On the surface, industries seem to differ, but the underlying driving forces will be the same. Porter contrasts the global automotive industry, the international art market and the regulated health-care industry in Europe, and observes that while each is different on the surface, the profitability of each is conditioned by the underlying structure of the five forces.[11] The principle is the same: to sustain an advantageous position, an organization has to compete in a way that takes account of its industry's five forces.

If the forces are intense, an organization is likely to be unable to earn attractive returns on its investment. If they are weak, then above-average returns are possible. Many factors have an influence on short-term profitability, but it is important to realize that the five **competitive forces** are factors that apply to the longer-term. For example, while the price of food moves up and down depending on the weather and the cost of fuel for storage and transport, the general and longer-term profitability of supermarkets rests favourably on the bargaining power of the retail chains in relation to their suppliers and to their customers (albeit to a lesser extent). The threat of new entrants is low, and the scope for substitutes for groceries is very limited.

An individual organization must consider the health of its industry structure, as well as its own strategic position within the industry, if it is going to

FIGURE 4.3 The five competitive forces[10]

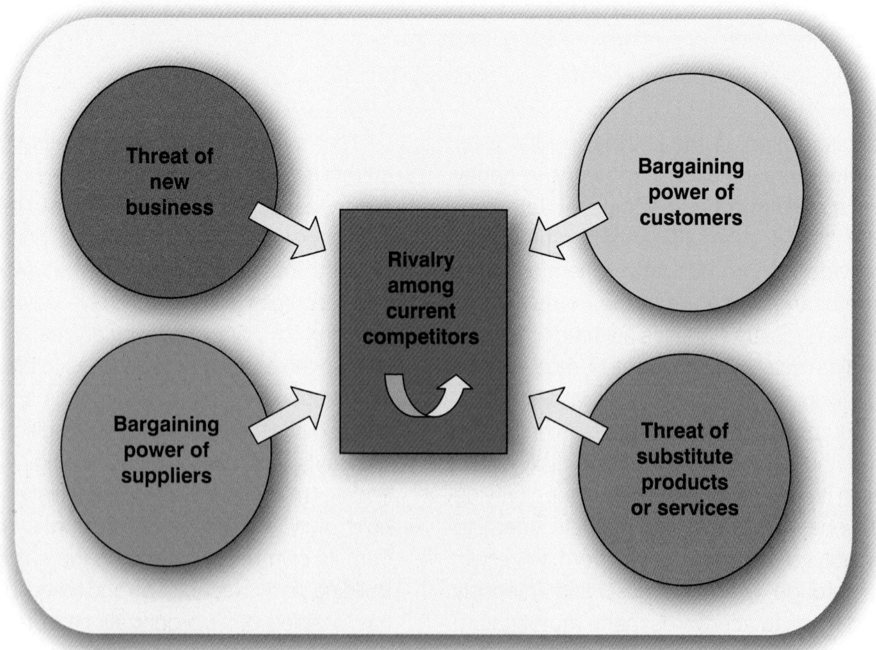

defend itself and shape an industry's forces in its favour. The nature of the forces differs by industry, and the strongest force may not be obvious. Traditionally, the value created for customers of supermarkets lies in their convenience and low costs, which critically depends for the customer on the location of the outlets. However, for Internet shopping, location and low cost may be less important than reliability in delivery, so that the organizations most likely to succeed may be those that are first to build up a critical mass of customers and a reputation for quality.

The threat of new entrants (new business)

New competition from outside brings additional capacity pressures on existing market shares that influence prices, costs and investment in an industry. If the new competition is strong in other sectors it can leverage its capabilities and cash flows to disrupt existing business. For example, the giant shadow of Microsoft falls menacingly across the Internet. In 2009, Microsoft bought control of Yahoo's internet search technology, which instantly tripled the number of US users of Microsoft's new search service: Bing in an attempt to compete with the more successful Google. Microsoft was late to the Internet, but it has one of the world's largest R&D budgets. While its key software products like Windows and Office are still very profitable, its personal computing business is becoming less important, and although it lost heavily on broadband and cable television in the late 1990s, it has enough cash and marketable securities to afford moves in other directions.

It is the threat or possibility of entry that holds down profitability in an industry. This is because when entry barriers are low enough for an outside rival, and profitability in the industry is high, then new business can enter the industry and drive down prices and raise costs for the existing competitors, or the existing organizations must spend more to raise entry barriers. There are eight sources of barriers to entry.

1 *Supply-side economies of scale:* These are economies that result when an organization is able to reduce its fixed costs per unit of an increasing output. It is probable that a larger organization is able to lower its costs – and therefore offer lower prices and increase its market share still further – more easily than a smaller organization. This will in turn enable more investment to be made in improved technology and to negotiate better terms from its suppliers. An outsider to compete effectively is likely to need to come into the industry on a

AN INDIVIDUAL ORGANIZATION MUST CONSIDER THE HEALTH OF ITS INDUSTRY STRUCTURE, AS WELL AS ITS OWN STRATEGIC POSITION WITHIN THE INDUSTRY, IF IT IS GOING TO DEFEND ITSELF AND SHAPE AN INDUSTRY'S FORCES IN ITS FAVOUR. THE NATURE OF THE FORCES DIFFERS BY INDUSTRY, AND THE STRONGEST FORCE MAY NOT BE OBVIOUS.

large scale, either on the basis of dislodging existing competitors, or by accepting a cost disadvantage. Scale economies are possible at any point in the supply chain; for example, large corporations, such as Tata Steel, dominate iron and steel manufacturing.

2 *Demand-side benefits of scale*: These benefits arise in industries when a customer's willingness to pay for an organization's product increases with the number of customers who already buy from the organization. An organization's image, its reputation and general awareness about its products and services, increase with size.

3 *Customer-switching costs*: These are costs customers will incur if they change suppliers. If these are high, entrants will find it expensive to make switching worthwhile to customers. For example, in many industrial markets, a supplier's input or service is important to the quality of a large customer's own products; changes in supply are likely to increase uncertainty and require modified working and extra investment.

4 *Capital requirements*: Where the cost of entry is high, access to large financial resources is necessary. If the values of capital, or the expectations of the owners of capital, are influenced by uncertain financial markets and interest rates, then the associated costs may reduce the viability of any investment. An important consideration is the potential resale value of assets.

5 *Incumbency advantages independent of size*: The existing organizations in an industry may have other advantages that potential entrants may not be able to match. Many of these are associated with early advantage, such as proprietary technology, preferential access to established materials and labour, perhaps because of favourable geographical locations, especially for existing customers, and a history, with established brands and an accumulated experience that is important to a particular organization's competitive advantage. Entrants may attempt to bypass such advantages.

6 *Unequal access to distribution channels*: The fewer the wholesale and retail channels, the more likely it is that existing competitors will have them tied up and the harder it will be for entrants to break in and replace existing customes. Sometimes new competitors have had to bypass existing distribution channels or even develop new markets altogether.

7 *Restrictive government policy*: Government policy and regulation, licensing and other controls that favour national interest or even facilitate trading agreements, can work to limit or even foreclose entry to industries.

8 *Expected retaliation*: The ability and history of competitors to retaliate when faced with new competition will influence how potential entrants see the attractiveness of an industry. Incumbents often use public statements and responses to one entrant to send an aggressive message to others. Considerations concern the abilities of competitors to manage all of the above barriers to entry, and to consider the possibility of new growth and customers, the power of competitors to weather or lower prices, and the underlying health of their balance sheets.

The challenge 'is to find ways to surmount the entry barriers without nullifying, through heavy investment, the profitability of participating in the industry'.[12]

The bargaining power of customers

Powerful customers, or groups of customers, can force suppliers in an industry to lower prices, demand more customized features, and force up service and quality levels. This activity drives down an industry's profitability and shifts the balance of power and value in favour of the buyers. Customers have an advantage if the following conditions apply:

1. Customers are few and buy in quantities that are large in relation to the size of suppliers. If suppliers' fixed costs are high and marginal costs are low there are likely to be attempts to keep capacity filled through discounting.
2. The industry's products are standardized or undifferentiated. If buyers can find equivalent products elsewhere, then it is possible to play suppliers off against each other.
3. Customers have low switching costs in changing suppliers.
4. Customers are able to threaten backward integration and can produce the product themselves if a supplier is too costly.

Buyers are likely to be sensitive to suppliers' prices if the cost of the product or service is a major concern to a buyer and takes a significant portion of its costs or available funds. A buyer is likely to search for best deals and negotiate hard in this situation, but the opposite is true when price is a low percentage of a buyer's costs. Price is less important when the quality of the supplied product and its influence on the buyer's own products are vital considerations; the importance of service, especially when quick response and advice are involved, can be much more important to the buyer. In general, cash rich and profitable customers with healthy enterprises may be less sensitive to levels of price.

Producers often attempt to reduce the power of channels through exclusive arrangements with distributors and retailers. Sometimes suppliers may market directly to consumers. Component manufacturers seek to influence assemblers by creating preferences for their components with downstream customers. Intermediate customers and customers who are not the end-user, such as buyers in the distribution channels, are similarly motivated, but with the difference that if they can negotiate favourable deals some of the gains can be passed downstream to strengthen their own trading positions.

The bargaining power of suppliers

If suppliers can influence the flow of products and resources to an industry's competing organizations, they can negotiate higher prices, or shift costs to other participants in the industry. Suppliers are able to act independently in relation to an industry's customers if any of the following conditions apply:

1. Suppliers are more concentrated than a particular industry and its customers.
2. Suppliers are not dependent upon a single industry for their revenues. Where a supplier is serving a number of different industries a supplier may extract high returns from each. Alternatively, suppliers may want to protect an industry through agreed and reasonable prices, and assist in other supply chain activities such as quality management or promotion.
3. Suppliers have customers with high switching costs. Suppliers may have favoured supplier status and may be clustered close to large customers.
4. Suppliers have differentiated products and services.

5 Suppliers have products and services for which there are no substitutes.

6 Suppliers have a potential to integrate forward and enter the industry and a customer's market.

The threat of substitute products and services

A substitute is a product or service of another industry, which creates an equivalent value for the customer. The threat of substitution can work indirectly or downstream in the industry. Substitutes are nearly always present, but are difficult to identify if they appear different in form from an industry's products or services. This is particularly so when conditions are fluid and changing radically in other industries and markets, so that it is difficult for an industry's participants to understand what is happening. The threat of substitutes influences an industry's profitability because prices must remain attractive or customers may go elsewhere.

The threat of substitutes is high if it is apparent to a customer that an alternative offers an attractive price/performance trade-off to the industry's offer. The customer's switching cost must also be low, not just in terms of costs but also in terms of convenience and assurance. The possibilities work both ways: it may be possible to exploit emerging opportunities in one's own industry to develop substitutes for products in other industries.

Rivalry among existing competitors

The degree to which competitors' rivalry influences an industry's profitability is influenced broadly by the intensity of competition and the basis on which rivals compete.

The intensity of rivalry is strong when competitors are roughly of equal power and size and are numerous. In this case it is difficult for any organization to win customers without taking them from rivals. Unless there is an industry leader to set the competitive conditions for the industry, the competitive behaviour is likely to be unstable and costly for the industry as a whole.

Slow industry growth can stimulate intense competition for market share. This is especially so when exit barriers are high, because, for example, competitors are locked into technologies and own specialized resources of limited value in other industries. This may lead to a chronic excess capacity and encourage discounting. Organizations may also be present for a variety of reasons that do not give a central role to profitability. Competitors may be part of a larger organization, which has a presence in other industries; these units may be there to search for opportunities for growth or to gain experience of the industry's technology and business. Other competitors may have social as well as profit-seeking objectives, which influence how they compete; for example, a public service may aim to keep its prices low.

The costs of competition can work to raise prices and reduce the number of customers. Price competition, however, works to win new customers. This may reduce the opportunities for such non-price enhancing factors as product functionality, and if it reduces the share of value created by the industry by passing it on to consumers, it can reduce an industry's profitability and limit investment and industry development. Intermediate customers and customers who are not the end-user, such as buyers in the distribution channels, are similarly motivated, but with the difference that if they can negotiate favourable deals some of the gain can be passed downstream to strengthen their own trading positions.

Price competition can occur, especially when the products and services of rivals are very similar and switching costs for customers are low. High fixed costs and low marginal costs lead to pressures for rivals to lower prices below average costs and win customers to help cover fixed costs. Essential investment often requires unavoidable large additions to capacity, which also tempts suppliers to discount prices to grow sales. Other impulses to cut prices involve cases of perishable goods, which must be sold quickly to prevent losses from sales because of poor quality, obsolescence or changing product information.

Non-price factors, such as product and service features, branding, and experience, allow market segmentation to take place, when a low price segment can be clearly managed apart from segments with more economically stable and higher prices that reflect the extra value these factors create for customers. In this way, non-price competition is less likely to erode an industry's profitability than price competition, since market segmentation can support above-average profitability.

The five competitive forces determine how the economic value created by an industry is retained by the organizations operating in the industry, and how much of it is bargained away by customers and suppliers, limited by substitutes, or constrained by potential new entrants. It is necessary for a strategist to keep the overall structure in mind rather than only one of the forces. To quote Michael Porter:

> **Every company should already know what the average profitability of its industry is and how it has been changing over time. The five forces reveal *why* industry profitability is what it is. Only then can a company incorporate industry conditions into strategy.**

Understanding the forces that shape industry competition is the starting point for developing strategy. Every company should already know what the average profitability of its industry is and how it has been changing over time. The five forces reveal why industry profitability is what it is. Only then can a company incorporate industry conditions into strategy.[13]

An organization's strategy, in Porter's view, can be based on building defences against the competitive

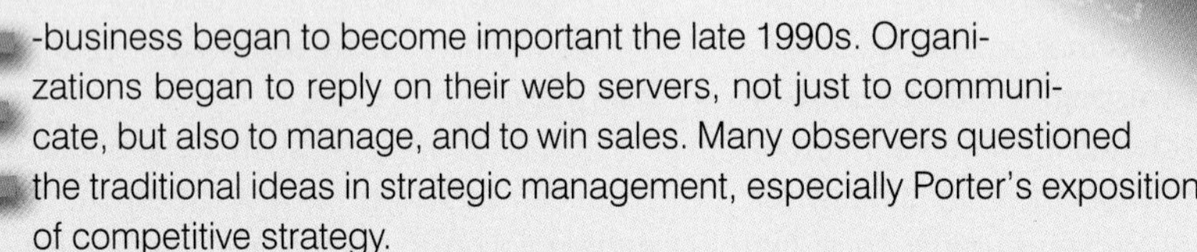

PRINCIPLES IN PRACTICE 4.2

The five competitive forces and the Internet

E-business began to become important the late 1990s. Organizations began to reply on their web servers, not just to communicate, but also to manage, and to win sales. Many observers questioned the traditional ideas in strategic management, especially Porter's exposition of competitive strategy.

Porter struck back in 2001, when he argued that the Internet, as many were suggesting, is not a strategy, but only a means for doing business.[22] Sustained competitive advantage is about strategic positioning: the need to deliver a value proposition.

He applies the five-force framework to the Internet as follows:

Threat of new business
Barriers to entry are reduced as the Internet requires a smaller sales force, ease of access and fewer physical and costly assets. The nature of software and Internet applications normally enables easy imitation by rivals, thus allowing entry into the market.

Bargaining power of customers
Powerful channels are eliminated or bargaining power over traditional channels is improved. General bargaining power is shifted to the end user, and switching costs are reduced.

Bargaining power of suppliers
Intervening companies are reduced as the Internet allows direct access from suppliers to end users. There is a shift of power to suppliers as barriers to entry are reduced.

Threat of substitute products or services
The size of the market can be expanded as the overall industry becomes more efficient. New substitute threats are created as the Internet becomes proliferated.

Rivalry among existing competitors
Visible differences between competitors are difficult to see by customers, thus creating more rivalry. The geographical market is increased, thus increasing the number of competitors. The likely differentiable variable is likely to shift to price, rather than company differences.

The survival of the organization, Porter argues, depends on assessing the external environment in respect of the five forces. In the long-term, Internet provision will be standardized and it will become difficult for customers to distinguish differences.

Question: Is the Internet an industry, or is it something else?

forces, or in finding a position where the forces are weakest. However, he warns that in shaping its strategy, an organization should be careful not to set in motion dynamics that will undermine the attractiveness of the industry in the longer term.

Competitive advantage depends on doing things differently from rivals, and in ways that take account of possible future competition. This is in contrast with doing things well, such as those that sustain an organization's fitness for purpose. Competitive advantage, of course, depends on doing both effectively, but doing things differently is essential. Organizations must ensure their practices are effective and are being continuously improved so that the health of the business is sustained over time. However, good and best practice can be learned through benchmarking, so rivals can often emulate each other. Competitive advantage is sustainable if it is specific to the organization and rivals find it too expensive and difficult to emulate (or perhaps even to understand).

Hypercompetition

The five forces are about how an organization can understand an industry to establish what determines the level of its average profits over the long term. However, for some industries, especially those emerging from new technologies, shorter-term profits can be very important. This is especially so in conditions of **hypercompetition**, described by Richard D'Aveni to explain a dynamic competitive state of constant disequilibrium and change.[14] The concept gained widespread use in strategic management during the time of the rise of the dot.com enterprises trading on the Internet in the late 1990s.

D'Aveni argues that in emerging and rapidly changing markets, competitive advantage is transient rather than sustainable and rivals typically move on before competitors can react. So there is an emphasis on renewing, rather than protecting, an organization's sources of competitive advantage. Rindova and Kotha call this activity 'morphing', after a children's television character called Morph, a shape shifter who constantly changes shape to suit his circumstances.[15] This behaviour calls for an ability to focus short-term, a honed ability to read a market and to generate creative innovations continuously.

A related idea is **disruptive innovation**, a concept introduced by Christensen to signify a revolutionary product that replaces existing ways of competing.[16] There are two basic forms: the first acts to create new competition with new markets and customers; the second acts to generate new value for existing customers, but who are located in a low-value-added part of a market where the established competitors will typically move offers up-market rather than defend low-end segments.

For example, the Virgin group has consistently entered traditional industries, such as insurance and air travel, and offered new value based on new products and services, and the excitement of its brand, to steal market share from the existing players. At Virgin the strategic question is one of why not, rather than why, according to Gordon McCallum, Virgin's former group strategy director. Virgin has articulated this perspective in terms of guidelines: Virgin will enter a market if it can challenge an industry's existing rules; if it can give customers a better break; be more entertaining and 'put a thumb in the eye' of any complacent incumbents.

Strategic groups

The observation that an industry's competitors respond in similar ways to competitive forces is reflected in the concept of **strategic group**. This is a small number of competing organizations which

Morph – an inspiration for modern business?

have a similar strategy and which compete with each other within the group, rather than with rivals from outside. Cool and Schendel show there have been systematic and significant differences in performance among organizations which belong to the same strategic group within the US pharmaceutical industry.[17] Within a group, rivals offer similar products to the same customers and competition can be intense. The significance is that within a single industry it is possible that the fundamental strategic differences of the different rivals, such as the positions they take in relation to the five forces, can be captured and understood by a small number of groups. The main competitive differences can be contrasted figuratively in the form of a **strategic map** (see Figure 4.4).

The term 'strategic map' should not be confused with 'strategy map' (used in association with the balanced scorecard: see Chapter 3). The strategic map is associated only with strategic groups. It is used to identify the competitive characteristics that differentiate an industry's groups. For example, these may include variables such as price, differentiation of product range, geographic coverage, the degree of vertical integration and use of distribution channels, and service. Pairs of such differentiating features can be used to plot the locations of organizations on the strategic map to see how these cluster and form a similar group. The figure illustrates five strategic groups, which are shown in the form of irregularly shaped pie-charts. The shape of the group will vary depending on the competitive characteristics (made up of combinations of the two axes).

In the example, the characteristics are geographical coverage (as a percentage of the whole market) and marketing intensity of the organization (as a percentage of marketing cost to sales revenue). Hence, three zones of **strategic space** become apparent. Strategic space 3 (represented by the dark-blue boxes at the bottom-right) concerns an uncompetitive position as marketing costs are high, covering only a small area of the market; the strategic position

FIGURE 4.4 A strategic map

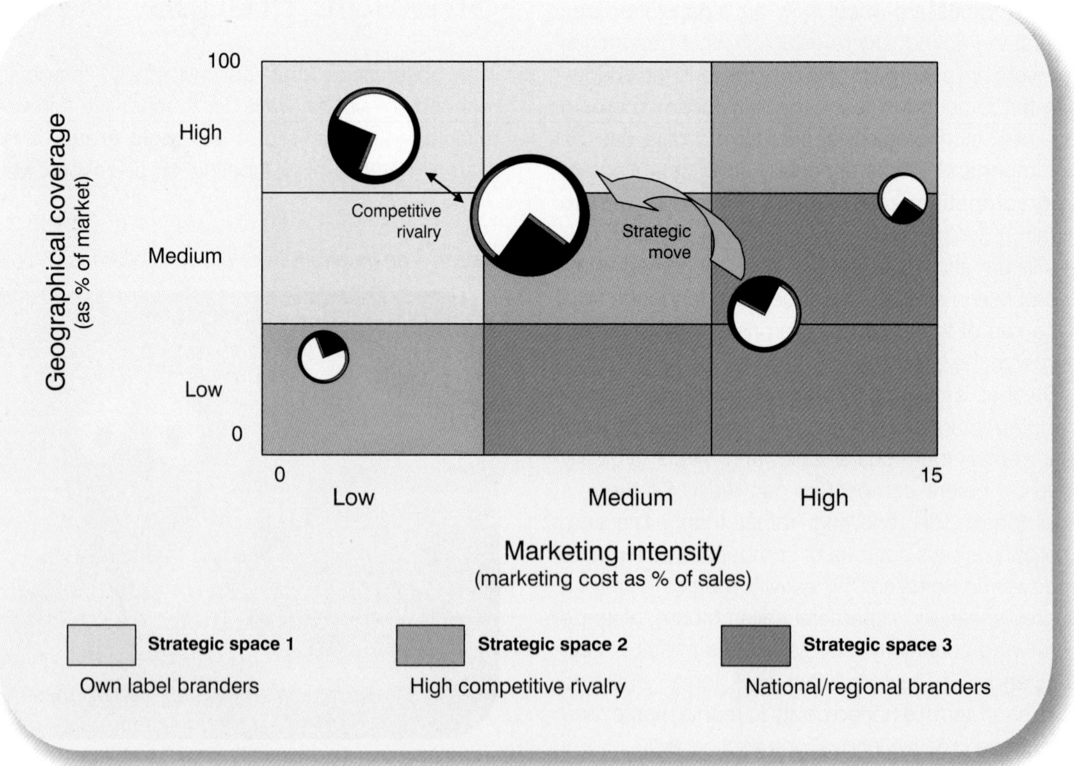

achieved is therefore of national or regional branders only. Strategic space 1 (represented by the light-blue boxes at the top-left of the figure), by contrast, concerns companies with many advantages that enable them to sustain a position that has small marketing costs (in relation to sales) but achieves a high geographical coverage. This is a high-performing competitive position, and the result is that the market will have mainly own-labels. Strategic space 2 (represented by orange boxes) is betwixt the two extremes, and can include characteristics of low marketing cost with low geographical coverage, high marketing cost with high geographical coverage or an intermediate quantity of both.

It is normally desirable for an organization to move away from strategic space 3 to strategic space 1, as strategic space 2 is highly competitive. This is because the gap in-between the two strategic groups represents the degree of competitive rivalry (the narrower the gap, the greater the degree of competitive rivalry). Note however that it is not always the case that organizations will desire to move in this direction, as it depends on the dimensions of the axes, and what opportunities are presented within each strategic space, and an organization will need to analyse carefully the gains when making each **strategic move** (a move in the direction that better achieves its longer-term strategy).

In drawing a strategic map, circles are marked around each strategic group, making each proportionate to the size of the group's respective share of the industry's sales revenue. The dual variables should not be highly correlated, and should expose differences between the groups in how they position themselves in the industry. It may be possible to draw several maps, using different axes to give a good overview of how organizations are competing. The shape of an industry is likely to be influenced by

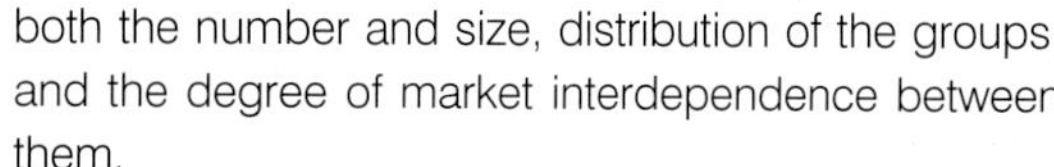

both the number and size, distribution of the groups, and the degree of market interdependence between them.

Individual organizations focus on improving their competitive position within their strategic group. However, these typically have similar market shares and respond in similar ways to external trends and the moves of other groups. For example, the photography industry is affected by the photonics and digital technology industries, as well as the creative arts industry. An organization operating in any of these three industries is affected by the development of and changes in the levels of competition within them.

Using the strategic map

The strategic map is useful as it enhances our understanding of the nature of **strategic choices** within a given industry. It is helpful for understanding competition; managers can identify more accurately who are the immediate competitors rather than those in the whole industry, thereby saving time and money by focusing only on those dimensions that distinguish the organization from its rivals. Another benefit of using the map is that it helps to identify unconquered strategic space. It will also help to identify what are the likely mobility barriers that prevent an organization from moving from one position to another (these are like barriers to entry); by recognizing these, it helps the organization to strengthen its position by preventing others from imitating its characteristics.

In identifying strategic groups, organizations may differ in terms of the scope of activities and the resource commitment. The scope of activities may include any of the following:

- The extent of product/service diversity. For example, a computing company may just sell PC software or it may also sell accessories,as Microsoft sells computer mice and keyboards, as well as computer software.
- The extent of geographical coverage. For example, the market for Asus, a Taiwanese laptop producer, is predominantly Asia, whereas the market for Acer, also a Taiwanese

laptop producer, includes Europe and other continents.

- The range of distribution channels in use. For example, Dell's main distribution channel is through the Internet, whereas Hewlett Packard sells through both the Internet and computer stores.

Resource commitment includes:

- The extent of marketing effort. For example, this could be in the form of advertising effort and spend as a proportion of sales.
- Quality, or even perceived quality, of a product or service. Assuming there is a trade-off between price and quality, then some customers may prefer to buy some products over others.
- Size of the organization. This depends on the mid-term purpose of a given company and where it wants to be in the future.

Blue ocean strategy

Blue ocean strategy is the name of a book written by W. Chan Kim and Renee Mauborgne.[18] They argue that organizations should not compete in over-crowded markets, which is (bloody) red ocean strategy, but seek opportunities where competition is weak. Organizations should create 'blue oceans of uncontested space': blue ocean demand is created, rather than through trying to win customers with the same products and service attributes that rivals have. This is done through the creation of new types of business or by finding a gap in a red ocean. They introduce the **value curve** (see Figure 4.5), which is a depiction of how market rivals compete on relative value-creating attributes, such as price, delivery, quality, functional aspects, service and so on.

The figure has value curves for two existing airlines. The area where existing competition seems to offer least value is located towards the lower left-hand corner of the figure. There might be space here

FIGURE 4.5 A value curve showing areas of blue and red oceans

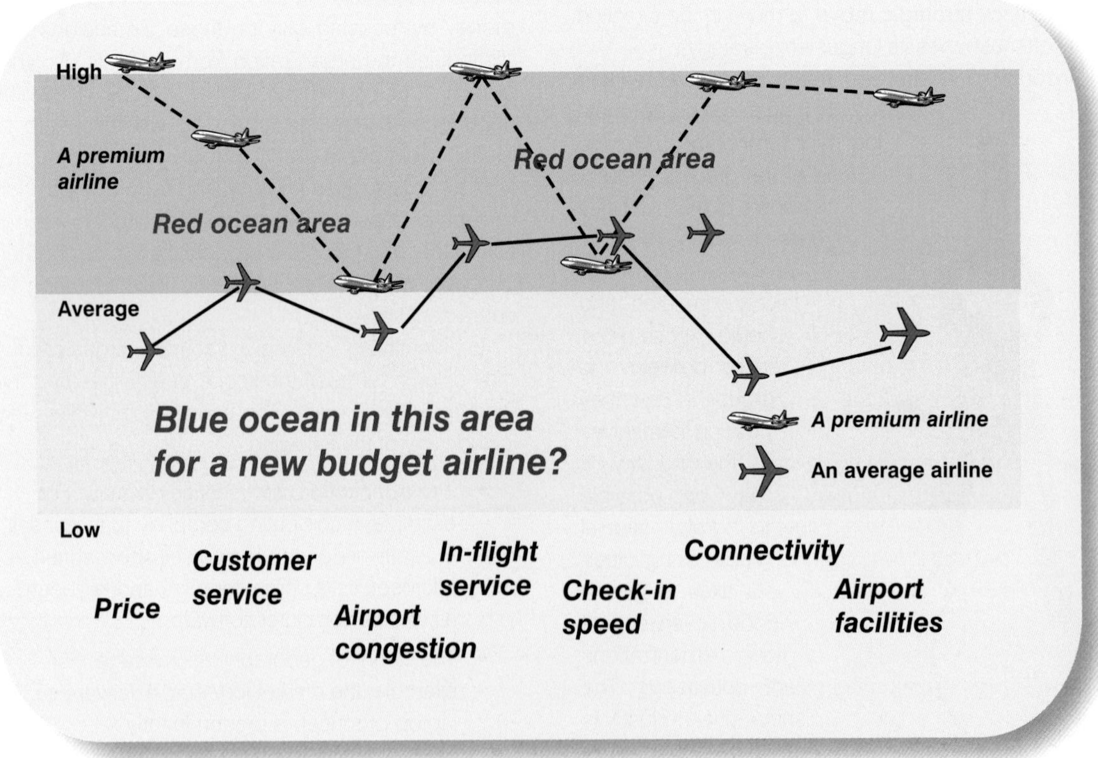

KEY DEBATE 4.1

Is it possible to do too much thinking?

On the whole practitioners seem to favour straightforward and no-nonsense approaches to thinking about strategy and the external environment. Evidence suggests 'a real world that is simple'; for example, the responses to the moves of competitors may be limited and short-term.[24]

Writing about sensing and seizing opportunities, David Teece[25] argues that entrepreneurial management, in particular, has little to do with analysing, but it does involve recognizing problems and trends. Kenichi Ohmae[26] thinks effective business strategies come from particular states of mind rather than analysis.

The rumbustious Gary Hamel has declared that: 'The dirty little secret of the strategy industry is that it doesn't have any theory of strategy creation'.[27] Of course, theories are frameworks used only as aids for thinking and understanding. It is not an exact science and the tools do not constitute judgement, which is more an art, based on experience and imagination.

Question: Are frameworks such as the industry life cycle, strategic groups and the five forces too complex to be practically useful?

for a new budget airline, which offers low price, low customer service, low airport congestion and in-flight service.

Non-profit sectors

Non-profit sectors of the economy include registered charities, educational institutions, professional bodies, campaigning organizations, and public or quasi-public sector agencies. Peter Drucker, writing from an American perspective, saw government and the public sector as a distinct and separate category from non-profit, although he includes schools and hospitals in his description of these sectors.[19] Usually these organizations aim to make a surplus of revenue over expenditure, which can be used to benefit a target group or activity. These often function in competitive environments: for example, charities compete for a given amount of available money, while others may also compete for customers and beneficiaries, as a university does for students and research funds. Thus, non-profit organizations can define their industry in terms of the five competitive forces.

However, ethics and ideology in some non-profit organizations may make overt competitive behaviour inappropriate. A charity places an emphasis on collaboration and partnerships with other rival charities to a degree that is impossible for commercial organizations, when in a regulated industry co-operation may be mistaken for collusion in some markets. The meaning of 'customer' is also often ambiguous; for example, in the commercial sector, customers usually pay directly for products and services, but in the non-profit case donors or other sources also pay to help cover the cost of resources, while others, such as clients, receive the direct benefits.

KEY DEBATE 4.2

Are the five forces still relevant for today?

Michael Porter introduced his competitive forces in the *Harvard Business Review* in 1979, and the journal invited him to revise the paper which was published in 2008.[28] His ideas continue to be (probably) the most influential in strategic management.

Nevertheless, the five-force model has been criticized as it seems to underplay the importance of factors such as an industry's growth rate, technology and innovation, and government. Porter argues that these are not competitive forces, but factors. While they are important, they are neutral in competitive terms because they offer opportunities as well as threats for the profitability of an industry. The five forces also appear to downplay the importance of industry collaboration and co-operation, most notably in terms of complementary products and services. However, there seems to be little reason for not considering this within the existing parameters of the framework.

One issue is the question about how to define an industry. Porter uses the official industrial classifications. It is perhaps not exactly what defines an industry so much as how the competitive forces influence a position within the industry that is crucial.

George Yip argues that most of the examples used by Porter, such as Southwest Airlines and IKEA, are already enjoying an established profitable industry position.[29] Porter notes the importance of time for building up a unique competitive position.[30] For some industries with high velocity markets there may be little time to do this (see hypercompetition).

Question: Porter's five forces help an organization to sustain a long-term competitive position within its industry, but how can a new entrant to an industry achieve such a position?

However, this is similar to many commercial situations, for example, in the media industry, where sponsors and advertisers contribute a significant portion of the industry's revenue. In cases such as this, segmentation is necessary to delivery distinct forms of value, and any conflict of interests between stakeholder groups has to be reconciled and accommodated. The degree and nature of formality in governance may be a factor; Rangan, for example, has argued in the pages of the *Harvard Business Review*, that strategic choices are less important to non-profit organizations, because these are not subject to the discipline of the capital markets.[20]

PRINCIPLES IN PRACTICE 4.3

Balancing revenue and creativity in local radio

For some organizations the returns may not come directly from the people it serves, but from sponsors, such as government and public sector agencies, which aim to provide general standards of public service, or commercial organizations whose income comes from promoters. BBC Radio One DJ, Chris Moyles, describes what happens in local radio:

DJs are scum. This is so true. In the world of commercial radio, it's all about the money. How little they pay you, and how much they can make and keep. The sales department is where the money is made, and that keeps the station going. The sales team sell the airtime to whoever they can and DJs end up doing a competition giving away fish fingers because the local fish-finger factory agreed to spend five

Chris Moyles

thousand pounds on a month-long competition. The sales team are gods with company cars and paid-for holidays, and the DJs are merely the idiots who have to present a road show from the local summer fete or present their show live from a bus station because the bus company also paid for a big promotion. God forbid that you want to do creative radio that actually costs money. Besides, you probably won't have time because you're giving away cough sweets as its National Cough Sweet Week and the National Cough Sweet Association has also spent money on a big promotion.[23]

Getting the balance right depends upon the external environment. Sometimes the means seem to be getting the best of ends. How an organization copes with its external environment can get in the way of its purpose.

Question: How do PESTEL factors influence the management of a radio station?

KEY DEBATE 4.3

Should strategy be stable over time, or should it be changing?

Constantly changing strategy is bad for morale if it creates an impression that an organization's senior managers do not know their own minds, so frequent changes in strategy should be avoided. It is also difficult to sustain and make a strategy stronger if changes are always taking place. This suggests taking a constrained or even a conservative view of the external environment.

Some observers, on the other hand, think that organizations should be ever changing, even inconsistent, if they are to be truly creative, innovative, and are to keep their competitors on their toes. The iconoclast, Tom Peters is well known for slogans such as 'Incrementalism is innovation's worst enemy', and 'Obsolete ourselves or the competition will win'.[31] In a sense, constant change is a strategy, or at least a strategic posture. The Virgin group of companies was strongly influenced by Peters. Similarly, Gary Hamel, perhaps inspired a bit too much by the creativity and innovation of the dot.com boom, argues that strategy should be revolution and based on innovation.[32]

Question: Strategic management is about achieving a consistency of purpose; does constancy matter as much?

SUMMARY OF PRINCIPLES

1. The starting point for effective strategic analysis is to understand the external environment.
2. The factors that relate to the general environment can be summarized in the form of a mnemonic, PESTEL: political, economic, social, technological, environmental, and legal.
3. Competitive advantage depends on doing things differently from rivals, and in ways that take account of possible future competition.
4. The Industry life cycle goes through five distinctive stages: introduction, growth, shakeout, maturity and aging; each stage is subject to different competitive conditions.
5. An industry's attractiveness is determined by the intensity of competition, which is influenced by the threat of new entrants; the bargaining power of customers; the bargaining power of suppliers, and the threat of substitutes.

6 During times of hypercompetition, an organization may need to consider immediate decisions for the short-term to deal with states of disequilibrium and change.

7 A strategic group analysis identifies strategic space, which is important for making strategic moves and to assess the extent of competitive rivalry in the industry.

GLOSSARY OF KEY TERMS

BRIC countries the countries Brazil, Russia, India and China, which are fast developing economies.

competitive forces the forces (or major impact factors) of the industry that affect the level of competition and management of strategy.

competitive strategy the view of Michael Porter about how competitive advantage is sustainable – this mainly requires close assessment of the impacts of the external environment.

Disruptive innovation a revolutionary product that replaces existing ways of competing.

External environment those conditions that influence the external changes in its industry, especially ones that influence the intensity of competition.

forecasting a prediction of future trends and possible outcomes.

Hypercompetition a dynamic state of constant disequilibrium and change in the industry.

Industry life cycle the distinctive stages of the life of an industry or product/service.

non-profit sectors organizations which are not commercial organizations.

PESTEL a mnemonic framework to understand factors that are Political, Economic, Social, Technological, Environmental, and Legal.

project an organized and finite series of activities that is finite.

regulation the control of an organization or industry in which an adequate level of competition does not exist, normally by specially established governmental bodies to protect the interest of the public against monopolistic abuse.

scanning an overview assessment of the external environment.

scenarios the evaluation of critical success factors for varying contexts and their outcomes.

strategic choices the options open to an organization in deciding on the strategy to adopt to achieve its purpose.

Strategic groups groups of organizations in an industry that share similar competitive characteristics.

Strategic map a pictorial assessment of the relative positions of strategic groups, used to assess and predict the possible strategic moves of competitors, and for the identification of strategic space.

strategic move a move of an organization in the direction that better achieves its longer-term strategy.

Strategic risk management a systematic and overall approach for managing those external events and trends that could seriously harm an organization's effectiveness for achieving its longer-term purpose.

strategic space a gap identified in the strategic group analysis of potential gain for an organization to move into.

strategizing an activity such as thinking about, formulating and crafting strategy to take account of reality and possibilities.

Structural break a fundamental and unpredictable event in the general environment, which is likely to require organizations to rethink their purpose and strategy.

Value curve a depiction of how market rivals compete on relative value-creating attributes, such as price, delivery, quality, functional aspects, service and so on.

GUIDED FURTHER READING

Strategic risk management has emerged during recent years as an important area, especially in terms of enterprise management: the report published by the Professional Accountants in Business Committee is one of the best reviews. The most cited article about risk management is by Slywotzky and Drzik:

The Professional Accountants in Business Committee (eds.) (2004) *Enterprise Governance: Getting the Balance Right,* PAIB Committee report, New York: International Federation of Accountants.

Slywotzky, A. J. and Drzik, J. (2005) 'Countering the biggest risk of all', *Harvard Business Review,* April: 78–88.

For further reading on the strategic groups, which explains the theory in more detail and the usefulness of strategic group analysis, see:

McGee, J and Thomas, H (1986) 'Strategic groups: theory, research and taxonomy', *Strategic Management Journal* 7(2):141–60.

Fiegenbaum, A. and Thomas, H. (1990) 'Strategic groups and performance: the US insurance industry 1980–84', *Strategic Management Journal* 11:197–215.

REVIEW QUESTIONS

1 What does a PESTEL analysis do?

2 Why is the global financial crisis a structural break?

3 What is strategic risk management?

4 Why is it helpful to know the stages of an industry's life cycle?

5 Why should organizations consider an industry's attractiveness in terms of its five competitive forces?

6 What kinds of industries are sensitive to hypercompetition?

7 Define the meaning of strategic groups.

8 What are 'strategic space' and 'blue oceans of uncontested space'?

SEMINAR AND ASSIGNMENT QUESTIONS

1 Why is it important for strategic management to see the 'strategic wood, rather than the operational trees'? Discuss this in relation to another idea that a 'whole is greater than the sum of its parts'. Consider the implications of these ideas for how a strategist should look at and evaluate the general external environment.

2 Choose an industry and work out how the intensity of competition is influenced by the five forces. Define and compare the different competitive positions of the main players. Give your opinion on the strengths and weaknesses of the five force model for your chosen industry. Reach a conclusion and provide a summary of the logic for you reaching your conclusion.

3 When economic times are good, popular business books and gurus are apt to say that

change is necessary because the environment is dynamic. When economic times are bad, they are still apt to say that change is necessary, but this time it is because change is needed to recover and get ahead of the competition before the economy recovers. Is there any other advice you could offer?

CHAPTER REFERENCES

1 Wilson, D. and Purushothaman, R. (2003) *Dreaming with BRICs: The Path to 2050,* global economics paper, 90, New York: Goldman Sachs.

2 'PEST' was developed by Andrews, K. (1987) *The Concept of Corporate Strategy* (1st and 3rd edns), Homewood, IL: Irwin; and developed by Steiner, G. A. (1979) *Strategic Planning: What Every Manager Must Know,* New York: Free Press.

3 Taleb, N. N. (2007) *The Black Swan: The Impact of the Highly Improbable,* New York: Random House.

4 Rumelt, R. P. (2008) 'Strategy in a "structural break"', *McKinsey Quarterly* December: www.mckinseyquarterly.com

5 Jiang, B., Koller, T. M. and Williams, Z. D. (2009) *McKinsey Quarterly* January: www.mckinseyquarterly.com

6 Sharman, R. and Smith, D. (2004) Enterprise risk management, chapter 6, in the Professional Accountants in Business Committee (eds), *Enterprise Governance: Getting the Balance Right,* PAIB Committee report, New York; International Federation of Accountants.

7 United States Securities & Exchange Commission (2006) The Electronic Data Gathering, Analysis and Retrieval System, www.sec.gov/edgar.shtml

8 Abernathy, W. J. and Utterback, J. M. (1978) 'Patterns of industrial innovation', *Technology Review* 80(7):40–7.

9 The five forces were introduced in Porter, M. E. (1979) 'How competitive forces shape strategy', *Harvard Business Review* March-April; the article was updated in Porter, M. E. (2008) 'The five competitive forces that shape strategy', *Harvard Business Review,* January:79–93.

10 Adapted from Porter (1979) *op cit.*

11 Porter (2008) *op cit.*

12 *ibid.* p. 82.

13 *ibid.* p. 88.

14 D'Aveni, R. (1994) *Hypercompetition: Managing the Dynamics of Strategic Manoeuvring,* NY: Free Press.

15 Rindova, V. P. and Kotha, S. (2001) 'Continuous morphing: competing through dynamic capabilities, form and function', *Academy of Management Journal* 44(6):1263–280.

16 Christensen, C. M. (1997) *The Innovator's Dilemma: When New Technologies Cause Great Firms to Fail,* Boston, MA: Harvard Business School Press.

17 Cool, K. and Schendel, D. (1988) 'Performance differences among strategic group members', *Strategic Management Journal* 9(3):207–23.

18 Kim, W. C. and Mauborgne, R. (2005) *Blue Ocean Strategy: How to Create Uncontested Market Space and Make the Competition Irrelevant,* Boston, MA: Harvard Business School Press.

19 Drucker, P. F. (1990) *Managing the Nonprofit Organization: Principles and Practices*, NY: HarperCollins.

20 Rangan, V. K. (2004) 'Lofty missions, down-to-earth plans', *Harvard Business Review,* March:112–19.

21 Welch, J. (with Welch S.) (2005) *Winning*, New York: HarperCollins, pp. 165–66.

22 Porter, M. E. (2001)'Strategy and the Internet', *Harvard Business Review,* March: 2–19.

23 Moyles, C. (2006) *The Gospel According to Chris Moyles: The Story of a Man and his Mouth*, London: Ebury Press, p. 134.

24 McKinsey (2008) 'How companies respond to competitors: A McKinsey global survey', *McKinsey Quarterly:*www.mckinseyquarterly.com

25 Teece, D. C. (2007) 'Explicating dynamic capabilities: the nature and microfoundations of (sustainable) enterprise performance', *Strategic Management Journal* 28:1319–350.

26 Ohmae, K. (1982) *The Mind of the Strategist*, New York: McGraw-Hill.

27 Hamel, G. (1997) 'Killer strategies that make shareholders rich', *Fortune* June 23:70–88.

28 Porter (1979) and Porter (2008) *op cit.*

29 Yip, G. S. (2004) 'Using strategy to change your business model', *Business Strategy Review* 15(2):17–24.

30 Porter, M. E. (1996) 'What is strategy?' *Harvard Business Review,* November–December: 61–78.

31 Peters, T. (1997) *The Circle of Innovation*, London: Hodder & Stoughton, pp. 26, 85.

32 Hamel, G. (1998) 'Strategy innovation and the quest for value', *Sloan Management Review,* Winter, 7–14.

CASE 4.1 How PESTEL Shapes Transco

Transco (part of National Grid Transco) is a monopoly gas pipeline company that transports natural gas to households in the UK and is responsible for ensuring public gas safety. This case illustrates how the PESTEL framework is important to its long-term survival.

Minding Transco's own business

National Grid Transco is a large organization that operates in the USA and the UK. It is made up of the UK's combined electricity transmission network (The National Grid Company) and gas transportation piping system (Transco). This case is only interested in its UK gas business, Transco. Its main work is described as follows:

> *We take gas from the terminals and transport it nationwide, through our transmission system, to areas of demand, where we hand over responsibility to distributors. We are also the largest distributor in the UK, and we take gas, which is at high pressure for efficiency, and deliver it on behalf of suppliers to consumers, dropping the pressure on the way to make it safe for use. We are responsible for ensuring we are able to meet the varying demand each day, using storage mechanisms to compensate for a flat rate of input and constantly changing output. We [also] run the UK national*

emergency call centre and respond to all reported gas escapes within our service area.[1]

Transco's legacy belongs to its history of being a part of the British Gas Company which covered all businesses of gas before being privatized in 1986. It was a national monopoly for gas supply and transportation. In 1996, the transportation business was separated, which became Transco. In 1998, the UK gas supply business was opened up to competition so British Gas was no longer a monopoly supplier of gas, but Transco remained a monopoly of the piping and emergency services. So when a UK household calls the emergency gas escapes hotline (0800-111-999), it is expected that the call is responded to in a timely manner. The economic regulator, Ofgem (Office of Gas and Electricity Markets), ensures that a whole suite of service standards in relation to responding to gas escapes and a range of other essential services are maintained.

While Transco may generally be regarded as a solid company in terms of what it does and how it does it, its scope of business activity is still constrained by the six macro-environmental factors, PESTEL, as follows.

Political – always risky

The lack of intensive competition in the industry, with Transco being the sole transporter company of gas through the UK pipelines, has meant that the gas industry has become a heavily regulated one. Ofgem was set up as its economic regulator to oversee most of Transco's business activity, and stand as a super-complainant for any anti-customer-friendly disputes. In addition, a number of other governmental bodies govern Transco's activities. A national networks director at Transco expressed these in the form of risks: 'There are all sorts of … risks: worrying about share prices … you've got your other stakeholders – the different regulators: … Energywatch to worry about consumer interests … the Health and Safety Executive to make sure you run safely … and Ofgem who are saying you do it at minimum costs. If safety goes, you lose your reputation. You get so preoccupied with cost reduction and internally focused you forget about your external customers. We have a risk management process which is an ongoing list of risks … new things come along and we're always updating that.'

In the event of Ofgem finding any wrongdoing of Transco, Ofgem may impose a financial penalty upon the company, or insist on individual cases of customer compensation.

Economic – counting on Transco

The role of Ofgem also includes conducting periodic reviews of the work of Transco, known as the periodic price control review. This quinquennial review, often nicknamed 'the contract' between Transco and Ofgem (because it dictates the activities that are permitted by Transco), can lead to severe financial consequences in the event of Transco's failure to comply or deliver. Ofgem can impose further financial penalties for poor performance, as well as set even tighter quality standards by which Transco is to comply. The specific set of quality standards is called GOSPs (Guaranteed and Overall Standards of Performance Scheme) which covers a range of safety standards. This is reviewed regularly and forms a key component of the periodic review. The importance of the 2002 review, for example, is emphasized by a representative of Transco: '[*It was a*] … tough settlement. It was probably pitched pretty carefully by Ofgem. It was enough to make us sweat …. It was tough, but we should accept it because we could just still maintain safety and deliver the economic changes needed to deliver the outcome.'

In other words, the amount of income (and therefore profit) Transco can make is affected by the agreement of the levels of service standards and expenditures between Transco and Ofgem.[2,3]

Social – living with the times

In establishing GOSPs for Transco, much consultation with Transco and surveys from market research groups were conducted by a number of independent consultants. This was to ensure that the changing social trends in household expectations about gas safety would be reflected in any modification to the quality standards. This in effect was also to imitate as accurately as possible the equivalent levels of service standards that would be achieved had it been subjected to competitive forces. In response to Ofgem's consultation questions, Transco qualifies that:

> *Transco agrees that the price control review provides a suitable opportunity to review what the appropriate qualitative and quantitative standards of service should be. Transco believes it to be important that standards of service are not considered in isolation. Transco believes that there would be some merit in tailoring certain outputs and performances in order to meet the individual service needs of customers – this would also support innovation and further competition.*[4]

Implementing GOSPs is a task of considerable difficulty due to the nature of its stochastic demand. Noticeably, 'the establishment of various standards of performance in the gas industry has been an ongoing and continuous process, subject to many amendments and changes'.[5] This has been marked by a series of preparatory activities. For instance, Ofgem's preparation of this set of new standards comprised a series of its own consultations with Transco in assessing its strategic business plan for 2002–2007 and further empirical research into customer preferences. This eventually led to the enactment of the *Utilities Act 2000*, which aimed to strengthen the incentives on Transco to increase efficiency and reduce costs, so that resultant benefits may be passed on to consumers in the form of lower prices, as well as to have enough money to continue to ensure good quality levels:

> *Consumers are interested in quality as well as prices. Therefore the price control review has involved consideration of the appropriate guaranteed and overall standards of performance and other quality indicators. [It] ... should ensure that Transco has sufficient resources to provide an appropriate quality of service and establishes targets that will reward efficient management.*[6]

The result is that the development of gas service standards has followed similar schemes used in other sectors (ie, electricity distribution) where penalties for failure to perform amounts to similar sums of revenue exposure.[7]

The views of quality regulation vary. One pessimistic view expressed by a Transco employee is: 'The regulator's there to control prices; that's fundamentally their objective ... why they have to keep whacking the service standards up is a complete mystery to me. I can't believe they get a massive representation of consumers saying the emergency service should attend at 97, not 96, per cent of the time within an hour ... Who cares? Nobody cares about that kind of stuff! How would they know? They're just one case in a set of statistics – they don't enjoy our service ten or twenty times a year, every year; they only see it once in a lifetime. It means nothing to them. Once every ten years, they ring up with a gas leak and we're there within half an hour – that's their experience.'

Technological – no choice?

The survival of Transco is much dependent on the need for the UK's use of gas. Substitute products to gas, such as electricity, are not direct substitutes to Transco's main line of work (which is the piping system itself). Despite technological developments over the years, there is no more effective alternative way to bring gas to households than through the piping system (discarding the very minor use of gas containers in some rural areas). However, Transco's other work – responding to emergency calls – could arguably be substituted by an alternative service; suggestions include amalgamating this to the national 999 emergency telephone service, but some fairness of financing issues are associated with this, as not all households are consumer of gas.

The operations of Transco have not only improved over the years because of regulatory pressure, but also because of the technological improvements from within the organization. For example, sophisticated call centres are now operated to ensure timely responses (as specified by Ofgem), and engineers on call are scattered around the country with laptop computers and other GPS navigation equipment to respond to gas escapes.

Environmental – that's natural!

For Transco the environmental concern is not the exhaustion of the supply of gas (this is the concern of gas supply companies), Transco's business is the transportation of gas. However, the gas transportation network is classed as a natural monopoly because economies of scale are so significant that costs are only minimized when the entire output of an industry is supplied by a single producer. This is a key environmental concern as less disruption to the landscape by way of laying pipes is paramount.

Legal – getting it right

Prior to GOSPs (which was implemented in 2002), Transco's levels of customer service standards were subject to obligations under Condition 19 of the Gas Transporter Licence, the Network Code and a set of its own voluntary standards. Transco's gas piping system is also subject to a number of regulatory and legal frameworks, such as those set out in the *Gas Act 1986*, as amended by the *Utilities Act 2000*. GOSPs made many of the previously voluntary standards an obligatory requirement, as well as consolidated the numerous obligations under different authorities.[8]

Specifically, GOSPs comprises two types of quality standards – guaranteed standards (GS) and overall standards (OS). Guaranteed standards are those that warrant a specified penalty payable to the customer for each failure to comply with the service specification (for example, £20 directly to the customer for failing to offer and keep an appointment, under standard GS3). Overall standards do not lend themselves to a direct penalty, but have attached with them negative reputational consequences; for example, the emergency gas escapes call centre must answer a telephone call within 30 seconds of ringing, 90 per cent of the time, under standard OS1, and the results are reported back to the general public.

This case has illustrated that the PESTEL framework is useful for understanding the external environment that affects the way in which the core business of Transco is managed, as well as how its daily operations may be constrained. Further, it has shown that even a company that operates in an industry that lacks competition is still subject to environmental constraints.

Discussion questions

1. What is the present core business of Transco and what options are available for it to grow?
2. What is the meaning of quality in gas transportation? Give an example of a quality standard currently in place. Are such standards transferrable to other sectors or industries?
3. How is understanding the external environment for a regulated monopoly industry such as Transco different from a commercially competitive one?

Case references

1. National Grid (2008) 'National grid annual review 2007/08', National Grid.
2. Chau, V. S. and Witcher, B. J. (2005) 'Implications of regulation policy incentives for strategic control: An integrative model', *Annals of Public and Cooperative Economics* 76(1):85–119.
3. Waddams Price, C., Brigham, B. and Fitzgerald, L. (2008) 'Service quality in regulated network industries', *Annals of Public and Cooperative Economics* 79(2):197–225.
4. Transco (2000) 'Review of Transco's price control – initial consultation document: Transco's response', July, Transco UK: London, p. 26.
5. Chau, V. S. (2002) 'Report on customer service performance measures in UK network industries: Squeezing hard to improve quality', Centre for Competition and Regulation, Working Paper 02–03, May, UEA, Norwich, p. 47.
6. OFGEM (2001) 'Review of Transco's price control from 2002: Final proposals', September, Office of Gas and Electricity Markets: London, p. 3.
7. Chau, V. S. (2009) 'Benchmarking service quality in UK electricity distribution networks', *Benchmarking: An International Journal* 16(1):47–69.
8. Transco (2002) 'Guaranteed and overall standards of service: Transco's consumer service standards', April, Transco UK, London.

This case study was prepared using only publicly available sources of information for the purposes of classroom discussion; it does not intend to illustrate either effective or ineffective handling of a managerial situation.

Chapter 5

THE INTERNAL ENVIRONMENT

Introduction

Chapter 4 considered the importance of the external environment to strategic management, and this chapter covers the internal environment. This includes strategic resources and their relation to competitive difference and value. It will introduce the key concepts of the value chain, core competences and dynamic capabilities; a distinction is drawn between strategy and operational effectiveness. Finally, we show how a SWOT analysis brings both the external and internal influences together for thinking about strategy and making strategic decisions.

The external environment is largely beyond an organization's control. An organization's competitive advantage rests on the ability to sustain a unique position. The internal environment, on the other hand, is subject to far more control. An organization's competitive advantage rests more on the organization's ability to adapt a unique behaviour to changing conditions. A **competitive advantage** is the reason for an organization's ability to compete effectively with its rivals or potential rivals. From an inside-out perspective there are four levels in building and sustaining a competitive advantage (see Figure 5.1): strategic resources, core capabilities, core competences and dynamic capabilities.

LEARNING OBJECTIVES

By the end of this chapter you should understand:

1. How strategic resources convey competitive advantage.
2. The concepts of core competences, dynamic capabilities and the value chain.
3. The strategic importance of lean production, total quality management, performance excellence and benchmarking.
4. The role of SWOT analysis for auditing the external and internal environments.

Business vignette Using the nature of what you are, to manage authentic Chinese food strategically, which is easier, lighter, fresher and healthier ...

What you are, can give you a competitive advantage, if it works to serve up something special that makes your products and services stand out.

The choice of which strategy an organization should adopt to achieve its strategic objectives is based heavily on its ability to carry it out and the appropriateness of its internal environment. This also concerns the need to ensure that all the competences of how an organization, or an entity that needs to be successful, configures all of its strengths in a way which allows it to take full advantage.

For example, Ching-He Huang, a Taiwanese-born British celebrity chef, earned fame when she first appeared on television in 2005, and recently in 2008 in a BBC cookery series, *Chinese Food Made Easy*. This was accompanied by her two cookery books, *China Modern* and *Chinese Food Made Easy*, which immediately became best-sellers. Her success may have been due to a number of factors, but what lies in the very heart of her style is

the Chinese philosophy of yin and yang (balancing negative and positive forces that affect existence), which she has used in all her accompanying business activities.

She first set up a healthy foodstuff company called Fuge Ltd,[1] followed by the release of a healthy drink product called Tzu,[2] made from sorghum vinegar. The name links the drink to a Buddhist charity called the Tzu-Chi Foundation, which is headed in the United Kingdom by her father. These activities are premised around the core belief of managing yin and yang.

Huang commented: 'we believe there is this philosophy of yin and yang, a balance of cooling foods and heating foods, to give you a good balance of life force (or chi) energy ... in any dish, you combine this balance for ingredients and cooking methods.'[3]

Strategic resources

Strategic resources are organizational assets, or attributes, which when combined in ways that are uniquely specific to an organization, constitute its competitive advantage. Strategic resources are not economic resources, because they are valuable only to the organization that uses them and they have no external value.

The resource-based view of strategy

By definition, because strategic resources are organization-specific, they are different from the strategic resources of other organizations. Organizations are always going to be different to some degree. What really matters though is an organization's ability

FIGURE 5.1 Building and sustaining an organization's competitive advantage

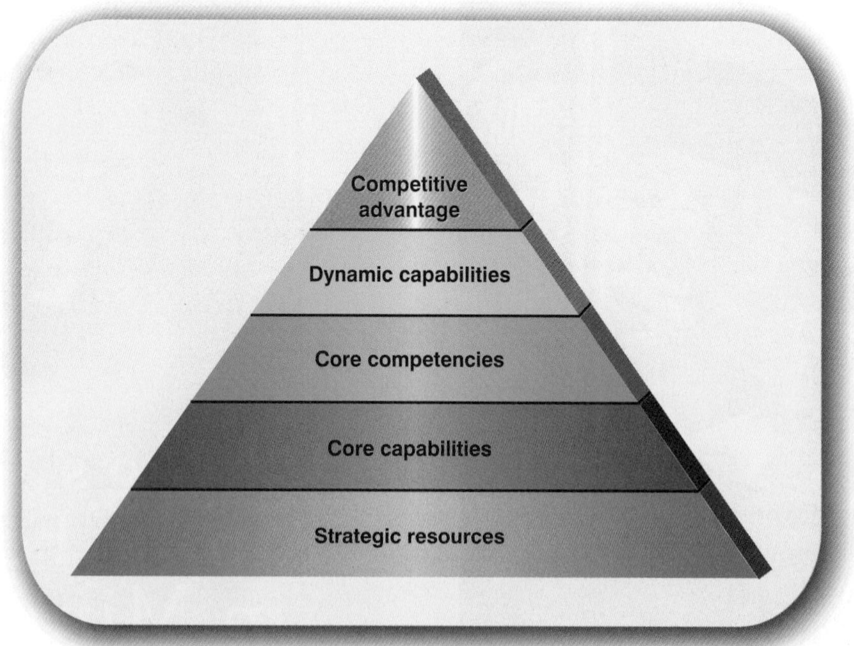

Strategic resources are organizational assets, or attributes, which when combined in ways that are uniquely specific to an organization, constitute its competitive advantage. Strategic resources are not economic resources, because they are valuable only to the organization that uses them and they have no external value.

PRINCIPLES IN PRACTICE 5.1

Creating strategic resources at McDonald's

The McDonalds were ... the true heroes of the fast-food revolution, and by any measure they were remarkable men. They had moved to California from New Hampshire (or possibly Vermont; sources conflict) during the depression years, and opened their first drive-in restaurant in 1937 near Pasadena. It didn't sell hamburgers. Then in 1940 they opened a new establishment at Fourteenth and E Street at the end of Route 66, in San Bernardino, in a snug octagonal structure. It was a conventional hamburger stand and it did reasonably well.

In 1948, however, the brothers were seized with a strange vision. They closed the business for three months, fired the twenty car-hops, got rid of all the china and silverware, and reopened with a new, entirely novel idea: that the customer would have to come to a window to collect the food rather than have it brought to the car. They cut the menu to just seven items – hamburgers, cheeseburgers, pie, crisps, coffee, milk and pop. Customers no longer specified what they wanted on their hamburgers but received them with ketchup, mustard, onions and pickle. The hamburgers were made smaller – just ten to a pound – but the price was halved to fifteen cents each.

The change was a flop. Business fell by 80 per cent. The teenagers on whom they had relied went elsewhere. Gradually, however, a new type of clientele developed, the family, particularly after they had added French fries and milk shakes to the menu, and even more particularly when customers realized the food was great and that you could feed the whole family for a few dollars. Before long McDonald's had almost more business than it could handle.

As volume grew, the brothers constantly refined the process to make the production of food more streamlined and efficient. With a local machine-shop owner named Ed Toman they invented almost everything associated with the production of fast food, from dispensers that pump out a precise dollop of ketchup or mustard, to the Lazy Susans on which twenty-four hamburger buns can be speedily dressed. They introduced the idea of specialization – one person who did nothing but cook hamburgers, another who made shakes, another to dress the buns, and so on – and developed the now universal practice of having food prepared and waiting so that customers could place an order and immediately collect it.[39]

Question: Is McDonald's different from its imitators?

to manage its strategic resources strategically so that customers prefer its offers to those of the competition. The idea that competitive advantage rests on an organization's strategic resources is the **resource-based view of strategy**.

The term appears to have been used first by Birger Wernerfelt,[4] but Edith Penrose had argued in the late 1950s that 'resources' should be broadly defined for economic analysis; for example, she pointed out that while water is often a free resource, its availability is important.[5] Penrose is important because her contribution was one of the first managerial perspectives to emerge from economics. This is important for understanding the important difference between the resource-based view of the firm and the resource-based view of strategy.

In economics an evolutionary tendency in thinking about markets has downplayed the role of firm-specific managerial intentionality, especially the part played by managers in sustaining long-term competitive advantage. The normative inclinations of the resource-based view of the firm lean towards a general understanding of markets, rather than an understanding of the managerial attributes of the individual firm.[6] The focus is on the characteristics of firms and how they survive in their environments. The resource-based view of strategy, on the other hand, is centred on the role of managerial intentionality in the single firm: how managers can identify and manage strategic resources. The management literature has offered up two approaches: the VRIO framework and value chain model.

The VRIO framework

Jay Barney offers criteria to identify strategic resources, which he calls the VRIO framework.[7] He suggests that above-average profits are likely if an organization's attributes are:

- Valuable: When they enable an organization to implement strategy that improves its effectiveness and efficiency.
- Rare: Few, if any, other competing organizations have these valuable attributes.
- Inimitable: Attributes may be too difficult to emulate because they have a unique history, their nature is ambiguous, or socially complex.
- Organizable: The organization can exploit the competitive potential of the other three.

In the instance of a university, attributes are valuable when they are core to the university's competitive difference. For example, its teaching and research distinguish it clearly from other universities. The university may have areas of expertise that other institutions lack; this rareness will attract students for courses in certain subjects. The established reputation, traditions, physical surroundings and the facilities (perceived and associated with how and what the university does), make it difficult for a rival to attract funding to develop a similar expertise and offer the same **quality** of course. Finally, the university should be able to organize these attributes in ways to build and reinforce its competitive difference.

Differences may be enhanced in many different ways: for instance, through the recruitment of people with certain aptitudes and knowledge, patents and proprietary technologies, physical assets like buildings and other facilities, location, social and business networks, alliances, and so on. However, the importance of intangible resources, such as corporate image, brands, customer service, is fundamental in establishing how people perceive the difference between organizations and the things they offer. Intangibility is quintessentially a holistically sensed quality. All organizations are to some extent unique bundles of attributes and it is how these are used and managed that determines differences in organizational performance.

The key thing is to integrate resources so the intangibility of the whole creates an image that puts the organization apart from its rivals. Robert Grant uses the example of McDonald's.[8] The organization has outstanding functional capabilities in product development, market research, human resource management, financial control and operations management; however it is how all these are integrated to provide a consistency in its products and services in thousands of its restaurants across the world that really accounts for its success.

VRIO is a framework for identifying strategic resources. By itself it does not constitute a source of competitive advantage, since the identified resources must be combined and managed as an integrated set.[9] This is the role and purpose of a value chain.

The value chain

The **value chain** is a model of an organization's value creating chain of strategically-relevant activities. It is used to identify those organizational strategically-related activities that are relevant to the organization's competitive advantage. The concept was originally introduced by Michael Porter.[10] **Value** is the satisfaction and benefits customers receive from buying and using products and services. This is represented in the value chain as the amount customers are willing to pay for the organization's products and services. This is measured by total revenue derived from the prices and the number of units that are sold. An organization is profitable if the value it commands exceeds the costs of creating the value; this is indicated as the margin (see Figure 5.2). Value activities consist of two broad types: primary and support activities.

Primary activities add value through the transformation of resources into products and services through the following stages:

- Inbound logistics: activities bringing in inputs.
- Operations: activities turning inputs into outputs.
- Outbound logistics: activities getting finished products to customers.
- Marketing and sales: activities enabling customers to buy and receive products.
- Service: activities maintaining and enhancing value.

FIGURE 5.2 The value chain[11]

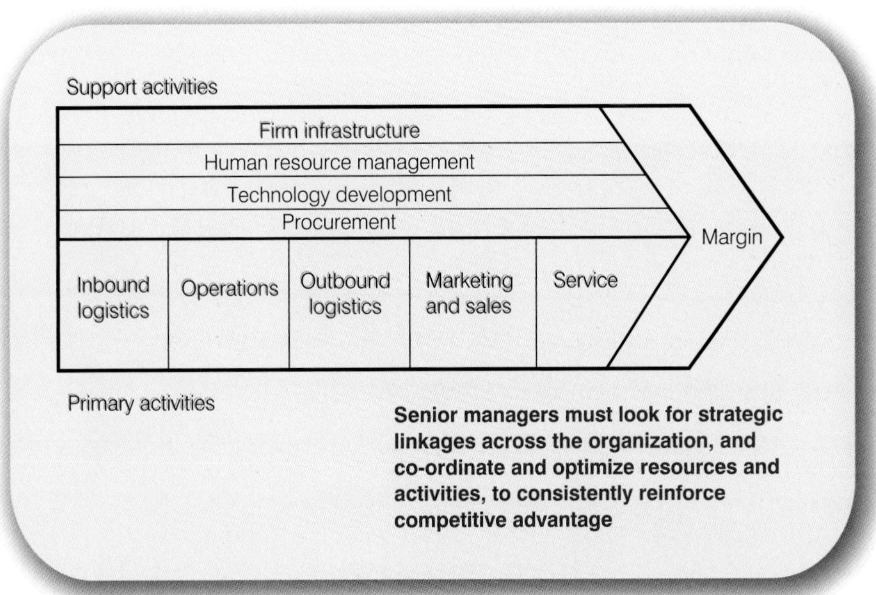

Conventionally, these activities are associated with the line functions of a business. However, a value chain is concerned only with those attributes and activities that are strategically relevant, and the value chain is concerned with how these interact and can be integrated as a whole system, and not in isolation from the perspective of any one functional part of the organization.

Support activities add value by facilitating and assisting the primary activities. Conventionally, support activities are typically staff functions and the responsibility of a dedicated department, although they are normally cross-functional in orientation. Figure 5.2 shows four examples (it is possible to have additional and other support activities, such as quality management):

- Firm infrastructure: activities, such as planning, legal affairs and finance and accounting, which support the general management of the primary activities.
- Human resource management: activities that support the employment and development of people.
- Technology development: activities such as the provision of expertise and technology, including research and development, that support the production and delivery process.
- Procurement: activities to support buying.

A value chain is used not just as a framework to identify strategic resources, but also to manage those resources once strategy is in place (examples are given for business-level strategy in Chapter 6).

The value chain concept can be extended beyond the boundaries of the organization to include those strategic resource related activities positioned in distribution and the supply chain. This can be illustrated diagrammatically as a series of linked value chains for the relevant distributors and suppliers.

Value chain resources and activities are inter-dependent, and must be evaluated as a whole set, so it is possible to optimize and co-ordinate activities so they work together effectively to sustain a coherent strategy. The linkages between the strategic resources and the associated activities are as

VALUE CHAIN RESOURCES AND ACTIVITIES ARE INTER-DEPENDENT, AND MUST BE EVALUATED AS A WHOLE SET, SO IT IS POSSIBLE TO OPTIMIZE AND CO-ORDINATE ACTIVITIES SO THEY WORK TOGETHER EFFECTIVELY TO SUSTAIN A COHERENT STRATEGY. THE LINKAGES BETWEEN THE STRATEGIC RESOURCES AND THE ASSOCIATED ACTIVITIES ARE AS IMPORTANT AS THE INDIVIDUAL RESOURCES AND ACTIVITIES THEMSELVES.

important as the individual resources and activities themselves. Changing the nature and management of one set of resources and activities in any one area of the organization is likely to affect what happens in other areas; for example, lowering costs in one area is sub-optimal if it works to raise costs elsewhere, and increases costs overall. Co-ordination is necessary for linking activities to each other; for example, it is necessary to co-ordinate delivery, service and payment, so that these things work with, rather than against, each other in producing value for the customer. A distinctive customer relationship management requires both optimization and co-ordination to control those activities that influence every part of the customer experience, rather than relying, say, on separated specialist functions, such as sales or customer orders.

Distinctive capabilities

John Kay argues that corporate success derives from a competitive advantage that is based on distinctive capabilities, which are derived from an organization's relationships with its suppliers, customers, or employees.[12] The continuity and stability of relationships allows for flexible and co-operative responses to change. There are three types of distinctive capabilities:

- Architecture: these are structures created to co-ordinate employees, customers and suppliers, to build a mutual commitment in an organization's distribution and supply chains to its unique ways of working.

KEY DEBATE 5.1

Is competitive advantage found in the industry, or the organization?

In an influential paper, Richard Rumelt suggests that competitive advantage is associated with factors at the individual firm level, such as through resources and the specific strategy that is adopted, rather than the structure (and therefore the attractiveness) of the industry.[42] He found that industry factors explained about 9 to 16 per cent of variations in profit, against around 46 per cent for factors that were specific to individual organizations. This supports taking a resource-based view of strategy.

Industry structure plays a central role in Porter and a 'successful strategy' primarily relates to how an organization takes this into account in choosing its position within the industry.[43] Scholars, such as Priem and Butler, assert that the resource-based view defines strategic resources too inclusively, and is poor at discriminating between resources that can be practically manipulated, and those which are beyond managerial control.[44] Hoopes and others argue that the perspective assumes what it seeks to explain and defines, rather than hypothesizes.[45] In short, the resource-based view is not very helpful to practitioners.

On the other hand, industry analysis also has its difficulties, not least in working out what are an industry's boundaries. If an industry and its competitive influences seem unknowable, it may be better to configure an organization around its core competences to give the organization a competitive uniqueness and a dynamic capability it would otherwise lack in the face of change.

Question: How can competitive advantage found within the organization and in the industry be reconciled?

- Reputation: this is built up through a customer's own experience, the organization's marketing and how the organization seems to compare with its rivals.

- Innovation: usually this can be copied, so what counts is how an organization can support innovation with strategies that are designed to make this difficult; for example through patents or secrecy that make it difficult for a rival to copy.

A key requirement is that an organization's people should have the necessary knowledge and skills to be proficient in delivering the unique value that customers want and expect. In other words, an organization must have the necessary core competences.

Core competences

Core competences are the organization-specific abilities that work together, and the knowledge and learning that manage strategic resources in ways that create competitive advantage. It embodies an organization's collective learning, particularly how to co-ordinate diverse production skills and integrate multiple technologies. Core competences have the following advantages:

- They are hard for rivals to understand how they work, and difficult to emulate: how people work together and the context of any particular organizational culture is difficult for an outsider to understand.
- They are suitable to influence a range of markets and industries: it may be possible to use an organization's core competences to produce a varied range of products and services.
- They help with an understanding of management's priorities: core competences provide a shared understanding of an organization's purpose, and top-down objectives are likely to be better understood and more easily implemented.

- They are useful for cross-functional working: people from different technical and departmental backgrounds are more likely to understand each other's needs if they share core competences, and they improve team working and project management generally.
- They facilitate common approaches for managing strategically-related objectives; core competences are typically associated with a common language of objectives, which are managed in a similar way across the organization.
- They promote a common set of learning-based tools and working principles: a common approach to learning and knowledge is likely to promote similar approaches and methods for solving problems.
- Bottom-up management is facilitated: effective responsibility for decision making is passed down to the lowest level that is capable of accepting it.

knowledge and supporting resources, which give to the organization its idiosyncratic competences that are core to its strategic purpose. These develop in part from organizational learning and are typically reinforced and strengthened over time, so that they follow a path or trajectory. This can mean that core competences are sticky and difficult to change quickly.[13] If knowledge and learning become too institutionalized then organizations run the risk of seeing their core competences turn into core rigidities.[14]

Prahalad and Hamel argue that risk is manageable if core competences are used to develop a foundation of core products that can be used to develop end-products and services in different industries.[15] Core products are areas of organization-specific expertise and resources. Core competences, on the other hand, are the collective learning abilities of employees, which include how to develop and manage the integration of technologies through cross-functional management and collaborative working.

For example, Canon used core competences to develop its technical competences in optics, a core

A core competence is not simply an ability to be good, or even to excel at something, if this something can also be achieved by a rival. ... it is not a retailer's ability to retail as such, but rather how this is done differently from the competition, such as how the retailer's staff work to enhance the customer's shopping experience to confer greater value than is available elsewhere.

A core competence is not simply an ability to be good or even to excel at something, if this something can also be achieved by a rival. So, for example, it is not a retailer's ability to retail as such, but rather how this is done differently from the competition, such as how the retailer's staff work to enhance the customer's shopping experience to confer greater value than is available elsewhere. An organization's strategic resources can be characterized as bundles, or patterns of skills,

product, to serve different sectors as diverse as cameras, copiers and semi-conductor equipment. This flexibility is possible because Canon has a core competence, or capability, where people come together and work in common ways. This gives Canon its organization-specific competitive advantage, which is unseen and is difficult for rivals to understand. The important thing with this example is that the competences involved in building up technology and developing products are different from the core competences required to manage those technologies in a unique way.

Many of the examples used in the resource-based view of strategy literature in the 1990s came from Japanese organizations like Canon, and the quality-improvement and deployment methods associated with them have become important tools for the development of competences. They offer a systematic approach that uses a shared set of business methodologies and management philosophies, which gives to everybody in an organization a common language for team working. Approaches, such as total quality management, allow a deeper understanding of cause-and-effect relationships, so that the organization is able to refine, test and validate constantly, its core competences.[16] The ability of an organization to manage its core competences over time is referred to in strategic management as a dynamic capability.

Dynamic capabilities

Teece, Pisano and Shuen define a **dynamic capability** as an organization's ability to integrate, build and reconfigure core competences to meet change.[17] This is a high level management process equivalent to strategic management itself, which acts to influence lower-level capabilities and competences. It is possible to imagine an organization as a hierarchical nest of dynamic capabilities, which are inserted into each other like a set of Russian dolls. Thus, a dynamic capability is a systematic and holistic business process. Its 'dynamic' quality is based on 'a learned and stable pattern of collective activity through which the organization systematically generates and modifies its operating routines in pursuit of improved effectiveness'.[18] In other words, a dynamic capability drives continuous improvement. Teece, Pisano and Shuen give the example of Fujimoto's account of production activities in the Japanese auto industry and identify the Toyota Production System as an example.[19]

Most auto-makers now have similar production systems to the Toyota system, which means it is not necessarily the dynamic capability itself that is organization-specific, so much as what it does in managing core competences. Eisenhardt and Martin agree that dynamic capabilities are often similar, but point out that there are likely to be real differences in the detail of their application.[20] Common features exist that can be benchmarked and shared as best practice between organizations, but because organizational context varies, so does the effectiveness. They define a dynamic capability less holistically than the others, as any organizational process used to configure core competences to influence markets: for example, a dynamic capability can be product development routines, alliance and acquisition capabilities, and routines for resource allocation, knowledge transfer, and relocation.

Eisenhardt and Martin suggest there is nothing uniquely distinctive in the learning processes involved; these can be easily copied by a rival organization. However, they give an organizational ability to manage resources in particular combinations that can be designed to achieve a series of short-term competitive positions. Each position sustains and builds a longer-term competitive advantage, much in the same way that Hamel and Prahalad suggest Japanese organizations run strategic marathons as a series of short-term challenges to achieve a longer-term strategic intent[21] (see Chapter 3).

The debate about dynamic capabilities reflects many ideas that emerged during the final decades of the twentieth century, when the so-called 'new competition' of the Japanese began to eat into western industries and markets. Originally Japanese[22], many of these have a capacity to manage internal resources strategically, and have now become mainstream to the strategic management of organizations across the world. These include:

- Lean production.
- Just-in-time management.
- Total quality management.
- Performance excellence models.
- Benchmarking.

Lean production

Lean production is a management system for ensuring any non-value contributing activity is eliminated in an organization's activities. The basic principle is that customers should pull the value they want from the system, and the system should be flexible enough to adapt to their changing needs. Lean production emerged in Japanese manufacturing in the 1960s as a production system approach, and many of its associated management methodologies were developed at Toyota.[23] Lean ideas have since been developed for a wide range of different industries, including services, such as retailing and banking. The story of the Toyota Production System is well documented in the operations management literature.

The central principle is to manage an organization's core business processes to remove those activities continuously that do not contribute to value. This is not the same thing as waste and cost reduction, although these may be subsidiary objectives: value takes precedence. Practitioners sometimes call their core processes 'key business areas', and the idea has much in common with Rockart's CSFs (Chapter 3) and Porter's value chain (above). These are critical to the effective management of those activities that contribute to value; so senior managers should specify what these areas are, and manage a system for setting objectives and reviewing improvement, to ensure that the organization is fit for purpose. Peter Hines and others at Cardiff University give an example for the car industry[24] and suggest the following:

1. Strategy formation and deployment: The strategic management of the company, focusing of change, managing critical success factors and ensuring all employees are fully aligned and empowered.
2. Order fulfilment (new cars, used cars, parts): Taking orders, processing the orders, scheduling planning, taking delivery, inspecting, delivery to customer and payment management.
3. Order fulfilment (car servicing and repairing): taking booking, receiving car, serving car, returning to customer and payment management.
4. Winning business: identifying and targeting new customers or business opportunities in order to trigger the order fulfilment process.
5. People life cycle management: the identification of needs, recruitment, motivation, training, development and reward of people together with the management of their eventual retirement.
6. Information technology: the management of electronic support systems.
7. Legal and financial management: the management of the legal function as well as costs, financial and management.

The nature of services is not necessarily as different from manufacturing as is sometimes supposed. Instead of a factory, there is an administrative office block, and the organization of routines can be as formal as those in a manufacturing plant. The major difference is normally a greater variation in the nature of demand; as John Seddon, formerly of Toyota, and now advising public services, says about lean working:

> *'So instead of thinking of the system as one that pulls physical things together to manufacture at the rate of customer demand (the essence of the Toyota system), you have to think of the system as one that brings (largely) intangible expertise together in response to the variety of customer demands. This different purpose leads to different methods, because there are different problems to solve. Solving these problems teaches how to design services from which customers can "pull" value – in other words, get what they want.'*[25]

The most advanced form of lean working is **just-in-time management (JIT)**. The customers say what they want, and the supplier then pulls all the components together, as and when they are needed in the production process. In Japan no car is built until the customer orders what they want. For western markets it is slightly different because buyers tend to make purchases when they see the car at a showroom. However, Toyota only starts to make cars when dealers place specific orders for them. General Motors, on the other hand, is organized around a much larger inventory system, and will often offer discount incentives to prevent its system becoming clogged. This is an important reason why Toyota's product turnaround in the United States averages about 30 days, while GM and Ford turnover on average after 80 days or more.[26]

In principle just-in-time removes the need for buffer stocks and reduces costs. It also requires a strict discipline through the supply chain to ensure that parts are delivered exactly to specification every time. This requires excellent quality management.

© Photolibrary

Total quality management

Total quality management (TQM) is an organization-wide management philosophy where quality is defined by the customer; it is supported by various business methodologies that are used by everybody in their work to satisfy the customer and create value. Quality in this sense is not an absolute product or service attribute. It is possible to have poor quality in a luxury car, as it is to have high quality in an economy car. If a customer's expectation is not being met, then quality is poor. The word, 'total', means that the philosophy must apply at every business level and to every process. Quality is only as good as the weakest link in the quality chain (see Figure 5.3). Every part of the production and delivery chain has to be good enough to give the next work process exactly what it wants for it to be able to produce what is exactly needed by the following process, and so on.

If everybody has control over their work to the extent that they have a responsibility to meet their immediate customer's requirements, then they are likely to see their work not as a static, stand-alone process, but as a dynamic activity which must change with the needs of the ultimate customer. The guiding principle is that every process is managed according to the **PDCA** cycle (see Figure 5.4), where 'P' is plan (the work), 'D' is do (carry out the work to plan), 'C' is check (to see if progress is satisfactory), and 'A' is act (take corrective action if progress is unsatisfactory). The principle should be used for any process, including the organization's strategic management. It forms the basic mechanism for all types of organizational learning.[26]

Another principle of TQM is to solve problems in ways to make sure they do not recur. PDCA should be about finding root causes and ending them, no matter where they originate from in the organization, especially if they are a result of management. This calls for enabling and facilitating styles of senior management and an organizational culture that is

PRINCIPLES IN PRACTICE 5.2

The Toyota Production System

The Toyota Production System is a production system that involves the elimination of 'muda', which is any non-value-creating activity. It is based on two key concepts: jidoka (translated from Japanese to mean, automation with a human touch) and just-in-time (producing only enough necessary for the next stage of the production process).

Jidoka: highlighting/visualizing the problems

1. Jidoka means that a machine safely stops when the normal processing is completed. It also means that, should a quality or equipment problem arise, the machine detects the problem on its own and stops, preventing defective products from being produced. As a result, only products satisfying the quality standards will be passed on to the next processes on the production line.
2. Since a machine automatically stops when processing is completed or when a problem arises and is communicated via the 'andon' (problem display board), operators can confidently continue performing work at another machine, as well as easily identify the problem cause and prevent its recurrence. This means that each operator can be in charge of many machines, resulting in higher productivity, while the continuous improvements lead to greater processing capacity.

Just-in-time: productivity improvement

1. When a vehicle order is received, a production instruction must be issued to the beginning of the vehicle production line as soon as possible.
2. The assembly line must be stocked with small numbers of all types of parts so that any kind of vehicle ordered can be assembled.
3. The assembly line must replace the parts used by retrieving the same number of parts from the parts-producing process (the preceding process).
4. A process should only replace those parts that the operator from the following process has already taken.[40]

Question: Does the TPS constitute a competitive advantage?

conducive to organization-wide problem solving and project working. Nonaka and Takeuchi argue that effective knowledge management is a mixture of explicit and tacit knowledge (which is felt but hard to articulate).[27]

It is necessary to encourage people to interact and share the tacit skills they have developed, but to make this work, senior managers must establish a common working culture that is fully understood and supported by the organization's managers. The key thing is to enable people through the organization to take responsibility for managing their work. If anything is happening to influence somebody's work adversely, then management must ensure that the

FIGURE 5.3 Getting quality right at every stage of the supply chain

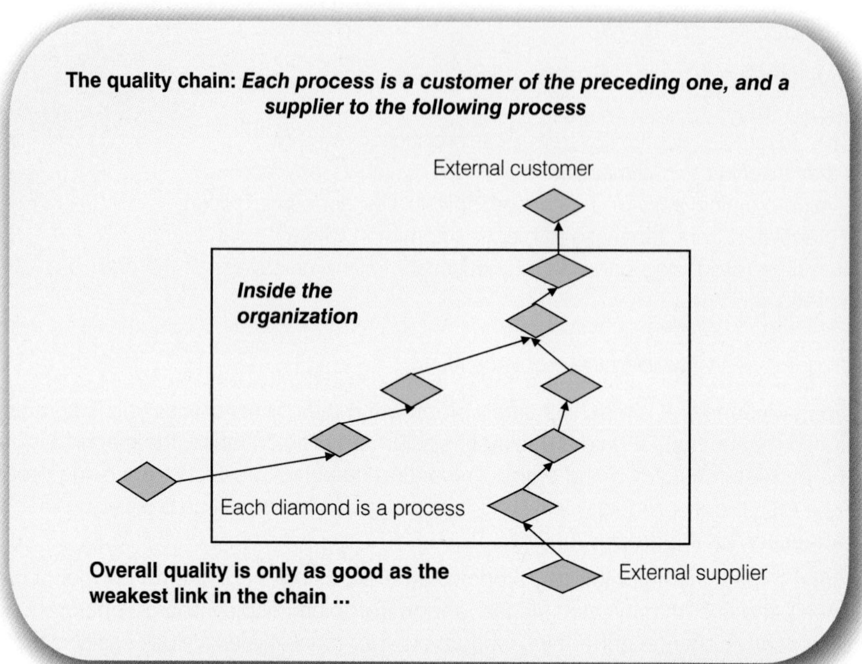

issue can be properly problem-solved, no matter where the source of the problem is. Otherwise PDCA stands for 'Please Don't Change Anything'.

A business process is influenced by five areas of quality (see Figure 5.5): (1) the quality of a plan (or design); (2) the conformance of work to plan (the fitness of the process); (3) the quality of inputs (from suppliers); (4) the perception of output (good insight and feedback from the customer is essential), and (5) the organizational support.

Corrective action is primarily a single-loop learning system where feedback is used to bring

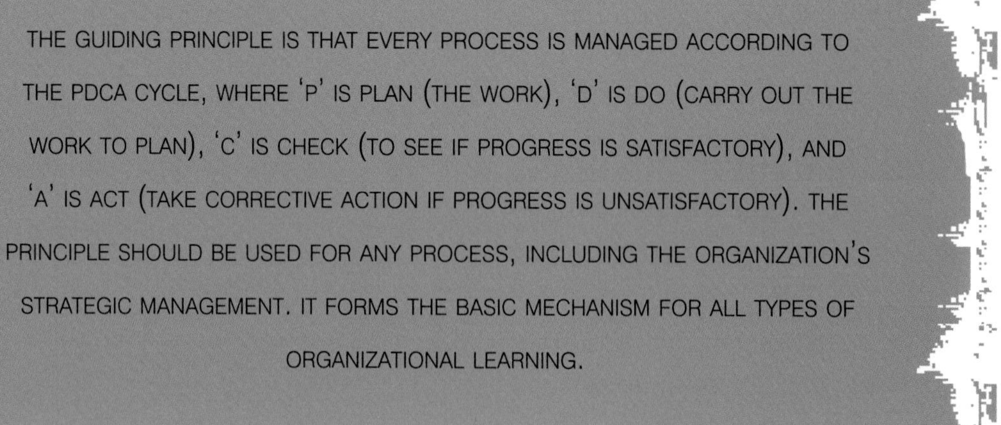
THE GUIDING PRINCIPLE IS THAT EVERY PROCESS IS MANAGED ACCORDING TO THE PDCA CYCLE, WHERE 'P' IS PLAN (THE WORK), 'D' IS DO (CARRY OUT THE WORK TO PLAN), 'C' IS CHECK (TO SEE IF PROGRESS IS SATISFACTORY), AND 'A' IS ACT (TAKE CORRECTIVE ACTION IF PROGRESS IS UNSATISFACTORY). THE PRINCIPLE SHOULD BE USED FOR ANY PROCESS, INCLUDING THE ORGANIZATION'S STRATEGIC MANAGEMENT. IT FORMS THE BASIC MECHANISM FOR ALL TYPES OF ORGANIZATIONAL LEARNING.

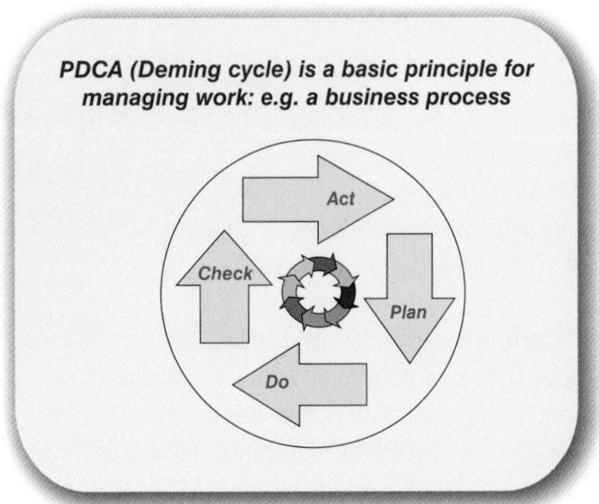

FIGURE 5.4 The PDCA cycle

performance back to the original plan. The PDCA principle, however, is a cycle that involves double-loop learning, which questions the assumptions of the plan itself.[28] This distinction is also used in Peter Senge's description of a learning organization when he contrasted adaptive and generative learning: the former is about dealing with symptoms, while generative learning involves understanding fundamental causes and seeing opportunities.[29] The main task of the strategist, according to Senge, is to facilitate organizational learning.

Japanese TQM is associated with a form of continuous improvement called *kaizen*, which is taken from *kai* meaning change, and *zen* meaning good.[30] Kaizen change is incremental and gradual, but the idea is that over time it adds up to a substantial improvement over the whole organization. However, the main influences on change, as shown in Figure 5.5, are driven by the need to satisfy customers, and are classically associated with the need to have organizational routines under control. Kaizen is also driven by strategic change. This involves senior managers in setting strategically linked objectives, which other levels take account of when forming their plans (see *hoshin kanri*, Chapter 10).

FIGURE 5.5 Process management and the areas of quality concern

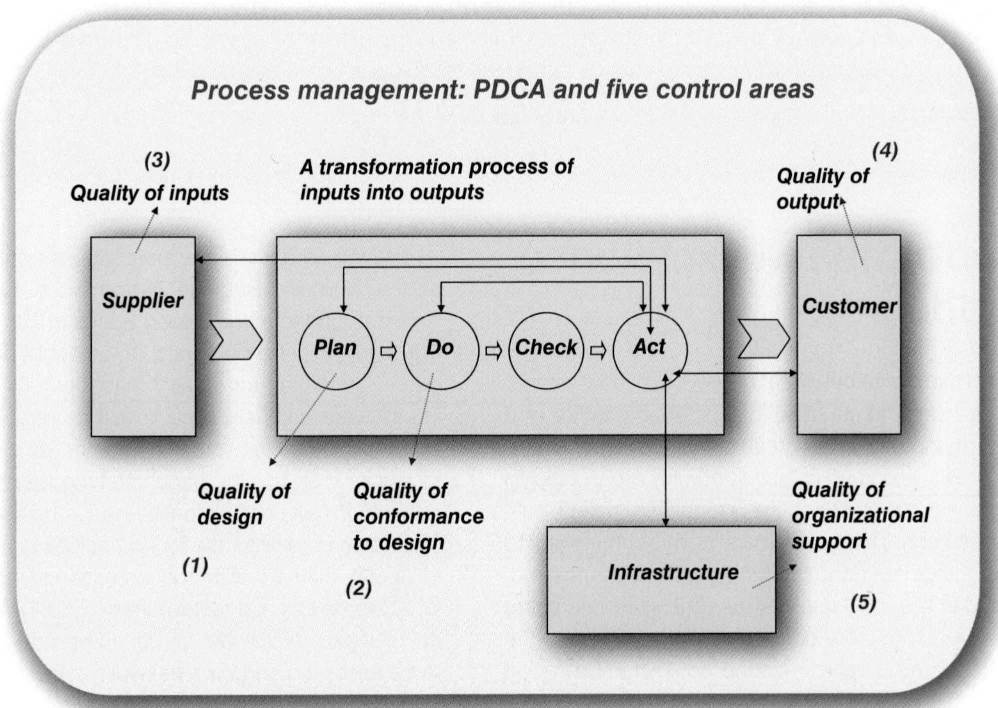

PRINCIPLES IN PRACTICE 5.3

General Motors and the Toyota Production System

An early example of benchmarking involved a General Motors–Toyota joint venture at a car plant in California. For GM this was an attempt to introduce American managers to the Toyota Production System (TPS). It was largely unsuccessful, and it was years later before GM was able to refine its own version of lean production.

Knowledge cannot be appropriately valued if it cannot be understood. Knowledge associated with the TPS was particularly difficult to understand because of its systemic and integrated nature, which leads to a second factor ... Within GM there was a belief that the 'secret' to the TPS was observable and transportable, i.e., 'if we could just get the blueprints for stamping'. However, the knowledge was not easily broken down into transportable pieces. The knowledge about TPS and lean manufacturing was deeply embedded in the Toyota context and was tied into an integrated system. As a manager said, 'You cannot cherry pick elements of lean manufacturing: you must focus on the whole system. Once you learn how the system works you need a good understanding of the philosophy that underpins it.'

The initial learning challenges are summed up in the following statement from a GM manager: 'We started with denial that there was anything to learn. Then we said Toyota is different, so it won't work at GM. Eventually we realized there was something to learn. The leaders initially said "implement lean manufacturing", but they did not understand it ... We went to Japan and saw "kanban" [*just-in-time management*] and "andon" [*where employees are empowered to stop the production line to solve problems*] but people did not understand why they work. We did not understand that the TPS is an integrated approach and not just a random collection of ideas ... We implemented parts of the system but did not understand that it was the system that made the difference ... We did not understand that the culture and behaviour has to change before the techniques would have any impact.'[41]

Question: Why did benchmarking not work for GM?

Performance excellence models

Performance excellence models are assessment frameworks that are used to audit good practice and performance in the key areas of the business.[31] When the activity is carried out involving only organizational personnel as auditors, the process is called self-assessment. The frameworks cover both enabling (how things are done), and business results, criteria. The idea is to evaluate how an organization is being managed in its core business areas, and to use the approach as a vehicle for the deployment of good practice and organization-wide learning.

Western organizations normally use the criteria of the Malcolm Baldrige Performance Excellence Award (founded in the United States in 1987), or the European Excellence Award (founded by the European Foundation for Quality Management in 1992). These were originally established as regional quality awards, but the term 'excellence' is now used to signify their role for benchmarking best practice, rather than just quality management. There are many other awards across the world, including the oldest in Japan, named after the American quality guru, W. Edwards Deming (established in 1951). The criteria for these awards are similar. Organizations apply to be assessed and if successful win the award. The assessment process involves external auditors who

W. Edwards Deming

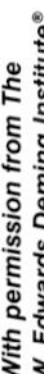

award scores for each category of the models. See the example of the European model, Figure 5.6.

The scores for the European Excellence Award are broken down as follows: leadership accounts for a potential 10 per cent of the overall points, people (8 per cent), policy and strategy (8 per cent), partnerships and resources (9 per cent), processes (15 per cent), people results (9 per cent), customer results (20 per cent), society results (6 per cent), and key performance results (15 per cent). The potential overall score is 1000 points, and an organization is rated excellent at over 700.

A version of the PDCA principle is central to how the assessors evaluate practices: that is, they expect processes to be planned, implemented effectively, subjected to monitoring and review and show evidence of effective follow-up, including where it is necessary to make modifications to the original plans. The model distinguishes between enablers and results, reflecting a balance between the drivers and the outputs of performance. Figure 5.6 shows the direction of influence of the categories from the enablers, which produce the outputs, and innovation and learning, which are fed back to inform the enablers.

Organizations typically apply for the awards to improve their organizational cohesiveness. Phil Francis, project manager, Capita Insurance Services says:

> *The company I work for was awarded a Recognized for Excellence in Europe award in 2005. We adopted EFQM and pursued the award for strategic reasons (differentiation from competitors in a contract tender). I would suggest that even without the focus being one of improving our end-to-end quality, there was a recognized benefit from the senior managers who were involved ... The perceived benefit in helping breakdown silos was sufficient that all the managers involved requested*

FIGURE 5.6 The European Excellence Model[32]

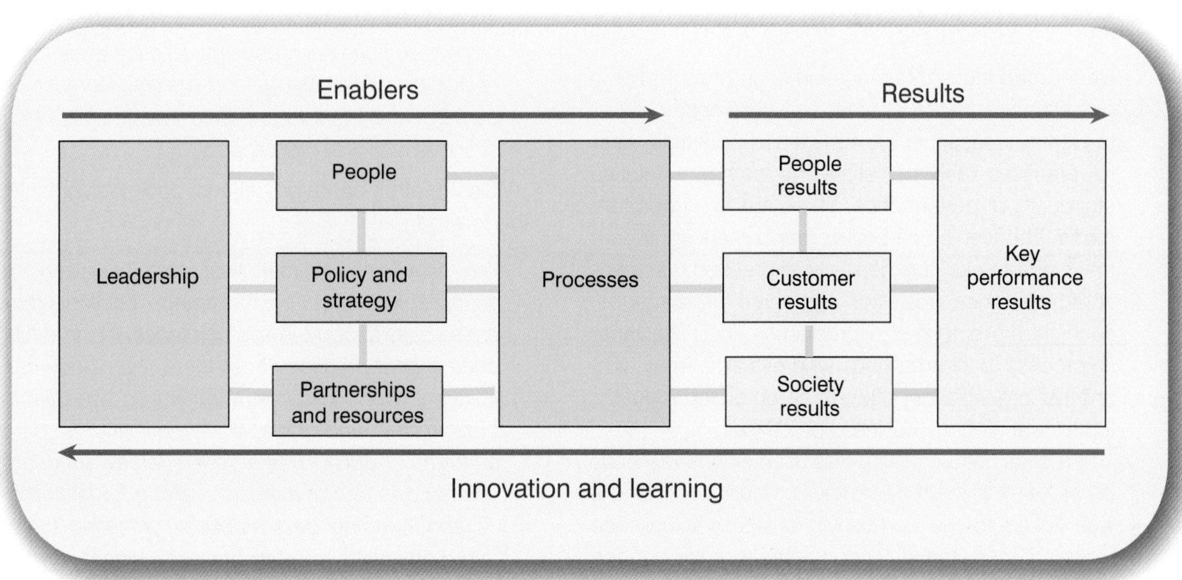

that we continue to work within the EFQM framework and aim for further awards.[33]

These models do not assess the content of an organization's actions' such as whether a purpose statement and a strategy are appropriate, but that certain processes should be in place and it must be proved that they are used. To win high marks for the 'policy and strategy' category, the European Excellence Model requires that an organization needs to show it has (1) policy and strategy based on the present and future needs, and the expectations of stakeholders; (2) these are based on information from performance measurement, research, learning and creativity related activities; (3) policy and strategy are developed, reviewed and updated; (4) deployed through a framework of key processes, and (5) communicated and implemented.

Performance excellence models require the organizations that use them to specify their practices. This has led some organizations to use the models as frameworks for benchmarking good or desired practice.

Benchmarking

Benchmarking is a comparison of an organization's practices with those of other organizations, in order to identify ideas for improvement and potentially useful practices, and sometimes to compare relative standards of performance. There are two important forms. The first is competitive benchmarking, where the benchmarks are normally expressed as measured reference goals for aggregate performance, such as the output of a production line. The other is process benchmarking, where teams may visit another organization, often in an unrelated industry, to study analogous business processes.

Process benchmarking was used extensively early on at Xerox to learn from other organizations, and it was linked to the company's business excellence model.[34] For instance, it used a study of the London ambulance service to improve its emergency call-out service for its engineers to visit customers. More recently, however, benchmarking has been scaled down and is used mainly as an internal activity to compare practices across Xerox's business units. Its internalization results from two difficulties: the problem of obtaining access to other organizations and the cost and time it has involved.

Benchmarking is useful for smaller projects, but as an approach for understanding organization-wide systems, it has problems. Part of the problem is that managers not only do not understand the other organization as a whole system, they also do not always understand their own in these terms. All generic frameworks are likely to need modification for individual applications and specific contexts. It is not a case of copying practice *per se*, but rather that benchmarking can be a useful catalyst for ideas and change.

From the resource-based view of strategy, the replication of best practice may be illusive, since the managerial practices that are most central to competitive advantage are likely to be specific to an individual organization, and irrelevant to another organization's strategic management. Michael Porter agrees, but for a different reason, when he thinks that those capabilities, categorized as originally Japanese, can be copied, and in that sense cannot be sources of lasting competitive advantage, but only of operational effectiveness:

> *The more benchmarking companies do, the more they look alike. If every company offers more or less the same mix of value, customers are forced to choose on price. This inevitably undermines price levels – and devastates profitability. At the same time, competitive convergence leads to duplicate investments and a strong tendency to overcapacity.*[35]

On the other hand, practitioner Jack Welch thinks this is wrong:

> *I've heard it said that best practices aren't a sustainable competitive advantage because they are so easy to copy. That's nonsense. It is true that once a best practice is out there, everybody can imitate it, but companies that win do two things: they imitate and improve ... imitating is hard enough ... But to make your strategy succeed, you need to fix that mindset – and go a lot further ... about finding best practices, adapting them, and continually improving them. When you do*

that right, it's nothing short of innovation. New product and service ideas, new processes, and opportunities for growth start to pop up everywhere and actually become the norm. Along with getting the right people in place, best practices are all part of implementing the hell out of your big idea and to my mind, it's the most fun. It's fun because companies that make the best practices a priority are thriving, thirsting, learning organizations. They believe that everyone should always be searching for a better way. These kinds of companies are filled with energy and spirit of can-do. Don't tell me that's not a competitive advantage![36]

Using SWOT analysis for strategic decisions

To be effective, a strategy must be consistent with the need to take account of both the opportunities and threats of the external situation, and the strengths and weaknesses of the organization's internal situation. This must be worked out in relation to purpose and the strategic objectives (see Figure 5.7).

SWOT is a mnemonic used to analyse an organization's strengths, weaknesses, opportunities, and threats. It is used to match an organization's strengths and weaknesses of its internal environment, with opportunities and threats in the external environments. The origins of SWOT go back to a similar technique that was used by Albert Humphrey, at Stanford University, to see why corporate planning failed in large American companies; although the first use of the actual acronym, SWOT, seems to be by Urick and Orr at a conference in 1964. It can be a quick and ready tool or a detailed and comprehensive organizing framework.

It is important that a SWOT starts with a desired end-state. Otherwise relative terms like 'strength in customer service' are meaningless without a context to explain what it is actually being compared with. A strategic SWOT generally involves the

I've heard it said that best practices aren't a sustainable competitive advantage because they are so easy to copy. That's nonsense. It is true that once a best practice is out there, everybody can imitate it, but companies that win do two things: they imitate and improve ...

KEY DEBATE 5.2

Is quality strategic?

In Porter's value chain, quality management is a support function for primary activities and quality is not a principle for managing the core areas of a business (as happens for lean production); but he does write that quality can be used as a basis to choose a differentiation strategy. However, he is critical of those who think of TQM as a competitive strategy, since TQM can be benchmarked and copied.[46]

The perspective from proponents of TQM is straightforward: strategy consists of understanding what customers want and aligning the organization with a set of plans to deliver it to them.[47] If Porter is right then the strategy of rivals in the same industry will converge.

However, the resource-based view of strategy suggests there are different ways for delivering value to customers. Powell argues that TQM is difficult to copy and, because of its complexity, it will take different and even unique forms, so it is a competitive advantage.[48] A major survey of 500 American hospitals suggests a positive link between its use and competitive advantage.[49]

Question: Has the strategy of Japanese rivals in the auto industry converged over the last 20 years?

FIGURE 5.7 SWOT analysis in its role for developing a strategy

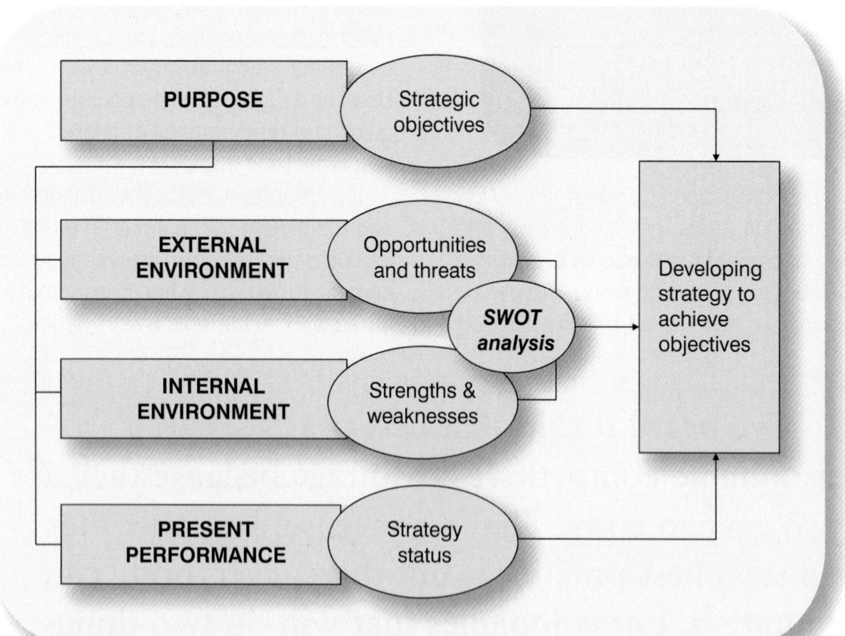

specification of strategic objectives and identifying the external and internal influences that are favourable and unfavourable in achieving these objectives (see Figure 5.8).

A strategic SWOT is comprised of the following:

- Strengths are attributes of the organization that are helpful for achieving the strategic objectives.
- Weaknesses are attributes that are unhelpful or require attention to make them helpful to achieve the strategic objectives.
- Opportunities are external influences, which are helpful for achieving the strategic objectives.
- Threats are influences that could harm, or prevent, the achievement of strategic objectives.

These are indicated on the right hand side of the figure. The opportunities and threats relate to the strategic objectives of the financial and customer perspectives of the balanced scorecard, where the outside-in influences of the external environment are important. The strengths and weaknesses relate to the strategic objectives of the internal processes and learning and growth perspectives, where the inside-out influences of the internal environment are considered.

The SWOT analysis process is driven by four basic questions:

1. How can each strength be used and developed to advance the strategic objectives?
2. How can each weakness be improved and converted into a strength?
3. How is it possible to exploit and benefit from each opportunity?
4. How can each threat be addressed, and possibly converted into an opportunity?

SWOT is a simple, but much abused, idea.[37] If it is not to become a simple list of bullet points of equally weighted factors, prioritization is necessary to determine which strengths, for example, matter more than

FIGURE 5.8 Using SWOT with strategic objectives

SWOT ANALYSIS

Financial performance	**Financial objectives and measures**	**OPPORTUNITIES THREATS** ***PESTEL factors*** ***Industry profitability and competitive forces*** ***Changes in industry groups*** ***Market life cycle***
Environmental and competitive situation	**Customer objectives and measures**	
Core capabilities	**Internal process objectives and measures**	**STRENGTHS WEAKNESSES** ***Value creation process management*** ***Price and quality*** ***People skills and values*** ***Location***
Core competences	**Learning and growth objectives and measures**	

BALANCED SCORECARD

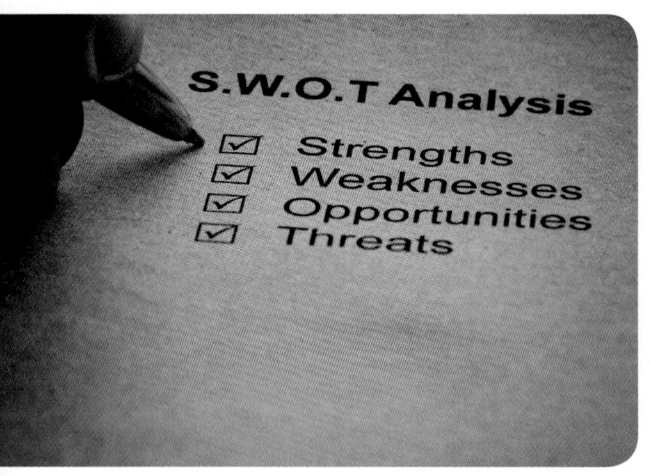

© iStockPhoto.com

others. In the case of strategic objectives, SWOT analysis should be centred on the critical success factors for achieving the objectives. It is therefore helpful if it is carried out alongside the use of strategy map. This can be used to identify the primary cause-and-effect relationships and will help the participants to identify and sort out the most important SWOT factors.

In carrying out a SWOT analysis, generally the following principles should be observed:

- Be as realistic as possible.
- Distinguish where the organization is now, and where it wants to be in the future.
- Be as specific as possible to avoid ambiguity and confusion.
- Keep the SWOT short (for example, focused on a small number of CSFs) and comprehensible.
- Question several times to clarify the logic of why a factor is relevant.

The composition and number of participants are important. As a team they should be representative of the core business areas and be able to see the overall and complete picture. The ideal number for an open discussion is eight. Using a balance scorecard approach for SWOT analysis helps to bring a balance of external and internal considerations to the process. Otherwise there is a tendency to favour either exploratory or exploitative sources of information depending upon the focus and location of the SWOT team in the organization.

For example, strategy making in the periphery of an organization may be more externally oriented than the case at the centre, which could be more internally focused. So, for example, decision-making that is closer to markets may involve more exploratory learning activities, such as scanning and scenarios. Decision-making at the centre of an organization may involve more exploitative forms of learning, such as monitoring and forecasting.[38] The aim should be to strike an overall balance.

We have explained SWOT as an approach to help review or choose a strategy. Of course, a SWOT can be used for other purposes, including for strategically-related decisions in any part of the organization. The important point remains, however, that the objective of the SWOT must be clear at its start, if it is to be a meaningful activity.

SUMMARY OF PRINCIPLES

1. The resource-based view capitalizes on how the internal strategic resources of the organization are managed in a particular way to sustain a competitive advantage.
2. An organization's strategy should take into account its strategic resource strengths and possibilities, in terms of those core competences and dynamic capabilities in which it is particularly effective.
3. A core competence contributes to competitive difference. It is not so much what people do that matters so much as that they should do it in a way that is unique to their organization.

4 A dynamic capability enables an organization to manage its core competences to give a competitive advantage.

5 The central principle of lean production is to manage an organization's core business processes to remove those activities that do not contribute to value.

6 In TQM, quality is defined by the customer, and the guiding principle for managing a process is the PDCA cycle.

7 To be effective, a strategy should be consistent with the need to take account of both the opportunities and threats of the external situation, and the strengths and weaknesses of the organization's internal situation.

8 SWOT analysis must start with a desired object to make it work properly.

GLOSSARY OF KEY TERMS

Benchmarking a comparison of an organization's practices with those of other organizations, in order to identify ideas for improvement and potentially useful practices, and sometimes to compare relative standards of performance.

Competitive advantage the reasons for an organization's ability to compete effectively with its rivals or potential rivals.

Core competences the organization-specific abilities people have to work together, and use knowledge and learning to manage strategic resources in ways that create competitive advantage.

Dynamic capabilities processes that help ensure that the resource configurations of an organization are congruent with the changing external environment.

Just-in-time management the management of production so that it responds to the needs of customers as and when the product or service is needed; it involves pulling all the components together, as and when they are needed in the production process.

Lean production a system for ensuring that wastage (or any non-value contributing activity) is eliminated in the production/management process.

PDCA an acronym representing the Plan-Do-Check-Act cycle, which is a principle for good process management.

Performance excellence models assessment frameworks that are used to audit good practice and performance in the key areas of the business.

quality defined in TQM by customer requirements.

Resource-based view of strategy the school of strategy that believes competitive advantage is based on strategic resources – those resources that uniquely give an organization its competitive advantage.

strategic resources are organizational assets, or attributes, which when combined in ways that are uniquely specific to an organization, constitute its competitive advantage. Strategic resources are not economic resources, because they are valuable only to the organization that uses them and they have no external value.

SWOT a mnemonic used to analyse an organization's Strengths, Weaknesses, Opportunities and Threats.

Top executive audit (TEA) a senior level business-wide audit of how the organization is managing its strategic priorities.

Total quality management (TQM) An organization-wide management philosophy for improving customer specified quality.

Value the satisfaction and benefits customers receive from buying and using products and services (it can also refer to the value that other stakeholders receive from the organization).

Value chain an organization's value creating chain of strategically-relevant resources and activities.

GUIDED FURTHER READING

Ideas about dynamic capabilities are still developing. The most comprehensive review is given by:

Helfat, C. E., Finkelstein, S., Mitchell, W., Peteraf, M. A., Singh, H., Teece, D. J. and Winter S. G. (2007) *Dynamic Capabilities: Understanding Strategic Change in Organizations,* Oxford: Blackwell Publishing.

Total quality management takes a wide variety of confusing forms. Cole gives an excellent retrospective commentary, and Witcher explains how 'quality' has been interpreted in different ways.

Cole, R. E. (1998) 'Learning from the quality movement: What did and didn't happen and why?' *California Management Review* 41:43–73.

Witcher, B. J. (1995) 'The changing scale of total quality management', *Quality Management Journal* 2:9–29.

REVIEW QUESTIONS

1 What is a strategic resource?

2 What makes a company competence a 'core competence'?

3 What is the difference between how a dynamic capability is defined by Teece *et al*. and Eisenhardt and Martin?

4 What is the meaning of 'lean' in the context of lean production?

5 Is 'please don't change anything' the correct meaning of the acronym PDCA?

6 What does 'total' mean in the context of total quality management, and who defines the level of 'quality' and why?

7 What is the purpose of benchmarking?

8 In SWOT analysis, how do we know how strong, weak, or what an opportunity or threat, is?

SEMINAR AND ASSIGNMENT QUESTIONS

1 Use a performance excellence model to evaluate an organization known to you personally. Don't forget to use PDCA!

2 Examine Michael Porter's 1996 *Harvard Business Review* paper, about real strategy and operational effectiveness. Discuss evidence and other arguments for and against his point of view. Reach a definite conclusion.

3 Make a list of different organizations and compare their unique features. Come to definite conclusions about how these differences are important to their strategic management. Discuss how they manage this difference.

CHAPTER REFERENCES

1 Fuge (2008) home page, www.fuge.co.uk

2 Tzu (2008) www.tzu-balanceyourself.com

3 British Broadcasting Corporation (2008), 'Chinese food made easy', www.bbc.co.uk, August 5.

4 Wernerfelt, B. (1984) 'A resource-based view of the firm', *Strategic Management Journal* 5:171–80.

5 Penrose, E. T. (1959) *The Theory of the Growth of the Firm,* Oxford: Basil Blackwell.

6 Nelson, R. R. and Winter, S. (1982) *An Evolutionary Theory of Economic Change,* Cambridge, MA: The Belknap Press of Harvard University Press.

7 The original Barney model was VRIN, where 'N' denotes non-substitutability (that the other three attributes do not have substitutes which rivals can apply), see Barney, J. B. (1991) 'Firm resources and sustained competitive advantage', *Journal of Management* 17(1): 99–120. The VRIO version is found in Barney, J. B. (1997) *Gaining and Sustaining Competitive Advantage,* Harlow: Addison-Wesley.

8 Grant, R. M. (1991) 'The resource-based theory of competitive advantage: implications for strategy formulation', *California Management Review* 33:Spring, 114–35.

9 Some of the RBV literature defines 'strategic resources' broadly to include not only an organization's distinctive collection of tangible and intangible resources, but also the core competences and dynamic capabilities required to manage these bundles. Taking a managerial perspective, we prefer to distinguish between the things that are being managed (strategic resources) and those things that help people manage (core competences).

10 Porter, M. E. (1985) *Competitive Advantage: Creating and Sustaining Superior Performance.* London: Collier Macmillan.

11 Adapted from Porter (1985) *op cit.,* Figure 2.2.

12 Kay, J. (1993) *Foundations of Corporate Success,* Oxford: Oxford University Press.

13 Dierickx, I. and Cool, K. (1989) 'Asset stock accumulation and sustainability of competitive advantage', *Management Science* 35(12):1504–11; Tushman, M. and Anderson, D. (1986) 'Technological discontinuities and organizational environments', *Administrative Science Quarterly* 31:439–65.

14 Leonard Barton, D. (1992) 'Core capabilities and core rigidities', *Strategic Management Journal* 13:111–25.

15 Prahalad, C. A. and Hamel, G. (1990) 'The core competence of the corporation', *Harvard Business Review* May–June:79–91.

16 Doz, Y. (1996) 'Managing core competency for corporate renewal: Towards a managerial theory of core competences'. In Dosi, G. and Malerba, F. (eds) *Organization and Strategy in the Evolution of the Enterprise,* London: Macmillan Press, pp. 155–78.

17 Teece, D. C., Pisano, G. and Shuen, A. (1997) 'Dynamic capabilities and strategic management', *Strategic Management Journal* 18:509–33.

18 Zollo, M. and Winter, S. G. (2002) 'Deliberate learning and the evolution of dynamic capabilities', *Organizational Science* 13:339–51, 340.

19 Teece, D. C., Pisano, G. and Shuen, A. (2000) 'Dynamic capabilities and strategic management'. In Dosi, G., Nelson, R. R. and Winter, S. G. (eds) *The Nature and Dynamics of Organizational Capabilities,* Oxford: Oxford University Press, pp. 334–62.

20 Eisenhardt, K. M. and Martin, J. A. (2000) 'Dynamic capabilities: what are they?' *Strategic Management Journal,* 21(10–11):1105–121.

21 Hamel, G. and Prahalad, C. K. (1989) 'Strategic intent', *Harvard Business Review*, May–June:63–76.

22 Kenneth and William Hopper (2009) argue that the origin of the success of the large American corporations is owed to basic cultural attributes, and these were transferred to Japan by engineers on loan from AT&T during America's occupation in the 1940s. These attributes included an aptitude for the exercise of mechanical skills; a moral outlook that subordinated the interests of the individual to the group, and exceptional organizing ability.

23 For example, see Monden, Y. (1998) *Toyota Production System: An Integrated Approach to Just-in-Time,* (3rd edn), Norcross, Georgia: Engineering & Management Press; published

in Japan, 1983, Institute of Industrial Engineers; Womack, J. P., Jones, D. T. and Roos, D. (1990) *The Machine That Changed the World*, New York: Rawson Associates.

24 Hines, P., Silvi, R. and Bartolini, M. (2002) *Lean Profit Potential*, Cardiff: Lean Enterprise Research Centre, Cardiff Business School, Cardiff University.

25 Seddon, J. (2008) *Systems Thinking in the Public Sector: The Failure of the Reform Regime and a Manifesto for a Better Way,* London: Triarchy.

26 Deming, W. E. (1986) *Out of the Crisis: Quality, Productivity and Competitive Position*, Cambridge: Cambridge University Press.

27 Nonaka, N. and Takeuchi, H. (1995) *The Knowledge-Creating Company,* Oxford: Oxford University Press.

28 Argyris, C. and Schon, D. (1981) *Organizational Learning*, Reading, MA: Addison-Wesley.

29 Senge, P. (1990) (2006 rev. edn), *The Fifth Discipline: The Art and Practice of the Learning Organization*, New York: Doubleday.

30 Imai, M. (1986), *Kaizen: The Key to Japan's Competitive Success*, New York: McGraw-Hill.

31 Performance excellence models are used in a wide variety of organizations. They formed the basis of the British government's 'Public Sector Excellence Programme' (Cabinet Office, 2003). Although some observers have alleged that the model has been used for controlling civil servants rather than as a framework that helps learning, in Massey, A. and Pyper, R. (2005) *Public Management and Modernization in Britain,* Basingstoke: Palgrave.

32 European Foundation for Quality Management (EFQM) (2008) *The EFQM Excellence Model,* Brussels: EFQM. http://www.efqm.org

33 Francis, P. (2007) email, *Performance Management Forum*, February 20.

34 Camp, R. C. (1989) *Benchmarking: The Search for Industry Best Practices that lead to Superior Performance*, Milwaukee: ASQC Quality Press.

35 Porter, M. E. (1996) 'What is strategy?' *Harvard Business Review,* November–December:61–78.

36 Welch, J. (with Welch, S.) (2005) *Winning,* New York: HarperCollins.

37 Hill, T. and Westbrook, R. (1997) 'SWOT Analysis: it's time for a product recall', *Long Range Planning,* 30(1):46–52.

38 See Regner, P. (2003) 'Strategy creation in the periphery: inductive versus deductive strategy making', *Journal of Management Studies* 40(1):57–82; March, J. G. (1991) 'Exploration and exploitation in organizational learning', *Organization Science* 2(1):71–87.

39 Bryson, B. (1995) *Made in America,* London: Minerva, pp. 402–406.

40 Toyota (2008) www.toyota.co.jp/en/vision/production_system/

41 Inkpen, A. C. (2005) 'Learning through alliances: General Motors and NUMMI', *California Management Review* 47(4):114–36, 120–21.

42 Rumelt, R. P. (1991) 'How much does industry matter?' *Strategic Management Journal* 12(3):167–85.

43 Porter, M. E. (1985) *Competitive Advantage: Creating and Sustaining Superior Performance,* New York: Free Press.

44 Priem, R. and Butler, J. E. (2001) 'Is the resource-based "view" a useful perspective for strategic management research?' *Academy of Management Review* 26(1):22–40.

45 Hoopes, D. G., Madsen, T. L. and Walker, G. (2003) Guest editors' introduction to the special issue: 'Why is there a resource-based view? Toward a theory of competitive heterogeneity', *Strategic Management Journal* 24:889–902.

46 Porter (1996) *op cit.*

47 Dean, J. W. Jr. and Bowen, D. E. (1994) 'Management theory and total quality: improving research and practice through theory development', *Academy of Management Review* 19:392–418.

48 Powell, T. C. (1995) 'Total quality management as competitive advantage: a review and empirical study', *Strategic Management Journal* 16:15–27.

49 Douglas, T. J. and Judge, Q. (2001) 'Total quality management implementation and competitive advantage: the role of structural control and exploration', *Academy of Management Review,* 44(1):158–69.

CASE 5.1 Nissan's management of its core competences

Nissan has a statement of values it calls 'The Nissan Way'. This reflects the importance to the company of its employees working in similar ways to be able to communicate and help each other. This is central to the executive team's ability to manage its competitiveness dynamically as the Nissan businesses and the environment change.

Nissan seeks to develop corporate-wide 'business methodologies and management philosophies'. These are designed to help cross-functionality and to assist its employees to solve problems easily and quickly, to modify behaviours as necessary, and to identify and take advantage of opportunities as they arise.

Nissan defines 13 cross-functional processes as its core business areas. These are critical for maintaining the overall value-adding capability of the firm and must be managed effectively across the organization. They are: (1) hoshin kanri, (2) fundamental daily management (nichijo kanri), (3) production maintenance, (4) standardization establishment, (5) productivity improvement activity, (6) inspection, (7) production control and logistics, (8) personnel and labour management, (9) cost management, (10) quality control (including just-in-time management, process control), (11) engineering capability, (12) parts localization, and (13) purchasing.

The inclusion of hoshin kanri is significant. Hoshin kanri is explained later (see Chapter 10), but note

© David Ball/Alamy

here that it is an organization-wide methodology for the deployment and management of strategically-related objectives, and is therefore important to the implementation of strategy. A 'hoshin' is a strategic objective with a brief explanatory guideline about its context.

Top Executive Audits (TEAs)

A **top executive audit** is an annual examination by executive management of the organization's management of Nissan's core business processes. Its purpose is given such that:

'A top shindan audit is defined as a detailed audit performed to obtain an overview of each activity that is supporting the company's stated strategic goals and objectives. The senior executive of the company always conducts the audit, which is focused on an individual's function and proposed improvement activity.' (The word, 'shindan', translates into English avs 'executive'.)

Nissan specifies seven business methodologies and management philosophies. These are: (1) daily control, (2) the determination of hoshins (the review of hoshin-related work and set up activity), (3) the co-ordination of hoshin development and deployment for hoshin/business plan and control items, (4) the establishment of control items, (5) analytical and problem-solving abilities, (6) check and action taken, and (7) leadership and participation by high-ranking personnel.

They constitute the core competences that everyone is expected to apply. These are used by senior managers to audit the organization's proficiency in managing the 13 business processes. There are other important competences, but these are functionally-based rather than cross-functional and value-centred. During the course of the audit the seven competences are called diagnostic items. The audit's activity examines the application of the seven competences in all of Nissan's units and determines how they are used in the 13 core processes; this is done in the light of Nissan's broader corporate purpose and medium-term plan.

Assessments are made by the executive management auditing team for each of the core business processes on a one-to-five scale of competency. This scale is similar to that used by the Philip Crosby's maturity grid – a scheme that offers five stages in the development of company-wide quality management. At Nissan the idea is expressed simply as: 'stage one, not aware'; 'stage two, aware'; 'stage three, starting'; 'stage four, getting there', and 'stage five, arrived'. This scale is used by the auditor to summarize progress on the condition of the diagnostic items found in the core business processes, and only after reaching stage four on all seven categories would head office consider that an overseas company had implemented 'The Nissan Way' philosophy successfully.

The status of competency for each of the diagnostic items is judged against a benchmarked series of standards that are specified through the engineering department at head office. These provide guides to what competency and practice should look like for each of the five stages. So, for example, taking one of the core business processes, '*hoshin kanri*', and one of the diagnostic items, '*hoshin determination – its review and set up activity for hoshin content*', the five stages that are used to evaluate the progress of a Nissan unit, are specified as follows:

- 1st step:
  - Hoshins are contained in slogans meant for everybody. Measures are not determined even though objectives exist.
- 2nd step:
  - Hoshins resulting from precise definition of desired objectives.
  - Not concentrated to the vital subjects in this year.
  - Objectives and measure have been determined.
  - Measures determined without understanding present situation.
- 3rd step:
  - Accurate formation of aim arrived at through distillation of the year's important points.
  - Annual plan and mid-term plan (3 years) are not matched.
  - Understanding is present and is related to objectives, which establish measures.

- No analysis done, but have decided measures through experience.
- 4th step:
  - Stress is made on the formulation of hoshins with solutions given for important problems, based on review.
  - Annual plan and mid-term plan are matched.
  - Set up measures by using QC method for grasping problem.
  - Procedure of hoshin determination has been laid down as rule.
- 5th step:
  - Formulation of the year's hoshins, which bear a relation to middle term plans.
  - Understood present situation, make clear contribution rate of each factor.
  - Revision of hoshins is appropriately being done.

Each business unit is notified about its competence level. So, for example, Nissan South Africa's hoshin kanri competency was judged at a level of 4.5, which in fact made its hoshin kanri one of the better-managed of the Nissan group. All the units are given advice about how they should follow up the audit for each of the seven competences. In the Nissan South Africa case, for the 'hoshin kanri determination' competency, the following advice for improvement was:

- To clarify the main activity, to become more priority oriented and to reduce the number of control items.
- To clarify responsibility and accountability.
- To follow up the last actions at review time.

Discussion questions

1 How does Nissan use its values statement, 'The Nissan Way', to manage strategic objectives?

2 What is the difference between Nissan's core business processes and its seven core competences? Why is it important for senior managers to conduct the audit?

3 If the top executive audit is a dynamic capability, how does it work to configure and reconfigure strategic resources?

Case reference

1 Witcher, B. J., Chau, V. S. and Harding, P. (2008) 'Dynamic capabilities: Top executive audits and hoshin kanri at Nissan South Africa', *International Journal of Operations and Production Management* 28(6):540–61.

This case study was prepared using only publicly available sources of information for the purposes of classroom discussion; it does not intend to illustrate either effective or ineffective handling of a managerial situation.

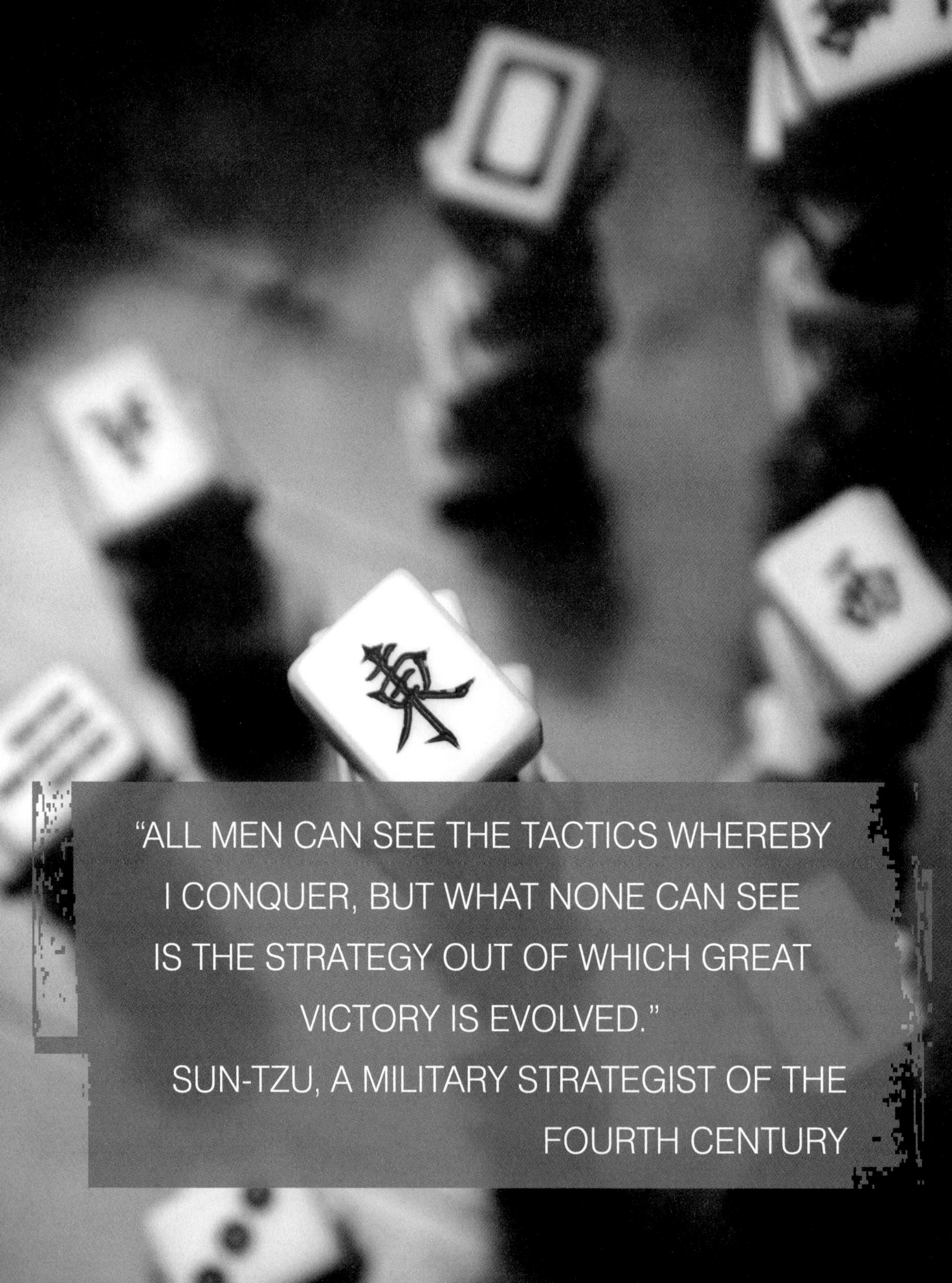

"ALL MEN CAN SEE THE TACTICS WHEREBY I CONQUER, BUT WHAT NONE CAN SEE IS THE STRATEGY OUT OF WHICH GREAT VICTORY IS EVOLVED."

SUN-TZU, A MILITARY STRATEGIST OF THE FOURTH CENTURY

Strategy

PART I WHAT IS STRATEGY?

CHAPTER 1
Overview of strategic management

CHAPTER 2
Purpose

PART II DETERMINANTS OF STRATEGY

CHAPTER 3
Strategic objectives

Balanced objectives

CHAPTER 4
The external environment

SWOT analysis

CHAPTER 5
The internal environment

PART III STRATEGY

CHAPTER 6
Business-level strategy

CHAPTER 7
Corporate-level strategy

CHAPTER 8
Global-level strategy

PART IV STRATEGY DEVELOPMENT

CHAPTER 9
Organizing

CHAPTER 10
Managing implementation

CHAPTER 11
Leadership

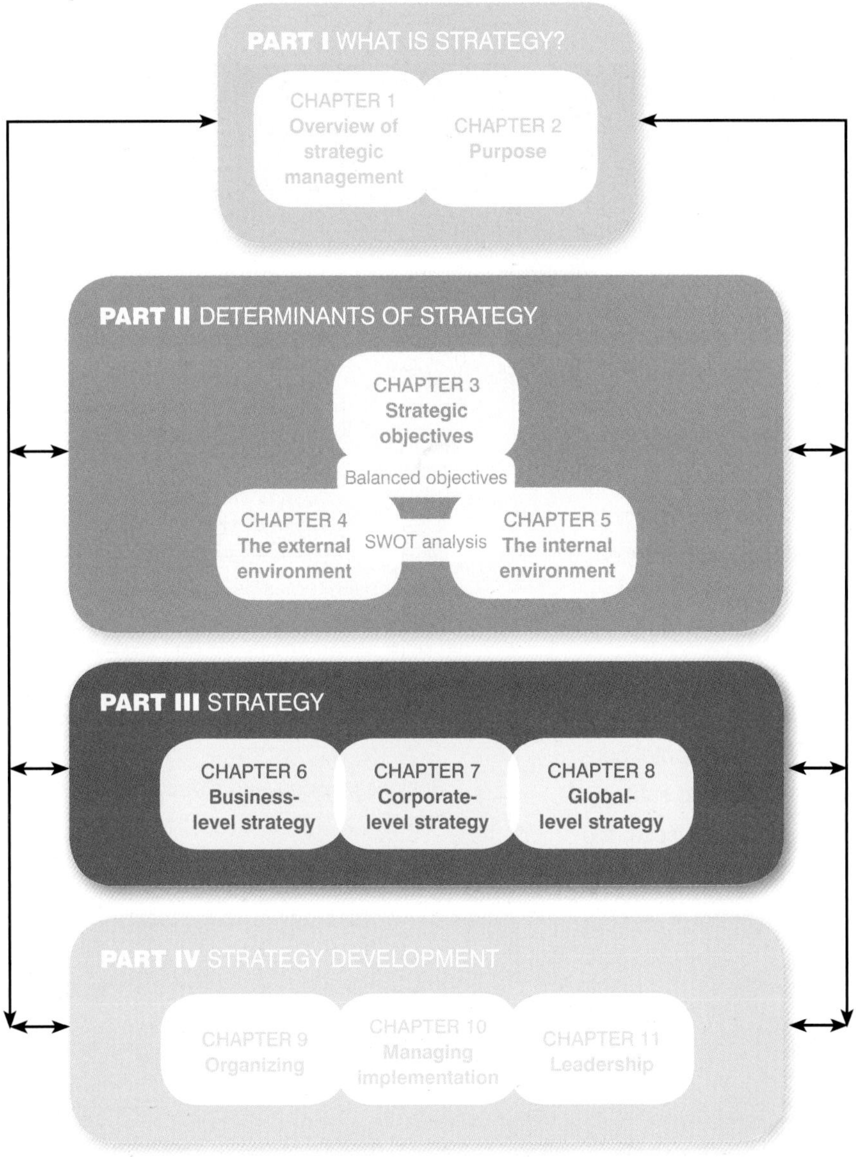

Chapter 6

BUSINESS-LEVEL STRATEGY

Introduction

Chapters 4 and 5 were about the external and internal environments; once an organization understands these, it must manage its overall strategy for achieving its purpose. This chapter is about business-level, or single business, strategy. A **business level strategy** can be defined as the organization's fundamental strategic choice of what approach to adopt to achieve its competitive advantage from the given options at the business unit level. Corporate-level, or multi-business, strategy is discussed in the following chapter. This chapter considers competitive advantage and generic strategy; the role of the value chain for managing these; the concept of the business model; and strategy activity mapping.

LEARNING OBJECTIVES

By the end of this chapter you should understand:

1. The meaning of a business-level strategy.
2. Generic strategies as a basis for competitive advantage.
3. The value chain as a vehicle for managing generic strategy and strategic activities.
4. Business models and strategy activity maps.

Image courtesy of IKEA UK

Business vignette Strategies involve inter-connecting activities ...

In an interview in 2004, Henry Mintzberg tells how much he admires strategy at IKEA, the Swedish home furnishings retailer: 'An organization that I think has a wonderfully integrated strategy is IKEA. Think about all the intricate interconnections and how that strategy has worked out piece by piece in all kinds of intricate, fascinating ways by people living every aspect of it.'[1]

Similarly Michael Porter writes about how effectively the company manages its activities: 'IKEA targets young furniture buyers who want style at low cost. What turns this marketing concept into a strategic position is the tailored set of activities that make it work ... to perform activities different from its rivals.'[2]

Anders Dahlvig, the IKEA ch... explains his organization's competitive ... as a totality of many things: 'Many co... ...itors could try to copy ... The difficulty is when you try to create the totality of what we have. You might be able to copy our low prices, but you need our volumes and global sourcing presence. You have to be able to copy our Scandinavian design, which is not easy without a Scandinavian heritage. You have to be able to copy our distribution concept with the flat-pack. And you have to be able to copy our interior competence – the way we set out our stores and catalogues.'[3]

Competitive advantage and generic strategies

Strategic management aims to provide a strong long-term competitive position that over time will benefit the organization's stakeholders more lastingly than, for example, short-term profitability. Because the external environment is subject to sudden shocks as well as continuous change, it is necessary to ensure that the organization's strategic priorities are consistent and, as far as possible, constant, so that the organization's people are clear about purpose and can adjust to change accordingly; in this way, customers and other stakeholders continue to receive value.

To achieve sustainable competitive advantage, organizations must compete in one of two distinct ways. In what is probably the most influential book about competitive advantage, Michael Porter writes that advantage 'grows fundamentally out of value a firm is able to create for its buyers that exceeds the firm's cost of creating it. Value is what buyers are willing to pay, and superior value stems from offering lower prices than competitors for equivalent benefits or providing unique benefits that more than offset a higher price.'[4]

Porter maintains that effective competitive strategy is based on two broad strategic approaches based on either cost or differentiation. The use of the word 'generic' means that all competitive strategy, no matter what its form or detail, should relate to one of the two sources of competitive advantage.

Generic strategy takes four forms, depending on the organization's competitive advantage and the competitive scope of its activities (see Figure 6.1). If the organization is targeting the whole industry, then the relevant strategies are cost leadership and industry-wide differentiation; if the organization is targeting only part of the industry, perhaps a market segment, the relevant strategies are cost focus and differentiation focus. There is a stark and important distinction between generic strategy that is industry-wide, and generic strategy that is focused on only a part of an industry.

> **Competitive advantage ... grows fundamentally out of value a firm is able to create for its buyers that exceeds the firm's cost of creating it. Value is what buyers are willing to pay, and superior value stems from offering lower prices than competitors for equivalent benefits or providing unique benefits that more than offset a higher price.**

FIGURE 6.1 Four generic strategies[5]

		Competitive advantage	
		Lower cost	Differentiation
Competitive scope	Broad target	***Cost leadership***	***Differentiation***
	Narrow target	***Cost focus***	***Differentiation focus***

Cost leadership generic strategy

For an organization to have a **cost leadership generic strategy** it is necessary for it to have lower costs per unit produced than its competitors and any potential rivals can achieve in that industry. The word 'leadership' is important, since this requires the organization to be *the* cost leader, and not just one of several organizations competing on costs. If an organization has a larger share of its industry's markets than its rivals, then it can achieve relatively greater economies of scale and scope. Economies of scale are obtained through cost savings that occur when higher volumes allow unit costs to be reduced. Economies of scope involve cost savings that are available as a result of separate products sharing the same facilities.

The advantages of scale and scope are associated with the experience curve effect, an idea introduced by the founder of the Boston Consulting Group, Bruce Henderson.[6] He argued that when the accumulated production of an organization doubles over time, unit costs when adjusted for inflation have a potential to fall by 20–30 per cent. This is not just the result of scale, but of a combined effect of learning, specialization, investment and scale. To paraphrase: the more that an organization does, the lower the cost of doing it. When cumulative volume doubles, the extra costs, including those in administration, marketing, distribution, and manufacturing, fall by a constant and predictable percentage.

The experience curve idea has encouraged organizations to try to gain a large market share quickly by investing heavily and aggressively down-pricing products and services; the high initial costs can be recovered in the longer-term once the organization has become the market leader. Organizations should certainly seek to learn and improve continuously before their competitors do. However, while there is (probably) a discernable effect like an experience curve in many industries, its exact nature is difficult to understand.

The sources of cost advantage are varied, and include such things as proprietary knowledge and technology, preferential access to industry distribution channels and sources of supply, as well as effective cost management. Low-cost leaders often sell a standard or no-frills product and service. They place considerable emphasis on taking advantage of scale, but also are likely to take advantage of any other opportunities to lower costs.

A low cost leader does not necessarily have to lower its prices below those of its rivals. It may do this to win more customers, and to reap more economies of scale, but if its costs are lower than the industry's average, then to earn above average returns all it has to do is command prices at or near the industry average. However, a cost leader cannot ignore differentiation completely, since its products and services must be perceived by customers as broadly comparable to those of its rivals, or the cost leader may be forced to discount its prices well below those of its competitors to achieve sales.

Differentiation industry-wide generic strategy

A **differentiation industry-wide generic strategy** requires an organization to have unique product and service attributes to (or which are different from) the industry's competitors, and which are valued by customers, such as special qualities, delivery and reliability features, corporate and brand images, technological, service and support arrangements, and so on. These enable a differentiator to attract returns that more than offset the extra costs of differentiation. Of course, the organization concerned will seek to reduce its costs, but only in a way that does not affect the sources of differentiation. A differentiation industry-wide generic strategy is one that covers the whole or a major part of the industry and its markets. In contrast to cost-leadership, there can be more than one successful competition position in an industry, based on differentiation strategy, especially if there are significantly different and distinctive customer groups that value product and service attributes in contrasting ways.

An example of differentiation is the case of Canon's success at creating an industry position in relation to Xerox, which dominated the corporate copier market, by following a clear strategy with machines that offered high-speed and high-volume reproduction. The big industrial customers required a direct sales force, and Xerox machines were leased, instead of sold, to the customers. Canon decided to target small and medium-sized organizations and produced smaller machines for individual use. These were sold through a dealer network rather than leased. Canon decided to differentiate its offer from Xerox by offering quality and price. Unlike Xerox's machines, Canon's copiers would not break down (they had TQM), and there was less need for a customer to rent a machine. The copier markets now had two successful organizations, each with a different strategy.

Cost focus and differentiation focus generic strategy

A **focus generic strategy** is narrowly based on a particular part of the industry, such as a market segment or niche, where an organization can design its strategy to meet the needs of customers more closely than its competitors. A focuser does not have an overall industry competitive advantage, but is able to achieve one in its target segment based on a low cost base, or differentiation. Both these strategies depend on the perception that a target segment is different from others in the industry.

The implication of a focus generic strategy is that more broadly-targeted competitors cannot deliver a comparable value to the focuser's target customers. The competitors may be under-performing in the sense that in meeting the needs of more general customers they are unable to meet the more specialized needs of the segment, or over-performing in the sense that they are bearing a higher than necessary

cost in serving the segment. Both will produce returns in that segment that are likely to compare unfavourably with those of a focused competitor. However, there is normally room for a number of focus strategies within an industry if the focusers choose different target segments.

A good example of focused differentiation is H&M (Hennes & Mauritz). The Swedish company designs cheap but chic clothing for men and women aged 18 to 45, children's apparel and its own brands of cosmetics. It opened its first store for women in 1947 as Hennes (Swedish for 'hers'), and bought the men's clothing store, Mauritz Widforss, in 1968. Since then it has consistently focused on its segment of the retail market and has grown to more than 1500 stores in about 25 countries.

Generic strategies are mutually exclusive

The important thing to note about the four generic strategies is that an organization must choose one, and not a combination, of them. An organization that chooses a strategy that is part cost and part differentiation is called a **straddler**. In Porter's view an organization must avoid becoming a 'jack of all-trades and master of none' – 'Being "all things to all people" is a recipe for strategic mediocrity and below-average performance, because it often means that a firm has no competitive advantage at all'.[7] Being stuck in the middle is typically a result of an organization's unwillingness to make choices about how to compete. Each strategy is a fundamentally different approach for sustaining a competitive advantage, which calls for a different set of strategically relevant activities.

The value chain (see Chapter 5) is used to identify these activities and to manage them in line with an organization's chosen generic strategy. It is important to remember that the primary and support activities in the value chain cover only those that are central, or core, to an organization's chosen strategy (see Figures 6.2 and 6.3).

The value chain illustrated in Figure 6.2 is an example for an insurance company that offers low price policies and aims to achieve economies of scale through taking a large market share. Its internal organization is formal, where an emphasis is placed on efficiency. The value chain tasks are then to coordinate and optimize costs across these activities to reduce the cost base continuously.

The value chain in Figure 6.3 is an electronics engineering company that supplies office equipment to industrial customers. It offers relatively high prices but a good and responsive maintenance service.

BEING 'ALL THINGS TO ALL PEOPLE' IS A RECIPE FOR STRATEGIC MEDIOCRITY AND BELOW-AVERAGE PERFORMANCE, BECAUSE IT OFTEN MEANS THAT A FIRM HAS NO COMPETITIVE ADVANTAGE AT ALL. BEING STUCK IN THE MIDDLE IS TYPICALLY A RESULT OF AN ORGANIZATION'S UNWILLINGNESS TO MAKE CHOICES ABOUT HOW TO COMPETE.

FIGURE 6.2 Cost leadership

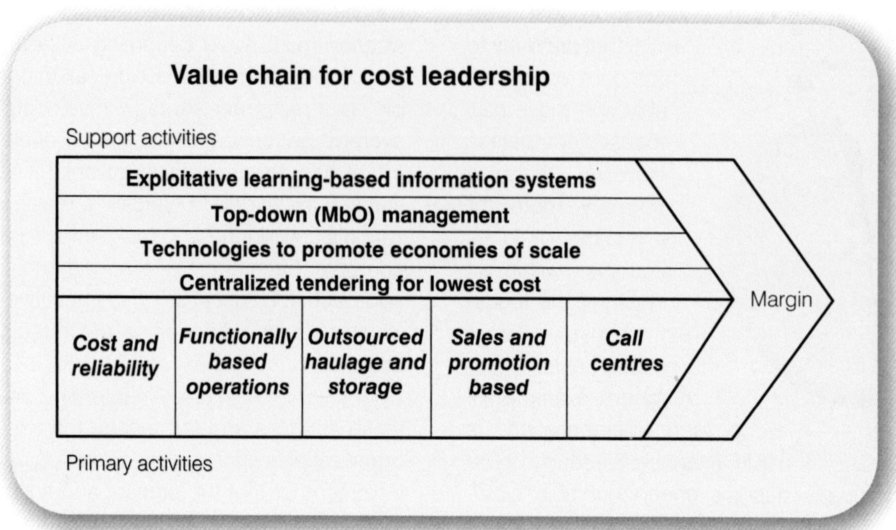

FIGURE 6.3 Differentiation

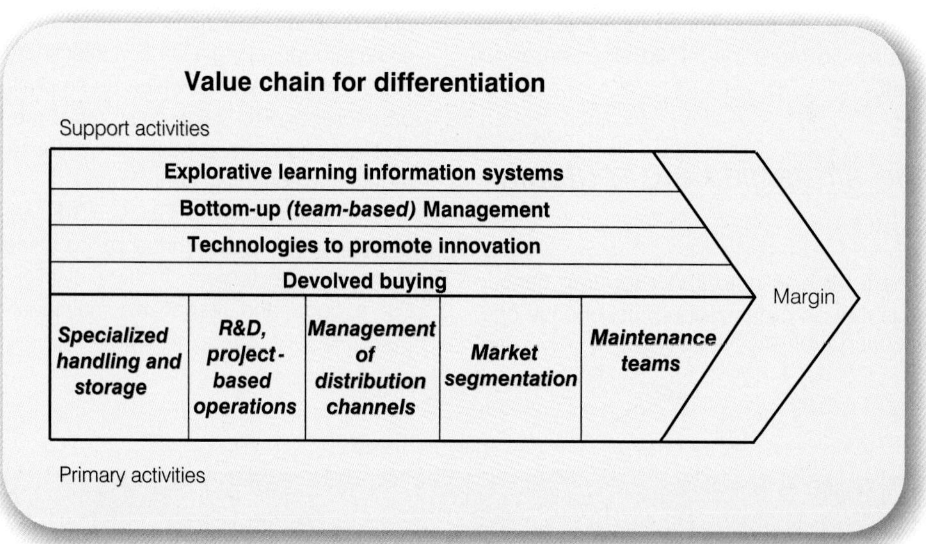

Its organizational culture is collegiate and informal, and there is a strong tradition of innovation. It takes a relatively large market share, which is based on providing its customers with a customized service. The value chain tasks are to co-ordinate and optimize the effectiveness of activities that support a customized service.

Hybrid generic strategy

The rise of new Japanese competition during the last part of the twentieth century called into question the choice of either cost- or differentiation-based competitive advantage. The Japanese seemed to offer differentiation simultaneously with lower costs in several industries. They did this largely through superior organizational capabilities, such as lean production and its associated core competences, such as those relating to business process management and customer focused organizing (see Chapter 5). The Japanese were in effect following a hybrid generic strategy (see Figure 6.4).

The **best-cost differentiation hybrid generic strategy** aims to offer superior value to customers by meeting their expectations on key product and

FIGURE 6.4 Hybrid generic strategy

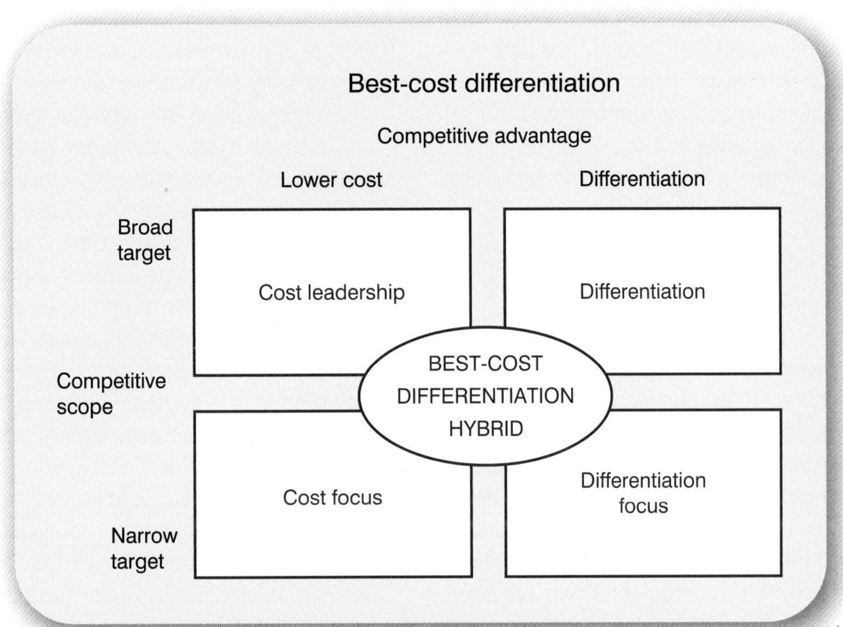

FIGURE 6.5 Best-cost differentiation

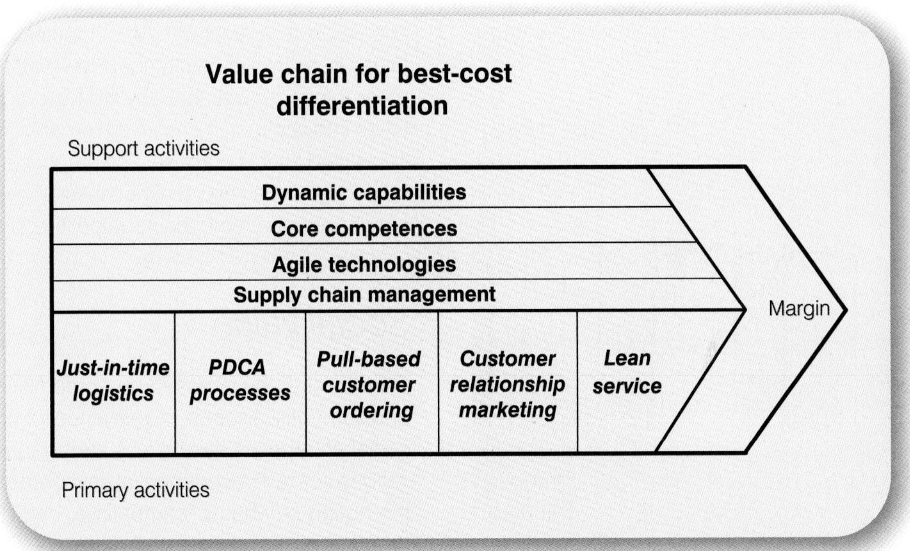

service attributes, while also exceeding their expectations on price. This in effect extends beyond value for money, to a definition of quality that incorporates a perception and expectation of continuous improvement (see Figure 6.5).

The value chain illustrated in Figure 6.5 is an example for an auto company. While it aims to minimize its costs through economies of scale, lean production and just-in-time management facilitate a more customized approach. Both efficiency and effectiveness are important: hoshin kanri is used to deploy top-down policies to encourage bottom-up strategies that are designed to achieve both. The value chain tasks are to co-ordinate and optimize activities that continuously improve the value for customers.

Strategy with thresholds

Treacy and Wiersema offer a similar view to hybrid strategy, which they term 'generic value disciplines', and which are based on strategy thresholds.[8] They suggest organizations should choose and *excel* in only one strategy and act on this consistency. However, at the same time the organization should ensure that appropriate threshold standards are maintained in relation to the other strategies. There are three generic strategies.

The first is operational excellence, where the organization aims to excel by providing a reasonable quality at a very low price: this focuses on efficiency, lean operations and supply chain management. This is essentially a low-cost-based competitive advantage, where high turnover and basic service are important. The second is product leadership, where the organization is strong in brand marketing and innovation, and operates in dynamic markets. The focus here is on development, design, time-to-market and relatively high margins. The third is customer intimacy, where an organization aims to excel in customer attention and service. The focus is on customer relationship marketing, where service and delivery are reliable and are relatively customized. These last two are primarily differentiation strategy.

© iStockPhoto.com

An organization should excel in only one of these and maintain basic standards in the other two. This seems to be like straddling. Nonetheless, a hybrid strategy may be effective, as the success of companies like Toyota and other Japanese organizations suggests.

Porter's ideas have been contrasted with the resource-based view of strategy. For example, while the insurance and electronic engineering companies above are said to be instances of generic strategy, the hybrid case is a strategic resource-based example, because there are obvious dynamic capabilities such as lead production and hoshin kanri, and bottom-up strategies point to superior core competences.

In fact, both the external (outside-in) and internal (inside-out) influences should be considered (see SWOT, Chapter 5). The real question concerns the extent to which an organization should be focused on Porter's two sources of competitive advantage. There is no doubt that a strong preoccupation with a strategy that is clear and obvious provides a discipline for everyone to be conscious that everything they do should be consistent with (and hopefully helps to sustain) a competitive advantage. However, there may be *other* things as well that are strategic and should be taken into account to ensure the organization achieves its desired overall purpose. The emphasis that is given here to 'other' is important because an overall strategy may have to be more than competitive strategy.

Social value

Generic strategy is based on competitive advantage and competitive scope. Its relevance for non-profit and social enterprises seems less strong than for organizations active in a commercial environment. However, the notion of what is 'competitive' can be translated broadly for organizations in terms of efficiency and

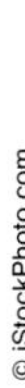

effectiveness. Much administration in non-profit organizations is centred on efficiency. Efficiency is about minimizing the quantity (especially in terms of cost) of inputs in relation to the achieved outputs, and typically concerns the optimal use of resources.

Effectiveness is more about the quality of resources in terms of their fitness for purpose. This can be about how efficiency is achieved, but it is primarily concerned with differentiation: how a range of services can be supplied effectively to (albeit non-market) demand. In the shorter-term, efficiency and the need to keep within budgets are important, but the success of longer-term policies and service depends more upon the effectiveness of achieving those things.

The idea of 'social value' has been proposed for social enterprises by Mark Moore.[9] This involves an entrepreneurial role for public sector managers; for example, managers should be explorers of why and how the public can make use of services in a way that goes beyond the (mere) administration of policy. For example, a librarian with responsibility for an adult library with restrictive opening hours realizes that after school, children are waiting for parents coming home from work. The result is that the librarian develops a proposal and wins funds to extend opening hours to accommodate this need at the library. The new demand for the library is likely to improve local educational levels and raises the social value of the library.

Ideas such as this are an extension of strategic effectiveness, which is as much about the continuous improvement of what an organization does now, as it is about achieving a strategic vision. This is properly a subject that concerns an organization's business model rather than a 'strategy' as such.

Business models

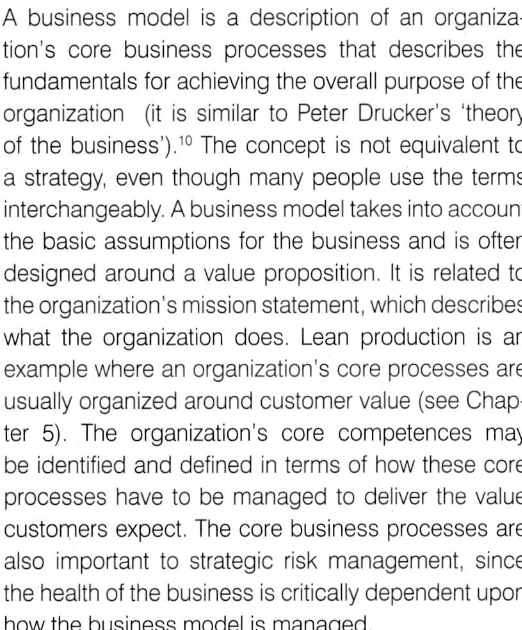

A business model is a description of an organization's core business processes that describes the fundamentals for achieving the overall purpose of the organization (it is similar to Peter Drucker's 'theory of the business').[10] The concept is not equivalent to a strategy, even though many people use the terms interchangeably. A business model takes into account the basic assumptions for the business and is often designed around a value proposition. It is related to the organization's mission statement, which describes what the organization does. Lean production is an example where an organization's core processes are usually organized around customer value (see Chapter 5). The organization's core competences may be identified and defined in terms of how these core processes have to be managed to deliver the value customers expect. The core business processes are also important to strategic risk management, since the health of the business is critically dependent upon how the business model is managed.

Chesbrough and Rosenbloom, and also Teece, argue that the function of a business model is to 'articulate' the value proposition, select the appropriate technologies and features, identify target market segments, define the **structure** of the value chain, and estimate the cost structure and profit potential[11]. Teece, in particular, writes that the design of business models is as fundamental as the development and adoption of physical technologies, since they depend upon each other for success: 'Business models implicate processes and incentives; their alignment with the physical technology is a much overlooked component of strategic management. The understanding of the institutional/organizational design issues is typically more limited than the understanding of the technologies themselves.'[12] Magretta makes the point

KEY DEBATE 6.1

Do straddler and hybrid strategies work?

Porter argues that organizations should choose only one of the generic strategies, and avoid becoming a straddler and hybrid strategy. There is no broad empirical consensus that the pursuit of a pure business strategy does result in a superior performance. However, Stewart Thornhill and Roderick White, in a study of 2351 businesses, report that there is a significant positive relationship between the purity of strategy and performance.[27]

This is unlikely to still the critics. Teece questions whether a static position can shield an organization from competition. He argues that market structure is determined by the competing organizations themselves and he advocates that organizations should build a dynamic capability to build strategic resources.[28]

Miller and Dess suggest that if one looks beneath the surface of a generic strategy, its methods of implementation and execution are diverse: it is not so much the choice of the generic strategy that is important as is how activities complement and reinforce each other.[29] Campbell-Hunt, on the other hand, finds the opposite: it is the choice of a strategy, rather than its detail, that really matters.[30]

Question: What do you consider to be the main strengths and weaknesses of Porter's ideas about generic strategy?

that a business model should reflect systems thinking about how all the elements of a business fit together, and should not factor in only one critical dimension of performance, such as competition.[13]

FedEx's business model is based on the idea that the fastest, cheapest way of delivering parcels is to fly

them to a central hub. There they can be sorted, put on different aircraft and transported with others sharing similar destinations. Fred Smith, the founder of FedEx, speaking about his 'hub-and-spokes model', recalled his systems thinking – 'I simply used a mathematical formula about how to connect a lot of points to a lot of other points ... If you take [*a*] transaction out of the aggregate, it looks very inefficient ... Take the aggregate out of all of them, rather than 9900 couriers connecting 100 points, you have 99. It's more efficient by a factor of 100.'[14]

George Yip makes a distinction between a 'strategy' and a 'business model'[15]. The former, he argues, should be used to change the underlying business model. We think it is important that strategic management should involve both the management of the organization's business model and the overall strategy. The former is essentially about controlling the health of the business to make sure it is fit for purpose, while the strategy concerns the management of strategic change that will take the organization forward. You cannot consider one without the other.

Yip suggests strategy relates to those dynamic activities that are used to change either a market or a competitive position, while a business model is comprised of elements that make up a static position. He asserts that most of the examples used by Porter and other strategy writers tend to describe static business models, in the sense that they are stable and their management reinforces the sustainability of the strategy. This is confusing a business model with a stable strategy. An overall strategy should be relatively stable over time; otherwise the strategy will lack discipline and the opportunity for sustaining a competitive position is difficult. This is clear when we consider strategy activity mapping.

Strategy activity maps

Michael Porter has consistently seen his ideas as an **activity-based view of strategy**, arguing that activities 'are narrower than traditional functions such as marketing or R&D and are what generate cost and create value for buyers; they are the basic units of competitive advantage'.[16] He argues that much of the thinking associated with modern management, especially about 'processes' (a term he sees as a synonym for activities) is about how strategically-relevant activities cut across functional units.

Porter gives a visual representation, which he calls a 'strategy activity map', for the American carrier, Southwest Airlines, and IKEA, to show how an organization's activities are tailored to deliver a competitive advantage.[17] (Note that this is *not* the same as a strategy map: see Chapter 3. An example of a strategy activity map is given for Ryanair in Case 6, at the end of this chapter.) The tighter a degree of activity fit, the more likely it is that the organization concerned will lock out its competitors, making it difficult not only to emulate, but also to understand its competitive advantage. An inter-locking array of activities makes it difficult for a rival to get any equivalent benefit from imitation unless they can match the whole system successfully.

PRINCIPLES IN PRACTICE 6.1

The easyGroup business model

The speed and flexibility of the Internet allows customers of the easyGroup of companies to take advantage of dynamic pricing, when prices are adjusted to match demand, with the best deals offered to advance bookers and off-peak users. EasyGroup has a number of different businesses in entertainment, leisure and travel, but all of them have the following features.[24]

- A clear value proposition: The 'easy' concept brings cheap and efficient services to the mass public.
- Standard resources: Only one type of aircraft, the Boeing 737, while the easyCar car fleet has just two or three car models.
- A common, pervasive technology, the Internet: Most customers book online, creating strong brand awareness.
- Simple outputs: Offer no-frills and stripped-down services.
- A common type of customer: Most easyGroup customers are young, urban and hip (or think of themselves that way), with more time than money.

Question: The easyJet business is often thought of as a budget airline. Does it have a cost-based (leadership or focus) or a differentiation (whole industry or focus) generic strategy?

Generic strategy guides managers in their choices of activities. This requires discipline. It is not possible, for example, to do everything or meet every need a customer expresses, without eventually blurring the organization's distinct positioning by becoming all things to all customers. The essence of a generic strategy is in choosing to perform activities differently, or to perform different activities from competitors. Porter observes for IKEA that it targets young furniture buyers who want style at low cost; what turns this into a strategic position is the company's tailored set of activities that makes it work.

Strategies require decisions that involve **trade-offs** between strategically incompatible activities. A trade-off occurs when doing more of one activity necessitates less of doing others. For example, a budget retailer may seek to emulate an up-market rival by extending its customer services; however, this is likely to increase pressure on prices, and may work to blur the perceived difference customers have of the two retailers. An organization's competitive advantage comes from the way activities fit together and reinforce one another. A generic strategy brings stability and should be chosen for the longer-term, which is for at least a decade or more, since it takes time to build an organization's competitive position, and the capabilities and skills needed to manage it. Porter emphasizes the role of senior management:

> *General management is more than the stewardship of individual functions. Its core is strategy: defining and communicating the company's unique position, making trade-offs and forging fit among activities... Managers at lower levels lack the perspective and the confidence to maintain a strategy. There will be constant pressures to compromise, relax trade-offs, and emulate rivals. One of the leader's jobs is to teach others in the organization about strategy – and to say no. Strategy renders choices about what not to do as important as choices about what to do ... Thus strategy requires constant discipline and clear communication. Indeed, one of the most important functions of an explicit, communicated strategy is to guide employees in making choices that arise because of trade-offs in their individual activities and in day-to-day decisions.*[18]

Complementarities

Work by economists, Peter Milgrom and David Roberts, has been influential in emphasizing the part played by **complementarities** in strategic management.[19] An activity is complementary when doing more of it increases the returns to doing more of another. This is a view of thinking about strategy as a complementary set of activities that reinforce each other as a complex set of inter-relationships.

Practices that are mutually complementary tend to be adopted together. When Xerox Corporation developed a strategy to become 'the document company', in order to meet its customers' requirements for managing office documents, it improved its multi-skilling capabilities, and the improvement it brought in terms of service reliability made it more attractive to the company to introduce a comprehensive customer satisfaction guarantee. Complementarity can also extend beyond the boundaries of the organization and may be used to develop markets. For example, Intel, the manufacturer of microprocessors, encouraged other companies to come up with products to open new end-markets, which would incorporate the Intel chip.[20]

The principle behind effective complementarity is organizational synergy: the management of the whole must be greater than the sum of the management of its parts. The idea that organizational practices should be mutually reinforcing is basic to the reasons for having an organization in the first place.

Prospectors, analysers, defenders and reactors

In their influential 1978 book, *Organization Strategy, Structure, and Process,* Raymond E. Miles and

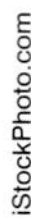

One of the leader's jobs is to teach others in the organization about strategy – and to say no. Strategy renders choices about what not to do as important as choices about what to do ... Thus strategy requires constant discipline and clear communication. Indeed, one of the most important functions of an explicit, communicated strategy is to guide employees in making choices that arise because of trade-offs in their individual activities and in day-to-day decisions.

Charles C. Snow, argue that strategy comes about from how organizations decide to address three fundamental problems.[21] The first is the entrepreneurial issue of how to choose a general and a target market; the second concerns an engineering issue of how to decide the most appropriate means to make and offer products and services and the third is about the administrative issue of how to organize and manage the work. They suggest there are four distinct types of organizations: prospectors, analysers, defenders and reactors. This is commonly known as the Miles and Snow Typology.

Prospector organizations put an emphasis on new opportunities and choosing the right products and services, so that the organization's growth comes through the development of new markets. These organizations use a variety of technologies and are characterized by flexibility: co-ordination and facilitation are important, and the nature of planning is broad and sensitive to external changes. Prospectors are likely to be first-movers: for example, Amazon.com was the first major online bookstore. It established an early lead over later entrants, which it has continued to hold. The traditional booksellers could have been much more powerful rivals if they had become online book sellers earlier. The Amazon success has provided a foundation for moves into other markets.

Defender organizations target a narrow market and concentrate mainly on the engineering issue of how to produce products and services to deliver value. They seek improvement in what they do, concentrating on core technologies, where control is relatively centralized and sensitive to internal conditions; such organizations are more functionally-based with finance and production dominant. In China, state-owned organizations have tended to adopt defender strategies.[22]

Analyser organizations are a combination of these two strategies. They avoid excessive risks, but hope to do well in the delivery of new products and service. These are represented by the larger companies, which cover a variety of markets and industries. In China these may be organizations that are foreign-owned.[23]

Reactor organizations respond to change in ways that are inconsistent and inappropriate; typically the reason is a mismatch in the management of the three issues. They often have little control over their external environment.

Miles and Snow argue that an organization's strategy, structure and processes should be consistent, although different strategies can be used by a single organization for different projects. In fact they suggest that no single strategy is best, but what determines the ultimate success of an organization is the fact of establishing and sustaining a systematic strategy that takes into account the organization's environment, technology and structure. In other words, pick a strategy and stick to it. The Miles and Snow model remains an attractive scheme for scholars who are interested in typologies or the study and interpretation of types. On the whole, research tends to confirm the general

PRINCIPLES IN PRACTICE 6.2

Strategy at Whole Foods Market

Founded as a small store in Austin, Texas, Whole Foods Market now claims to be the world's largest retailer of natural and organic foods with more than 270 stores.[25]

Whole Foods Market's strategy is focused on differentiation. Its products are 'unadulterated by artificial additives, sweeteners, colourings and preservatives', and the company aims to give an 'extraordinary customer service'.

Its employees are 'passionate about food'. They are 'well rounded human beings' who are expected to be involved in community service work, neighbourhood events and the work of non-profit organizations. In particular, the company aims to educate its customers and gain their loyalty on the basis of their knowledge about natural and organic foods, health, nutrition and the environment.

Whole Foods Market is still focused only on parts of the North American and the United Kingdom retail food industry. Its focus is on natural produce and so its costs require the company to charge premium prices. The extra costs take in those other unusual activities, which are carried out to an extent that is unusual, such as its community service work.

Many supermarket chains offer organic produce and participate to some extent in neighbourhood projects, but Whole Foods Market makes these central to what it does in ways that are impossible for the larger retailers.

Unlike its rivals, Whole Foods Market tailors its activities to sustain a perception among its customers that 'whole foods' are desirable for community and whole earth reasons.

Question: Is WFM's differentiation strategy an industry-wide, or a focused one?

idea and the terms, prospector, analyser, defender and reactors have common usage in the strategy literature.

End-note

This chapter has been about strategy at a single business level. This may apply to a single business, or to a business division, such as a company that is part of a larger corporation. Porter's generic strategies in particular apply to a single industry or market, where a specific approach is required to position the organization against its rivals. Business strategy can be used for a large corporation as a whole, but in this case, the organization is typically operating in a single (typically international) industry. The next chapter considers the multi-business organization.

PRINCIPLES IN PRACTICE 6.3

A strategy is creeping up on Twitter

Twitter is a service run by a Silicon Valley company of around 30 employees. It was started in 2006 and since late 2008 it has shown signs of becoming very popular. The service is used to broadcast short messages (of no more than 140 characters) about what people are currently doing, their moods and thoughts. The messages are mostly one-liners. The service could one day become as popular as blogging and social networking.

Twitter users post short messages, called tweets, either from a personal computer or a cell (mobile) phone. They are made public although they can be limited to a select few. The people who read them are called followers.

© Steven May/Alamy

© AP Photo/Jeff Chiu

Birds of a feather: Evan Williams and Biz Stone, founders of Twitter

The messages that followers find interesting can be retweeted and broadcast to friends. A stream of messages becomes available, whether from friends or a large group that has celebrities, politicians and so on. All messages are received on an equal footing, are received in real time and can also be searched.

There is a lot of interest from possible investors, and Twitter has already received $35 million. But the service has no income yet, nor does it seem to have a picture of what it will be in the future – it is a strategy of 'build it, and it will come'.

Biz Stone, a co-founder, says Twitter will never charge a fee for its basic service, although it has considered charging business users for extra functions. Many think that if it develops as a mass medium, the service is likely to provide a platform for related products and advertising that existing social networking services like YouTube and Facebook have provided. The Internet barriers to entry are low so new competition is possible. But it is also possible that tweeting will just be a passing craze.[26]

Question: Would complementarities require a certain kind of generic strategy to be successful?

SUMMARY OF PRINCIPLES

1 There are two sources of competitive advantage: lower costs and differentiation.

2 Generic strategy is based on sources of competitive advantage and scope.

3 Organizations must choose and sustain only one of the four generic strategies: cost leadership, differentiation, cost focus, and differentiation focus.

4 With generic strategy it is possible to vary strategy providing the activities that sustain strategy keep within the four groups.

5 The value chain is used to co-ordinate and optimize organizational activities so that they reinforce the chosen strategy.

6 Both an organization's business model and its strategy should be managed together as an integrated part of the strategic management process.

7 Strategy involves making trade-offs and is as much about what not to do, as it about what to do.

GLOSSARY OF KEY TERMS

activity-based view of strategy a view that strategically-relevant (typically cross-functional) activities should be tailored to sustain strategy.

Best-cost differentiation hybrid generic strategy a customer-satisfaction-based strategy that meets expectations on key product and service attributes, while exceeding their expectations on price.

Business-level strategy the organization's fundamental strategic choice of what approach to adopt to achieve its competitive advantage from the given options at the business unit level.

Complementarities activities where doing more of them increases the returns to doing other activities.

Cost-leadership generic strategy a cost-based strategy that involves having a lead in terms of lower costs per unit produced than the rest of the participants in the industry.

Differentiation industry-wide generic strategy a strategy based on having unique, or different, product and service attributes, which other organizations in the industry do not have, and which generates returns that more than offset the costs of differentiation.

Focus generic strategy strategy based on a particular part of an industry, such as a market segment or niche; this is based on either low cost or differentiation.

Generic strategy a type of strategy to achieve a competitive advantage that is based either on cost or differentiation.

Straddler an organization that competes on both sources of competitive advantage: cost and differentiation.

structure the organization of effort into a coherent and working entity.

Trade-off choosing to do one activity that involves a reduced ability to do another activity.

GUIDED FURTHER READING

A business model is sometimes described as a unique dynamic capability. Makadok gives examples as the yield management system of American Airlines, Wal-Mart's docking system, Dell's logistics system and Nike's marketing capacity.

Makadok, R. (2001) 'Towards a synthesis of resource-based and dynamic capability views of rent creation', *Strategic Management Journal* 22(5):387–402.

REVIEW QUESTIONS

1 What are the sources of competitive advantage?

2 What is meant by leadership in a cost leadership generic strategy?

3 Why are generic strategies mutually exclusive?

4 What is a hybrid strategy?

5 Why were the Japanese successful?

6 Why should a value chain differ for different generic strategies?

7 How is a strategy activity map different from the strategy map (see Chapter 3)?

8 What are complementarities?

9 What are trade-offs?

SEMINAR AND ASSIGNMENT QUESTIONS

1 Compare four organizations that use cost-leadership, differentiation, cost focus and differentiation focus, generic strategies. Consider in each case how each organization holds its competitive position in its industry in relation to its main competitor.

2 Sketch out value chains for the organizations you used in question 1 above.

3 Use a strategy activity map to sketch out the linkages between the important activities at your college, or university, that sustain your institution's overall strategy.

CHAPTER REFERENCES

1 de Holan, P. M. (2004) 'Management as life's essence: 30 years of the "Nature of Managerial Work" ', an interview with Henry Mintzberg, *Strategic Organization* 2(2):205–12, 208.

2 Porter, M. E. (1996)' What is strategy?', *Harvard Business Review,* November–December:61–78, 65.

3 Borwn-Humes, C. (2003) 'An empire built on a flat-pack, an interview with A. Dahlvig', *Financial Times,* November 24,12.

4 Porter, M. E. (1985) *Competitive Advantage: Creating and Sustaining Superior Performance,* New York: Free Press, p. 3.

5 Adapted from Porter (1985), *op cit.* p. 12.

6 Henderson, B. D. (1974) 'The experience curve reviewed, II. History', *Perspectives,* The Boston Consulting Group; and 'The experience curve reviewed, III: Why does it work?', *Perspectives,* The Boston Consulting Group, www.bcg.com

7 Porter (1985) *op cit.* p. 12.

8 Treacy, M. and Wiersema, F. (1995) *The Discipline of Market Leaders: Choose Your Customers, Narrow Your Focus, Dominate Your Market,* Reading, MA: Addison-Wesley.

9 Moore, M. H. (1995) *Creating Public Value: Strategic Management in Government*, Boston: Harvard University Press.

10 Drucker, P. F. (1997) *Managing in a Time of Great Change,* Oxford: Butterworth-Heinemann.

11 Chesbrough, H. and Rosenbloom, R. S. (2002) 'The role of the business model in capturing value from innovation: evidence from Xerox Corporation's technology', *Industrial and Corporate Change* 11(3):529–55.

12 Teece, D. C. (2007) 'Explicating dynamic capabilities: the nature and microfoundations of (sustainable) enterprise performance', *Strategic Management Journal* 28:1319–350, 1327.

13 Magretta, J. (2002) 'Why business models matter', *Harvard Business Review,* May:86–92.

14 Baer, J. and Guerrera, F. (2007) 'The man who reinvented the wheel', *Financial Times* December 3,18.

15 Yip, G. S. (2004) 'Using strategy to change your business model', *Business Strategy Review* 15(2):17–24.

16 Porter, M. E. (2004) *Competitive Advantage* (export edn), London: Free Press, p. xv.

17 Porter (1996) *op cit.*

18 Porter, M. E., Takeuchi, H. and Sakakibara, M. (2000) *Can Japan Compete?* London: Macmillan, p. 77.

19 Milgrom, P. and Roberts, J. (1995) 'Complementarities and fit: strategy and organizational change in manufacturing', *Journal of Accounting and Economics* 19(2/3):179–208.

20 Gawer, A. and Henderson, R. (2007) 'Platform owner entry and innovation in complementary markets: evidence from Intel', *Journal of Economics & Management Strategy* 16(1):1–34.

21 Miles, R. E. and Snow, C. C. (1978) *Organizational Strategy, Structure and Process,* London: McGraw-Hill.

22 Peng, N. M., Tan, J. and Tong, T. W. (2004) 'Ownership types and strategic groups in emerging economies', *The Journal of Management Studies,* 41:1105–129.

23 Peng *et al.* (2004) *op cit.*

24 Delbridge, R., Gratton, L. and Johnson, G. (2006) *The Exceptional Manager,* Oxford: Oxford University Press.

25 Whole Foods Market (2008) *Welcome to Whole Foods Market*, www.wholefoodsmarket.com

26 Waters, R. (2009) 'Sweet to tweet', *Financial Times,* February 27, 10.

27 Thornhill, S. and White, R. E. (2007) 'Strategic purity: a multi-industry evaluation of pure vs hybrid business strategies', *Strategic Management Journal* 28:553–61.

28 Teece, D. C. (2007) 'Explicating dynamic capabilities: the nature and microfoundations of (sustainable) enterprise performance', *Strategic Management Journal* 28:1319–350.

29 Miller, A. and Dess, G. (1993) 'Assessing Porter's 1980 model in terms of its generalizability, accuracy and simplicity', *Journal of Management Studies* 30(4):553–85.

30 Campbell-Hunt, C. (2000) 'What have we learned about generic competitive strategy? A meta-analysis', *Strategic Management Journal* 21:127–54.

CASE 6.1 Ryanair's Strategy

Ryanair is an Irish-owned and European-based short haul airline. Growth of the company has been spectacular – it was founded by Tony Ryan in 1985 and in 2008 it was operating in 26 countries and carried around 22m passengers over 730 routes.

During its early years, Ryanair was unable to turn rapidly rising passenger numbers into profits. Ryan brought in his personal assistant, Michael O'Leary, an accountant, to investigate the airline's problems. 'Scrabbling through the undergrowth of the company, O'Leary started to work out where the money was flowing to, and how it could be saved. He had yet to formulate the rigorous business model that would transform Ryanair into the leanest and most profitable airline in the world, but he could identify waste and he could identify ways of doing business more cheaply'.[1]

It took him about two years to work out where the money was going, and at one point, he was pessimistic enough to suggest to Ryan that the company should be sold. In the end O'Leary became CEO and saved the company.

Two things stand out about O'Leary's strategic management: (1) a cost-based strategy, which is used as a discipline to focus everybody (including customers) on Ryanair's competitive advantage; and (2) a set of business activities, or business model, that is consistent with, and sustains, this strategy.

O'Leary always attributed Ryanair's success to its 'simple' business model. 'We have the lowest cost base of any airline in Europe. Business is simple. You buy it for this, you sell it for that, and the bit in the middle is ultimately your profit or loss. We have low-cost aircraft, low-cost airport deals, we don't provide frills, we pay travel agents less [*than other airlines*], our people are well paid but work hard and we deal in efficiencies.' Other airlines were failing to implement the same formula with success because, he said, 'nobody else has our discipline'.[2]

According to O'Leary strategy is about focus and discipline ... It was not, he says, about saving paper clips but about instilling discipline. 'It's the decision that one guy down in operations can make on one Friday evening on leasing in an aircraft that can cost you £10 000 or £20 000 at a stroke,' he says. 'It's those decisions that we have to clarify and clear up in people's minds'.[3]

'If Ryanair could have lower costs than anyone else, it could also have lower prices. And if prices were low enough, it could fill seats on almost any route ... led Mr O'Leary to three further conclusions. The first was to increase capacity relentlessly, even during downturns in a notoriously cyclical industry. The second was that there are all manner of ways of wringing money from the business other than selling tickets. Passengers were not only captive customers for food and drink but, from Ryanair.com, they could be sold car hire, insurance, hotel bookings and airport transfers. The third was that those marginal, out-of-the-way airports would pay Ryanair to bring them passengers.'[4]

If these three 'conclusions' can be thought about as strategic themes it is possible to illustrate how these link Ryanair's key activities by using Porter's activity map (see Exhibit 6.1). The three themes are the emboldened circles, and the other circles are the

© Tupungato/Dreamstime.com

AP Photo/Peter Morrison

Michael O'Leary

supporting activities. Ryanair seeks to increase its profits not only simply by saving costs, but also by raising ancillary revenue, achieving favourable conditions at airports, and maximizing the number of passengers.

Dynamic pricing

Fares vary according to purchase dates. Around 70 per cent of passengers get low fares for early booking, but late bookings are expensive. A dynamic pricing system allows Ryanair to price up to its rivals when they raise their prices, and also offer relatively low prices when it is necessary to gain market share. This process is facilitated by the absence of travel agents and the ability of Ryanair through its website to react immediately to prevailing market conditions. There are no special programmes such as a frequent flyer programme and penalties for 'no show' passengers. However, there is no airline policy of over-booking and so there is no risk to the passenger of missing the flight.

Promotion

This is low cost promotion, with the same simple message of cheap fares. Its advertising is often controversial, involving attention-grabbing issues. The emphasis is on promotions that advertise special deals, discounts via the web, and email advertisements. Ryanair has an uncompromising corporate image – cheap, but no concessions. Ryanair has a history of bad publicity, such as charging for wheelchairs and uncompensated damage to baggage. Many of these incidents are trivial cost concerns, but they reinforce the company's image that Ryanair is cheap, and offers no concessions. The company's

EXHIBIT 6.1 Ryanair's activity mapping system

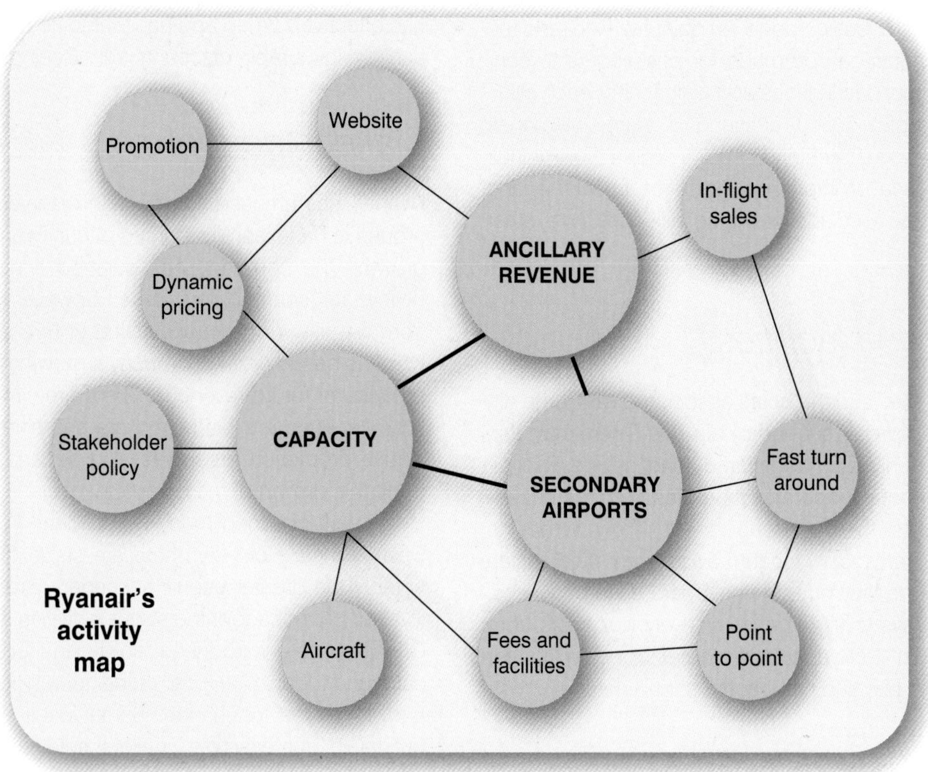

aggression also makes it seem a formidable competitor and negotiator. O'Leary likes to project himself as the underdog scrapping for a fair chance to take on the big guys. That sense of smallness, of being an entrepreneurial company in a world of state-owned or recently privatized behemoths, is critical to the company's cost conscious culture and low fares corporate image.

Website

No travel agents are used to sell tickets and there are no Ryanair retail ticket outlets. Passengers have to book their flights through the company's website. This saves on the costs of using travel agents and gives Ryanair an immediate flexibility to adjust prices as needed. In September 2007, the airline ended its on-line booking fee (although there is a significant credit card charge), and introduced extra charges for passengers choosing to use the check-in facilities at the airport (travellers with limited mobility, or who are visually impaired, families with infants, and groups of more than nine, must check-in). Passengers are encouraged to check flights and print boarding passes from the website. The website is also used to raise ancillary revenue, such as hotel accommodation, car hire and insurance.

In-flight sales

Ryanair does not offer in-flight free services such as free sweets, newspapers, food and beverages. This, and the sale of on-board items, such as insurance, adds to revenue. Passengers have to pay for in-flight services and this reduces the quantity of items and helps to simplify cleaning and speed up turnaround.

Point to point

Ryanair is a basic, point to point service and no arrangements can be made for passengers to connect to other destinations and airlines. For each additional leg of a journey passengers must collect their bags, clear customs and check in again. For Ryanair the absence of interlining simplifies check-ins and avoids any need for interlining alliances with other airlines.

Fees and facilities

Landing fees and the costs associated with large airports are lower at secondary airports. There may also be opportunities for negotiated concessions. Ryanair believes that if it operates its routes from the cheapest airports, then passengers will follow. While the airports are typically located away from major urban destinations they offer to customers ease of access, fewer delays to flights and relatively low costs from congestion. To Ryanair this creates opportunities for deals with bus and hire-car firms, and hotels.

Fast turnaround

Check-in is kept simple and there are no seat allocations. The relative lack of congestion and delay at secondary airports, and their smaller size, which enables passengers to walk directly on to their planes, helps to speed up Ryanair's aircraft turnaround time. This is typically under 25 minutes and compares very favourably with about one hour for the major airlines using large airports. O'Leary is very clear about the advantage: 'We can fly six aircraft a day where Aer Lingus or British Airways could fly four...Where they get six in the air, we fly eight. So we're 20–25 per cent more efficient from the very start. It's so simple a four-year-old could work it out.'[5]

Aircraft

Ryanair uses one class of plane: the Boeing 737-800, and accommodates only the ordinary traveller (there is no business class), which facilitates more seats per aircraft and a higher load factor. The single plane means that staff training time and maintenance costs are simplified. It is also believed that Ryanair has effectively timed and negotiated its purchases to achieve favourable discounts from Boeing.

Stakeholder policy

Ryanair has amassed large cash reserves, which it argues is necessary to pursue capacity and organic growth. The company has pursued a no-dividend policy; its shareholders have, however, benefited from the rise in the capital value of Ryanair shares, which is based on the company's growth record and promise of future revenues. There are similar incentives for Ryanair's staff, who are shareholders, and whose promotion prospects also depend upon the profitable growth of the company.

O'Leary obtained many of his ideas from Southwest Airlines. However, there are some differences, notably the greater use of secondary airports. Also, Ryanair did not adopt the above activities all at once. Changes were introduced slowly and opportunistically, and today's low-cost model took time to evolve and continues to change. Some ideas were tried, but failed: for example, in-flight entertainment was announced at the end of 2004, but was soon abandoned when it was found passengers would not pay over short flights. The Ryanair offer is not a low quality one in the sense that its service represents low customer value; rather it is a choice of high fares and a full flight service of the traditional airline, against a no-frills service and low fares offered by the low-cost model.

Discussion questions

1. O'Leary describes his business model and strategy. Do you agree with O'Leary's description of these concepts, and what kind of generic strategy is he following?
2. Is Ryanair really very different from easyJet and the other low budget airlines competing with Ryanair in the European market? What is the company's competitive advantage?
3. Compose a value chain for Ryanair. Note the differences from Ryanair's strategy activity map. How might the two tools be used to fulfil different roles in the airline's strategic management?

Case references

1 Ruddock, A. (2007) *Michael O'Leary: A Life in Full Flight,* Dublin: Penguin, p. 75.

2 Ruddock (2007) *op cit.* p. 223.

3 Ruddock (2007) *op cit.* p. 75.

4 *Economist* (2007) 'Snarling all the way to the bank'. Review of Ruddock (2007) *Michael O'Leary: A Life in Full Flight,* Penguin, August 23.

5 Ruddock (2007) *op cit.* p. 223.

This case study was prepared using only publicly available sources of information for the purposes of classroom discussion; it does not intend to illustrate either effective or ineffective handling of a managerial situation.

Chapter 7
CORPORATE-LEVEL STRATEGY

Introduction

The previous chapter was about business-level strategy. This chapter considers the nature of **corporate-level strategy**: the strategy of organizations when they grow to a sufficient size to manage several businesses, or become a large business that operates in several markets, or a combination of these things. The primary focus is on a corporate centre's strategic management of a multi-divisional or multi-unit organization.

This chapter covers the growth of organizations through market development and mergers and acquisitions; it then explains different approaches to the strategic management of diversification and corporate parenting.

LEARNING OBJECTIVES

By the end of this chapter you should understand:

1 The definition of corporate-level strategy.

2 Product-market expansion.

3 Mergers and acquisitions.

4 Related and unrelated diversification.

5 The management of diversification through portfolio analysis and parenting.

Business vignette Corporations grow, given the opportunities facing them, but also because of the choices corporate management gives itself ...

In the late 1980s, Microsoft had a corporate commitment to the computer software industry. There was, however, strategic uncertainty about how best to compete in that space. And so the company pursued a number of different trajectories simultaneously. MS-DOS was their bread-and-butter product for both personal and corporate computing customers. Yet Microsoft was collaborating with IBM on the OS/2 graphical interface operating system, even as it was developing its own graphical Windows systems, while exploring a version of Unix, targeted at commercial markets. And on the applications front, the company was writing Excel and Word for the Apple OS.

This was not diversification designed to create a portfolio with uncorrelated fortunes and cash flows. Rather, it was a carefully constructed set of hedges, some of which could prove enormously useful to each other. Some of these strategic options, like OS/2, never ripened and were abandoned. Others, in particular the Windows OS and its complementarity with Word, Excel, and other applications, became the foundation of decades of profitability and industry dominance.

Today, Microsoft continues to build and manage a portfolio of strategic options. The Windows OS platform and Office applications suite are the company's current bread-and-butter, but strategic uncertainties abound. What will the next platform, or platforms, for personal computing be? Mobile devices? Game players? What about content, search, or online services? From the perspective of the corporate office, Microsoft's investments in Windows mobile, X-box, MSNBC and MSN can be seen as strategic options

Bill Gates

that create the ability, but not the obligation, to morph the OS division in a number of very different ways, depending on how the industry evolves over the next five to seven years, arguably the long term in this industry. The result is an ability to mitigate strategic risk in ways that the divisions, and shareholders, cannot replicate.

It would appear that … managers responsible for each of these product groupings – Windows Mobile, Xbox and MSN, for example – quite likely view the ventures they guide not as options but commitment. That is, each manager must choose how best to make the operation as successful as possible in the medium term – say, three to five years.[1]

Corporate synergy and corporate development

A concern for any organization, especially for an organization made up of multi-businesses like a large corporation, is how to manage strategically so that the different organizational parts work together effectively to achieve strategic purpose. Igor Ansoff explained **corporate synergy** as 'the "2+2 = 5 effect"' … the firm seeks a product-market posture with a combined performance that is greater than the sum of its parts'.[2] It is achieved through a simultaneously corporate-wide sharing of operational activities and resources and capabilities between the different corporate businesses, so that the value added of each individual business is enhanced. Synergy provides the rationale for the development of the organization. There are two broad types of strategy that are associated with corporate development (see Figure 7.1): growth, and multi-business strategy.

The product-market growth grid

Ansoff explains there are four main directions to take in developing an organization's markets and products; see his product-market growth grid, sometimes called the growth vector matrix (Figure 7.2).

Depending upon whether products and markets are new or not, four growth strategies are possible. The four distinctive positions are formed through different combinations of current and new products (represented by P) and markets (represented by μ): market penetration, market development, product development and diversification. The size of each of the four quartiles that make up Figure 7.2 symbolizes both the potential gain opportunities for that given option as well as the potential risk associated with it, the smallest being market penetration and the largest being diversification.

Market penetration

This involves using the existing product range to increase an organization's share of its existing markets. This is the least risky strategy of the four options. An organization, for example, should be able to understand its existing customers and be able to use existing activities to encourage them to buy more. Prospective customers, who may be currently buying a competing offer, or additional prospects that can be added through geographical extensions, for example, may also be encouraged.

Igor Ansoff explained corporate synergy as 'the '2+2 = 5 effect' … the firm seeks a product-market posture with a combined performance that is greater than the sum of its parts.

Market development

This strategy introduces an organization's existing products and services into new markets. The move into new areas usually requires good research and marketing strategy to provide an initial entry, target segments, and effective organizational learning about the new market. There are likely to be potential differences between existing and new markets.

FIGURE 7.1 Two broad types of strategy for corporate development

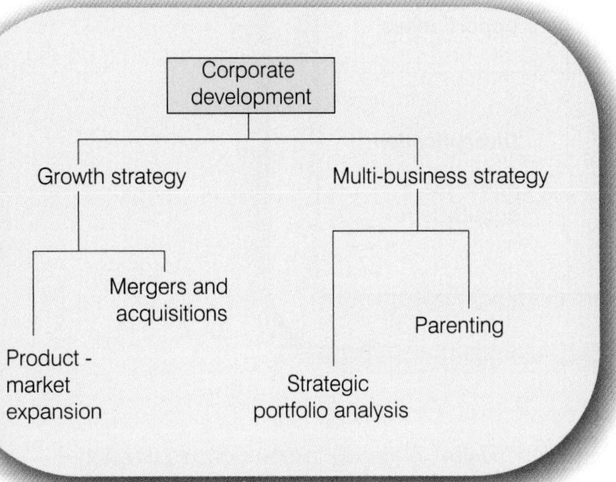

Product development

This strategy introduces new products and services into existing markets. Ideas for new products typically come from understanding the needs and behaviour of existing customers. The risk of new product failure can be minimized if innovation is piloted or developed with familiar customers.

Diversification

This strategy involves introducing new products and services into new markets. This is the riskiest option if the organization has to take time to develop new resources to understand its products and market. For large organizations that can command the backing of investors, mergers and acquisitions offer an opportunity by which to enter new markets and industries.

The American conglomerate, 3M, has built its reputation and grown through using innovation to develop new products and markets. It has four overall

FIGURE 7.2 The product-market growth grid[3]

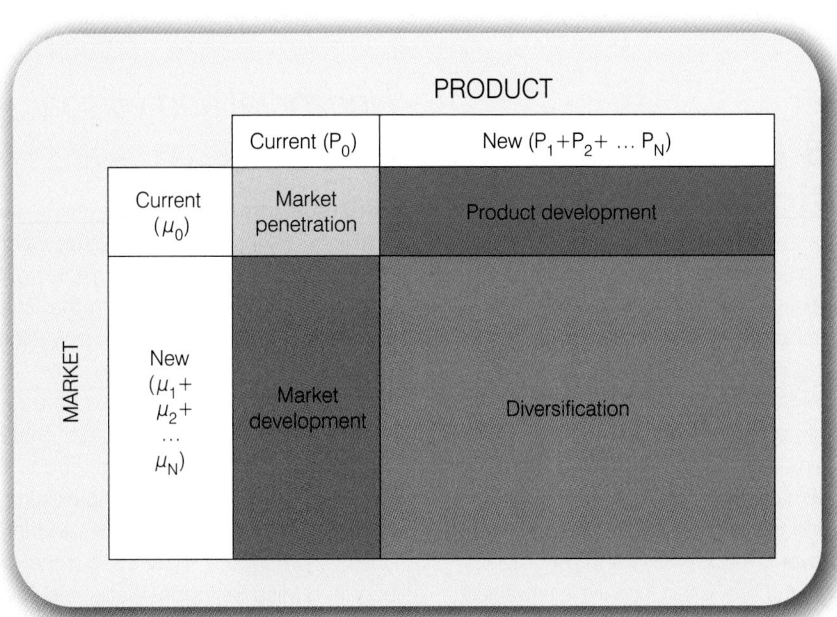

FIGURE 7.3 Corporate strategy at 3M[4]

MARKET \ PRODUCT	Current	New
Current	**Market penetration** Growing core business	**Product development** Emerging business opportunities
New	**Market development** World	***Diversification*** *Strategic acquisitions*

strategies; each of these corresponds to an Ansoff quartile (see Figure 7.3). 3M aims to continue expanding sales of its existing core products and will find new world markets for these. It is taking advantage of the opportunities offered by its research and development to develop new products. Finally, it will continue to diversify through acquisitions.

Mergers and acquisitions (M&A)

A **merger** is the agreement of two organizations to integrate their operations as a combined organization under a common ownership. A merger of equals is unusual, since one of the organizations is usually more dominant, and its management is likely to be favoured by post-merger negotiations and reorganization. An **acquisition** is when one organization buys a controlling interest in another, with the aim of creating a larger entity, or with a view to restructuring the acquired organization to re-sell at a profit. A **takeover** is made when the target organization has not sought the acquisition, and if it is unwanted, it is called 'hostile'. A friendly takeover occurs when the target's board of directors endorses the terms of the bid and recommends it as a desirable offer for the shareholders. The reasons for mergers and acquisitions are often about growth through integration. Organizations can benefit through horizontal and vertical forms of integration.

Horizontal and vertical integration

Horizontal integration occurs when an organization grows by taking over, or merging with, competitors, or organizations that offer complementary products and services. For example, in the United Kingdom, Sir Philip Green founded a new clothing retailing company, Arcadia Group, in 1997 out of the old Burton Group. Green revitalized the group by growing it horizontally to take a larger share of the clothing retail business on the high street. This has been done organically by developing existing brands, such as Dorothy Perkins and Evans, and introducing new ones, Topman and Topshop, but the group has also acquired Miss Selfridge, Wallis and Outfit.

KEY DEBATE 7.1

Can (should) organizations grow and grow?

Edith Penrose suggested there were limits to the growth of the firm.[22] It does not seem like it with the largest organizations. Companies such as General Electric, IBM, Microsoft, Toyota Motor and Wal-Mart Stores, earn around ten billion (US) dollars or more annually. Richard Foster and Sarah Kaplan in their book, *Creative Destruction*, argue that the growth of the large corporations is ending; this is largely because they lock-in fixed ways of doing things, and the assumption that success will continue deadens the sensitivity of senior managers to the need to accommodate change and adapt to new cultural philosophies.[23] In a similar view, Miller has suggested that success is susceptible to an Icarus paradox, where success leads to hubris and organizations over-reach themselves.[24] Success fuels growth but growth brings complexity and this can divert attention from the detail that was responsible for the success.

Industries may also come to the end of their life cycles if new technologies and markets emerge.[25] There are also the slings and arrows of competition and economic cycles and so on. It seems hard sometimes just to keep going.

Even so, many companies have been household names for over a century. Longevity may be because large organizations have more resources and can better adapt than other organizations. The German firm, Siemens, was founded in 1847 and continues to prosper in engineering. Of the top 30 companies that comprised the *Financial Times Stock Exchange Index* in 1947, 12 are still in today's list.

Question: How should senior managers manage very large organizations?

Vertical integration can move in two directions: forwards, when an organization expands its operations through parts of the distribution chain towards the ultimate customer, and backwards, through the supply chain towards the primary sources of supply. Backward vertical integration enables an organization to control some of the resources that are used as inputs in the production of its products and services. For example, Suzlon Energy, an Indian wind energy company, which started manufacturing wind turbines with just 20 employees, has now grown substantially to around 13 000 employees; it has started to develop manufacturing capabilities for all its critical components, which, in the words of Mr Tani, the company's founder, brings into play economies of scale, quality control, and assurance of supply.[6]

Forward vertical integration enables an organization to control the distribution centres and retailers where its products are sold. In 2006 Alliance UniChem, a pharmaceutical wholesaler, acquired the Boots Group, a UK-owned pharmaceutical retailer, to form Alliance Boots. This forward move up the supply chain enables Alliance to position itself as an industry leader with expertise in distributing brands in pharmacy-led health and beauty retailing, as well as in wholesaling.

In fact, the exact forms of horizontal and vertical integration vary. An organization's control of an industry's participants in a supply chain varies, not so much according to how much of a supplier it owns, as the influence it exerts through its purchasing power. This is often a preferred strategy if the organization wants to spread its risk over several suppliers. For example, the five competitive forces are important influences in the auto-industry for their conditioning of the nature and the extent to which a car manufacturing company can manage its supply chain in ways to be sure it gets the desired quality, just-in-time, from its primary suppliers.

The success and failure of M&A

In general, M&A activity is a fast way for an organization to increase its market power. This may be achieved through horizontal and vertical integration, especially if growth brings new knowledge, technologies, competencies and resources. It can take the acquiring organization into new markets and industries. M&A is classically associated with new and expanding industries and markets.

Vodafone, the mobile/cellular phone company, is a classic example. The company's M&A activity was a dash for growth during the de-regulation of national telecommunication services, and the expansion of the industry was spurred on by the emerging new technologies. The acquisitions included taking over Airtouch in the United States for £42.7 billion, and Mannesmann in Germany for £101 billion. However, Vodafone spent relatively little cash on its global expansion, less than £15 billion; the rest was raised through shares issues. The strategy had aimed to capture the mobile phone sector as it was going through rapid consumer growth. It coincided with a strong general rise in shares, which gave Vodafone 'an acquisition currency'. More recently, Vodafone's chief executive, Arun Sarin, has said, he 'inherited a company that was created out of a lot of M&A. There was no operating principle to the company.' Now this period is over, he says, 'Today this feels like a good well-run company'.[5] Does this mean that Vodafone was lucky?

Some companies in other sectors of telecommunications were not: notable failures included WorldCom and Marconi, which through a combination of bad timing, and perhaps some ill-thought-out

M&A ACTIVITY IS A FAST WAY FOR AN ORGANIZATION TO INCREASE ITS MARKET POWER. THIS MAY BE ACHIEVED THROUGH HORIZONTAL AND VERTICAL INTEGRATION, ESPECIALLY IF GROWTH BRINGS NEW KNOWLEDGE, TECHNOLOGIES, COMPETENCIES AND RESOURCES. IT CAN TAKE THE ACQUIRING ORGANIZATION INTO NEW MARKETS AND INDUSTRIES. M&A IS CLASSICALLY ASSOCIATED WITH NEW AND EXPANDING INDUSTRIES AND MARKETS.

KEY DEBATE 7.2

Does M&A work?

It can probably never be proved, but most people seem to think that most M&As fail. It is hard to know what that means since most of the large corporations have grown as much through M&A as through organic growth, where growth is generated internally.

Porter found in a study of corporations between 1950 and 1986 that a majority of them had divested more acquisitions than they had, in the end, integrated.[26] This may simply reflect an active use of strategic portfolio analysis. The notion that acquisitions, like jobs, are forever, is problematic. Many acquisitions involve re-structuring and the reselling of some or parts of the acquired organization is profitable for shareholders.[27]

When a very large organization merges with another, it is difficult to tell what 'success' means. Is not the size of the majority of today's large corporations due to M&A? The Hewlett-Packard/Compaq merger was undoubtedly painful for its first few years. Today, with H-P's process management and Compaq's PCs (and perhaps problems at Dell), things seem better. The truth may be that it takes years, rather than months, to achieve a high level of organizational synergy, especially in terms of organizational culture.[28]

Question: Is growing your organization a personal thing for some chief executives?

ambition, disappointed their shareholders and fell into bankruptcy. A major problem is the integration of the acquired company.

Acquisition integration

Success requires a clear strategy before an acquisition is completed. To achieve synergy the integration process needs to be prompt and decisive once the financial transaction is over. Without planned integration a company achieves little but financial diversification. A basic understanding of the acquired company is needed on the part of senior management and this is difficult. Some of the most successful mergers have been between companies with a previous history of partnerships such as through joint ventures or alliances (see Chapter 8).

A McKinsey study that followed the progress of 160 deals consummated in 1995 and 1996, found that only 12 per cent managed to accelerate sales growth in the three years after a merger.[7] The reason was that mergers typically create uncertainty. The top salespeople became recruitment targets for rivals, post-merger redundancies damage morale, and consumers are sensitive to signs that product or service quality is slipping. While cost cutting and rationalization boost profits and earnings for a short time, long-term progress is impossible if management is damaged or stagnates.

Philippe Haspeslagh and David Jemison offer a matrix for classifying integration approaches (see Figure 7.4).[8] This is based on the need for strategic interdependence after the merger, and the need for the acquired organization to have autonomy.

Strategic interdependence is conditioned by the need to create extra value from the acquisition. There are four main sources:

1 Sharing resources at the operating level.
2 Transfer of functional skills by moving people or sharing knowledge.

> **A McKinsey study that followed the progress of 160 deals consummated in 1995 and 1996, found that only 12 per cent managed to accelerate sales growth in the three years after a merger . The reason was that mergers typically create uncertainty.**

3 Transfer of management to improve control and insight.
4 Combined benefits created by leveraging resources, borrowing capacity, added purchasing power and greater market power.

Managers should not damage the value of the acquired organization and a judgement about the need for the degree of required organizational autonomy is necessary. This can be determined by asking three questions: (1) Is autonomy essential to preserve the strategic capability that was bought? (2) If so, how much autonomy should be allowed? (3) In which areas specifically is autonomy important?

Depending on whether strategic interdependence, and organizational autonomy, are low or high, the preferred acquisition approaches are (see Figure 7.4):

Absorption: the acquisition should be fully integrated into the organization.

Preservation: the focus should be to keep the source of the acquired benefits intact.

Symbiosis: integration should be gradual, while the existing boundary is maintained, it should be permeable.

Holding: no intention to integrate, advantages can from financial transfers, risk sharing, general management capability only.

FIGURE 7.4 Acquisition integration approaches[8]

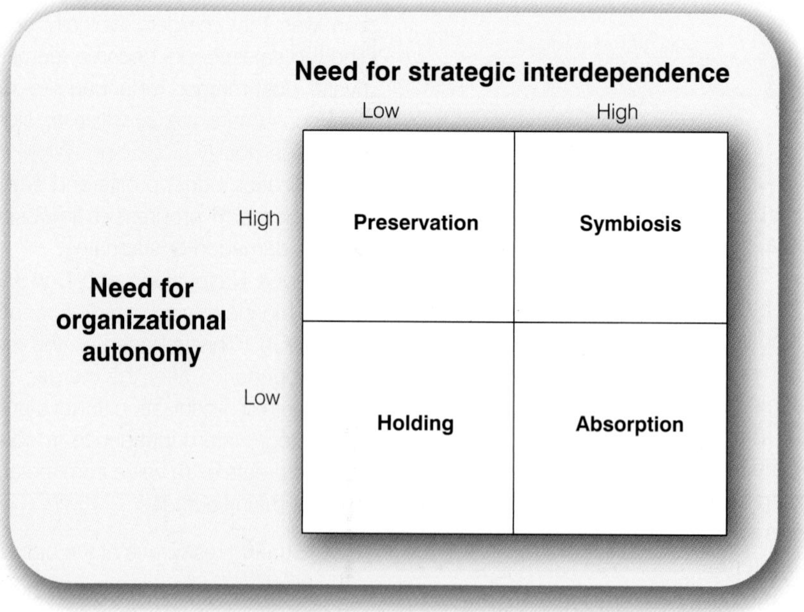

Need for organizational autonomy	Need for strategic interdependence: Low	Need for strategic interdependence: High
High	**Preservation**	**Symbiosis**
Low	**Holding**	**Absorption**

In recent years some important mergers have come to grief. Two of the most prominent were the breakup of the American-German car company, DaimlerChrysler, and the troubles and changes in senior management at the American-French telecoms equipment group, Alcatel-Lucent.[9] Jack Welch, an M&A master, emphasizes the importance of **'cultural fit'**, where the organizational culture of the acquisition should be compatible with that of the acquiring company (see organizational culture, Chapter 1). It is relatively easy, he writes, to evaluate strategic fit (and possibly also strategic interdependence) since most managers have the tools to assess whether two companies complement each other in geography, products, customers or technologies. But cultural fit is difficult because companies have unique and often very different ways of doing business:

> *I passed over deals on the west coast in the '90s because of my concerns about cultural fit ... The booming technology companies in California had their cultures – filled with chest thumping, bravado, and sky-high compensation. By contrast our operations in places like Cincinnati and Milwaukee were made up of hard working, down-to-earth engineers, most of whom were graduates of state universities in the Midwest. These engineers were every bit as good as the west coast talent, and they were paid less well but not outrageously. Frankly, I didn't want to pollute the healthy culture we had. Every deal affects the acquiring company's culture in some way, and you have to think about what is going in. The acquired company's culture can blend nicely with yours. That's the best case. Sometimes, a few of the acquired company's bad behaviours creep in and pollute what you've built. That's bad enough, but in the worst case, the acquired company's culture can fight yours all the way and delay the deal's value indefinitely.*[10]

PRINCIPLES IN PRACTICE 7.1

Integrating Compaq at Hewlett-Packard

Burgelman and McKinney argue that the Hewlett-Packard/Compaq merger had focused too much on operational integration at the expense of longer-term strategic integration:

'... the strategic integration process was not clearly recognized as a distinct one by top management... [*and*] resulted in insufficient top management attention to executing the multi-year strategic activities necessary to meet the longer-term goals.'

'[*The*] integration team's role was to work with the new company's Executive Committee members to agree on short-term and long-term goals, define exactly how the new organization and related decision-making would work, and to develop comprehensive plans required for the new company to successfully implement all aspects of the operational and strategic integration. Part of the integration planning team was chartered to prepare the go-to-market strategy for the new company and to start the development of the multi-year strategic initiatives related to the further development of HP's direct distribution model (to compete with Dell) and global accounts to solution delivery capability (to compete with IBM). Eventually over 1500 senior people became involved full-time with integration planning. The remainder of the 150 000 people of the two companies continued to compete with each other in the market place.'[20]

Working principles were devised to deal with post-merger issues as they emerged:

- 'Clean teams' – The managers who worked on the integration were removed from daily management to free up time and distance them from vested interests.
- 'Adopt and go' – Where practices differed, the best one was chosen regardless of whether it came from Hewlett-Packard or Compaq.
- 'Launch-and-learn' – The emphasis was given to taking action quickly, providing the activity concerned was good enough to close down a problem.
- 'Put the moose on the table' – Differences had to be brought where all concerned could see them, with an emphasis on reaching agreement quickly.
- 'Fast start' – A priority was placed on getting people to learn quickly about changes to reconcile these with the longer-term culture.

Question: Where does the H-P/Compaq merger fit into the acquisition integration approaches model?

Related and unrelated diversification

Diversification is when an organization is active in different types of business area. The degree of difference varies. For example, Citigroup is a large American company that offers many different products and services in distinct business areas, but these are nearly all in financial services. This form is called **related diversification**, since it typically offers up a strong degree of corporate synergy through corporate parenting. **Unrelated diversification**, on the other hand, involves an organization offering contrasting products and services in different markets and industries that have little or no similarities. Ansoff argued that unrelated diversification has risks associated with the unfamiliar. However, selling multiple products and services to different

KEY DEBATE 7.3

Is related better than unrelated diversification?

In their book about the growth of large American corporations, from the end of the nineteenth century to the global financial crisis of this century, brothers Kenneth and William Hopper argue that the move into unrelated businesses began when the senior managers of the corporations became professional managers.[29]

Managers become expert and mobile in the sense they believe they can manage any sort of business, without the necessary domain knowledge. The Hoppers blamed this on the rise of the business schools in the 1950s in America. In the early 1970s the large corporations began to diversify and strategic portfolio analysis became popular. Up to the early 1970s, the growth of the large corporations had been driven by internally financed investment; after that time, external borrowing became important and a greater emphasis was placed on the shorter-term performance of the corporate businesses.

The generally favoured response given to the work of Goold *et al.*[30] about parenting and the rise of Japanese competition, with organizations built around related diversification, saw a swing away from unrelated diversification.

Andrew Pettigrew and others suggest that European organizations have been narrowing their 'spheres of activity', toward a dominant business and a set of related businesses.[31] Even so, conglomerates, such as General Electric and the Virgin Group, continue to do well.

Question: Is it possible for a large company to grow without diversification?

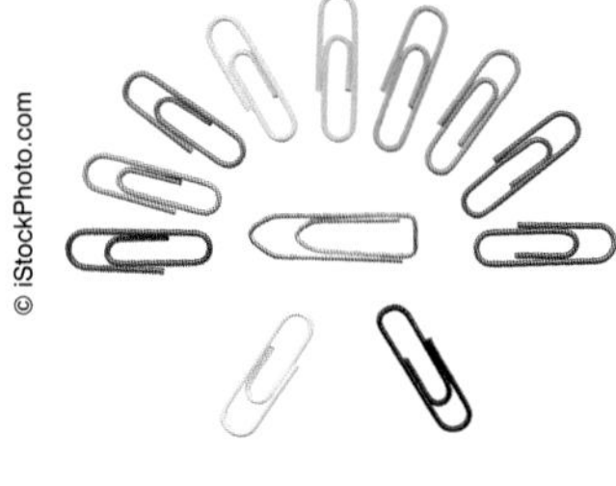

markets can potentially provide security by spreading the risk of market failure in any one industry. A frequently used term for an organization of this kind is a 'conglomerate'.

The middle of the twentieth century saw a strong growth in conglomerates when companies such as Litton Industries in the United States, and Hanson Industries in the United Kingdom, developed as corporate groups of autonomous operating companies, which seemed to offer little or no synergies. Many of these conglomerates added value for their financial stakeholders by imposing radical rationalization and aggressive management on the acquisitions; in its extreme form, this kind of M&A activity is known as asset stripping, when an acquired organization is broken up and its parts sold off.

In recent times, some important conglomerates have emerged in developing countries, where industrial groups had been encouraged by government policies that both limited foreign competition and encouraged indigenous economic development. In India, for example, many of these are long-established family firms, such as the 140-year old Tata group, which developed a range of diversified infrastructural-based businesses in India and has now become an important global corporation. Many of the world's largest corporations are American, and the greater proportion of these are diversified organizations. They are typically made of many separately organized large businesses. There are two main ways for managing these complex organizations: strategic portfolio analysis and corporate parenting.

Strategic portfolio analysis

Strategic portfolio analysis is used at a corporate level by executives and central management to appraise the performance of a portfolio of the corporate businesses. It is used primarily as a corporate framework to manage a group of corporate businesses as a single set of distinct investments. It is not meant to be a vehicle for analysing the internal management of the businesses, although it can be used to identify problem businesses, which may then lead to corporate interventions. The two best-known portfolio approaches are the Boston Consulting Group **growth-share matrix** (sometimes called the 'Boston Box'), and the **General Electric/McKinsey matrix** (otherwise known as the 'GE-McKinsey Screen').

The growth-share matrix

The growth-share matrix was introduced in 1970 by the Boston Consulting Group to group businesses by overall market growth and market share (see Figure 7.5). The principle is to review the performance of its businesses in an analogous way to a portfolio of investments. A balance of businesses is maintained where each is at a different stage of competitive power and growth. The individual businesses will then each have different investment needs and these are balanced by the centre in the interests of the corporation as a whole. The matrix is similar to the industry life cycle, which can be used in a similar way to fund the investment needs of the new and growing businesses (the businesses of the future), by transferring money from today's successful businesses (today's breadwinners).

The matrix is comprised of high and low relative positions of growth and market share. Market growth rate is ranged between 0 and 25 per cent, and relative market share (to competitors) is ranged between 0.2 × (20 per cent) and 2 × (200 per cent) on a logarithmic scale against the product or service's largest competitor (normally a rival). The size of the circles inside each quartile represents the extent to which a wise organization should invest in its products/services. Figure 7.5 indicates a balanced portfolio of investments – that being only a few small investments that are of low market share and growth, some medium-sized investments that are of high growth but still have low market share, and greater investment in those of high growth and low/high market share. These distinctive quartiles can then be represented diagrammatically (in the right half of Figure 7.5) through the use of the well-known business metaphors, 'cash cows', 'stars', 'question marks' and 'dogs'.

The stars and cash cows are businesses in industry leadership positions in expanding, and mature markets respectively. Question marks and dogs

FIGURE 7.5 The Boston Consulting Group's growth-share matrix[11]

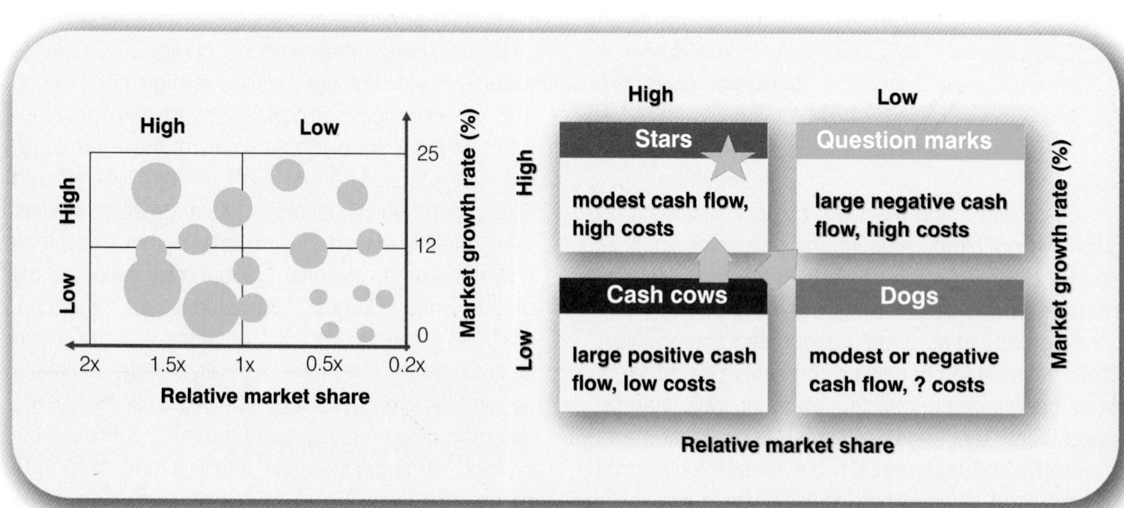

are in weak competitive positions in uncertain, and declining, markets respectively. Cash cows provide investment funds for stars and question mark businesses. Dogs should be divested.

Cash cow businesses

These have a high market share in a slow growing, typically mature, industry. They are likely to generate cash in excess of the amount needed to invest to maintain the health of the business. The excess cash can be milked off to provide investment funds for stars and question marks. Of course, the managements of cash cows may not be happy to have investment funds transferred from their business to another, especially if a local management is prevented from diversifying into new business itself. From the perspective of the corporate whole, however, the principle is that these generally slow-growing, but cash-rich, businesses should provide the investment necessary for the milk cows of the future.

Star businesses

These have a high market share and are in expanding markets. The expectation is that stars will become the cash cows of tomorrow. For the present, however, they are likely to require more funds than they can generate if their high growth rates are to translate into sustainable leadership positions. The principle is to grow star businesses as fast as possible by removing any resource constraints; for example, growing businesses typically need to add capacity ahead of demand.

©iStockPhoto.com

Question mark (or problem child) businesses

These have a low market share, but are in fast growing markets. A question mark business is sometimes called a problem child because typically it does not generate much cash and its future is uncertain. While a question mark has the potential to become a star, it is likely they will require a lot of cash, especially when a market begins to turn upwards. This is typically the commercialization stage of innovation, when the cost of R&D and market development becomes much more expensive. Corporations are typically involved in a number of promising, but unproven, businesses, where the corporate centre is essentially watching developments. At this stage, these may be relatively inexpensive, but the principle is to be prepared to move resources into expanding businesses, but at the same time, noting that caution is necessary as well.

Dog businesses

These have a low market share and are located in low-growth markets. While these may break even, they may not generate enough cash to maintain their present market share. If they add little value to the corporate whole, then they should be divested, or closed down. They are sometimes called pet businesses in that they have in the past contributed significantly to the success of the corporation, so that psychologically it can be

difficult to put them to sleep and close them down. Dogs may previously have been cash cows which enjoyed a loyal market which is now replaced by a new rival. The decision of whether or not to 'shoot the dog' is a difficult one. Even if it may only be marginally profitable or loss-making, it may still be prudent to keep it alive if the dog is: (1) a 'guard-dog', that blocks existing competition; (2) a 'guide-dog', that complements other activities; or (3) a 'sheep dog', that creates customers at the bottom of the product's range which may trade up to one of its better products later on. However, if dogs are products that originally built up a business, managers can be sentimental and reluctant to let 'pet' businesses die. The principle is that these businesses should be terminated as soon as conditions allow.

Strengths of the growth-share matrix

The advantage of a growth-share matrix is that it is a straightforward approach for identifying the most attractive corporate businesses into which to put cash. It helps senior managers to compare the businesses on their competiveness. Of course, cash flow is influenced by more than simply market share and industry growth and many external considerations are ignored that could have a significant impact upon decisions. Return-on-investment and the opportunity costs of not investing in new and alternative investments are not necessarily a consideration. The emphasis is on the internal competition for funds. However, the approach is not meant to be deterministic, and is only a framework to help guide decisions and as such it is useful for periodic reviews. The approach has been used for a long time, but its form is generally modified to suit a particular organization; an example is the General Electric /McKinsey matrix.

The General Electric/ McKinsey matrix

The GE/McKinsey matrix was developed in the 1970s by consultants McKinsey and Company, for General Electric. It was based on the Boston Box, but was designed to include more detail and to overcome some of the problems associated with the Boston Box. It therefore utilizes a nine-cell matrix, and instead of market share and market growth, it uses industry attractiveness and competitive strength (see Figure 7.6). The nine cells are grouped into three zones, and investment decisions are offered for each zone: zone 1, investment for further growth; zone 2, selective investment because of weakness; and zone 3, short-term gains only or pull out.

The factors that typically determine the market attractiveness of a business include variables such as market size, growth and profitability, pricing trends, the intensity of competition, the overall risk of return to the industry, entry barriers, the opportunity to differentiate products and services, variability in demand, the segmentation and distribution structure, and, lastly, the stage of technology development.

The factors that typically influence the competitive strength of a business include: strategic assets, competencies, relative brand strength, size and growth of market share, customer loyalty, relative cost structure and profit margins compared to competitors, distribution strength, capacity, ability to innovate and develop technology, quality, access to financial and other investment resources and management strength.

The sizes of circles plotted on the matrix represent market size; the sizes of circle segments represent the market share of the business. The arrows represent the expected direction and movement of a business in the future. The order of the stages of analysis are:

1 The specification of the drivers of each dimension.
2 Weight each driver to prioritize its relative importance.
3 Score each business on each driver.
4 Multiply weights by scores for each business.
5 View the resulting graph and interpret what it means.
6 Perform a sensitivity analysis (adjust weights and scores accordingly).

A strategic portfolio analysis helps corporate analysts to decide which businesses to develop, from which ones to draw funds to support development and which businesses should be divested or sold. However, if a corporate organization's businesses are unrelated and diversified, the corporate management may know very little about the nature of the work being

FIGURE 7.6 The GE/McKinsey matrix[12]

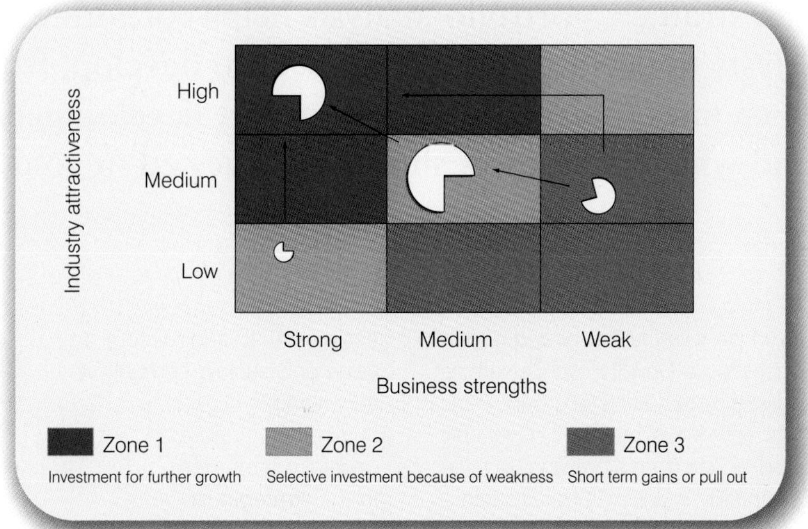

carried out. In this case corporations are really only collections of autonomous operating companies with no apparent corporate synergies, except financial transfers. From the level of a corporate perspective, it is the overall performance of a business that matters. The advantage to corporate strategic management is to reduce the risk of business cycles by investing in a diversified portfolio of businesses. Also, a spread of different businesses offers opportunities to cover a wide range of possibilities for growth in areas that could become the profitable industries of the future.

General Electric simplified the approach to make it more straightforward when Jack Welch began his term as chief executive, although he kept to its principles (see Case 7.1).

The strategic business unit (SBU)

When conglomerate organizations are structured into divisions that have a strong degree of strategic independence from the corporate centre, they are called **strategic business units** (SBUs). Each SBU has a general manager who is assisted by a staff that includes the functional heads working in the division; these are middle managers in the sense they report to senior executives at the corporate headquarters or centre. However, corporate executives are not directly involved with running the strategic management of the divisional businesses; instead, their role is to evaluate the performance of the divisions and to manage the overall allocation of resources.

SBUs are designed to stand alone within the corporate structure, and are typically single business-based enterprises, with perhaps their own business-level generic strategy, and distinctive organizational cultures and competencies. However, a corporate structure with SBUs can help facilitate a corporate-level portfolio approach, in that individual SBUs can be added or divested without any significant knock-on effects on the other SBUs in the portfolio. The investment and divestment of SBUs have helped some diversified corporations transform themselves from one type of industry to another.

For example, since the eighteenth century Whitbread had been a successful brewing company in the United Kingdom with its own estate of public houses. In 2001, it sold its alcoholic beverage-based businesses; the Whitbread beer brand is now managed by another company called InBev. Whitbread's present businesses include Premier Inn (hotels) and Costa Coffee, as well as several more restaurant businesses including Brewers Fayre and Beefeater. The brewing business was at best a cash cow that had started to bark and Whitbread saw the industry as unattractive. Since 2001 it has followed an active

A strategic portfolio analysis helps corporate analysts to decide which businesses to develop, from which ones to draw funds to support development, and which businesses should be divested or sold.

portfolio approach which saw the arrival and departure of such businesses as David Lloyd Leisure, a chain of fitness clubs; the Marriott Hotel group; Pizza Hut; and Britvic, its soft-drinks business. Over this short time Whitbread moved from a brewing, to a leisure, and now a hospitality, industry. It has worked a very successful corporate transformation, which continues through Whitbread's active management of its portfolio of separately-managed businesses.

Downscoping and strategic re-structuring

Downscoping is a divesture, spin-off, or some other means of eliminating businesses, which are unrelated or are not core to an organization's overall business or mission.[13] The aim is to refocus an organization on those activities that are central, a principle described by Tom Peters and Robert Waterman as 'sticking to the knitting': organizations should concentrate on those activities that add directly to value and sustain competitive advantage.[14]

© Photolibrary

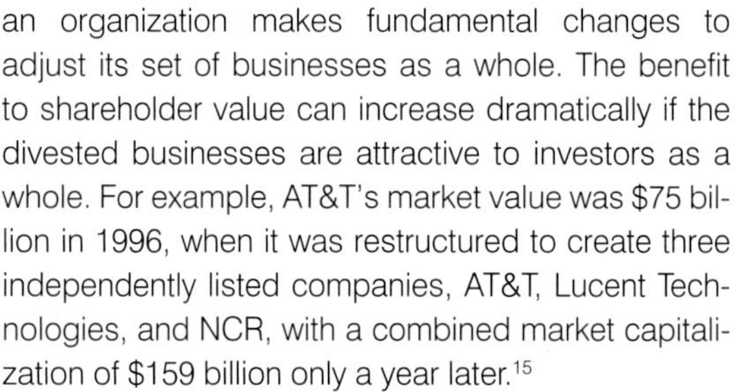

©iStockPhoto.com

Another, more general, term for this is **strategic re-structuring**, when an organization makes fundamental changes to adjust its set of businesses as a whole. The benefit to shareholder value can increase dramatically if the divested businesses are attractive to investors as a whole. For example, AT&T's market value was $75 billion in 1996, when it was restructured to create three independently listed companies, AT&T, Lucent Technologies, and NCR, with a combined market capitalization of $159 billion only a year later.[15]

Re-structuring is typically related to a serious crisis, when the organization may be experiencing a loss of resources such that its viability is doubtful. A topical example is how some financial institutions have had to restructure their businesses away from investment banking and financial derivatives, to more traditional forms, such as private lending and clearing bank activity. Then a head office will plan a 'corporate turnaround', when an extraordinary (typically an internal organization-wide) effort is put underway to enable the organization to resume routine working and viability.

Fundamental changes are difficult to accomplish quickly since it is likely that new skills and new specialized resources must be developed, and employees have to learn new ways of working. The classic case is IBM, which almost destroyed itself in the early 1990s by mishandling the transition from mainframes to personal computers. Yet it managed to reinvent itself under new management as a supplier of 'solutions' to emphasize its computer services and software, rather than hardware. It sold its personal computing business to Lenovo in 2004; it also took a near 20 per cent stake in the Chinese company.

The McKinsey Consultants have argued recently that the right portfolio strategy is to be the 'natural owner' of the businesses; this is when the absolute level of returns is less important than the difference an owner can make to build the synergies of the organization, through operational synergies, distinctive skills, or specific strengths, such as superior access to capital and talent in emerging markets.[16] This, called by another name, is corporate parenting.

Corporate parenting and related diversification

Using the portfolio and SBU approaches may leave little room for intervening in corporate businesses to bring them back to health or to improve their performance directly. This is especially so for unrelated diversified businesses, when senior managers at the centre may know very little about the type of business. Michael Goold, Andrew Campbell and Marcus Alexander contrast unrelated with related diversification strategies, and introduce the concept of **corporate parenting.**[17] (This is not to be confused with the same term used in the public sector, to mean the responsibilities a public agency has for children within a local area.)

©iStockPhoto.com

Goold, Campbell and Alexander explain how a corporate centre acts like a responsible parent to the corporate businesses, by nurturing and growing them synergistically as dependent entities. Parenting aims to create a unique fit between the corporation's capabilities and the critical success factors for each of the individual businesses, so that the value added by the corporate headquarters to the value of the individual businesses can be maximized. In other words, the corporate centre should create more value for the corporate stakeholders from the businesses it looks after than the value would otherwise be if these same businesses were functioning independently. Otherwise the corporation would be wise to sell these businesses as going concerns.

Bad parenting is making bad decisions in allocating resources and setting direction. This is made worse if the centre and the corporate structure work to hinder at the business level, relations with markets, the development of emerging technologies, and flexible responses to the moves of competitors. This is serious if the centre causes delays in making decisions, and the centre does not respond effectively to emerging opportunities and threats.

In order to counter these possibilities some corporations organize their strategy around the needs of divisions, so that the direction of strategy formation is bottom-up rather than top-down. For example, Ed Arditte, senior vice-president of strategy and investor relations at Tyco International (2003-present), states that for large 'diversified companies, like Tyco, strategy is typically driven by the businesses, with appropriate input and guidance from the corporate centre. That has proved to be a better approach for us than approaching it from the centre outwards.'[18]

FOR LARGE DIVERSIFIED COMPANIES, LIKE TYCO, STRATEGY IS TYPICALLY DRIVEN BY THE BUSINESSES, WITH APPROPRIATE INPUT AND GUIDANCE FROM THE CORPORATE CENTRE. THAT HAS PROVED TO BE A BETTER APPROACH FOR US THAN APPROACHING IT FROM THE CENTRE OUTWARDS.

Parenting styles

A key consideration is organizational structure (see Chapter 9). Goold and Campbell offer a typology of three generic parenting styles: financial control, strategic planning and strategic control.[19] Financial control involves the portfolio approach. This is less about parenting and more about the centre achieving a better investment performance. SBUs manage their strategy within tight financial targets set by the centre. Strategic planning emphasizes linkages, where the centre co-ordinates and reviews strategy. The centre continues to set tight financial, but also, strategic targets. There is some attempt to create links between the different businesses to create competitive advantage. Strategic control is based on the management of the core business. The centre drives strategy around the development of important synergies and competences. There are strong co-ordinating actions and linkages between the businesses (see Chapter 11 for strategic control).

Franchising

Franchising is a contractual relationship between a parent organization (the franchiser) and its partners (franchisees) that specifies the control, sharing, and use, of the franchiser's strategic resources. Some very large corporations have used franchising to expand their overseas markets, where a franchiser's knowledge of local conditions is uncertain and the franchise model offers less risk. Some of the best-known names include the United States' McDonald's and Starbucks, but also Spain's Zara, Sweden's H&M and the United Kingdom's Mothercare.

The primary role of a franchiser is to develop these resources and capabilities and transfer them to the franchisees to compete effectively at a local level. Franchisees on their part should feed back to the franchiser knowledge about their competitiveness and how to become more effective. In other words, the franchiser works closely with franchisees to develop the whole business and strengthen the franchise's brand. The franchiser charges for the

Maurice Savage/Alamy

right to make use of its brand name, products, operating systems, marketing etc. The franchisee gains knowledge and skills quickly, and is able to exploit the reputation, systems (etc) of the larger group. For the franchiser it is a fairly economical way to grow without raising capital and the extra risk this entails.

The franchise model is based on a strong centrally controlled form of performance management, in terms of setting boundaries for franchisees and how local employees work and serve customers. This generally aims to impose centrally determined values to support the brand, the use of the associated logo, the necessarily core competence, or the common ways of working that people must be able to perform to provide the same standard of product and service, wherever it is made available.

Franchising is also an effective way for the senior management of a large multinational to retain control over the implementation and execution of its **business model** without too much structure. However, there may be an adverse trade-off in favour of centralized control, and against creativity and innovation at a local level. Toni Mascolo, owner of Toni and Guy, a chain of roughly 250 hairdressing salons in the United Kingdom, has no doubts. He says it encourages the franchisees to do things for themselves. The important things are the Toni and Guy brand, and the fact that it must be supported by hairdressing academies to teach the latest hair designs.

PRINCIPLES IN PRACTICE 7.2

Chief strategy officers as parents

Some large corporations have a central strategy function to manage the parent–children relationship between the corporate centre and the divisions. This function is typically a responsibility of a chief strategy officer (CSO).

These are different from chief executives, who are in overall charge. The job of a CSO is to craft and implement strategies. The actual job title varies, in a large American corporation they are likely to be called 'vice presidents of corporate strategy'.

CSOs grapple the challenge of balancing short- and long-term goals: handling the multifaceted demands of an increasingly global business environment, they strive to focus on growth without losing sight of productivity ... a closer relationship with the CEO is vital for instigating change.[21]

J. F. Van Kerckhove is vice-president of corporate strategy at eBay (2007-present), and he says:'The CEO is the ultimate owner of corporate strategy. A good strategy process finds the right balance between top-down and bottom-up engagement in developing strategy, building on the collective wisdom and exposing its main assumptions. While the formulation of strategy often goes through specific planning milestones, its development is on-going – at times explicit and at times not.

The CSO plays an important role in helping to co-ordinate and inject knowledge in the more formal strategy process, as well as fostering an environment for more spontaneous strategy creations. The latter often finds its roots in a close collaboration with the business units or field operations at the forefront of experimentation and learning. In a fast-paced industry like ours, the ability to rapidly learn from the field is a true competitive advantage.'

Question: Why is it necessary to have CSOs?

SUMMARY OF PRINCIPLES

1. Synergy is achieved when the centre can effectively add value for the group as a whole.
2. Corporate-level strategy concerns the strategic management of an organization's businesses at the corporate centre.
3. An organization grows in four main ways: through market penetration, product development, market development, or diversification.
4. M&A activity is a fast way to grow an organization, but success depends upon an effective integration strategy.
5. There are broadly two kinds of diversification: related and unrelated.
6. Strategic portfolio analysis is used to manage diversified businesses, especially SBUs, to allocate investment between them.
7. A corporate centre is a parent to its businesses when it is able to add value to the businesses that is greater than the centre's cost.

GLOSSARY OF KEY TERMS

Acquisition when one organization buys a controlling interest in another, with the aim of creating a larger entity, or with a view to restructuring the acquired organization to re-sell at a profit.

business model the clarification of how the organization fundamentally manages its core business activities.

Corporate parenting a corporate centre acts to nurture its dependent businesses to create a unique fit between the corporation's capabilities and the critical success factors of the individual businesses.

Corporate synergy a corporate performance that is greater than the sum of its parts.

Corporate-level strategy a corporate centre's strategic management of a multi-divisional or multi-unit organization.

Cultural fit where the organizational culture of an acquisition should be compatible with that of the acquiring company.

Diversification when an organization is active in different types of business area.

Downscoping a divesture, spin-off, or some other means of eliminating businesses, which are unrelated or are not core to an organization's overall business or mission.

Franchising is a contractual relationship between a parent organization (the franchiser) and its partners (franchisees) that specifies the control, sharing, and use of the franchiser's strategic resources.

General Electric/McKinsey matrix devised for GE by McKinsey, framework for managing a portfolio of corporate businesses, which are grouped according to a market's attractiveness, and the factors that affect the competitive strength of a business.

Growth-share matrix the Boston Consulting Group's framework for managing a portfolio of corporate businesses, which are grouped according to their share of a market, and the growth of that market.

Horizontal integration the growth of an organization by expanding its operations to offer complementary products and services, or to acquire a competitor with similar products and services.

Merger the agreement of two organizations to integrate their operations as a combined organization under common ownership.

Related diversification as different products and services in distinct business areas, but these are in related markets and/or industries.

Strategic business units (SBUs) are autonomous single businesses within a corporate structure, with perhaps their own business-level generic strategy, distinctive organizational cultures and competencies.

Strategic re-structuring when an organization makes fundamental changes to change its set of businesses as a whole.

Takeover an acquisition that is made when the target organization has not sought the acquiring organization's bid.

Unrelated diversification offers contrasting products and services in different markets and industries that have little or no similarities.

Vertical integration the growth of an organization by expanding its operations along the distribution chain towards the ultimate customer, and/or along the supply chain towards the primary sources of supply.

GUIDED FURTHER READING

For more detailed and up-to-date materials about their approaches to strategic portfolio analysis see the websites of the Boston Consulting Group (www.bcg.com), and McKinsey (www.mckinsey.com); they offer related articles and updates on their matrices.

The ideas of **corporate parenting** are examined closely by Goold with others. In particular, see their 'parenting fit matrix'; this is proposed as a means for assessing the critical success factors of an individual corporate business, and for comparing these with a centre's own value creation insights.

Goold, M., Campbell, A. and Alexander, M. (1994) *Corporate-Level Strategy: Creating Value in the Multibusiness Company*, New York: John Wiley & Sons.

For a review of the role of the centre in multi-business firms, Constantinos Markides has written an excellent article for the *Handbook of Strategy and Management:*

Markides, C.' Corporate strategy: The role of the centre'. In Pettigrew, A., Thomas, H. and Whittington, R. (2002) *Handbook of Strategy and Management,* London: Sage Publications.

REVIEW QUESTIONS

1 What is synergy?

2 What is corporate-level strategy and how is it different from business-level strategy?

3 What is the importance of integration to a successful merger?

4 What is related and unrelated diversification?

5 What is a strategic business unit and how does it facilitate M&A?

6 What defines whether a parent adds value to its businesses?

7 What are the advantages and disadvantages of franchising?

SEMINAR AND ASSIGNMENT QUESTIONS

1 Strategic and cultural fit are different things. Discuss their implications for strategic management.

2 Conduct a strategic portfolio analysis to group different businesses that are part of a single corporation. Recommend a strategy to help the corporate centre manage these. Discuss the reasons for the strategy and suggest any major disadvantages and how the corporate centre should allow for these.

3 How has the global financial crisis affected M&A activity? Review journal and newspaper commentary over the last year. What kind of M&A activity has been encouraged and which has been discouraged? Comment if you think the growing popularity of M&A up until 2008 has contributed to the crisis and come to a conclusion about how you think M&A activity should now be managed.

CHAPTER REFERENCES

1 Raynor, M. E. (2007) 'Solving the strategy paradox: How to reach for the fruit without going out on a limb', *Strategy & Leadership* 35(4):4–10, 7.

2 Ansoff, H. I. (1965) *Corporate Strategy: An Analytic Approach to Business Policy for Growth and Expansion*, London: Pelican edn (pub. 1968), p. 72.

3 Adapted from Ansoff, H. I. (1957) 'Strategies for diversification', *Harvard Business Review* 35(5):113–24.

4 3M (2007) *Annual Report: Leading Through Innovation*. Foreword by George W. Bockley, chairman. www.multimedia.3m.com

5 Burt, T. (2002) 'The winners are concentrating on cash-generation, cost controls and subscriber margins', *Financial Times*, November 23; Parker, A. and Edgecliffe-Johnson, A. (2007) 'Vodafone survivor sets a course for convergence', *Financial Times,* November 17, 16.

6 Suzlon Energy (2009) *Our Company, History*, www.suzlon.com

7 Reported in London, S. (2002) 'Secrets of a successful partnership', *Financial Times,* February 6, 12.

8 Adapted from Haspeslagh, P. C. and Jemison, D. B. (1991) 'Managing acquisitions: Creating value through corporate renewal', New York: Free Press.

9 Hall, B. (2008) 'Russo and Tchuruk are paying the price for failure', *Financial Times,* July 30, 20.

10 Welch, J. (with Welch, S.) (2005) *Winning,* New York: HarperCollins. p. 226.

11 Adapted from Henderson, B. D. (1984) *The Logic of Business Strategy,* New York: Ballinger Publishing.

12 Adapted from McKinsey (2008) www.mckinsey.com

13 Hoskisson, R. E and Hitt, M. A. (1994) *Downscoping: How to Tame the Diversified Firm,* Oxford: Oxford University Press.

14 Peters, T. J. and Waterman, R. H. (1982) *In Search of Excellence*, London: Harper & Row.

15 Anslinger, P. L., Klepper, S. J. and Subramaniam, S. (1999) 'Breaking up is good to do', *McKinsey Quarterly* 1:16–27.

16 McKinsey (2008) 'Is your company the natural owner of its business?' *McKinsey Quarterly Chart Focus Newsletter,* July 18, www.mckinseyquarterly.com

17 Goold, M., Campbell, A. and Alexander, M. (1994) *Corporate-Level Strategy: Creating Value in the Multibusiness Company*, New York: John Wiley & Sons.

18 Dye, R. (2008) 'How chief strategy officers think about their role: A roundtable', *The McKinsey Quarterly,* May, www.mckinseyquarterly.com

19 Goold, M. and Campbell, A. (1991) *Strategies and Style: The Role of the Centre in Managing Diversified Corporations,* London: Blackwell Publishers.

20 Burgelman, R. A. and McKinney, W. (2006) 'Managing the strategic dynamics of acquisition integration: Lessons from HP and Compaq', *California Management Review* 48(3):6–27.

21 Dye, R. (2008) *op cit.*

22 Penrose, E. T. (1959) *The Theory of the Growth of the Firm,* Oxford: Basil Blackwell.

23 Foster, R. and Kaplan, S. (2001) *Creative Destruction: Why Companies that are Built to Last Underperform the Market – and How to Successfully Transform Them,* New York: Doubleday.

24 Miller, D. (1991) *The Icarus Paradox,* London: Harper Business Books.

25 Frankl, P. and Rubik, F. (2000) *Life Cycle Assessment in Industry and Business: Adoption Patterns, Applications and Implications,* Berlin and Heidelberg: Springer-Verlag.

26 Porter, M. E. (1987) 'From competitive advantage to corporate strategy', *Harvard Business Review* 65(3):43–59.

27 Baghai, M., Smit, S. and Viguerle, S. P. (2008) 'M&A strategies in a down market', *McKinsey Quarterly,* August, www.mckinseyquarterly.com

28 Gerstner, L. V., Jr. (2002) *Who Says Elephants Can't Dance?* NY: Harper Business Books.

29 Hopper, K. and Hopper, W. (2009) *The Puritan Gift, Reclaiming the American Dream Amidst Global Financial Chaos,* London: I. B. Tauris.

30 Goold, M., Campbell, A. and Alexander, M. (1994) *op cit.*

31 Pettigrew, A. M., Massini, S. and Numagami, T. (2000) 'Innovative forms of organizing in Europe and Japan', *European Management Journal* 18(3):259–73.

CASE 7.1 Corporate strategy at General Electric

The American-based conglomerate General Electric (GE) is one of the world's largest corporations, employing around 327 000 people in 160 countries.[1] The company's origins lie with Thomas Edison, who established his Electric Light Company in 1876, and a merger with the Thomson-Houston Electric Company created the General Electric Company in 1892. In 2007, the company recorded $173 billion revenue and $22.5 billion in earnings. It calls itself a diversified technology, media and financial services company. It is an important company to strategic management, because no organization has probably contributed more to thinking about corporate-level strategy.

Changes in GE's corporate-level strategy

The history of GE shows how the strategic management of a large corporation develops in ways that reflect changes in corporate agenda and the management style of a chief executive. In a review of strategic planning at GE since the 1940s, Ocasio and Joseph observe that each chief executive of GE has changed the design of the strategic planning system to meet their own priorities, and to reflect their own experience, management style and background, as well as to take account of the changing market and institutional environments.[2]

During the 1960s and early 1970s Fred Borsch moved the group from a form of strategic management that was based on financial performance to one that took into account industry attractiveness and competitive strength, and established a large central corporate planning department. His successor, Reginald Jones, was more financially oriented and had a more detached management style, which was facilitated by building up a more elaborate system of SBUs, which reported to central planning.[3]

In the early 1980s, GE was hit by recession, and a new chief executive, Jack Welch, downsized the corporation and drastically reduced the corporate planning office. He re-structured the corporate divisions, and ended the strategic independence of the SBUs to make them more accountable to the centre. Welch followed an extensive M&A programme to reposition the group's strategy away from one based on commoditization to a value-added strategy.[4]

Jeffrey Immelt, the current chief executive, is following the Welch strategy, although there is probably more emphasis on organic (internally-generated) growth rather than on M&A. The corporation is now divided into four main businesses: technology infrastructure (made up of units in aviation, enterprise solutions, healthcare, transportation), energy infrastructure (energy, oil and gas, water and process technology), GE Capital (aviation financial services, commercial finance, energy financial services, GE Money, Treasury), and NBC Universal (cable, film, internal, network, sports and Olympics).

GE's strategy

'Our strategy was ... directional. GE was going to move away from businesses that were being commoditized towards businesses that manufactured high value technology products or sold services instead of things. As part of that move, we were going to massively upgrade our human resources – our people – with relentless focus on training and development. We chose that strategy after getting hammered by the Japanese in the 1970s. They had rapidly commoditized businesses where we had reasonable margins, like TV sets and room air conditioners ... Our quality, cost, and service – the weapons of a commodity business – weren't good enough in the face of their innovation and declining prices ... That's why we divested businesses like TV sets, small appliances, air conditioners, and a coal company, Utah International. It is also why we invested so heavily in GE Capital, bought RCA, which included NBC; and poured resources into developing high technology products in our power, medical, aircraft engine, and locomotive businesses.

Imagebroker/Alamy

Now, in such changing times, how and why did GE stick with one strategy over 20 years? The answer is that strategies, if they're headed in the right direction and are broad enough, don't really need to change all that often, especially if they are supplemented with fresh initiatives. To that end we launched four programmes to bolster our strategy – globalization, service add-ons, Six Sigma, and e-business. More than anything, though, our strategy lasted because it was based on two powerful underlying principles: commoditization is evil and people are everything. Virtually every resource allocation decision was based on those beliefs ... My advice, then, is when you think strategy, think about decommoditizing. Try desperately to make products and services distinctive and customers stick to you like glue. Think about innovation, technology, internal processes, service add-ons – whatever works to be unique. Doing that right means you can make a few mistakes and still succeed. That's enough theory!'[5]

Welch had been impressed by the returns to financial services at GE Capital. This was founded in the 1920s to offer hire purchase to help customers buy GE products. However, its involvement in real estate and commercial loans meant that when the global financial crisis came along in 2008, GE shares fell 70 per cent and it lost its triple-A rating, which it had safeguarded since 1965.

Corporate mission

According to Welch, the corporate mission was sometimes mistaken by outsiders as GE's strategy: 'From 1981 through 1995, we said we were going to be "the most competitive enterprise in the world". By being No. 1 or No. 2 in every market – fixing, selling, or closing every under-performing business that couldn't get there. There could be no doubt about what this mission meant or entailed. It was specific and descriptive, with nothing abstract going on. And it was aspirational, too, in its global ambition.'[6]

This 'mission' was used in combination with Welch's modified GE/McKinsey nine-cell matrix (see Exhibits 7.1 and 7.2). He grouped GE's businesses into three rings and one square.

'Invest and grow' were businesses that were number one or two in their markets, or were thought to be promising. While harvest businesses provided cash for the two groups, these others were divested.

Strategy at divisional level

At a divisional level, managements were advised to do strategy in three steps. 'Over my career, this approach worked incredibly well across varied businesses and industries, in upturns and downturns, and in competitive situations from Mexico to Japan.'[9]

The steps were (1) come up with the big idea (Welch calls it the 'aha') for the business, which must be a smart, realistic and a relatively fast way to gain sustainable competitive advantage; (2) put the right

EXHIBIT 7.1 Welch's three rings replaced the nine-cell matrix[7]

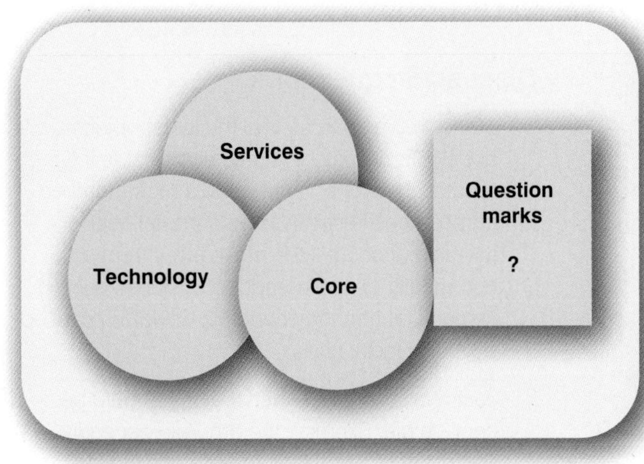

EXHIBIT 7.2 GE's businesses grouped in terms of four priorities[8]

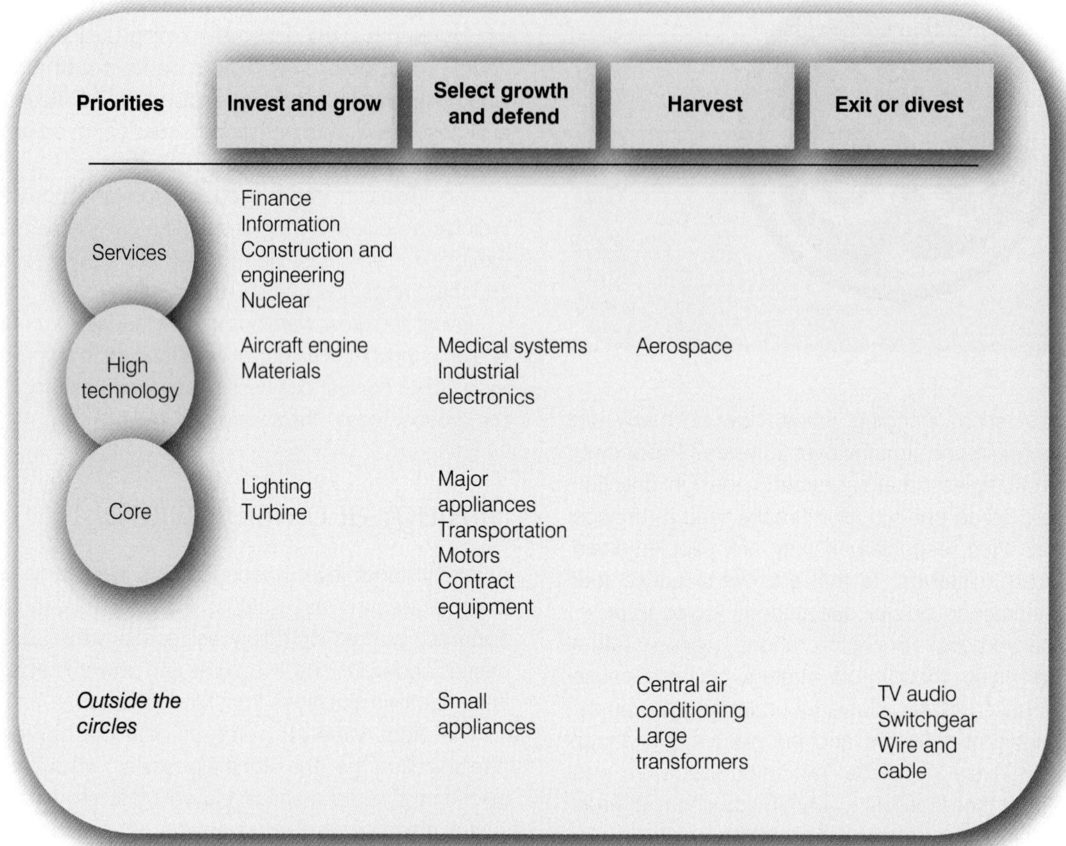

people in the right jobs to drive it forward; and (3) relentlessly seek out the best practices to progress your strategy (continuous improvement).

Discussion questions

1 Using web resources and the latest opinions about GE, critically evaluate and decide if GE's reputation as one of the world's most admired corporations is still deserved. In particular, take into account if the move away from a commodity to a value-added business has helped it during the economic downturn caused by the financial crisis.

2 Jack Welch believes that strategy should be kept simple. Examine the grounds generally for thinking along these lines in the strategic management literature.

3 Evaluate the job of a chief executive at GE. How does it involve 'synergy' and can a single person, such as Jack Welch, ever be said to be in control of an organization as vast as GE?

Case references

1 General Electric (2008) **www.ge.com**

2 Ocasio, W. and Joseph, J. (2008) 'Rise and fall – or transformation? The evolution of strategic planning at the General Electric Company, 1940–2006', *Long Range Planning*, 41:248–72.

3 Pascale, R. T. (1991) *Managing on the Edge,* New York: Simon & Schuster.

4 Welch, J. (with Welch, S.) (2005) *Winning,* New York: HarperCollins.

5 Welch (2005) *op cit.,* p. 170–71.

6 Welch (2005) *op cit.,* p. 15.

7 Adapted from Rothschild, W. E. (2007) *The Secret of GE's Success,* London: McGraw-Hill, exhibit 12.1.

8 *ibid.*

9 Welch (2005) *op cit.,* p. 167.

This case study was prepared using only publicly available sources of information for the purposes of classroom discussion; it does not intend to illustrate either effective or ineffective handling of a managerial situation.

Chapter 8
GLOBAL-LEVEL STRATEGY

Introduction

This chapter discusses global-level strategy, which is considered against the broader context of globalization. **Global-level strategy** is an organization's strategic management of its operations across multinational borders. **Globalization** is a phenomenon of changing commonalties and differences associated with a world-wide perception that the world is becoming smaller, more alike and more inter-connected.

This chapter covers the background of globalization before discussing the four types of **international strategy.** It then considers strategic alliances and partnerships and the rise of leveraged buy-outs.

LEARNING OBJECTIVES

By the end of this chapter you should understand:

1. Globalization.
2. The competitive advantage of nations.
3. The four strategic approaches for global-level business.
4. Strategies for local companies.
5. The influence of national cultures.
6. Strategic alliances and partnerships.

Patrick Eden/Alamy

Business vignette The world is flat

One of the most influential business writers on globalization is Thomas Friedman. He writes in his bestselling book, *The World is Flat*, how he thought of its title.

Friedman describes a visit to the Indian company, Infosys Technology, and its chief executive, Nandan Nilekani. He recounts that at one end of the company's conference centre was a massive wall-size screen. This had been constructed from forty digital screens and was probably the largest flat-screen TV in Asia. Infosys used it to hold virtual meetings with people, who Nilekani described as the key players in the company's global supply chain to discuss any project at any time. So, for example, American designers could be on the screen talking with their Indian software writers, and their Asian manufacturers, all at once.

According to Nilekani, 'We could be sitting here, somebody from New York, London, Boston, San Francisco, all live. And maybe the implementation is in Singapore, so the Singapore person could also be here ... That's globalization.' Above the screen there were eight clocks and these summed up the Infosys workday: 24/7/365. The clocks were labelled US West, US East, GMT, India, Singapore, Hong Kong, Japan and Australia.

Nilekani summed up the implications, 'Tom, the playing field is being levelled ...'

In Friedman's words: 'He meant that countries like India are now able to compete for global knowledge work as never before ... I kept chewing on that phrase: "The playing field is being levelled." What Nandan is saying, I thought, is that the playing field is being flattened. Flattened? Flattened? My God, he's telling me that the world is flat!'[1]

Thomas Friedman

Globalization

Globalization is a growing world phenomenon of connections, associations, differences and commonalities, which influence national markets and international industries. It is an idea that human activity, in particular commercial activity, is converging and becoming more inter-connected all over the world. Some observers have called the present period a post-industrial or post-modern age: a shrinking world that is growing basically more alike (or flat!), but at the same time is becoming more global and stylistically divergent.[2] This perception is heightened by the growth of world communications media and a pervasive feeling that the world ecology is not as safe as we used to think. If we can call this 'globalization', then it is the most important change phenomenon of our time, and is inextricably tied up with the great international debates concerning climate change and the economic management of our planet.

Technological developments, such as satellite broadcasting, computers, email and the Internet, and parallel developments in liberalizing trade and movements in international capital, have helped drive globalization. The concentration of investment activity through international banks and other financial institutions, in large companies, and in accompanying insistence on the part of international investors that commercial organizations should grow in size and adopt global practices, have been important influences.

For example, in a review of the pulp and paper industry, Lilja and Moen conclude: 'During the 1990s leading firms have become Europe-wide or even global as a result of their production systems ... The concentration process has transformed pulp and paper mills into multinational companies ... Investment banks have had a major role. They have acted as architects, messengers and bankers between firms ... As a result, leading firms have learnt to construct strategy projects that appeal to transnational investors and financial analysts.'[2]

The pressure to internationalize approaches to organizational management has been important in nearly all areas of administration, including those in government, religion, charity, sport – just about every human activity that requires organizing and management has been influenced by the idea that the world is somehow increasingly becoming joined-up. However, success in international markets may begin with a strong base at home.

Global-level strategy is an organization's strategic management of its operations across multinational borders. Globalization is a phenomenon of changing commonalties and differences associated with a world-wide perception that the world is becoming smaller, more alike, and more inter-connected.

PRINCIPLES IN PRACTICE 8.1

Think globally, act locally

According to Akio Morita, chairman of Sony Corporation, it is possible for a company to be both global and local.

'For companies operating worldwide, true localization is the first step towards becoming a global enterprise. Managers of such global enterprises must consider how to knit closely together or integrate each of their localized operations so that they function as a single corporate entity. What is essential to this end is a universally common management philosophy and technology on how to develop and market products.

'I introduced a slogan – "global localization" – to let Sony people know the importance of these concepts. It is another Sony word, like Walkman, and who knows, the phrase may one day appear in a Webster's dictionary either under the word, "global" or "local". I believe that I share the same idea with Mr. Gozueta [chairman of Coca-Cola], who in the past advocated the concept, "Think globally and act locally".'[39]

Lebrecht Music and Arts Photo Library/Alamy

Akio Morita

Coca-Cola was a single brand company for nearly a century, but it now has over 200 products and many of these are local brands (there are 47 in China). Coca-Cola gives some degree of autonomy to local marketing; however, the centre's overall strategy has been to give more prominence to Coca-Cola's global drive to expand its range of beverages beyond fizzy drinks. This has led to Coca-Cola buying Russia's second largest juice maker, Multon, in 2005.[40] The overall concept is now 'think globally, act locally'.

According to its chief executive, Douglas Daft, Coca-Cola had made the mistake of centralizing its decision-making and standardizing its practices. 'We were operating as a big slow, insulated, sometimes even insensitive global company and we were doing it in a new era when nimbleness, speed, transparency and local sensitivity had become absolutely essential to success.'[41]

Question: Is there not a basic contradiction in thinking globally and acting locally?

KEY DEBATE 8.1

Is globalization good?

As the world economy converges, countries are likely to become richer and consumer tastes will probably change. This is likely to be disruptive as traditional ways of being and thinking will be questioned. There are many who are concerned with the associated implications and consequences for socio-economic issues, such as an unequal distribution of income and the ecological effects on the health of the planet.

In particular, hostility over aspects of American foreign policy and questions about the business ethics of some conglomerates, have spilled over to influence how people see globalization. This has focused particularly on the power of brands such as Nike, Shell, Wal-Mart, Microsoft and McDonald's; see Klein's *No Logo*.[44]

Researching the thoughts of South American youth for Levi, Amaranta Wright is worried that 'Perhaps one day there will be no authentic thoughts and feelings left, only branded ones, formulated to inspire needs before needs exist.'[45]

A contributory factor may be a lack of scruples at board room level. American big business, say Kenneth and William Hopper, has forgotten the original reasons for making profits, which is to serve society.[46]

The tenants of current global business ideology, such as shareholder value, free trade, intellectual property rights and profit repatriation, are not universally accepted. The importance of the Internet and the threat of censorship and manipulative ideologies, are becoming major concerns.

The global financial crisis is probably the first big test for the principles of international integration: the deregulation and liberalization of trade. Things could go into reverse. However, it is likely that international forums will become more important, and groups such as G-20 will be more active. This is a group of around 20 nations which represent both the advanced and most important emergent economies; it was created in 1999 to promote international financial stability.

Question: Rather than coming closer together, will the world become more adversarial?

The competitive advantage of nations

The importance of a strong home base as a foundation for global expansion was made the subject of research by Michael Porter, which was sponsored by the government of the United States in the late 1980s.[3] He investigated 20 industrial sectors in 12 countries. It was found that many internationally leading industries were clustered in geographical regions. For example, the most successful global parts of the film industry, as well as the IT industry, are centred in California. Porter's research pointed out the importance of developing and nurturing a geographical concentration of suppliers, specialized resources, and the importance of getting a balance between an industry's home-based activities and those dispersed abroad. Porter argues that an organization's competitive advantage in part depends upon local advantages that cluster as a regionally localized industry. Porter illustrated the influences of the competitive strength of a nation as a diamond (see Figure 8.1).

Firm strategy, structure and rivalry

The intensity of domestic competition works to compel organizations to work for improved productivity and innovation. This follows on from Porter's ideas about industry competitiveness (see Chapter 4). An important factor is a country's capital market. When relatively short-term returns to investment are expected, such as in the United States, then industries with short investment cycles are encouraged, for example, computers and films. In countries where the investment cycle is longer, such as in Japan, then investment favours more radical technology, for example, Toyota's hybrid car, which the company started to develop in the 1990s.

Demand conditions

The presence of demanding and sophisticated customers will spur on greater efforts and competitiveness. Domestic industries are encouraged by open competition, since this raises expectations about the standard of service and products a market wants, and this spurs local organizations to innovate and improve. The large, important leather and footwear industries in eastern England succumbed quickly in the late twentieth century, when markets were opened up to competition from Italy and other countries, largely because they were unable to innovate after years of protected markets.

Related and supporting industries

This source of competitive advantage is concerned with the need for a sufficient density of related and

FIGURE 8.1 Porter's diamond of competitive advantage of nations[4]

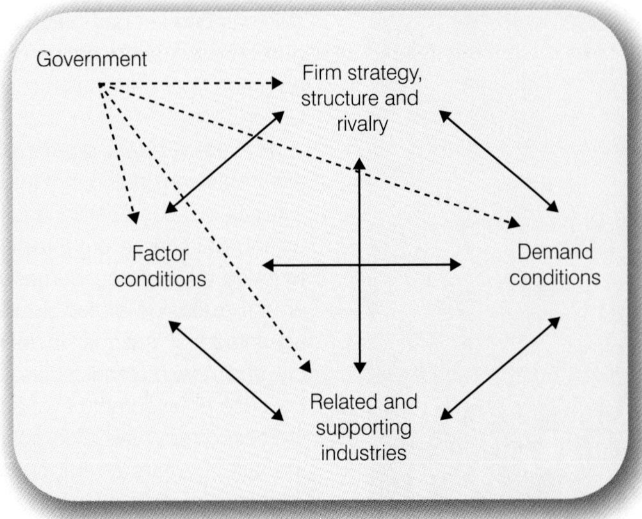

supporting organizations, especially the proximity of distributors, suppliers and other organizations, that facilitate an industry's activities. For example, the number and close proximity of clothing wholesalers and fashion houses in Milan have provided an important springboard for the Italian textile industry.

Factor conditions

These are the available specialized factors of production, which include skilled labour, capital and infrastructure. They do not include general-use factors, such as unskilled labour and raw materials, which are generally available and do not contribute to a nation's competitive advantage, such as general education, because specialized training is more important for generating innovation that leads to a sustainable competitive advantage. The Dutch horticultural industry is a world leader in produce that includes tomatoes and dahlias, but it has no natural resources that are particularly suited to these plants. The origins of Dutch horticulture lie in the seventeenth century when the Netherlands was internationally famous for tulips. Since that time the country has been able to build up its specialist marketing and other resources across the world.

The role of government

The purpose of government, according to Porter, is to provide and facilitate economic conditions that act as a catalyst and encourage enterprise. Local rivalry can be stimulated by policy that limits direct co-operation and enforces anti-trust regulations. In the diamond, 'government' is shown as a periphery influence. This reflects Porter's view that the role of government is neutral: in other words, government can be good or bad.

However, there is no denying that policy interventions often work well to build infrastructure, develop specialist resources and can boost investment to encourage innovation. According to Kenneth Galbraith, the mighty public investment in the American defence industry has been a primary driver of the country's dominance in key technologies, such as computing and aircraft.[5] Peter Drucker compared the success of Japan to the failure of the United Kingdom to support innovative industries that would have maintained the country's technological leadership.[6]

Regional clusters, of course, do not necessarily last. In the United States, there has been a discernible move of car manufacturing away from Detroit. This has been in part because of relatively high production costs and location of Japanese subsidiaries on green field sites in the less expensive parts of the United States.

However, Porter's diamond is important since he is effectively concluding that the success of a country's international competitiveness is dependent upon the growth of its large organizations, and this growth is founded on a strong domestic base. Porter's ideas are an extension of the old idea of the comparative advantage of nations. In fact, in terms of assembly and raw material costs in manufacturing, and because of favourable exchange rates, the developing economies have a comparative advantage. Over the last 30 years an important part of western and Japanese manufacturing has relocated to the emerging economies, including some aspects of services (notably call centres). It seems that a domestic base may not be as important now.

Value-added products and services and low manufacturing costs

In terms of overall employment some advanced economies have shifted significantly towards a service-based economy. However there is evidence from the OECD, for example, that suggests the value of sales in manufacturing as a proportion of the economy has been stable. The implication is that falling employment may be associated with rising productivity. It is, anyway, likely that employment in services will rise as general prosperity increases. The switch in employment from manufacturing to services is called de-industrialization.

Many large international organizations have adopted a strategy that moves them into product and service markets, where sophistication, speciality and intangibility are important benefits, and the value added is relatively high compared to more simple products, especially commodities. Some of these organizations come from the emerging economies. Robert Kaplan and David Norton observe that strategies for creating value have shifted from managing tangible assets to knowledge-based strategies. These utilize an organization's intangible assets, such as customer relationships, innovative products and services, high quality and responsive operating processes, skills and knowledge of the workforce, supporting IT infrastructure which link an organization to its suppliers and, finally, an organizational climate that encourages innovation, problem-solving and improvement.[7]

Undifferentiated products and services compete against each other on volume production, economies of scale and low price. It seems possible that mobile (cell) phones could become commodities if prices carry on falling as advances in technology continue to lower costs and competition intensifies. **Commoditization** makes it difficult for companies to control margins. Vodafone has used new technologies, such as the third-generation mobile format, to add new value-added services and extra revenue from existing premium users, rather than to win new sales of phones.

ICI decided in the early 1990s to focus on high value-added speciality chemicals, and become less reliant on bulk chemicals; it de-merged a large part of its bulk chemicals business, which became Zeneca Pharmaceuticals. It followed this up by an acquisition of Unilever's speciality chemicals business and sold its remaining bulk chemical business to its old rival, DuPont. Competition in bulk chemicals depends on price and delivery. Sales in speciality chemicals depend more on customizing chemical recipes to the specifications of large industrial customers, which involves close partnership working that adds value to the chemicals being used.

If international trends have reinforced differentiation, they have also encouraged others to relocate and reduce costs. The Swedish company, Electrolux, is the world's second largest producer of domestic appliances. It has presided over one of the biggest programmes of plant reorganization of any large company. It has closed 22 plants in high-cost nations over the five years to 2007, while opening up 12 new ones in Asia and Eastern Europe. About 40 per cent of its spending on components comes from low-cost countries, which is projected to rise to 60 per cent in 2009. In 2002, around 85 per cent of its production was in high-cost regions, but this has already fallen to 40 per cent. The change has resulted in a fall in the workforce from 75 000 in 2001, to about 55 000 employees in 2007. The main part of this reduction in labour has come in the high-cost regions, including the United States, Australia, Denmark, Germany and Spain.[8]

Emerging markets

The opening up of consumer markets in large and developing countries, particularly in China and India, with populations of well over a billion people each, has meant a growing interest in low-income consumers. For many large Western organizations the scope for expansion in their domestic markets is limited and the development of overseas' markets is important to maintain growth.

Procter & Gamble has changed its strategy to shift more of its resources to low-income customers in overseas' markets. The company is using new approaches in its consumer research involving time spent in the homes of low income consumers and the development of new forms of communication. At first glance this looks like an organization that focuses on low value-added products. However, Proctor & Gamble are using advanced technology and marketing to design low-income products in ways that local competitors find difficult to emulate. For example, it is producing a disposable nappy for no more than the price of a fresh egg (ten cents).

Overseas expansion is not all one way. Some large global players are emerging from within the developing economies. Tata Steel, for example, acquired the Anglo-Dutch Corus Group, which includes the old British Steel assets, in 2007. The Tata group retains its low-cost base in India, but it is also seeking access to the lucrative markets of the developed world by taking over western companies. Tata Steel has access to cheap supplies of government allocated iron ore, which it ships to its operations in south-east Asia and Corus' European markets. The strategy has been to combine low-cost production in emerging economies with the high-margin markets of the West.[9]

A example of a successful company that has emerged over the last decade is the Shenzhen-based and Chinese-owned BYD. This is now the world's largest producer of lithium-ion batteries for mobile (cell) phones. It is planning to use its expertise in batteries to dominate the Chinese market for electric cars. BYD does not actually stand for 'build your dreams' but it has now adopted this slogan.

Four strategic approaches for global-level business

There are four strategic approaches for global-level business (see Figure 8.2); these are multidomestic, global, international and transnational strategies.[10]

1 Multi-domestic strategy

Multi-domestic strategy is the use by organizations of different products and services for different markets in different countries. This is based on knowledge that markets in different countries or regional parts of the world are distinctly different and independent. A simple transfer of an existing strategy that has been effective in a domestic market may not work. The solution is to develop a strategy to take account of local conditions. It is necessary to give local managers considerable autonomy for strategic and operating decisions, perhaps as part of a corporate structure of SBUs with responsibilities for different regions of the world. Catering for local demand is likely to increase costs, but on the other hand, it may increase sales to a level that compensates.

Expansion into another country may involve the acquisition of companies that are familiar with local conditions. This can be risky if local knowledge and experience are turned against a parent organization, perhaps because there is a clash of organizational cultures, or the parent is thought to be ignorant, and too slow to support local decisions. The intervention in key issues at a local level could also be misinterpreted as uninformed interference.

For example, Unilever has favoured a decentralized approach and given local managers autonomy to make decisions. It works well for food because products can be adapted to meet local tastes. It is less effective in household and personal care, where the same products, such as nappies, toilet rolls, razors, can be marketed and sold

FIGURE 8.2 Four strategies for international markets

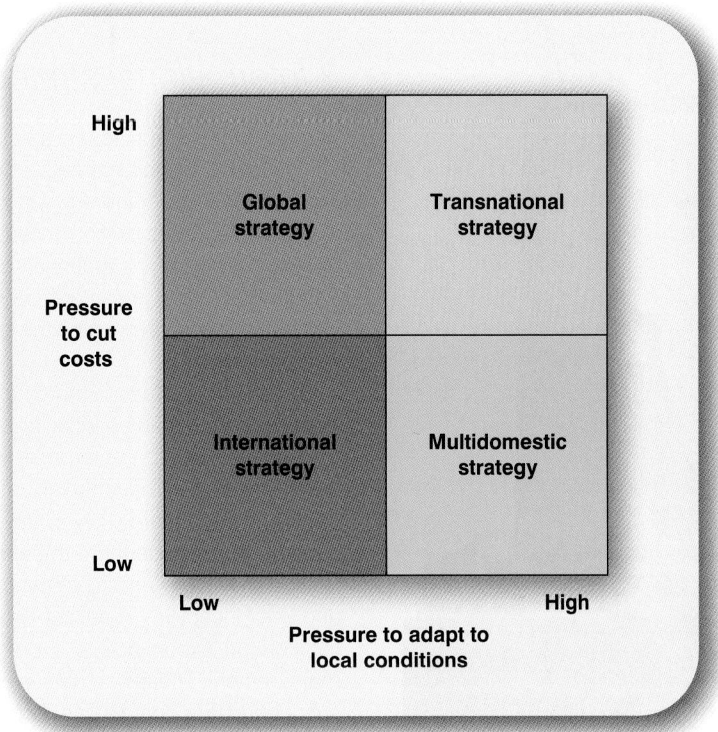

globally. So the company has been introducing changes for such products, and it has reduced its brands from about 1300 in 2000 to around 400 in 2008.[11] Most of these brands were local ones.

2 Global strategy

Global strategy is the use by organizations of a standardized product and service range to exploit markets in different countries. Theodore Levitt, writing about the globalization of markets, argues that organizations will be encouraged to develop a single standardized product to sell in the same way throughout the world.[12] This is likely to bring enormous economies of scale from centralized production, distribution and marketing. He argues that this will be possible because consumer lifestyles and tastes are likely to converge. IKEA does not tailor its stores to local markets: people buy the same things, and the same range is everywhere – 'beautiful functional items at the lowest prices'.[13] There are many other examples, usually associated with global brands.

A **brand** is a name or label that incorporates a visual design or image, which is associated with a product, service, or corporation, to differentiate it from others. Various positive attributes are associated with the brand through communication media and advertising to add a value that goes beyond the intrinsic functional value of the product or service bought. When branding is effective it offers attractive price premiums to the producer, and creates strong loyalty to the brand from the customer.

Brands are important to global strategy as they signify a standardized offer and a consistent promise of benefits regardless of where purchases are made. Companies may go to great lengths to ensure a brand retains its exclusivity and image: Levi, for example, fought a series of legal actions to stop retailers such as Tesco from selling its jeans in supermarkets at reduced prices.

One of the most successful brands of the last decade has been Apple, which has been built using new technology, smart design and strong advertising; it has had the benefits of a high profile founder, Steve Jobs, and has been supported by a customer service network based on own-name retail outlets. The iPod, a digital music player, was priced high when it was originally introduced, but demand quickly increased as it was seen early on a fashion statement.

Brands are a major motive for acquisitions. They are not always successful: Ford bought the luxury car brand, Jaguar, in 1989 and rashly tried to turn this niche brand into a mass-market one, building Jaguars on Ford platforms. In 2008 the brand was finally sold on again, this time to Tata Motors.

3 International strategy

International strategy is the use by organizations of innovation to exploit markets in different countries. Technologies, products and services are developed in the home countries and these are then extended to less-developed international markets. A survey of *Fortune*'s 'world's most admired companies' suggests that these companies fall into the international strategy group.

These companies are more focused on managing from the centre than on local initiatives. For example, they are focused on enterprise-wide objectives and these are better managed from the centre. These companies are more likely to develop new practices centrally and diffuse them to subsidiaries than other companies. They also have centralized pay policies and keep incentives consistent from country to country. Foreign experience is a prerequisite for senior management. These companies also claim they have succeeded in building a one corporate culture across all their divisions.[14] This includes common core competences.

4 Transnational strategy

Transnational strategy is used by organizations to exploit markets in different countries by using a combination of multi-domestic and global strategies. It is also called **'glocalization',** which is a combination of globalization and localization. Transnational strategy recognizes that the global market is not a single homogenous one but is made up of many locally different ones. The local markets are globally accessible, but they have different cultural conditions that require a more regionally customized one. A multinational organization must balance the interests of the greater organization with the needs of local management and its need to make local strategic decisions.

Strategic manufacturing platforms are one way of doing this. During the 1980s and 1990s General Motors (GM) and Ford both sought to develop a

© Photolibrary

world car. They aimed to gain economies of scale by selling the same car everywhere, rather than developing vehicles separately for each region. In the end they abandoned this in favour of platforms (or architectures), which involved a common group of basic models that are used and varied at the local levels of assembly and marketing units to suit local conditions. This is part of a policy for centralizing research and development and dispersing manufacturing to low cost assembly units and suppliers.

There were problems at GM when regional engineers made expensive modifications that raised the prices of its mid-sized cars. Broadly, however, it resulted in the same type of car being sold in Europe, the Vauxhall Cavalier and Opel Ascona, while in the United States it sold as a Chevrolet Cavalier, Pontiac Sunbird, Buick Skyhawk and Cadillac Cimarron. Problems surfaced when the models looked too alike: for example, the Cadillac failed due to its similarity to cheaper brands. There were also technical difficulties in that compromises were needed to achieve a car that in the United States was suitable for the long straight highways, and another version for the more twisty European roads. It was a hybrid strategy of trying hard to get appealing local differentiation, while at the same trying to get synergies and a reduced cost base. Cost savings did not always materialize because local regulatory standards and different manufacturing practices involved making adjustments to a car's design.[15]

Jim Press, president of Toyota Motor North America, says that whenever a global product is made you have to remember there are details that have to fit each specific market. However, at Toyota the emphasis is placed on learning the Toyota system as a non-national cultural guiding light of business and this does not change.[16]

PRINCIPLES IN PRACTICE 8.2

Wal-Mart uses the web as a strategic platform

Increasingly, global companies are using the Internet to develop platforms. Wal-Mart aims to emulate Amazon's global online expansion, saying it will invest 'millions of dollars' in a global e-commerce technology platform that can readily be deployed by its subsidiaries in China, Japan

charistoone-stock/Alamy

and Latin America. The retailer is increasingly looking to overseas sales to offset slowing growth in the US, and says the global Internet project will be a multi-billion dollar opportunity over the next three to five years.

A new global e-commerce unit at Wal-Mart's international division will oversee the creation of a platform that can sell groceries, general merchandise and digital products while linking up with its stores and with call centres. In the US, the Wal-Mart.com website has sales estimated at \$2bn a year and is the most visited US retailer's site after Amazon, the world's largest Internet retailer ...

Wal-Mart will build a 'globally saleable' system that would essentially act as a kit of online parts – that can be readily deployed in different markets ... The move also reflects growing interest among US retailers in the international possibilities of e-commerce, after their initial focus on the expansion of the US market. Online now accounts for about 13 per cent of total US retail sales excluding cars and groceries.[42]

Question: Is this really strategic, or a tactical and operational move?

KEY DEBATE 8.2

Should strategy be global or local?

Many observers believe that a successful worldwide strategy needs to be global; see Levitt.[47] Others argue that strategy rarely impacts upon global performance, because the advantages that underpin competitive advantage are rare; they think that competitive advantage is the creation of barriers to market entry, and that a global organization is only successful if it can pursue local strategies.[48] However, George Yip thinks that a local advantage is only available when local expertise and regulation are important.[49]

Alan Rugman questions the basis of globalization and thinks the real drivers are the network managers of large multinationals. Their business strategies are regional and responsive to local customers.[50]

Question: Is globalization as a single converging world economy a myth?

Strategies for local companies in emerging markets

Niraj Dawar and Tony Frost suggest a strategic framework for local companies to assess their competitive strength in an emerging market.[17] This is based on two parameters: the strength of globalization pressures in an industry, and the degree to which a company's assets are transferable internationally (see Figure 8.3).

If globalization pressures are weak, and the local company assets are not transferable, then the company should defend its own position. Dawar and Frost use the example of Shanghai Jahwa, a Chinese cosmetics group. The company has developed low cost mass-market brands that are positioned around beliefs about traditional ingredients. If globalization pressures are weak but the company's assets can be transferred, then the company may be able to extend its business to some other markets. Jollibee Foods is a family-owned chain of fast food restaurants based in the Philippines. After meeting fierce competition from McDonalds the company opened restaurants in Hong Kong, the Middle East and California, to offer its traditional meals to expatriate populations.

If globalization pressures are strong and a company's assets are suitable only for home, then it will need to depend on its ability to dodge the multinationals by re-structuring to serve those parts of the value chain where its local assets are still valuable. Skoda, the Czech Republic's car company, entered into a joint venture with Volkswagen; the alternative would have been to sell out entirely. If globalization is strong and a company's assets are transferrable, then it may be able to contend globally with the multinationals. Acer of Taiwan and Samsung of Korea have become very successful at the global level. Local companies typically start with a cost advantage over the multinationals and this can be used to give them a foothold in some markets.

National cultures

The importance to multinationals of one-company cultures was noted above in the context of international

FIGURE 8.3 Positioning for emerging market companies[18]

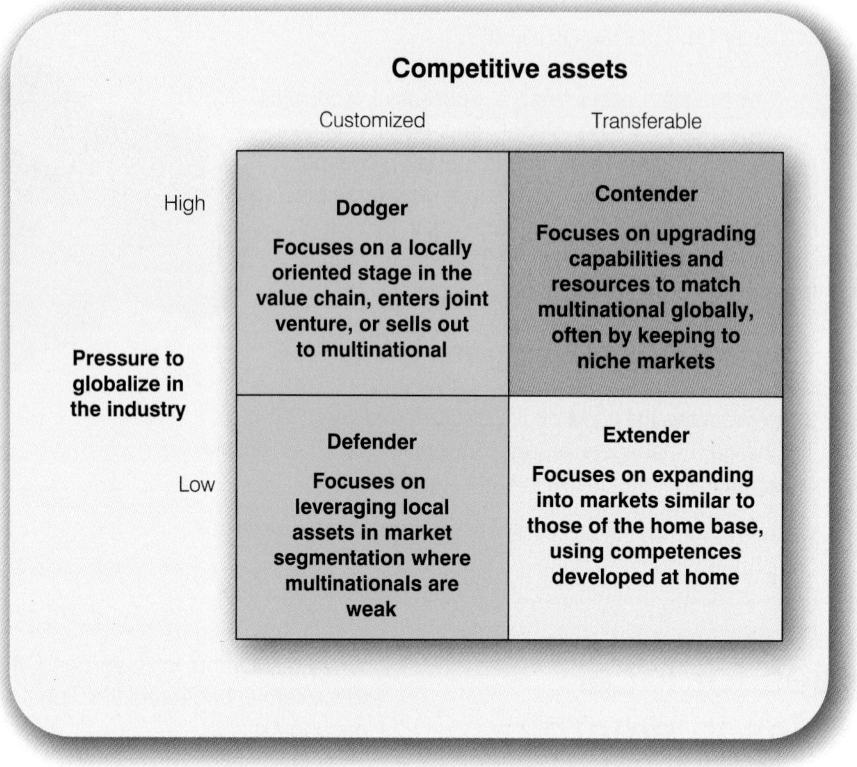

Competitive assets

Pressure to globalize in the industry	Customized	Transferable
High	**Dodger** Focuses on a locally oriented stage in the value chain, enters joint venture, or sells out to multinational	**Contender** Focuses on upgrading capabilities and resources to match multinational globally, often by keeping to niche markets
Low	**Defender** Focuses on leveraging local assets in market segmentation where multinationals are weak	**Extender** Focuses on expanding into markets similar to those of the home base, using competences developed at home

strategy. There is evidence that Japanese business methodologies and management philosophies do transfer effectively between countries.[19] This is important to organizations which, like Toyota, take a resource-based view of competitive advantage. If national cultures create insurmountable barriers to the transfer of organizational core competences and capabilities, then a competitive advantage built on strategic resources will be at risk.

Toyota's executive vice-president, Mitsuo Kinoshitsa, admits that adapting to individual communities can be challenging: 'In India the cultural differences are nothing like those in the United States. Indians are often quite sensitive to criticism, resisting Toyota's culture of constant improvement through problem identification, and deadlines are often not viewed with high importance ... The French and the Japanese have vast cultural differences ... Japanese are known to work long hours, but in France, a 35-hour work-week prevails for most professionals.'[20]

Of course, it may be the senior managers who are the real 'challenge'. Carlos Ghosn, chief executive of Renault-Nissan, thinks that the predominant national culture of an organization is a factor in how an executive sees its approach to the rest of the world: 'One of the great challenges that Renault has faced in its globalization is the fact that a part of its management still sees itself as exclusively French. It goes without saying that French culture is very important in the culture of the company, and again we mustn't lose sight of that fact. But we can't stop there.'[21]

Most of the theories about how to manage come from the United States. Hofstede finds there are no universal management styles because of differences in national cultures.[22] There are five dimensions that influence how organizations are managed:

1 Power distance – which is the degree of inequality a national culture considers normal.

PRINCIPLES IN PRACTICE 8.3

The Renault-Nissan Alliance

In 1999 Renault and Nissan entered an alliance. Renault assumed a 36.8 per cent stake (now 44 per cent) in Nissan. Renault was reducing its dependence on Europe and Nissan offered access to the North American and Asian markets. The Japanese car company had incurred huge debts during the Asian financial crisis. Renault invested $5.4 billion, which saved Nissan's investment grade status.

Renault's senior management agreed to three important principles during negotiations: (1) Nissan would retain its name; (2) the Nissan chief executive would be appointed by the Nissan board; and (3) Nissan would take responsibility for implementing a revival plan.

ALLIANCE VISION – DESTINATION[43]

The Renault-Nissan Alliance is a unique group of two global companies linked by cross shareholding. They are united for performance through a coherent strategy, common goals and principles, results-driven synergies, shared best practice.

They respect and reinforce their respective identities and brands.

The Alliance is based on trust and mutual respect. Its organization is transparent.

It ensures: clear decision-making for speed, accountability and high levels of performance, maximum efficiency by combining the strengths of both companies and developing synergies through common organizations, cross-company teams, shared platforms and components.

The Alliance attracts and retains the best talents, provides good working conditions and challenging opportunities: it grows people to have a global and entrepreneurial mindset. The Alliance generates attractive returns for the shareholders of each company and implements the best established standards of corporate governance.

Objectives

The Alliance develops and implements a strategy of profitable growth and sets itself the following three objectives:

1 To be recognized by customers as being among the best three automotive groups in the quality and value of its products and selling in each regional and market segment.

2 To be among the best three automotive groups in key technologies, each partner being a leader in specific domains of excellence.

3 To consistently generate a total operating profit among the top three automotive groups in the world, by maintaining a high operating profit margin and pursuing growth.

Question: To become the world's third car company, Renault-Nissan must overtake Ford. What is its strategy for doing so?

2 Individualism versus collectivism – the extent a culture thinks it is appropriate for people to look after themselves, and be cared for.

3 Masculinity versus femininity – the acceptable balance between dominance, assertiveness and acquisition on the one hand, and regard for people, feelings and quality of life on the other.

4 Uncertainty avoidance – the degree of preference for structured versus unstructured situations.

IN INDIA THE CULTURAL DIFFERENCES ARE NOTHING LIKE THOSE IN THE UNITED STATES. INDIANS ARE OFTEN QUITE SENSITIVE TO CRITICISM, RESISTING TOYOTA'S CULTURE OF CONSTANT IMPROVEMENT THROUGH PROBLEM IDENTIFICATION, AND DEADLINES ARE OFTEN NOT VIEWED WITH HIGH IMPORTANCE ... THE FRENCH AND THE JAPANESE HAVE VAST CULTURAL DIFFERENCES ... JAPANESE ARE KNOWN TO WORK LONG HOURS, BUT IN FRANCE, A 35-HOUR WORK-WEEK PREVAILS FOR MOST PROFESSIONALS.

5 Long-term versus short-term orientation – saving/persistence to reach a future, versus present, tradition and other social obligations.

Susan Schneider and Jean-Louis Barsoux, in their book, *Managing Across Cultures*,[23] contrast a 'controlling cultural model' with an 'adapting' one (see Table 8.1). In effect this contrasts the classical view of strategic planning and strategy with the emergent view (see Chapter 1).

Using Pascale's account of the Honda effect as evidence (see Key Debate 1.2), they argue that Japanese approaches are adaptive and contrast with western approaches. Similar to Porter's diamond they point out the importance of a domestic economy as an influence on the international strategies of organizations. So, for example, the conditions in Germany (see Table 8.2) may have influenced that country's organizations to follow an international strategy approach.

This characterization of German strategic management is consistent with Richard Whittington's observations that there is a German and Japanese model of close co-operation between banks and

TABLE 8.1 Cultural models of strategy[24]

Controlling	*Adapting*
• Formal and centralized planning	• Informal and decentralised planning
• Quantitative, objective, impersonal	• Qualitative, subjective, personal
• Top-down, expert driven	• Bottom-up, employee driven
• SMART objectives	• Broad, implicit
• Short term	• Long term
• Sequential plans	• Simultaneous plans
• Explicit performance measurement	• Vaguely monitored

enterprises, a paternalistic state and a communitarian view of manager–worker relations. This translates into a long-term view of strategy and a heightened propensity to invest in equipment and training, and a respect for the hands-on skill required for technology and production.[26] This contrasts with an Anglo-Saxon model, which is associated 'with turbulent financial markets, and impatient leaders, hostile takeovers and a hire-and-fire approach to labour. The consequences for strategy are an emphasis on short-term financial results, an aggressive external orientation to strategy and a high valuation put on speed and flexibility.'[27]

TABLE 8.2 The characteristics of the German organizational context[25]

German Model
• Long-termist, institutionally regulated markets, house banks
• Importance of family entrepreneurship
• Developed system of vocational education and training which encourages technologically sophisticated, quality products
• Consensus and cooperative decisions
• Administrative-legalistic personnel management (less strategic, slower adoption of things)
• Bureaucratic and personal controls, strong functional division of labour, specialist expertise

The German/Japanese model of strategy was generally successful between 1960–1990, when the demands of large-scale mass-production of traditional goods – cars, consumer electronics, chemicals, were strongly felt. However, 'The Anglo-Saxon economies ... have taken off, especially on the most recent period of the late 1990s, characterized by the shock of transition towards the new economy of information, services, and the Internet. It looks like the fast-moving, flexible and sometimes ruthless strategizing of the Anglo-Saxon economies is better suited to the emergent economic conditions of the twenty-first century than the careful instrumentalism of Germany and Japan.'[28]

If Whittington was right, he may not be now, if the arrival of the global financial crisis has exhausted the Anglo-Saxon model's credit. The nature of strategic leadership and the role of management in strategic management may have played their parts (see Chapter 11). The crisis has certainly called into question beliefs that unregulated markets are good for (any sort of) business.

The market state

The nature of a government's readiness to support industry is in part a cultural, but also an ideological, matter. The idea that free markets drive globalization has influenced how governments think about public sector organization. This is the idea of the market state, a concept used by Philip Bobbit in 2002 to describe an 'emerging constitutional order that promises to maximize the opportunity of its

... with turbulent financial markets, and impatient leaders, hostile takeovers and a hire-and-fire approach to labour. The consequences for strategy are an emphasis on short-term financial results, an aggressive external orientation to strategy, and a high valuation put on speed and flexibility.

KEY DEBATE 8.3

Do national cultures matter?

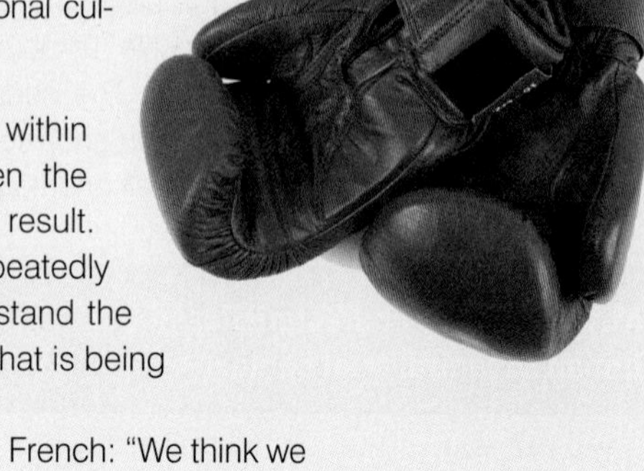

Referring to the Nissan-Renault alliance, Magee gives an example of how the Japanese and French national cultures influence communications:

'The communication methods and habits within the cultures are so different that even when the same language is used, different understandings can result. For instance, Japanese businessmen often say "yes" repeatedly when being told something. It is a sign that they understand the dialogue and are absorbing it, not that they approve of what is being said. Imagine the potential for confusion.

French: "We think we need to close a plant."

Japanese: "Yes."

French: "Jobs will be lost."

Japanese: "Yes."

French: "We have no choice. It must be done."

Japanese: "Yes."

'The conversation ends. The French are moving on, making plans to close a plant. The Japanese are only ready to begin considering it, having said "yes" simply as conversational confirmation that they understand what was being said. Confusion never occurred at this magnitude, but cultural communication differences made for some interesting moments during high-level meetings and discussions.'[51]

Question: The ideal of a 'global manager' seems some way off. Is it possible that a new class of global manager can emerge with globalization?

people, tending to privatize many state activities and making representative government more responsive to the market.[29] The market state is perceived as an ultimate replacement for the national state, which, according to Bobbitt, was the dominant constitutional order of the twentieth century, which had promised to improve the material welfare of its people.

Bobbit cites Michael Walzer: 'In the market state, the marketplace becomes the economic arena, replacing the factory. In the marketplace, men and women are consumers, not producers (who are probably offshore anyway). What can a hospital attendant, or a school teacher or a marriage counsellor or a social worker or a television repairman or a government official be said to make? ... More important than producers ... are the entrepreneurs – heroes of autonomy, consumers of opportunity – who compete to supply whatever all the other consumers want or might be persuaded to want ...

© iStockPhoto.com

competing with one another to maximize everyone else's options.'[30]

The idea does not necessarily imply a reduced role for the national state since government is still needed to regulate levels of service. These ideas have had profound consequences, especially in the United Kingdom, where much of the public service provision is now open to foreign competition. The market state is premised on the idea of globalization, and relies especially on the international capital markets to create stability in the world economy. The fear of many, now that the financial markets have suffered a reverse, is that national economies will impose trade restrictions and regulate financial markets, which could slow or even reverse globalization.[31]

Strategic alliances and partnerships

Strategic alliances and partnerships are formal and informal associations and collaborations between independent organizations. A formal alliance involves a legally binding collaboration between two organizations to work to a specified purpose and which may involve a major project and shared resources. It can involve forming an independent organization such as a joint venture. This involves establishing a legally separate company, in which the partners take agreed equity stakes. Agreements are made about a common purpose, standards, and contractual arrangements, covering such matters as licensing, franchises, distribution rights and manufacturing agreements. Organizations can also enter informal alliances, including customers who have major accounts, key distributors, preferred suppliers, major institutional shareholders, and other stakeholders.

The reasons for alliances and partnership are varied and numerous. Often it is to share knowledge about new technologies. Sony and South Korea's Samsung in 2007 announced a $2 billion joint venture to mass produce the next generation liquid crystal screens for flat-screen televisions. Sony has a leading share in cathode-ray tube televisions, but its share is falling as flat-screens take more of the market. Both companies will benefit in that Sony will gain from Samsung's technical knowledge and Samsung will be able to exploit Sony's market power.

Alliances also help organizations to find out about another company's management approaches, or about unfamiliar markets. They can help to reduce the cost of capital and spread risk, and sometimes they are a more acceptable form of market entry to regulators. eBay entered the Chinese online market in 2002 by acquiring EachNet, a leading auction site in China. Ebay modelled its site on its globally successful website design, but growth was slow because of strong local competition. Recognizing it needed to be more in tune with local customers, it entered into a joint venture with TOM online to form TOM eBay in 2006.

A consortium partnership involves companies that come together to bid for a mutual rival. In 2008 Heineken, and Carlsberg, two independent brewers, made a joint take-over of Scottish & Newcastle. Heineken aims to become number one or two in the beer markets in the countries it operates in, but prior to the bid only had one

© iStockPhoto.com

per cent of the British market; as a result of the acquisition it is now the largest brewer there. Carlsberg has taken over those parts of Scottish & Newcastle that are important in Eastern Europe and Russia. The Heineken and Carlsberg bid was designed to facilitate a break-up of the British company that would satisfy the European Union's competition laws. The companies would not have been able to bid independently. After the bid they were required to dismember Scottish & Newcastle in ways that reduced the threat to competition.

The rapid changes in communications technologies, especially the Internet, have given rise to new thinking about alliances. Two important developments are co-opetition and technology-based strategic platforms.

Co-opetition (competition and collaboration)

Co-opetition is a word collapsed from co-operation and competition. It takes its inspiration from e-business. Ray Noorda, the founder of Novell, may have been the first to use the term, and it has now been widely taken up in the IT industry. It means a form of business activity that involves competing organizations that also co-operate with each other. For example, organizations that belong to strategic groups may work together to create barriers to new or outside competition. Adam Brandenburger and Barry Nalebuff in their book, *Co-Opetition*, use examples from the e-economy and ideas from game theory to show how collaboration between rivals can work in the interests of all.[32]

Organizations should consider their industry to take into account how its network of customers, suppliers and competitors can be used to enhance the value of products and services. This involves identifying potential and actual complementors: those other organizations that through their own products will enhance the value of an organization's products and services. For example, a rival's software products may complement an organization's hardware products, and vice versa. The e-economy offers a change in strategy thinking from a 'bricks and mortar' approach, based on tangible resources, to one more intangibly centred on interacting with inter-organizational networks.[33] Organizations have to determine how possible relationships may be complementary and how they can be used to sustain their competitive advantage.

Technology-based strategic platforms

A **technology platform** is a standardized technical system over which an organization may have property rights, but it can be used by other organizations (and sometimes rivals as in co-opetition) as a platform to develop their own products and services.[34] Microsoft's strategic success is based upon its desktop operating system, which has provided a platform for software groups to develop their own products to use with the Microsoft system. Bill Gates, the former Microsoft chief executive, has been consistent in ensuring that changes to MS-DOS, or Windows, have not meant that customers have had to abandon their existing programs and accessories. This has added complexity and cost to the development process and may have made Windows less reliable. "Bill Gates insistence on the strategic imperative has infuriated some of his most talented programmers ... It just keeps plugging on. That is not very glamorous – and it often results in bloated code and feature-laden programs. But it is an extremely effective competitive weapon in an industry where products never get past the 'promising' stage".[35]

There is a strong functional interdependence amongst components of a technology-based system – what David Teece calls a multi-sided market phenomenon.[36] For instance, electronic game consoles need games, and organizations have to work together to co-specialize, and a platform provider must take such activity into account for its strategic decision making.

It may be difficult to implement platforms without forming alliances with other organizations to co-ordinate and respond to market changes. The French Minitel videotext system was co-ordinated by the French government as a telecommunications platform and involved a broad alliance of hardware manufacturers, software designers and information providers. This facilitated the joint development of organizational competencies that allowed Minitel to offer new products through its online access. A similar videotext service failed in the United Kingdom largely because it failed to develop a **strategic platform** that could be used profitably by its information providers.[37]

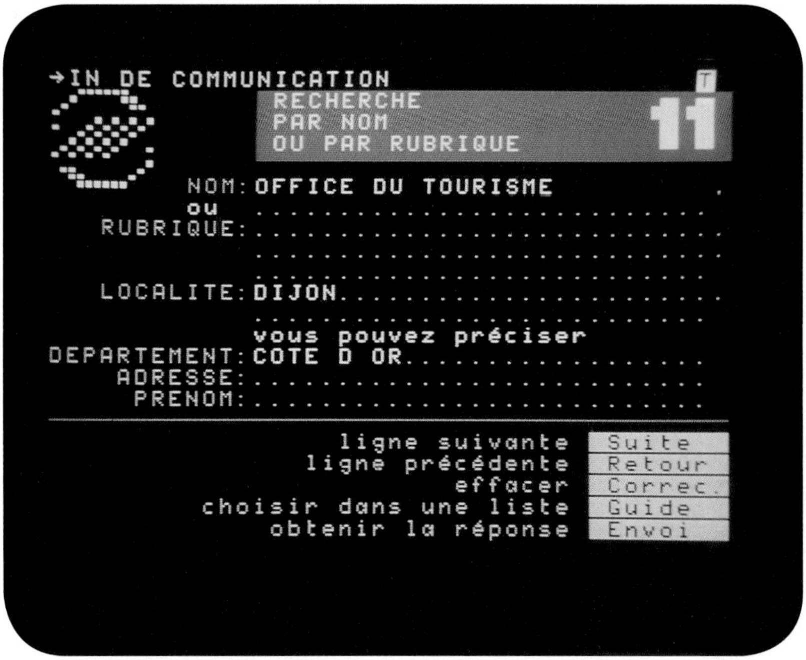

dk/Alamy

France Télécom's Minitel service

Private equity firms

Private equity firms are associated with **leveraged buy-outs** when they buy a publicly-quoted company and make it private, so that the acquired company's stock is no longer traded publicly. Private equity firms raise large amounts of debt to finance their purchases, and offset the costs by re-selling parts or the whole of the acquired companies, and sometimes building them up by adding other companies (called 'bolt-ons') to sell on to other companies. Traditionally, many of the private equity firms provide venture capital to new enterprises, but they have become increasingly involved with buying companies rather than taking shares in them.

Permira is Europe's largest private equity group: it owns several well-known brands, including Birds Eye, the AA (Automobile Association), and the retailer New Look. The world's biggest buy-out occurred in 2008, when Blackstone, founded in 1986, spent £19.8 billion to acquire Equity Office Properties, the largest commercial property group in the United States. Buy-outs, however, often involve consortia of investors rather than just a single firm or buyer.

Private equity firms have been criticized for their lack of public accountability, especially in terms of investor names and executive salaries, and also for the very large levels of borrowings they sometimes use to finance deals, which afterwards can burden purchased firms with large debt (which is of some concern to fans of Manchester United, a famous football club which was subject to a buy-out). There are also accusations of asset-stripping and short-term financial, rather than longer-term strategic management. Others see their role as usefully ruthless and better able to reinvigorate sluggish companies that might otherwise have changed very little. Silverfleet, a United Kingdom private equity firm, bought the Dutch-based TMF, a provider of outsourced administrative services, in 2004. It built up the business by making more than fifty bolt-ons, and then sold the business on making a six-fold return on its investment in 2008.[38]

Another form of private equity is the sovereign wealth fund; this is an investment fund held by a national government, which is used to invest in international companies. The history of these funds stretches back to at least the early 1950s, but they have more recently attracted attention for their participation in private equity buy-outs. The largest fund seems to belong to Abu Dhabi ($635 bn); others include Norway, Singapore, Kuwait, China and Russia. Some of these owe their existence to dollar surpluses accrued from oil. At the present time sovereign funds account for a low proportion of the world's financial assets, but they are expected to become a significant feature of globalization, prompting disquiet about the possibility that a hostile country can take control of companies that are strategically important.

Until the global financial crisis in 2008, private equity had been increasing very quickly. Private equity funding was about 4 per cent of the global M&A market in 2000 and rose to over 20 per cent in 2007. The importance of private equity is likely to remain but to what extent it will recover is at the moment open to question.

SUMMARY OF PRINCIPLES

1 Global-level strategy must be considered against the main drivers of globalization, but it is important to recognize that global changes are still uncertain, so that organizations should be adaptable.

2 A company's competitive advantage in part depends upon local advantages that cluster as a regionally localized industry.

3 There are four broad strategic approaches for global-level business: multi-domestic, global, international and transnational (glocalization) strategies.

4 The positioning for emerging market companies depends on the pressure to globalize in the industry and their competitive assets.

5 National cultures exert a large influence in the choice of international strategy.

6 Strategic alliances and partnerships enable organizations to learn about technologies, ways of managing and new markets.

7 Strategic platforms provide a basis for adapted or complementary products and services.

GLOSSARY OF KEY TERMS

Brand a name or label that incorporates a visual design or image which is associated with a product, service, or corporation, to differentiate it from others.

commoditization the transfer of unsophisticated production and service units from advanced economies to developing countries where the cost of labour is low.

Co-opetition when competing organizations also co-operate with each other.

Global strategy one of the four strategy approaches for global-level business; it is the use by organizations of a standardized product and service range to exploit markets in different countries.

Globalization a phenomenon of changing commonalities and differences associated with a world-wide perception that the world is becoming smaller, similar and more inter-connected.

Global-level strategy an organization's strategic management of its operations across multinational borders.

glocalization a combination of globalization and localization.

international strategy one of the four strategy approaches for global-level business; it is the use by organizations of their strategic resources to exploit markets in different countries.

Leveraged buy-out a group of private investors buys a publicly quoted company in order to take the company private.

Multi-domestic strategy one of the four strategy approaches for global-level business; it is used by organizations to supply different products and services to different markets in different countries.

Strategic alliances and partnerships formal and informal associations and collaborations between independent organizations.

strategic platform a basic design or technological system that provides opportunities for the provision of adapted and complementary products and services.

Technology platform a standardized technical system, over which an organization may have property rights, but it can be used by other organizations as a platform to develop their own products and services.

Transnational strategy one of the four strategy approaches for global-level business; it is used by organizations to exploit markets in different countries by using a mixture of multi-domestic and global strategies.

GUIDED FURTHER READING

An essential read for those interested in **globalization** is Thomas Friedman's *The World is Flat*. It is probably the most influential popular business book of a large and growing library.

Friedman, T (2005) *The World is Flat: A Brief History of the Globalized World in The 21st Century*, London: Allen Lane.

For an in-depth treatment of the management of global-level strategy, Bartlett, Ghoshal and Beamish, *Transnational Management,* is now in its fifth edition.

Bartlett, C., Ghoshal, S. and Beamish, P. (2008) *Transnational Management: Text, Cases, and Readings in Cross-Border Management,* (5th edn) London: McGraw-Hill.

One of the best up-to-date books about international business in China is by Xiaowen Tian.

Tian, X. (2007) *Managing International Business in China,* Cambridge: Cambridge University Press.

REVIEW QUESTIONS

1. What is the difference between the following: global-level, global strategy and globalization?
2. Is the dominance of western economies coming to an end?
3. What are the four drivers of the competitive advantage of nations?
4. What are the four strategic approaches to global-level strategy?
5. How can local companies compete in emerging economies?
6. Do national cultures influence strategic management?
7. What is a strategic platform and what are its complementors?
8. What are the advantages and disadvantages of alliances?

SEMINAR AND ASSIGNMENT QUESTIONS

1 Compare the Porter diamond with the Schneider and Barsoux example of the German model. Put together two lists that compare how national cultures may encourage and discourage any of the four types of global-level strategy.

2 Can international organizations be managed as a single company? Consider if a one-company culture is effective.

3 Are countries like China and India more likely to use the Anglo-Saxon rather than the German/ Japanese models for strategic management? Compare the two models and use contrasting examples from America, the United Kingdom, Germany and Japan.

CHAPTER REFERENCES

1 Friedman, T (2005) *The World is Flat: A Brief History of the Globalized World in the 21st Century,* London: Allen Lane.

2 Lilja, K. and Moen, E. (2003) 'Co-ordinating transnational competition: Changing patterns in the European pulp and paper industry'. In Djelic, M-L. and Quack, S. (eds) *Globalization and Institutions: Redefining the Rules of the Economic Game,* Cheltenham: Edward Elgar, pp. 187–60.

3 Porter, M. E. (1990) *The Competitive Advantage of Nations,* New York: Free Press.

4 Adapted from Porter (1990) *op cit.*

5 Galbraith, J. K. (1975) *Economics and the Public Purpose,* London: Pelican.

6 Drucker, P. F. (1969) *The Age of Discontinuity,* London: Pan Piper.

7 Kaplan, R. S. and Norton, D. P. (2001) 'Transforming the balanced scorecard from performance measurement to strategic management: Part 1', *Accounting Horizons* 15(1):87–104.

8 Marsh, P. (2007) 'Electrolux awaits results of clean-up, interview with CEO Han Straberg', *Financial Times,* February 13, 25.

9 Leahy, J. (2008) 'The burning ambition of the Tata Group', *Financial Times,* January 25, 5.

10 Bartlett, C., Ghoshal, S. and Beamish, P. (2008) *Transnational Management: Text, Cases, and Readings in Cross-Border Management* (5th edn) London: McGraw-Hill.

11 Wiggins, J. and Rigby, E. (2008) 'A break with history', *Financial Times,* October 3, 15.

12 Levitt, T. (1983) 'The globalization of markets', *Harvard Business Review,* July–August:92–102.

13 George, N. (2001) 'One furniture store fits all', *Financial Times*, February 8.

14 HayGroup (2006) 'Going global, in the world's most admired companies', *Fortune* 4–5.

15 Mackintosh, J. (2005) 'General Motors' quest for the elusive world car', *Financial Times,* November 8, 13.

16 Magee, D. (2007) *How Toyota Became # 1, Leadership Lessons from the World's Greatest Car Company,* London: Portfolio, Penguin Group, p. 169.

17 Dawar, N. and Frost, T. (1999) 'Competing with giants: Survival strategies for local companies in emerging markets', *Harvard Business Review,* March–April:119–29.

18 Adapted from Dawar and Frost (1999) *op cit.,* p. 122.

19 Hong, J. F. L., Easterby-Smith, M. and Snell, R. S. (2006) 'Transferring organizational learning systems to Japanese subsidiaries in China', *Journal of Management Studies* 43(5):1027–58.

20 Magee (2007) *op cit.*, p. 170

21 Ghosn, C. and Reis, P. (2003) *Shift: Inside Nissan's Historic Revival,* London: Currency, Doubleday, p. 166.

22 Hofstede, G. (1980) *Culture's Consequences: International Differences in Work-related Values,* London: Sage Publications. *(Culture's Consequences: Comparing Values, Behaviours, Institutions, and Organizations Across Nations,* 2001, 2nd edn); Holstede, G. and Holstede, G. (2005) *Cultures and Organizations: Software of the Mind* (2nd edn) New York: McGraw-Hill.

23 Schneider, S. C. and Barsoux, J-L. (2003) *Managing Across Cultures* (2nd edn) London: Prentice Hall.

24 Adapted from Schneider and Barsoux (2003) *op cit.*, p. 124.

25 Schneider and Barsoux (2003) *Op cit.*, p. 138.

26 Whittington, R. (2001) *What is Strategy – And Does It Matter?* (2nd edn) London: Thomson.

27 Whittington (2001) *Op cit.*, p. 5.

28 *Ibid.*

29 Bobbit, P. (2002) *The Shield of Achilles: War, Peace and the Course of History,* London: Allen Lane Penguin Press, p. 912.

30 Walzer, M. (1995) 'The concept of civil society'. In Walzer, M. (ed.) (1995) *Toward a Global Civil Society,* Berghahn Books, p. 17.

31 Wolf, M. (2008) 'Financial crisis tests durability of globalization', *Financial Times,* October 10, 12.

32 Brandenburger, A. M. and Nalebuff, B. (1996) *Co-opetition: A Revolution Mindset that Combines Competition and Cooperation – The Game Theory Strategy That's Changing the Game of Business,* NY: Doubleday.

33 Gnyawali, D. R. and Madhavan, R. (2001) 'Co-operative networks and competitive dynamics: a structural embeddedness perspective', *Academy of Management Review* 26(3):431–45.

34 Evans, D. S, Hagiu, A. and Schmalensee, R. (2006) *Invisible Engines: How Software Platforms Drive Innovation and Transform Industries,* Cambridge, MA: MIT Press.

35 Martin, P. (2001) 'Let's hear it for Microsoft', *Financial Times,* October 16, 23.

36 Teece, D. C. (2007) 'Explicating dynamic capabilities: The nature and microfoundations of (sustainable) enterprise performance, *Strategic Management Journal* 28:1319–350.

37 Witcher, B. J. (1982) 'Telepropinquity: Implications for Business Trading Systems'. In Didsbury, H. F. (ed.) *Communications and the Future*, Washington, DC: World Future Society, pp. 296–304.

38 Arnold, M. (2008) 'How the credit crunch threw a spanner in works for bolt-ons', *Financial Times,* August 22, 21.

39 Senn, J. A. (1995) Interview with Akio Morita, Chairman of Sony Corporation, *Global Management Challenges,* Computer Information Systems Department, Georgia State University, cis.gsu.edu/jsenn/morita.pdf.

40 Kwong, R. and Mitchell, T. (2008) 'Coke to squeeze more from China', *Financial Times,* September 4, 20.

41 Tomkins, R. (2003) 'As hostility towards America grows, will the world lose its appetite for Coca-Cola, McDonald's and Nike'? *Financial Times,* March 27, 19.

42 Birchall, J. (2008) 'Wal-Mart aims to go global with internet platform', *Financial Times,* February 1, 25.

43 Nissan (2004) *Alliance Vision – Destination,* Nissan Motor Company. www.nissan-global.com

44 Klein, N. (2001) *No Logo,* London: Flamingo.

45 Wright, A. (2005) *Ripped and Torn: Levi's, Latin America and the Blue Jean Dream,* London: Ebury Press.

46 Hopper, K. and Hopper, W. (2009) *The Puritan Gift, Reclaiming the American Dream Amidst Global Financial Chaos,* London: I. B. Tauris.

47 Levitt, T. (1983) *op cit.*

48 Greenwald, B. and Kahn, J. (2005) 'All strategy is local', *Harvard Business Review,* September:95–104.

49 Yip, G. S. (2005) 'All strategy is local', Letters to the Editor, *Harvard Business Review,* December:145–46.

50 Rugman, A. M. (2005) *The Regional Multinationals: MNEs and 'Global' Strategic Management,* Cambridge: Cambridge University; Rugman, A. M. and Hodgetts, R. (2001) 'The end of global strategy', *European Management Review* 19(4):333–43.

51 Magee, D. (2003) *Turnaround: How Carlos Ghosn Rescued Nissan,* New York: HarperCollins, p.135.

CASE 8.1 Global Strategy Caught Up in a Web

The Internet is a global system of interconnected organizational and individual computer networks that makes use of the Internet Protocol Suite (TCP/IP), the end results of which require little introduction for today's networked generation. It facilitates access to information resources and services, in particular the interlinked hypertext documents of the World Wide Web, and the infrastructure that supports email and other e-services involving voice and video. The origins of the technology lie in the 1960s and the United States military, but the commercialization and rapid development of services occurred in the mid-1990s. About a quarter of the world's population now uses the Internet, making it perhaps the most significant driver of globalization.

Business success with the web extends beyond just improving technology, to the delivery of new forms of information at lower cost. At the time of the dot.com boom the business models of many Internet organizations were similar and based on attracting 'lots of people to the website, try to keep them there as long as possible, and hope to "monetise the eyeballs" by selling advertising. In the early days this model only really worked for one company, AOL, and that not for long…The "razors and blades" model invented by King C. Gillette in 1901 is also going strong: sell the basic product at a low cost and make better margins on the blades (or ink cartridges for printers, or air time on mobile phone networks). Microsoft's Hotmail is a variation on this model – the basic product is free, but users pay for additional storage.'[1]

The most successful global web organizations started off with a very narrow focus, which was only broadened out with more markets as they established a leadership position on the web. Amazon kept to online bookselling until 1997 when it moved into music, by which time it had well-tested processes and capabilities, and these also worked well for CDs. Traditional and established book and record retailers were probably inhibited by their existing ways of doing business. Kieran Levis in his book, *Winners and Losers,* outlines eight essential attributes for successful web businesses, which are distinctive to web leaders[2]. Levis argues these hold for most of the web successes and latent demand and the availability of venture capital are particularly important.

- A clear strategic vision based on a radically different way of meeting a large, previously unsatisfied customer need.
- A set of highly distinctive capabilities – technological, marketing and logistical – tailored to the needs of the market.
- Value propositions that are so compelling that they change customer behaviour and shift loyalties.
- An entrepreneurial but disciplined organization that balances creativity with practicality, is innovative but pragmatic, and creates effective teams.
- A robust, radical business model that is not easily imitable.
- Genuine concern for quality and consistency of the customer experience.
- Leadership that ensures the clear communication of strategic direction and consistent implementation.
- Sharp focus on the chosen market.

The importance of market attributes such as transparency, and freely and easily available information are particularly important for some markets. The eBay feedback system gives every buyer and seller a score for every transaction, and these are publicly displayed for anyone to see. With this degree of transparency, trust ceases to be as it is for conventional auctions, since it is in everyone's interest to behave well. It means that total strangers can do business in second-hand items in confidence.

The nature of buying online makes it easier to supply information for consumers to conduct their product and service searches rather than using, say, hardcopy directories. The web brings shopping into the very place where the need for a product is felt most keenly; it moves the shopping context to where buying decision processes start, namely the home. The close proximity of computer-based information to the buying experience is called telepropinquity: the relation in the buying process of distant information, brought within the actual time of the action of the purchase[3]. Within the buying process businesses are able to place information and advertisements with platform providers, such as Google and others, in ways to link searchers directly to their web pages. The value to advertisers can be tapped directly if rates are linked to the number of clicks made by searchers and prospects for visiting the advertiser's website.

Another factor is network effects: a virtual global network is a community of users who interact with a common service or a product, and who have common sets of needs and interests. Malcolm Gladwell in his book, *The Tipping Point,* argues that trends and networks on the web develop (and become established) quickly once a critical mass is reached[4]. Once this occurs it is then difficult for other web businesses to tempt members to leave their established networks, such as a web dating agency or an events service.

Large Internet businesses are especially able to exploit what Chris Anderson, the editor of *Wired Magazine,* has called the 'long tail'[5]. In statistics a curve that charts high frequencies at the beginning and afterwards tails off so that the tail is very long relative to the head, is called a long-tailed distribution. Most conventional businesses are constrained in the range of products they can offer customers. So, for example, a book or music retailer can only offer the best-selling titles, since capacity and storage are limited. Those products for which there is a limited and infrequent demand – the long tail – are not stocked. There are also products wanted by small niche markets and specialist users, where premiums are necessary to cover the extra costs associated with meeting low demand. However, online retailers can profitably facilitate the sale of low-selling items by reaching a wider and more geographically distant market. Also online retailers are likely to have relatively lower storage costs. In total individual occasional and specialist demands can add up significantly. In meeting these kinds of demands the web has opened up buying opportunities for niche products and services for dispersed and far-flung consumers. These types of markets are now more attractive to small and medium-sized business because a website offers a more easy global reach.

Once they are established, web-based organizations seem to behave like any other, and many have moved from collaborative to acquisitive activity to crush their rivals or to take advantage of emerging opportunities, to deter threats in the future. 'A pattern [has] now emerged of eBay relying on its muscle and its money to eliminate or crush competition, rather than developing new organizational capabilities,'[6]. Microsoft has incorporated into its operating system features such as browsers that had previously been available as individual programmes, and has withheld information on Windows so that its own programs will interact with its operating system more smoothly than those of rivals.

Many industries are in turmoil because of the alternatives offered by the web. The impact of globalization and the Internet is a massive issue for the record, film, magazines, and the newspaper, industries. The basic problem is that the consumer now expects free content. Chris Anderson in his latest book, *Free,* argues that all content and services will inevitably, sooner or later, be free. This is because cost of processing, bandwidth and storage is falling at an annual deflation rate of 50 per cent. The cost of doing business on the web points to zero. The money opportunities will come around the fringes of free. Google gives its services free, but makes revenue and its enormous profits out of advertising. Business should accept this and think of the web as the ultimate advertising platform. The trick is to think of new ways of doing this. 'It's a consumer paradise: the web has become the biggest store in history and everything is 100 per cent off.'[7]

Even so, it seems that advertising is unlikely to pay for everything. The global financial crisis seems to have limited the money available. Some businesses have adopted a compromise, where a general product or information is offered free, but more specialist product is offered at a premium. In other words, hook visitors into a website, and then bait them with an add-on product or service. Online gamblers or gamers can play free, but paid options include time-saver cheats, and other add-ons to enhance games.

Even so, younger people no longer need to buy a DVD or a magazine when it is easy for them to download a movie or read the magazine's content online (legally or otherwise). Magazines are responding by giving away content for free. Men's weekly *Shortlist,* which is distributed free in major cities, is being followed by a woman's version, *Stylist,* which was launched in late 2009. All their income comes from advertising. The majority of profit from women's magazines comes from advertising, but the difference is that the magazines must need to prove to advertisers that the title is reaching the right people. For newspapers this is not a sustainable model, where journalists are struggling to work out how to make money from online content. The *Financial Times* charges for content that is fairly specialist, but for more general news and commentary, News International seems to have made a strategic shift to focus on the regular readers of its newspapers as subscribers, rather than to try to build as big an audience as possible[8]. The willingness of readers to pay a subscription for general content is unproven though.

The global film and record industries have experienced major technologically-based competition before through television and the video in film, and through recorders and cassettes in records. The web is unlikely to sweep away these industries. For example, in many retail areas customers will want to see and touch the things on sale; cinemas offer an intense and involving experience; record shops and bookshops offer the opportunity to browse and sense products.

Not everybody agrees: take this view from an LA film critic: 'The only films getting financing are Transformers, Batman, sequels, tentpoles etc. It's actually a terrible time for cinema, even though it looks like it's grossing more than ever. That's because ticket prices have gone through the roof. Far less people are actually going to the cinema now. In real terms, the industry is nowhere near as big as it used to be. And lots of distributors are now only picking up DVD rights to films, so far less is getting a theatrical release, and for a shorter amount of time as they rush out the DVD to try and combat piracy. The whole thing is a shambles.'[9]

Traditional industries are unlikely to disappear, but the organizations offering films, newspapers and records will probably have to look more closely than before at the exact nature of the value propositions that make them different from only from their competitors, but also from the emerging alternatives the web makes possible.

Discussion questions

1 Does the web replace and substitute, or does it offer opportunities for organizations to complement and enhance business? Consider examples using the web.

2 Are there business models that are unique to the web?

3 Is the film critic right? The media and entertainment industries have to find new strategy for dealing with the web. But what should they be?

Case references

4 Levis, K. (2009), *Winners & Losers: Creators & Casualties of the Age of the Internet,* London: Atlantic Books, p. 161.

5 Levis, *op cit.* pps. 167-168.

6 Witcher B. J. (1982), Telepropinquity: Implications for Business Trading Systems, *Communications and the Future,* Washington: World Future Society, 296-302.

7 Gladwell M. (2000), *The Tipping Point; How Little Things Can Make a Great Deal of Difference,* Boston: Little, Brown.

8 Anderson C. (2006), *The Long Tail: How Endless Choice is Creating Unlimited Demand,* London: Business Books.

9 Levis, *op cit.* p. 184.

10 Anderson C. (2009), *Free: The Future of a Radical Press,* London: Random House.

11 Tryhorn C. (2009), Times and Sunday Times target regular readers with membership scheme, *The Guardian,* October 5.

12 Witcher, Rosamund (2009), Los Angeles, October (personal communication).

This case study was prepared using only publicly available sources of information for the purposes of classroom discussion; it does not intend to illustrate either effective or ineffective handling of a managerial situation.

"CUTTING-EDGE FIRMS AND FLEXIBLE ORGANIZATIONS NEED PEOPLE WHO CAN LEARN NEW SKILLS RATHER THAN CLING TO OLD COMPETENCIES. THE DYNAMIC ORGANIZATION EMPHASIZES THE ABILITY TO PROCESS AND INTERPRET CHANGING BODIES OF INFORMATION AND PRACTICE … IN WORK TERMS A PERSON'S HUMAN 'POTENTIAL' CONSISTS IN HOW CAPABLE HE OR SHE IS IN MOVING FROM PROBLEM TO PROBLEM, SUBJECT TO SUBJECT."

ROBERT SENNETT

Strategy development

PART I WHAT IS STRATEGY?

CHAPTER 1 **Overview of strategic management**

CHAPTER 2 **Purpose**

PART II DETERMINANTS OF STRATEGY

CHAPTER 3 **Strategic objectives**

Balanced objectives

CHAPTER 4 **The external environment**

SWOT analysis

CHAPTER 5 **The internal environment**

PART III STRATEGY

CHAPTER 6 **Business-level strategy**

CHAPTER 7 **Corporate-level strategy**

CHAPTER 8 **Global-level strategy**

PART IV STRATEGY DEVELOPMENT

CHAPTER 9 **Organizing**

CHAPTER 10 **Managing implementation**

CHAPTER 11 **Leadership**

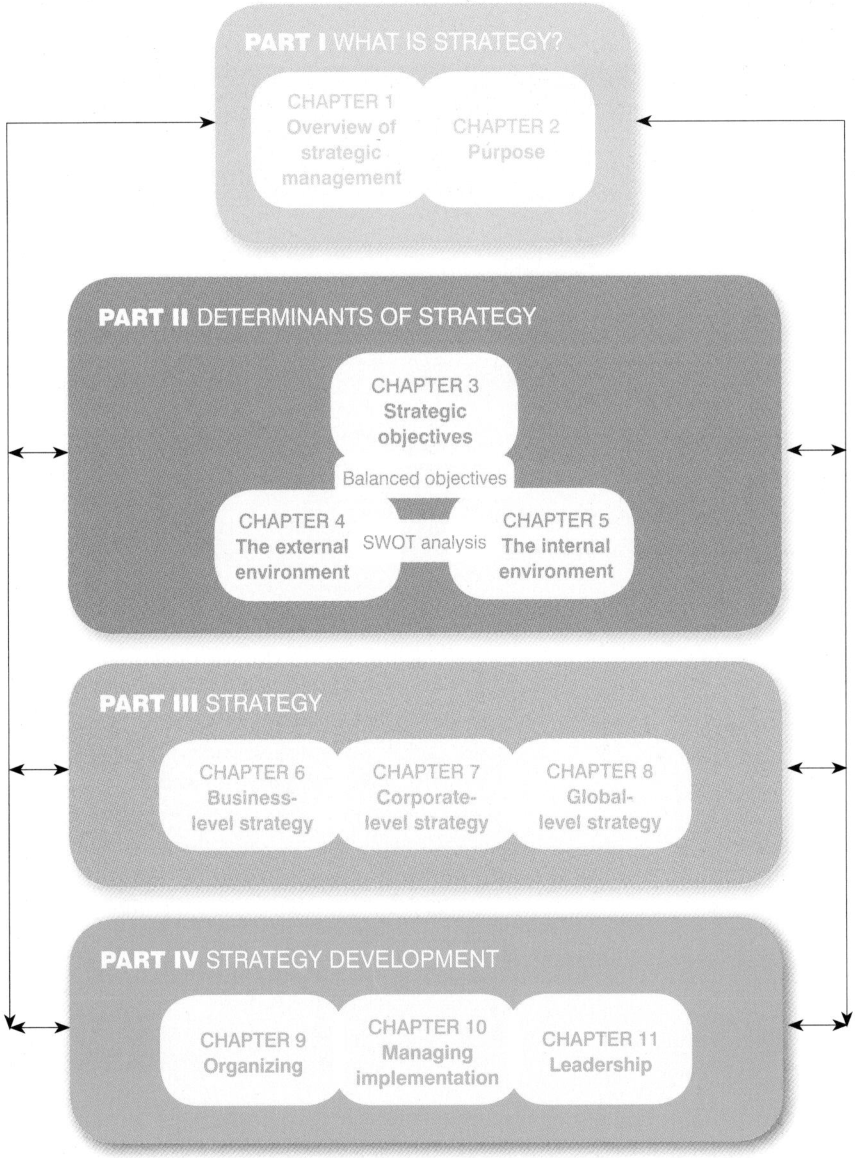

Chapter 9

ORGANIZING

Introduction

This chapter discusses the organizational needs of strategy. This is from the perspective that organizing structures and systems, including mid-term strategic planning, are parts of the implementation of longer-term objectives and strategy. The chapter covers structure, including process and cross-functional management. It discusses systems and systems thinking, including the 7S framework, and returns to strategic planning.

LEARNING OBJECTIVES

By the end of this chapter you should understand:

- Structure as an organizing capability.
- Types of organizational structure, functional, divisional, matrix.
- Forms of organizing that include networks, internal markets.
- The McKinsey's 7S framework.
- Cross functional structures.
- Business process re-engineering.

Business vignette Getting structure right at the oil companies

BP and its larger ExxonMobil rival differ in the degree of how they organize strategically. After a series of operating disasters, BP has been introducing a fundamental change to the way it is structured to counter views among investors that the company has a systemic operating problem. The BP revamp is expected to take five to ten years. The company was organized to be the most efficient cost-cutter in the industry. This may have influenced safety and maintenance has probably contributed to skill shortages within the company. The acquisition of Arco and Amoco complicated this. BP improved Amoco's safety record, but BP admits it failed to integrate fully different safety systems. Its plants still use a range of procedures that are entrenched by local custom and practice.

It seems a gap may have emerged between the corporate centre, which tries to establish clear business principles, and local management, which is focused on day-to-day operational performance. BP's organizational structure is made up of many business units which are profit centres. These contrast with the old school style of ExxonMobil, which uses a more centralized structure.

ExxonMobil is the only major oil company with a structure that allows it to face the challenge of taking

on huge, technologically-challenging projects. Exxon's success resulted from the bitter experience of the Exxon Valdez tanker oil spill in Alaska in 1989. The company overhauled its approach to safety and centralized its businesses, adding checks and balances, and created an internal communications system that improved everything from financial prudence to physical caution and technological innovation. Based on the approach taken by Dow Chemical, the company structure is now the same around the world. Therefore employees do not have to relearn Exxon's policies and procedures every time they move. It also allows problems to be communicated throughout the company so that others can help, or at least learn from them.

Mark Albers, president of ExxonMobil Development Company, who oversees all of Exxon's new production and development projects, says the centralized structure is key to its success. From concept to production, all of Exxon's big projects are managed from Houston:

'In terms of the management and service that we provide to each of our affiliates, it's all done in one location, which means we can provide the same world-class service to an affiliate in Angola as in Sakhalin, as in Qatar. And people are literally just down the hall from people who worked on a similar issue on a project somewhere else down the globe, so the information transfer and the best practice transfer is immediate.'

He points out that the projects Exxon operates are within 3 per cent of the unit costs expected at the time of funding, and the company finishes its projects about 5 per cent more quickly than it forecasts.[1]

Organizational structure

Structure is the organization of effort into a coherent and working entity. Its characterizing feature is a hierarchy to determine an order of responsibilities; only very small organizations can do without it. Structure can be categorized in terms of width and the degree to which decisions are centralized or not, and height, according to the number of levels of management, and a hierarchy formalizing the direction of reporting. A difference is sometimes made between local structure (the organization within functional and distributed units) and strategic structures (the organization of the total structure). Broadly, the overall structure of organizations can be grouped into four main types. In Figure 9.1 these are represented by functional, product, region, and matrix forms. The lines between the boxes show the main reporting paths between the different parts. These also reflect corporate parenting styles, as already discussed in the last chapter.

Functional structure is based on **functional management**. This involves the division of work into specialist activities. Typically these are organized into departments that specialize in purchasing, manufacturing, marketing, finance and so on. This specialization is characteristic of the division of labour, when work is split into parts so that individuals are

> **Structure is the organization of effort into a coherent and working entity. Its characterizing feature is a hierarchy to determine an order of responsibilities; only very small organizations can do without it.**

FIGURE 9.1 Four basic types of organizational structure

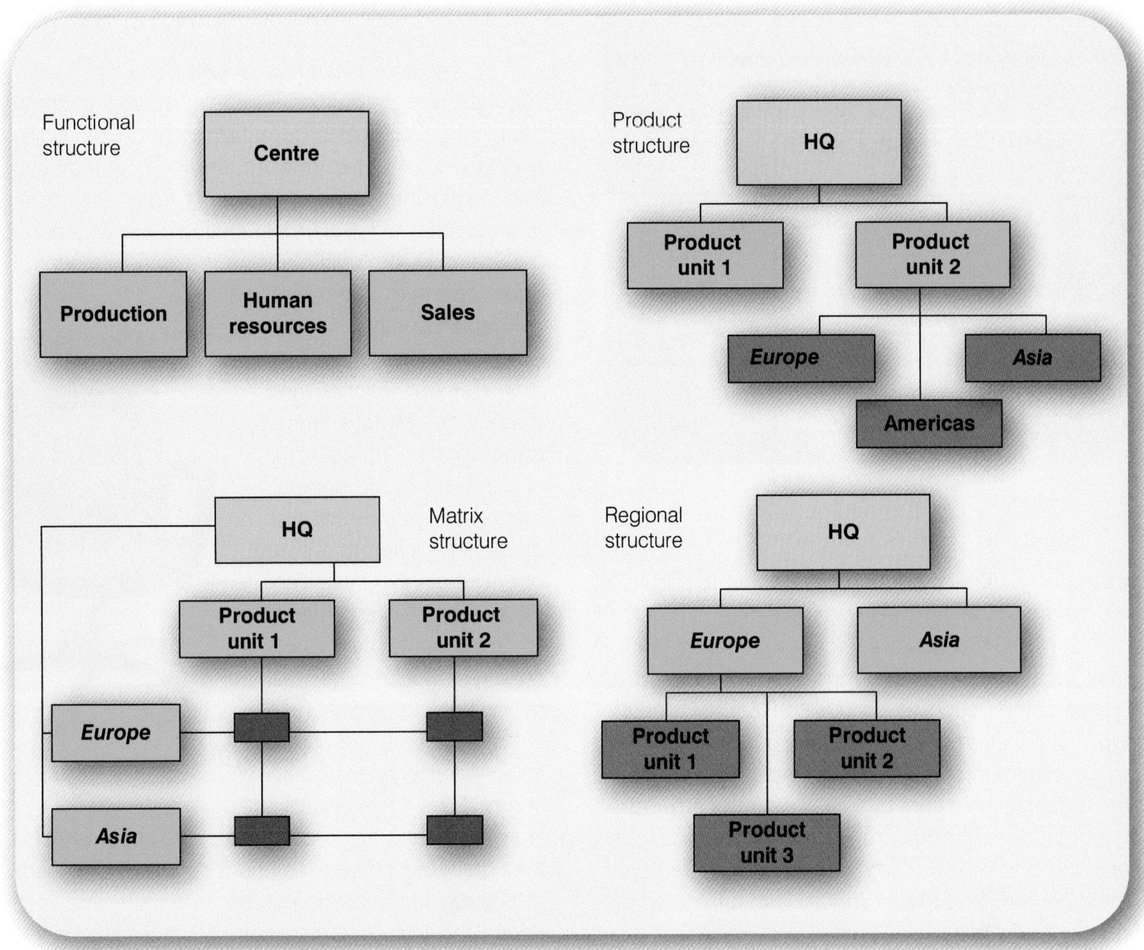

more able to carry it out effectively. To work as a complete system the separate parts must be co-ordinated effectively by a centre, so that the structure must be hierarchical where the centre is positioned at the top of the organization and controls the overall design of the inputs-into-outputs transformation process.

As some organizations grow in size, becoming multi-product and multi-market enterprises, they group their activities into divisions, based on products and geographical regions. These divisions are organized into functional activities with their own co-ordinating centre, and are typically under the control of a general manager, whose team reports to the organization's headquarters. The reasons for the multi-divisional form were first articulated by the economic historian, Alfred Chandler, who offered an account of corporate growth at General Motors and Du Pont.[2] The term used for multi-divisional structure by organizational scientists is the '**M-form**' organization.

The M-form enables each division to specialize on particular products (or brands), or on a distinct regional market. The divisions are thus focused and are closer to customers, so that they can pick up, and respond quickly to, the needs of the markets. The overall co-ordination of the divisions is effected by executives at headquarters. However, if there are needs for the divisions to collaborate with each other, this can be difficult to achieve formally within the product and regional structural form. If, for

example, a range of different products is required for distinct markets, then inter-divisional and inter-departmental projects are necessary. Project teams may be organized by a support function based at headquarters, such as corporate R&D, or marketing, with their membership drawn from the divisions. Where inter-divisional projects are central to the organization's core business a **matrix structure** is put in place. In this project teams and units are organized to report jointly to product and regional management, and to co-ordinate with others for ongoing project work.

ABB, a global electrical products company, made the product line-geographical matrix approach popular in the 1990s, when it organized its hundreds of local business units around the world. In the new structure, each local business unit reported to both a country executive and a worldwide line-of-business executive. This allowed the corporation to achieve the benefits of centralized co-ordination, functional expertise and economies of scale for product groups, while maintaining local divisional autonomy and entrepreneurship for marketing and sales activities. Matrix organizations have proved difficult to manage because of their inherent tension between the interests of the senior executives responsible for managing either a row or a column of the matrix. A manager at the intersection struggles to co-ordinate between the preferences of his 'row' and 'column' managers, leading to new sources of difficulty, conflict and delay. The ultimate source of accountability and authority in the matrix organization is ambiguous.

The degree, and levels, of organizational hierarchy vary in organizations. Chandler thought strategy should be made at an organization's centre, while divisions should be involved only with operations. The notion that strategy is distinct from operations is a central one for classical strategic management: the idea that strategic planning is primarily a central and long-term function, while its implementation is carried out through shorter-term management control and operations. **Middle management** (for Chandler this is made up of the general managers who lead the divisions) is used to report operational progress on the plan to the centre, and to relay any necessary changes decided at the centre back to operations.

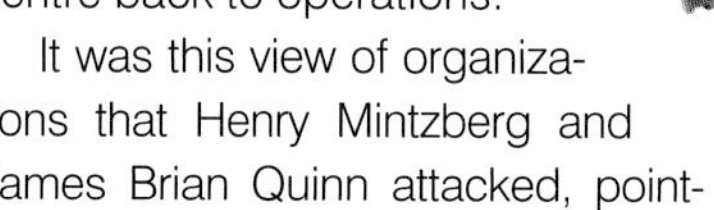

It was this view of organizations that Henry Mintzberg and James Brian Quinn attacked, pointing out the idea that a centre can control its divisions through detached analysis and a rational deployment of strategy is doubtful.[3] This became more apparent during the last years of the twentieth century when many large corporations began to de-layer, or take out hierarchical levels, to make their organization flatter. This reduced the ranks of middle-managers, and the size and functions at a corporate headquarters. In part this reflected a fashion for downscoping (discussed in Chapter 8), but it also reflected an awareness of Japanese business process and customer-based organizing: for example, total quality management and lean production (see Chapter 5).

Problems of functional organization

Functional working has many disadvantages from a strategic management point of view. Strategic

PRINCIPLES IN PRACTICE 9.1

Don't organize for specialization

Peter Drucker argues that functional thinking is bad for taking an overall view. Three stonecutters were asked what they were doing:

The first replied: 'I am making a living'.

The second kept on hammering while he said: 'I am doing the best job of stone-cutting in the entire country'.

The third one looked up with a visionary gleam in his eyes and said: 'I am building a cathedral'.

The third man is, of course, the true manager. The first man knows what he wants to get out of the work and manages to do so. He is likely to give a fair day's work for a fair day's pay. But he is not a manager and never will be one.

It is the second man who is a problem. Workmanship is essential; without it no work can flourish ... there is always the danger that the true workman, the true professional, will believe that he is accomplishing something when in fact he is just polishing stones or collecting footnotes. Workmanship must be encouraged in the business enterprise. But it must always be related to the needs of the whole. The majority of managers in any business enterprise are, like the second man, concerned with specialized work.[25]

Question: How is it possible to organize so that specialists become strategic?

priorities are likely to become fragmented, as critical business processes are chopped into disjointed pieces and scattered across several specialized departments. This can result in many hand-offs between activities, which lengthen completion time, and efforts to deal with delays increase the costs of co-ordination and overheads. There is a risk that essential details fall through the cracks. Breaking objectives down into specialized pieces is also to lose sight of the strategic imperative for an activity, so that employees go through the motions, and do not follow through to make sure the work is being done.

Process organization

A **business process** is a sequence of tasks necessary to deliver a business objective. In the organization science literature, 'processes' are classically understood as (normally) informal cross-functional activities, which flow horizontally across the vertical and hierarchical structure of the organization. The distinction is that a hierarchical structure provides a stable working framework, while processes are essentially the organizing activity within that framework. The new thing about this lies in the relationship of organization to organizing. In Japanese organizations, business processes are organized more directly around the pull of customer requirements, whereas in many western organizations, the requirements of the customer are less instant, and pushed through the organization through top-down planning and design. The practical difference for organizing is that in a Japanese context the processes decide, bottom-up, what they need from the specialists.

Reporting on the findings of a major international study of organizational forms in Europe and Japan, Andrew Pettigrew with others write that there is 'now an understandable tendency to drop the noun of organization and to use the more dynamic verb of organizing to try and capture the realities of

THERE IS NOW AN UNDERSTANDABLE TENDENCY TO DROP THE NOUN OF ORGANIZATION AND TO USE THE MORE DYNAMIC VERB OF ORGANIZING TO TRY AND CAPTURE THE REALITIES OF CONTINUOUS INNOVATION ... ORGANIZING AND STRATEGIZING ARE NOW RECOGNIZED AS TRULY COMPLEMENTARY ACTIVITIES EVEN TO THE POINT WHERE THE FORM OF ORGANIZING MAY BE SYNONYMOUS WITH THE STRATEGY OF THE FIRM.

continuous innovation ... Organizing and strategizing are now recognized as truly complementary activities even to the point where the form of organizing may be synonymous with the strategy of the firm.'[4]

Cross-functional structure

In fact, the process orientation of large Japanese organizations is still based within a functional structure, but the difference is that business processes are strategically managed to take account of top-down priorities. Japan has a strong top-to-bottom structure in its organizations that is likely to impede horizontal relations. The solution has been to use cross-functional committees to provide support for how key strategic **cross-functional** objectives are managed in the functional areas of the business. Ishikawa has compared this activity to making cloth, when the horizontal woof (sometimes called weft) of a textile is crossed to bind together the vertical warp into a strongly-held-together textile (see Figure 9.2).[5] The functional areas of a business are suggested at the top of the figure, and the work of the committees through review is indicated on the left-hand side of the figure.

The cross-functional committees are organized centrally and involve senior management. These work to review periodically the organization-wide progress of a limited number of strategically derived objectives. The objectives are characterized in a similar way to the perspectives of the balanced scorecard (Chapter 3), as quality, cost, delivery and employees. 'Quality' means those objectives that are linked directly to customer-oriented requirements; 'cost' to financial needs; 'delivery' to the strategic needs of the core business processes and 'employees' to the growth and learning needs of the workforce.

At the time when the Japanese were first introducing cross-functional structures, western corporations were moving away from management by top-down committee towards the devolved and divisional forms of corporate control.[6] In fact, western corporations never really use the woof-warp structure of review for strategic objectives. Instead, they use matrix

FIGURE 9.2 Cross-functional woof to weave functional warp

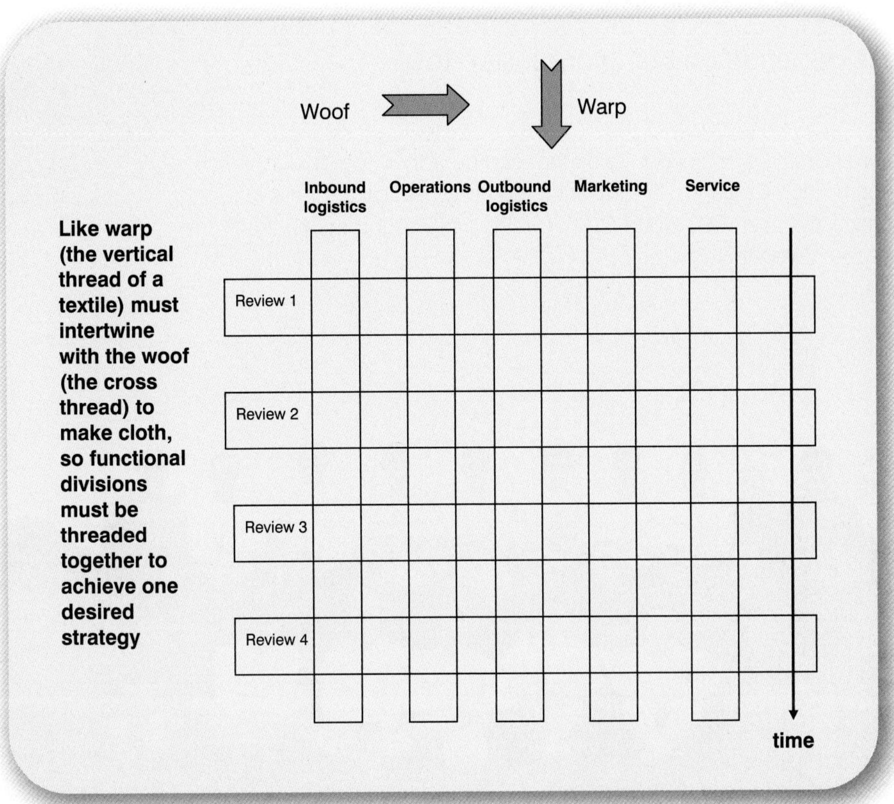

organization, where strategically-relevant project work is based around specially established multi-skilled teams.

The Japanese use matrix organization as well, but the work of the project teams is strategically linked to a review of progress carried out within the existing cross-functional structure. In this context, Kondo suggests Japanese organizations do not have as many centralized functions, such as quality planning, co-ordination, and auditing, as their western counterparts, but that instead these activities are carried out by line personnel, who have the necessary education and training for managing strategically-linked objectives.[7] He pointed out that Japanese central departments are typically small and perform only a limited array of activities, including objective deployment, review and consulting services.

Downsizing

Downsizing is a reduction in the size of a corporate entity. It reflects a wider revolution in thinking about organizations: a move from the bureaucratic pyramid to what the Yale sociologist, Richard Sennett, terms 'the flexible organization of the new capitalism':

'Cutting-edge firms and flexible organizations need people who can learn new skills rather than cling to old competences. The dynamic organization emphasizes the ability to process and interpret changing bodies of information and practice … In work terms a person's human "potential" consists in how capable he or she is in moving from problem to problem, subject to subject.'[8]

This results in smaller corporate headquarters for many organizations, and a reduced role for staff at the corporate office. However, downsizing has

PRINCIPLES IN PRACTICE 9.2

Success depends on being organized to achieve it

Jimmy Greaves, footballer, holds the record for the most goals scored for England. In his autobiography he puts England's success in the 1966 World Cup down to a new approach used by the England manager:

AP Photo

England's historic success was seen to be the result of players being 'professional' and 'doing a professional job'. Alf [the team manager] had had a game plan and he picked the players to suit that game plan. What he didn't do was create a game plan to suit the styles of the players at his disposal. Each player had a job to do within the game plan. They did it and England won the World Cup. Though players enjoyed a degree of freedom with this game plan, there was no place for a player who might want to stamp his own idiosyncratic style on the course of a game. No place for a maverick with a penchant for playing to the crowd. Players had to be professional and do the job they were being paid to do. The modernization of English football had picked up momentum since the late fifties. Even before 1966 coaches were having a bigger say in how the game should be played and teams were better organized … [it was] the death knell for players who were given to fully expressing themselves in the course of a game. Being 'professional' seeped into the subconscious of the game and any player who took it upon himself to play-act in the course of a match, or play to the gallery, was deemed to be 'unprofessional'.[26]

Question: What is the connection in strategic management between purpose and organization?

KEY DEBATE 9.1

Should structure encourage a competitive or a collaborative organizational environment?

There is an implicit assumption in much of the writing about strategy that the intensity of competition works to sharpen organizations and their managements through providing incentives for strong leadership and change. This belief can lead to problems when an organization's structure is designed to incentivize competitive behaviour. The logic for organizations (and hierarchies) is that (a market's) competitive behaviour is unfavourable to many purposes: see the original work of Arrow and Williamson.[28]

The link between competition and good management is uncertain.[29] When a financial perspective dominates a strategic portfolio approach; competition between SBUs within a corporate group may encourage short-termism (see Chapter 7).

The resource-based view argues that hierarchies are created spaces for organizing activity in a non-market-like fashion. The things that make an organization competitive are its unique core competences and capabilities; it is how structure facilitates organizing that really counts: *'The very essence of capabilities/competences is that they cannot be readily assembled through markets'*, write Teece et al.[29]

Initiatives to introduce market influences to achieve hybrid structures have worked against the very organizational complementarity that sustains a hierarchical structure, and have proved dysfunctional enough to spiral hierarchies toward fundamental transformation.[30]

Question: There is a paucity of evidence that favours the internal promotion of competition through structure. Can you think of any, and how has it worked?

attracted much adverse commentary, since in several instances its scale was huge. For example, BT cut its workforce from 232 000 in 1990, to 148 000 in 1995; the consequences for employee relations were such that, according to BT surveys, one-fifth of its workforce thought that managers could not be relied upon.[9]

Downsizing is associated with **business process re-engineering (BPR)**, which was originally defined as the use of information technology to redesign business processes radically,[10] but it quickly came to mean any breakthrough change in business processes that involves redesigning a set of activities to make them customer, rather than functionally, responsive. It involves establishing a senior management project team to question how the corporation should be structured if it were to be re-organized from scratch. Its focus is on creating an entirely new organization so that it can eliminate overheads that are incurred because of excessive specialization. While it produces new forms of flexible organization, because it typically de-layers organization to make it flatter, it also diminishes the role and influence of middle management, which can adversely take away a main support for organizing, and diminishes collective corporate memory.

Downsizing is associated with outsourcing. This concerns activities that do not contribute directly to value, and can be performed more effectively by external organizations. For example, Procter & Gamble has outsourced human resources, accounting and information technology; these are activities that had employed 8000 people in areas that had been considered back office operations.[11] Outsourcing

can be risky if things go wrong at the supplier over which the customer organization has no control. British Airways outsourced its in-flight prepared meals to Gate Gourmet, but in 2005 the caterer became involved in an industrial dispute that delayed BA flights and generated a lot of bad publicity.

Networks

Corporate memory is less important if organizations are in areas of dynamic change and networks offer a learning capability and a potentially valuable source of corporate knowledge. **Networks** are comprised of informal groups of individuals, who are typically based in distinct and different parts of, and are sometimes external to, the organization. However, they can be organized from the corporate centre.

This happens at Xerox, where specialists manage from the centre cross-functional networks of experts located, sometimes individually, in the different business units acting as consultants in areas like IT, quality and human resources. The networks are informal and involve forums across the organization where ideas are exchanged about best practice, matters of mutual interest are discussed, and intra-organizational learning is facilitated. These networks are also used to manage the Xerox Management Model (see performance excellence, Chapter 5) and the deployment of strategic objectives (see Case 10.1).

Nearly all organizations have some form of informal networks that are quasi-social in character, and which often cut across formal structure. Compared to hierarchical structure, which is indicative of authority, lines of command and reporting, informal networks are typically about the communication of information and support. In some countries they take on special qualities that are influenced by national cultural practices (for example, see China's *guanxi*, Chapter 2).

Systems and systems thinking

Systems are typically formal and documented codes, policies and procedures, which organizations prescribe as normal or best ways of working. Such systems are important to hierarchical structure to clarify responsibilities and reporting procedures. However, systems thinking is different. Broadly it likens organizations to organisms, especially the idea that problems can only be understood by looking at the whole context, rather than by examining the constituent parts. Organizations have sub-systems just as organisms do. Many have boundaries that span each other and many will have interconnected components that work together. A systems way of thinking implies that people will see the whole, whereas in a functionally top-down organization there is always a danger of sub-optimization. This is where one part will act in its own interest, and against the interest of the customer and the whole. A systems approach emphasizes the use of integrative conceptual frameworks to guide strategic decisions, which can provide a consistent and holistic view of an organization's activities. The best known is the McKinsey Consulting Group's 7S framework.

McKinsey's 7S framework

The **McKinsey 7S framework** was first published by Waterman with others in 1980, and made popular by Tom Peters and Robert Waterman a couple of years later in their very successful book, *In Search of Excellence.*[12] The authors were McKinsey

FIGURE 9.3 Organizing for interconnectivity[14]

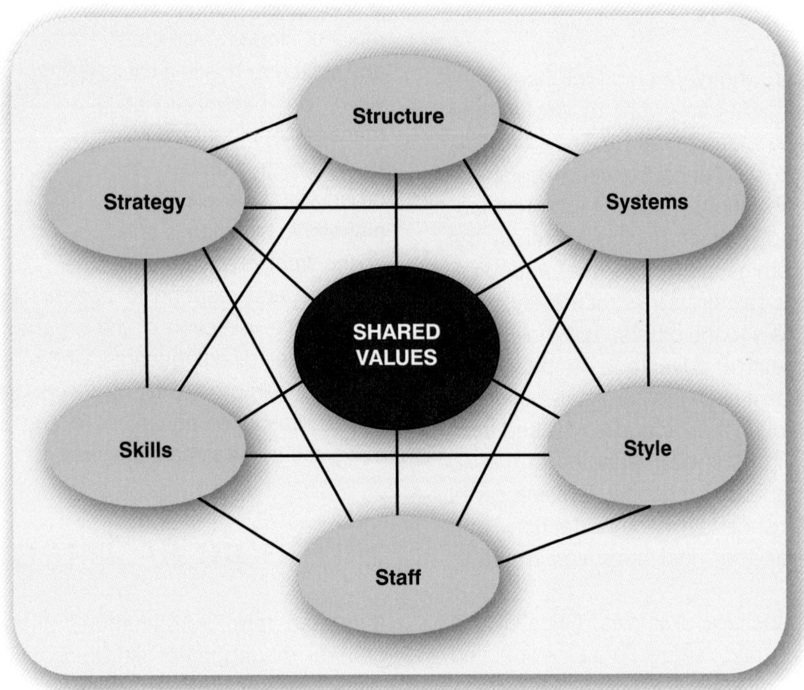

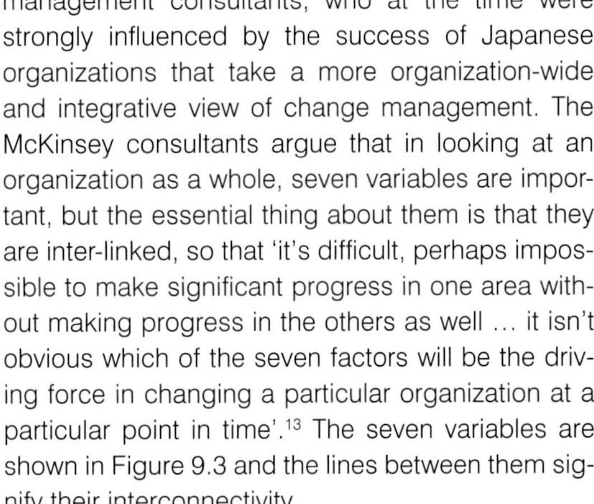

management consultants, who at the time were strongly influenced by the success of Japanese organizations that take a more organization-wide and integrative view of change management. The McKinsey consultants argue that in looking at an organization as a whole, seven variables are important, but the essential thing about them is that they are inter-linked, so that 'it's difficult, perhaps impossible to make significant progress in one area without making progress in the others as well … it isn't obvious which of the seven factors will be the driving force in changing a particular organization at a particular point in time'.[13] The seven variables are shown in Figure 9.3 and the lines between them signify their interconnectivity.

- Strategy: those actions an organization plans in response to, or in anticipation of, changes in the external environment, its customers and competitors.
- Structure: the organization that divides tasks and provides for their co-ordination.
- Systems: the processes, procedures, formal and informal, that 'make an organization go'.
- Style: the perception a senior management team creates of itself in the organization.
- Staff: the socialization of managers in terms of what the business is about.
- Skills: the characterization of the organization in terms of what it does best, its dominating attributes or capabilities.
- Shared values (or superordinate goals): the guiding beliefs, or fundamental ideas, around which an organization is built.

Making changes in strategy and structure by themselves can be implemented quickly. However, to be effective the other elements must be strategically managed, especially the central place of shared values, a concept that is virtually the same as core values (see Chapter 2). Changes in these other elements can take years to achieve, so that the real pace of change is ultimately a function of all seven variables.

Hard and soft strategic management

Pascale and Athos, who were also McKinsey consultants, used the 7S framework to explore the nature of Japanese management.[15] They find that while there is little difference between Japanese and western organizations in terms of the management of strategy, structure and systems, the Japanese give prominence to the other variables. Pascale and Athos call strategy-structure-systems 'hard-ball' variables and the others, 'soft-ball'. They stress that competitive advantage is based as much on soft-ball as it is on the hard-ball variables. The new competition of the Japanese resulted from a combination of the soft-ball variables of the 7S framework: the Japanese national 'culture gives them ambiguity, uncertainty, imperfection and interdependence as the most approved mode of relationship'.[16]

Using mostly Japanese examples, Ghoshal and Bartlett go further and argue for a soft-based approach to running organizations, based on purpose, process, and people.[17] These three things should replace strategy, structure and systems. This is a flat view of organizational management that favours a minimum number of organizational levels; where a strategic direction is reliant on the creative abilities of people to sense and respond to opportunities. Thus, 'purpose' is the direction of the organization; 'process' involves self-directing teams, where people plan, do, check, and improve their own work, and 'people' are the facilitation of commitment and involvement to make self-management possible.

Strategic architecture

A related term, 'architecture', is popular in the general management literature where it is 'used

KEY DEBATE 9.2

Is it implementation or strategy that matters?

Many observers argue that the reasons for ineffective strategic management concern poor implementation. Charan and Colvin argue that for 70 per cent of organizations that get into trouble, it was not because of a wrong strategy, but an inability to implement that caused the problems.[31] Floyd and Wooldridge argue the problem is caused by middle and operational management, which is either ill-informed or simply unsupportive.[32] The problems may result from structures that do not involve and encourage an effective cross-functional management, and effective company-wide understanding and effort.[33] Barney argues that the ability of organizations to implement strategies is itself a source of sustainable competitive advantage.[34]

Others, such as the processual, or learning school of strategy (see Chapter 1), argue that the distinction between strategy and implementation is a false one anyway.[35] Mintzberg thinks there is a disconnect between grand strategy and operations: this is due to the fact that senior managers do not understand their organizations.[36]

Question: What are the principal tasks of good strategy implementation?

to refer to such things as networks and infrastructural elements, including a mix of formal and informal management systems, frameworks, organizational structure and culture. Architecture can be understood as those co-ordinating features that link up activities and influence behaviour, which are 'hard-wired' into an organization in the same way that a building's design will condition how people work. A modern example relates to information architecture, where the design of a database in terms of its applications will determine how people work together.

Hamel and Prahalad give **'strategic architecture'** a central role: 'a company needs a point of view about the future (industry foresight) and must construct a blueprint for getting there (strategic architecture)'.[18] This 'blueprint' is a framework for core competence building and must ensure that existing core competences do not fragment across corporate business units. Although they do explicitly make the link, the role of a strategic architecture is to enable an organization's dynamic capability: the corporate-wide capability to reconfigure and sustain core competences, or strategic assets (see Chapter 5).

© iStockPhoto.com

Joined-up management

Joined-up management is 'a strategy which seeks to bring together not only government departments and agencies, but also a range of private and voluntary bodies, working across organizational boundaries'.[19] It aims to address complex social problems, such as social exclusion and poverty, in a comprehensive and integrated way. While such problems have a long history, especially in relation to problems of co-ordination in government, the term 'joined-up government' came into common use in public sector management in the late 1990s as a criticism of functional departmentalization. However, public sector strategic management has tended to move away from this to favour the possibility that competitive influences can 'incentivize public services' to improve services.

Internal markets

Internal markets are created as quasi-markets to simulate market behaviour inside a single organization or an organizational group, such as a large corporation. The purpose is typically to achieve efficiencies, say, based on competing cost centres and/or through formal contracts. This approach has been favoured by governments in the United Kingdom for parts of the public sector, notably the National Health Service, where service providers must negotiate contracts with internal suppliers and some types of customers. The aim is to create a more cost-conscious orientation, but this may have been at the expense of a patient-caring organizational culture. More generally, collaborative efforts that encourage learning and technology transfer may be jeopardized if incentives and rewards work to encourage individualism rather than collective behaviours.

Loosely-coupled strategic management

Karl Weick introduced a more fluid view of strategic organizing, when he argued that it is how organizational elements come together frequently and loosely that determines how an organization works as an entity. Using ideas originally associated with biology, Weick argues that frequently in organizations several different means lead to the same outcomes, so that it can be said that means are loosely coupled to an end, in the sense that there are alternative pathways.[20] Rationality and indeterminacy are both accepted, which contrasts with classical views of administrative science, for example, of Herbert Simon and his view that complex systems should be decomposed into stable sub-assemblies.[21] According to Weick loose coupling involves impermanence, dissolvability and tacitness; they are all the 'glue' that holds organizations together. Weick used a metaphor to start his essay about loosely-coupled systems:

> *Imagine that you're either the referee, coach, player or spectator at an unconventional soccer match: the field for the game is round; there are several goals scattered haphazardly around the circular field; people can enter and leave the game when they want to; they can throw balls in whenever they want; they can say, 'that's my goal!' if they want to; the entire game takes place on a sloped field; and the game is played as if it makes sense. If you now substitute principals for referees, teachers for coaches, students for players, parents for spectators and schooling for soccer, you have found an equally unconventional depiction of school organizations. The beauty of this depiction is that it captures a different set of realities within educational organizations than are caught when these same organizations are viewed through the tenets of bureaucratic theory.*[22]

In many ways strategic management looks more like Weick's unconventional soccer match than it does the old idea that an organization is like a car; you assemble the pieces, put in the oil and off it goes. In saying this, it does not necessarily mean we need less management (see 'what management means' in Chapter 11).

Strategic planning – revisited

One could be forgiven, especially if one works in them, for thinking that organizations are a mess or, in some cases, they seem to run themselves. Where does this leave strategic planning? How is it possible to be deliberate? The days of classical strategic planning, when long-range strategy, structure, and systems, were worked out at an organization's centre by planners for others to implement are now probably long gone. In the oil industry, for instance, Robert Grant concludes that strategic plans have become shorter term, more goals-focused, and less specific with regard to actions and resource allocations, which are worked out informally at local levels. The role of strategic planning systems within strategic management has also changed. It has become less about strategic decision making and more a mechanism for co-ordination and managing performance.[23]

Strategy implementation puts in place an organization's strategy. It is carried out through an organization's structure and control systems, and the outcomes are modified during daily management. 'Implementation' and 'execution' are often used interchangeably. However, an organization's structures and systems must be in place prior to execution, or the alignment of strategy with operational activity is unlikely. Strategic planning is today primarily an implementation activity, rather than one about formulation, for many large and complex organizations, and works through medium-term planning. It involves plans that are half-way between longer-term purpose, strategic objectives and overall strategy, and the strategic initiatives and priorities that are operationalized in daily management. These are called **medium and mid-term plans**.

PRINCIPLES IN PRACTICE 9.3

Two principles for structures and hierarchy

The most important sub-system in any organization is the managerial hierarchy

Hierarchies permit the systematic delegation of functions, roles and tasks. Delegation is not a simple concept as it might seem at first blush. When the American engineer Homer Sarasohn inquired into the weakness of Japanese manufacturing in the late 1940s, he observed that, when managers delegated a task to a subordinate, they thought they had also delegated the responsibility for it. He believed that the delegator retains that responsibility, just as if he were performing the task itself.

Hierarchy is sometimes attacked on the grounds that it inhibits the creation of cross-departmental teams designed to address problems that affect more than one area of a firm. Anyone who propounds this view has misunderstood the way in which such teams come into being and function. They do not simply materialize out of the thin air. Someone in authority has to appoint them and they are effective only if they report to the person whose position in the hierarchy is strong enough to ensure the recommendations are put into effect.

By permission of Lisa Sarasohn

Homer Sarasohn

The best type of hierarchy is bottom-up

This goes far beyond the simple delegation of tasks to appropriate levels that are characteristic of all well-run hierarchies. It superimposes an additional, informal structure which permits *de facto* operational responsibility to be pushed down to the lowest level capable of accepting it – which in a manufacturing plant would be a foreman – while not abolishing the formal line-of-command as the ultimate channel of communication and control. In a crisis, or when a major change of direction is required, a senior manager can reassert control over a subordinate at the drop of a hat and without upsetting the relationship.[27]

Question: Structure reflects a need for organizational control: if control must be different at different times, what does this suggest for structure?

These plans are expressed as a three-year, sometimes five-year, series of annual targets for year 1, year 2, year 3, and so on, for 3–5 years. They consist of grouped objectives, sometimes using an objective set based on perspectives like the balanced scorecard, or as a specified set of strategic initiatives grouped to suggest themes for strategic projects. Hamel and Prahalad explain similar plans as challenges, or stages that will move the organization forward to achieve its longer-term strategic intent (see Chapter 3). Medium-term objectives are developed with other levels, including functional management, and take into account the condition and progress of overall purpose (Chapter 2), the external and internal environments (Chapters 4 and 5), and the overall, and divisional, strategies (Chapters 6, 7 and 8).

These longer-term considerations are used as a loosely-related group to guide the more detailed development of medium-term objectives and means. However, even the specification of the mid-term objectives themselves is not meant to be prescriptive of the enablers. This view of strategic planning is similar to the 'programme' view favoured by Mintzberg and his related concept of an umbrella strategy, when a loose and directional form of longer-term strategy is used to guide more detailed short-term action planning.[24] The medium-term is essentially a guiding framework for the detail which is worked out more precisely at a daily management level. This is the subject of Chapter 10.

KEY DEBATE 9.3

Is the new flexible organization good for people?

The shift from a bureaucratic to a more fragmentary new form of capitalism, argues Yale sociologist, Richard Sennett, acts to reduce institutional loyalty, trust among workers and weakened institutional knowledge. He contrasts the 'bureaucratic pyramid' with the 'new flexible organization' of the new capitalism:

> *One vice of the old bureaucratic pyramid was its rigidity, its offices fixed, its people knowing exactly what was expected of them. The virtue of the pyramid was, however, accumulation of knowledge about how to make the system work, which meant knowing when to make exceptions to the rules or contriving back-channel arrangements. As in armies, so in big civilian bureaucracies, knowing how to manipulate the system can become an art form. Often people who have the most institutional knowledge of this sort are low down the corporate hierarchy … complements informal trust; in time, as experience accumulates, the bureaucrat learns how to oil bureaucratic wheels.*[37]
>
> *Cutting-edge firms and flexible organizations need people who can learn new skills rather than cling to old competences. The dynamic organization emphasizes the ability to process and interpret changing bodies of information and practice … In work terms a person's human 'potential' consists in how capable he or she is in moving from problem to problem, subject to subject. The ability to move around in this way resembles the work of consultants, writ large.*[38]

Sennett argued that this mobility puts an emphasis on a person's potential ability, rather than their experience as a measure of talent. The flexible firm is an influential model for government, but this organizing form is inappropriate for those public institutions that seek to deliver security and well-being to citizens.

Question: What types of strategy are favoured by these two different forms of organizing?

SUMMARY OF PRINCIPLES

1 Structure is necessary for hierarchy; there are four principal types: functional structure, product structure, regional structure and matrix structure.

2 Flat organization is associated with devolved decision-making and has become associated with new forms of flexible organizing, such as downsizing and business process re-engineering.

3 Cross-functional structure has the benefit of integrating the strengths of the horizontal (functional areas) and vertical (review areas) of an organization.

4 The McKinsey 7S framework is a systems view of organizations, when the key areas of an organization must be considered as a whole.

5 Strategy, structure and systems are 'hard-ball', while skills, staff, style and shared values are 'soft-ball' and the latter are as important as the former.

6 Joined-up management concerns the bringing together of governmental and private bodies across a range of organizational boundaries, mainly to address complex social problems.

7 A number of different means can lead to the same end; the recognition and management of this is called 'loosely coupled management'.

GLOSSARY OF KEY TERMS

Business process a sequence of tasks to deliver a business objective.

Business process re-engineering (BPR) the re-designing of business processes.

Cross-functional horizontal management/structure (normally used to work across the functional divisions of an organization).

Downsizing reduction in the size of a corporate entity.

Functional management the management of work involving its division into specialist activities that are normally organized into departments, such as design, purchasing, operations, marketing, finance, human resources, IT, and so on.

Matrix structure units/projects report to more one than one division/unit.

McKinsey 7S framework a framework of seven inter-related variables for managing organizational change.

Medium and mid-term plans statements of three to five year objectives (sometimes with guidelines about means).

M-form organization a multi-divisional organization.

Middle management managers placed between the senior/executive and operational levels.

Networks informal groups of individuals, who are typically based in distinct and different parts of, and sometimes external to, the organization.

Strategic architecture blueprint for an organizing framework that conditions how people work.

Strategy implementation the putting in place of an organization's strategy.

GUIDED FURTHER READING

Karl Weick, who is always interesting, has extended his ideas to situations where there is little or no existing reference frameworks for understanding an organization; see:

Weick, K. (1995) *Sensemaking in Organizations*, Thousand Oaks, CA: Sage.

The use of metaphors for understanding and managing organizations has been covered in several areas of organizational studies. Gareth Morgan uses images, such as plants, as sense-making tools to categorize organizations, and to understand the essence of different organizational forms.

Morgan, G. (1996) *Images of Organization* (2nd edn), London: Sage

Henry Mintzberg has proposed a new way for understanding organizational structure, called configurations; see:

Mintzberg, H. and Waters, J. A. (1985) 'Of strategies, deliberate and emergent', *Strategic Management Journal* 6257–72.

Mintzberg, H., Lampel, J., Quinn, J. B. and Ghoshal, S. (2003) (eds), *The Strategy Process* (4th edn), London: Prentice Hall.

REVIEW QUESTIONS

1 What is meant by an organization structure, and why is this important?

2 List the four main types of organizational structure.

3 What is a business process and how do process organizations facilitate this?

4 What is the defining characteristic of Japanese organizational structures?

5 Why has business process re-engineering (BPR) got a bad name?

6 What is the difference between 'hard-ball' and 'soft-ball' variables?

7 What is 'loosely-coupled' strategic management about?

8 How has strategic planning changed?

SEMINAR AND ASSIGNMENT QUESTIONS

1 What things need to be taken into account for developing an effective organizational structure that is appropriate to an organization's overall strategy?

2 Use a 7S framework to examine two contrasting organizations. Consider for each case how taking a system's view is likely to improve their strategic management. Are there any disadvantages to the 7S framework?

3 When is structure a strategy?

CHAPTER REFERENCES

1 Hoyos, C. (2006) 'BP battles to clear its Augean stables', *Financial Times* September 20, 23.

2 Chandler, A. D. Jr. (1962) *Strategy and Structure: Chapters in the History of the Industrial Enterprise*, Cambridge, MA: MIT Press.

3 Mintzberg, H. (1994) *The Rise and Fall of Strategic Planning,* London: Prentice Hall; Quinn, J. B. (1980) *Strategies for Change – Logical Incrementalism,* Homewood, IL: Irwin.

4 Pettigrew, A. M., Massini, S. and Numagami, T. (2000) 'Innovative forms of organizing in Europe and Japan', *European Management Journal* 18(3):259–73, 6.

5 Ishikawa, K. (1969) 'Company-wide quality control activities in Japan', *Proceedings of the 1st International Conference on Quality Control*, Tokyo:JUSE.

6 Jantsch, E. (ed.) (1967) *Technological Forecasting in Perspective,* Paris: OECD.

7 Kondo, Y. (1988) 'Quality in Japan'. In Juran, J. M. and Gryna, M. (eds), *Juran's Quality Control Handbook* (4th edn), London: McGraw-Hill, 35F1–35F30.

8 Sennett, R. (2006) *The Culture of the New Capitalism,* London: Yale University Press, p. 115.

9 Micklethwait, J. and Wooldridge, A. (1997) *The Witch Doctors: What the Management Gurus are Saying, Why it Matters and How to Make Sense of It,* London: Mandarin.

10 Hammer, M. (1990) 'Re-engineering work: don't automate, obliterate', *Harvard Business Review,* July–August, pp. 104–12.

11 Saigol, L. (2002) P&G begins global review of back office, *Financial Times,* February 26, 30.

12 Waterman, R. H., Peters, T. and Phillips, J. R. (1980) 'Structure is not organization', *Business Horizons,* June:14–26; Peters, T. J. and Waterman, R. H. (1982) *In Search of Excellence*, London: Harper & Row.

13 Waterman *et al.* (1980), p. 18–19.

14 Adapted from Peters and Waterman (1982) *op cit.,* p. 10.

15 Pascale, R. T. and Athos, A. G. (1982) *The Art of Japanese Management*, London: Penguin.

16 Pascale and Athos (1982) *op cit.*, p. 204.

17 Ghoshal, S. and Bartlett, C. A. (1997) *The Individualised Corporation: Great Companies are Defined by Purpose, Process, and People,* London: William Heinemann.

18 Hamel, G. and Prahalad, C. K. (1994) *Competing for the Future*, Boston, MA: Harvard Business School Press, p. 280.

19 Bogdanor, V. (2005) 'Introduction'. In Bogdanor, V. (ed.) (2005) *Joined-Up Government,* Oxford: Oxford University Press, pp. 1–2.

20 Weick, K. E. (1979) *The Social Psychology of Organizing* (2nd edn), Reading, MA: Addison-Wesley.

21 Simon, H. A. (1947) *Administrative Behaviour: A Study of Decision-Making Processes in Administrative Organizations,* New York: Free Press.

22 Weick (1979) *op cit.,* p. 1.

23 Grant, R. M. (2003) 'Strategic planning in a turbulent environment: evidence from the oil majors', *Strategic Management Journal,* 24:491–517.

24 Mintzberg (1994) *op cit.*

25 Adapted from Drucker, P. F. (1955) *The Practice of Management,* London: Heinemann-Butterworth, p. 20.

26 Adapted from Greaves, J. (2004) *Greavsie, The Autobiography,* London: Time-Warner, pp. 280–81.

27 Adapted from Hopper, K. and Hopper, W. (2009) *The Puritan Gift: Reclaiming the American Dream Amidst Global Financial Chaos,* New York: I. B. Tauris, pp. 280–81.

28 Arrow, W. (1974) *The Limits of Organizations,* London: W. W. Norton; Williamson, O. E. (1975) *Markets and Hierarchies: Analysis and Antitrust Implications,* New York: Free Press.

29 Teece, D. C., Pisano, G. and Shuen, A. (1997) 'Dynamic capabilities and strategic management', *Strategic Management Journal* 18:509–33, 517.

30 Zenger, T. R. (2002) 'Crafting internal hybrids: complementarities, common change initiatives, and the team-based organization', *International Journal of the Economics of Business* 9(1):79–95.

31 Charan, R. and Colvin, G. (1999) 'Why CEOs fail', *Fortune Magazine,* June 21.

32 Floyd, S. W. and Wooldridge, B. (1996) *The Strategic Middle Manager,* London: Jossey-Bass.

33 Kano, N. (1993) 'A perspective on quality activities in American firms', *California Management Review*, 35:12–31.

34 Barney, J. B. (2001) 'Is the resource-based "view" a useful perspective for strategic management research? Yes', *Academy of Management Review* 26(1):41–56.

35 Mintzberg, H., Lampel, J., Quinn, J. B. and Ghoshal, S. (2003) (eds), *The Strategy Process* (4th edn), London: Prentice Hall.

36 de Holan, P. M. (2004) 'Management as life's essence: 30 years of the "Nature of Managerial Work", an interview with Henry Mintzberg', *Strategic Organization* 2(2):205–12.

37 Sennett, R. (2006) *The Culture of the New Capitalism,* London: Yale University Press, p. 69.

38 Sennett (2006) *op cit.,* p. 115.

CASE 9.1 Cross-functional structure at Toyota

Toyota is organized around the way it manages its strategy. It is commonly believed that the company's competitive advantage is based on the Toyota Production System, its lean production approach. In fact, all the global car makers use their own version of Toyota's production system. Corporate management in Japan say (privately) its competitive advantage is based on the company's cross-functional structure, of which its lean production is only one part.

Cross-functional committees

Cross-functional structure began at Toyota in 1961, when it was designed to ensure that company-wide quality control worked at departmental level.[1] Quality assurance and cost management were regarded as purpose activities (core to the reasons for the organization), while others, including engineering (product planning and product design), production (manufacturing preparation and manufacturing), and commercial (sales and purchasing), were called means activities (enablers). This is similar to Porter's distinction between support and primary activities in the value chain.

Each area of activity has its formal reviews that are separate from departmental ones although they have a shared membership, but both types report to the corporate executive. The flow of the relationship is that cross-functional reviews take corporate strategic decisions, which the departments implement, acting in effect as line management to the cross-functional committees. Once the cross-functional policy is

Artpartner-images.com / Alamy

known, a department establishes its plans and holds meetings with its sections. The exact shape and membership of the cross-functional meetings vary according to the urgency and reach of a cross-functional concern at any one time. The cross-functional reviews constitute a formal and permanent structural arrangement, and involve bi-monthly and monthly meetings on quality and cost (although a significant agenda is also required). The immediate purpose of these meetings is to take remedial action on plans and reviews. A more substantial evaluation of progress is carried out in the middle and at the end of the planning year, and this involves the participation of top level, functional, and departmental, managers; the purpose is to provide feedback on the functional policies.

In the following exhibit, Toyota's strategic management starts with Toyota's overall purpose, a vision statement and its values expressed as a set of 'guiding principles'. These are used as reference frameworks to develop Toyota's basic policies and guidelines (see Exhibit 9.1). These are used as a basis for the mid-term plan. This is managed using cross-functional structure as described above. A key element is Toyota's hoshin kanri (policy management), an approach to policy execution discussed in more detail in Chapter 10. Senior managers translate the mid-term plan into action guidelines and goals (called hoshins) for each division of Toyota.

Toyota's guiding principles

- Honour the language and spirit of the law of every nation and undertake open and fair corporate activities to be a good corporate citizen around the world.
- Respect the culture and customs of every nation and contribute to economic and social development through corporate activities in local communities.
- Dedicate ourselves to providing clean and safe products and to enhancing the quality of life everywhere through our activities.

EXHIBIT 9.1 Toyota's organizing pyramid[2]

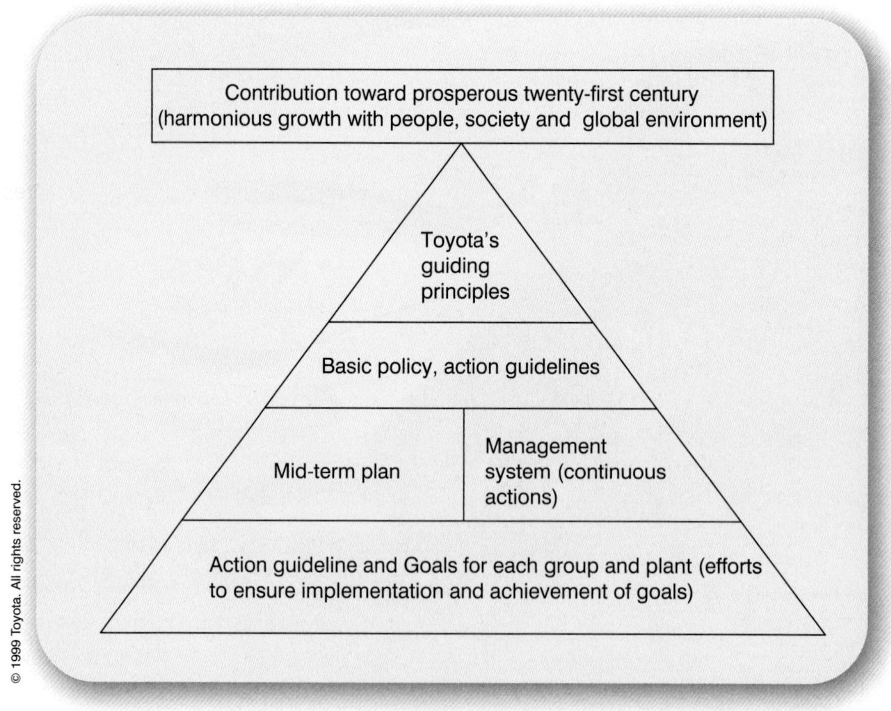

- Create and develop advanced technologies and provide outstanding products and services that fulfil the needs of customers worldwide.
- Foster a corporate culture that enhances individual creativity and teamwork, while honouring mutual trust and respect between labour and management.
- Pursue growth in harmony with the global community through innovative management.
- Work with business partners in research and creation to achieve stable, long-term growth and mutual benefits, while keeping ourselves open to new partnerships.

Example of a basic policy: environmental policy[3]

An over-arching concern is environmental policy. However, few firms actually manage the execution of environmental policy through the deployment of related objectives and means as closely as Toyota. This involves the formulation by senior management of three basic policies to last five years; each policy is linked to a number of action guidelines, which are managed continuously, or 'promoted' (the Japanese term), by senior management committees chaired by the president.

Each action guideline is in turn translated into several 'action items' put together as a 'mid-term' (five-year) plan. Generally, in Japanese companies, an 'item' is understood as an item of control, so that in this instance, the items are used to control the implementation of the three policies.

The mid-term plan gives each item its own 'action policy', with its specific goals and implementation items, and which are continuously reviewed by senior management for current status against expected achievement. For example, one of the three basic policies is written thus:

'Recognize that the manufacture of automobiles is deeply related to the earth's environment. Combine the strength of all groups with the company and co-operate with suppliers and distributors worldwide to develop technologies that are gentle on the earth and serve to promote environmental measures.'

This policy has seven action guidelines. One of these, for example, is: 'Always be concerned about the environment. Promote programmes to protect the environment: (i) develop low-pollution vehicles; and (ii) develop low-pollution production processes.'

Each action guideline has its own action items, or a statement, which is used as a guide for finding the means to achieve the policy. So, for example, the action guideline to achieve '(i) develop low-pollution vehicles', has five action items:

- reduce exhaust emissions
- reduce noise pollution
- increase fuel efficiency
- develop clean-energy vehicles
- use alternative refrigerants.

In the 2001–2005 mid-term plan, the seven action guidelines had in aggregate 23 action items, and each action item had its own 'action policy' and 'specific goals and implementation items'. For example, for the action item, 'reduce exhaust emissions', the mid-term plan had the following:

Action policy:

Promote appropriate emissions reduction responses considering specific urban needs in each country and region.

Promote technological development challenging zero emissions.

Respond to regulations in developed countries prior to their enactment.

Expand emission control measures immediately in developing countries.

The specific goals and implementation items are translated at divisional or business unit level into local mid-term plans. The ones shown immediately below are an example, in this case, for business units and plants in Japan. Local units will translate the mid-term plan into annual priorities or objectives, typically grouped under QCDE targets, for everybody to align and integrate into daily management.

Specific goals and implementation items (Japan only):

Further reduction in emissions in gasoline vehicles.

- Systematically introduce low emission vehicles which emit a quarter of the emissions permitted under Japan's 2000 regulation, starting with Prius.

Development and introduction of clean diesel vehicles.

- Introduce vehicles that accommodate the new Japanese diesel long-term regulation prior to its enactment.
- Development of ultra-clean diesel vehicles.

This deployment of its environmental policies through its mid-term plan is used by Toyota for its other policies. The unusual aspect is the continuous use of top level management committees to review and drive the action policies against expectations, once the mid-term plan is in place. This continuous review activity is cross-functional and takes priority over the company's departments and functional areas. It is at the heart of Toyota's management system referred to in Exhibit 9.1.

The world's first hybrid car

One of the great successes of Toyota's environmental policies has been its hybrid car. This was launched in Japan in 1997, and was offered for sale in the United States two years later. The former Toyota chairman, Eiji Toyoda, believed Toyota needed to put its time and money into creating a unique product for the next generation of customers, shareholders and employees. Toyota engineers had been working to develop a hybrid engine technology, a system that reduces gasoline usage by integrating electric power.

After several years in development, the project resulted in the revolutionary Prius Sedan. Using Toyota's own hybrid technology, dubbed the Hybrid Synergy Drive, the Prius was the world's first bona fide twenty-first century vehicle intended for sale on

AP Photo/Paul Sakuma

Eiji Toyoda

a mass, commercial level. Its development was one of the most difficult challenges in the history of global product design, engineering and manufacturing. Total costs, including the development of the hybrid technology, exceeded $1 billion. Difficulties arose all along the way, but the project received strong encouragement and direction from the highest corporate levels.

'...There will be great significance in launching the car early,' said former Toyota president Hiroshi Okuda, who took charge of the company in the midst of the Prius project, 'this car may change the course of Toyota's future and even that of the auto industry.'[4]

Some observers of the industry had felt that developing a new model for a mass market was an expensive mistake. There was no demand for a small car, a hybrid-engine car, especially as growing world prosperity seemed to favour larger cars. However, the gamble paid off and the company now puts hybrid engines into a range of popular models, and Toyota is now widely considered the leader in alternative transportation, at a time when global warming and rising oil prices are major world concerns.

Discussion questions

1. How does Toyota use organizational structure to implement its strategy?
2. Consider the strengths and weaknesses of a large multinational corporation of a Toyota pyramid (see Exhibit 9.1).
3. Is Toyota a truly visionary organization, and what constitutes its competitive advantage?

Case references

1. Koura, K. (1990) 'Survey and research in Japan concerning policy management', *ASQC Quality Congress Transactions*, San Francisco, 348–53; Kurogane, K. (1993) (ed.), *Cross-Functional Management: Principles and Practical Applications,* Tokyo: Asian Productivity Organization; Monden, Y. (1998) *Toyota Production System: An Integrated Approach to Just-in-Time* (3rd edn), Norcross, Georgia: Engineering & Management Press. (Published in Japan, 1983, Institute of Industrial Engineers.)
2. Toyota (1999)'Ensuring the achievement of the second action plan (FY2000) and taking actions for the 21st century', *Toyota Environment Management,* company document. (available at www.toyota.co.jp/environment/report/index.html)
3. Information taken from Toyota (1999) *op cit.*
4. Magee, D. (2007) *How Toyota Became # 1, Leadership Lessons from the World's Greatest Car Company,* London: Portfolio, Penguin Group.

Chapter 10

MANAGING IMPLEMENTATION

Introduction

Once an organization has in place organizing structures and systems, including medium-term strategic plans, it then has to ensure that its strategic priorities are implemented by everyone. This is sometimes called Strategy Execution. This chapter considers strategic performance management and how strategy is used to link daily management to strategic objectives.

LEARNING OBJECTIVES

By the end of this chapter you should understand:

1 Strategic performance management and how it is used to support strategic objectives.

2 The importance of using strategically-related objectives to focus the organization for alignment and integration, and the part played by strategic review at a daily management level.

3 The importance of 'delivery' in the public sector and the associated delivery chain.

4 CompStat and its use as a strategic review system for identifying patterns and achieving strategic objectives.

Business vignette Management does not join up by itself, the implementation of strategy should be managed

Dan Simpson, vice-president (head of Strategy and Planning at Clorox for 16 years), says: 'Execution problems are often symptoms of trouble upstream in the strategy-development process – the strategy process has failed to realistically assess current reality, to honestly understand organizational capabilities, to align key players with those who do real work, or, at the end of the day, to create a compelling, externally driven vision of success.'[1]

Strategic performance management

Organizations, in addition to organizational structures for implementing strategies, need to install an organizing framework for realizing them. In general, senior managers deal with implementation that is effective immediately after decision making by putting in place organizational structures and systems, but implementation that is executed through an organizational-wide effort requires strategically managed systems to link daily management to strategy: these are called **strategic performance systems**.

If a strategic objective and its strategy crafted at a senior level are to work at an operational level, then they must be linked-in effectively with all the different things the organization is doing already. Without making and managing these connections an all-involving effort to achieve the organization's overall priorities is unlikely to happen. This requires more than a calendar of dates and deadlines; it requires the proactive involvement of senior managers in strategic performance management. This helps them to understand their organization better so that they are able to manage strategy implementation.

This does not assume a top-down strategy formulation, followed by a strategy implementation approach, as in classical strategic planning. Senior managers in organizations are more likely today to set the overall direction and the organization's strategically-related priorities, which the rest of the organization uses to develop bottom-up action plans for the year. It is within these parameters that local managers have to work out the other organizational activities, such as determining budgets, functional priorities as well as departmental control and incentive systems. Good strategic performance management mobilizes an organization-wide effort to achieve four main things: focus, alignment, integration and review **(FAIR)** (see Figure 10.1).

FIGURE 10.1 The FAIR framework for managing implementation

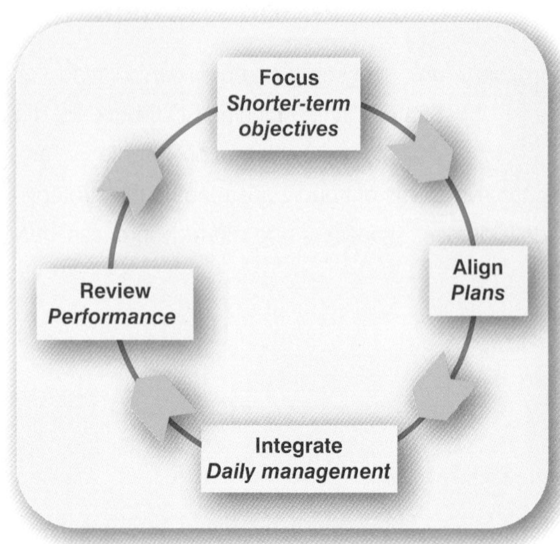

Managing implementation involves focusing the organization on the needs of the medium-term plan by crafting objectives that the rest of the organization

> Good strategic performance management mobilizes an organization-wide effort to achieve four main things: focus, alignment, integration and review (FAIR).

uses to align action plans. When the plans are managed in daily management the objectives are progressed, and towards the end of the planning cycle performance is reviewed and the lessons are used to inform the re-crafting of the objectives for the next turn of the planning cycle.

Focus

The primary participants in the focus phase of the cycle are senior managers (see Figure 10.2). The senior management team (top left of the figure) is

FIGURE 10.2 The determination of shorter-term objectives

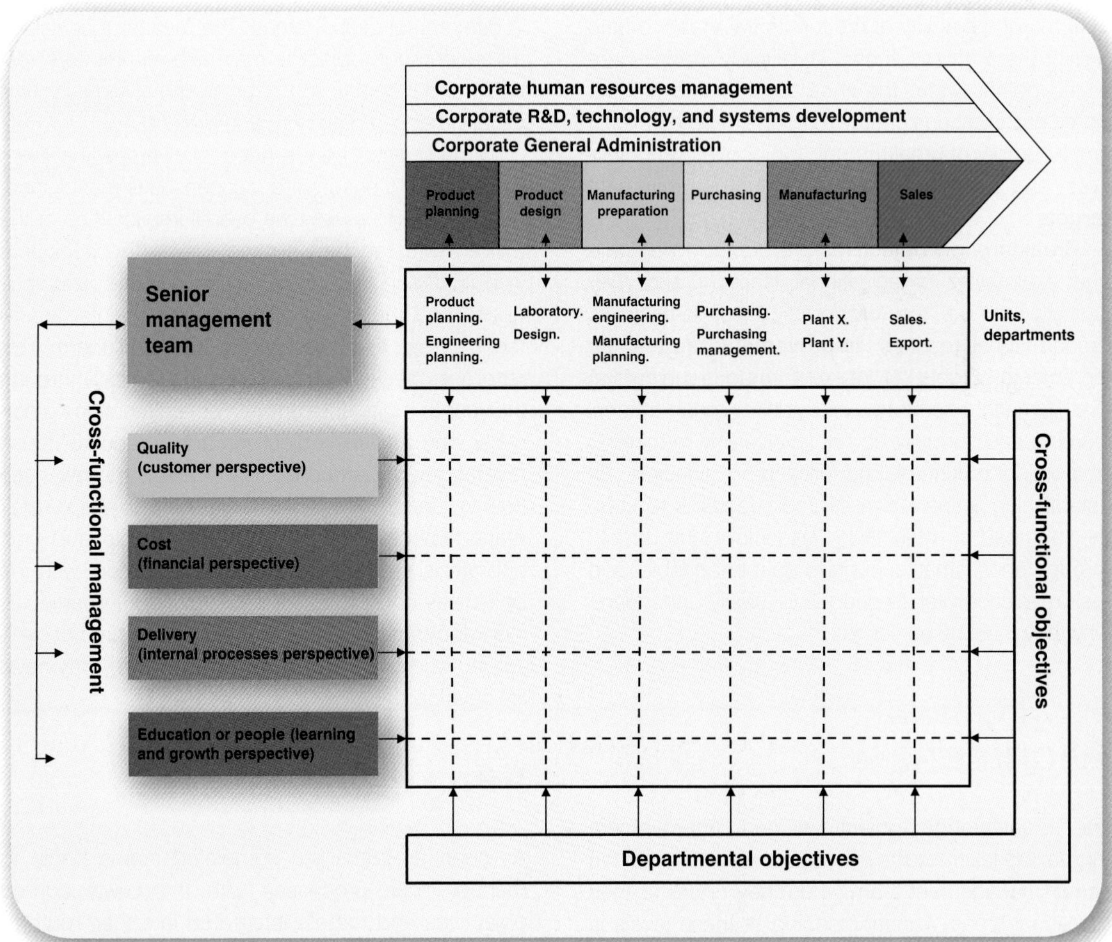

typically comprised of departmental and functional heads. The first consideration in crafting the annual objectives is to sort out the needs of the departments (the relationship of a department to the organization's value chain is shown at the top of the figure). This is done within the framework of longer-term purpose (vision, mission, and values), strategic objectives (the balanced scorecard), and overall strategy, and is centred on the organization's need to progress the medium-term plan over the coming year. This involves establishing the opportunities and threats facing the departments, as well as working out the strengths and weaknesses in relation to achieving the objectives of the plan.

The second consideration is to do the same but to identify the critical needs of the medium-term plan in terms of cross-functional objectives. These are explored from the four perspectives of the scorecard (see left of Figure 10.2). Then the two are brought together to determine the cross-functional objectives that are both critical for the organization and practical in terms of the ability of the functional areas to help deliver them (this is shown stylistically in the figure at the points where the lines cross in the matrix). Some organizations craft two groups of objectives: a small number of breakthrough (or innovatory) objectives, and a larger number of annual improvement **targets**.

Breakthrough objectives are crafted to encourage exploratory organizational learning and they typically require the organization to re-think its organizational routines. **Improvement targets** are incremental targets (or key performance indicators) that primarily encourage exploitative organizational learning and normally do not involve any re-thinking of existing routines.[2] The organizing principle for establishing a short-term strategic focus is to keep the number of objectives, especially the breakthrough ones, small enough to be manageable, and their relevance vital so people will easily understand why they must be achieved.

Alignment

The breakthrough objectives and improvement targets are taken by the individuals who make up the senior management team when they return to their functional areas. Annual planning at these levels is primarily centred on local priorities, but the objectives and targets take priority in working out everything else. This involves crafting draft action plans and passing them between teams to reach agreements with everybody involved about how the objectives and targets can be achieved (see Figure 10.3).

The objectives and targets are provisionally incorporated into team plans for the coming year. The implications for third parties, and especially for other team plans, are sounded out. This is an iterative process of throwing ideas and possibilities backward and forward like a game of catchball. It is likely that teams will have to change their targets and their proposed means (the strategies to achieve a target), perhaps several times.

Some breakthrough objectives are difficult and may therefore need a long planning or development period to sort out their implications. Typically these objectives need to be developed to clarify the full relevance for a department, or a number of departments, in different functional areas. The means of achieving a breakthrough objective may take months to investigate and then this sort of problem-solving activity is usually made into an on-going project.

Departmental heads need to oversee the planning period to ensure that consensus is established, but primarily to review the overall implications of the agreements reached among teams to check that workload and resources, especially the responsibilities and the timing of the critical events, are all recorded so that everyone is aware of them. This record is checked and reviewed periodically through the year to make sure operations are functioning normally, and that the objectives are on course (these reviews are departmental, not strategic, reviews; see below). Departmental heads also have to ensure their management systems, such as budgets and staff appraisals are harmonious, and consistent with the objectives and the associated working. In particular, it is important to be sure that individuals are not overloaded and can receive the support they may need for development.

Integration

As soon as plans are completed teams begin to manage their processes with the newly agreed objectives and targets integrated into their routines

FIGURE 10.3 Agreeing team plans

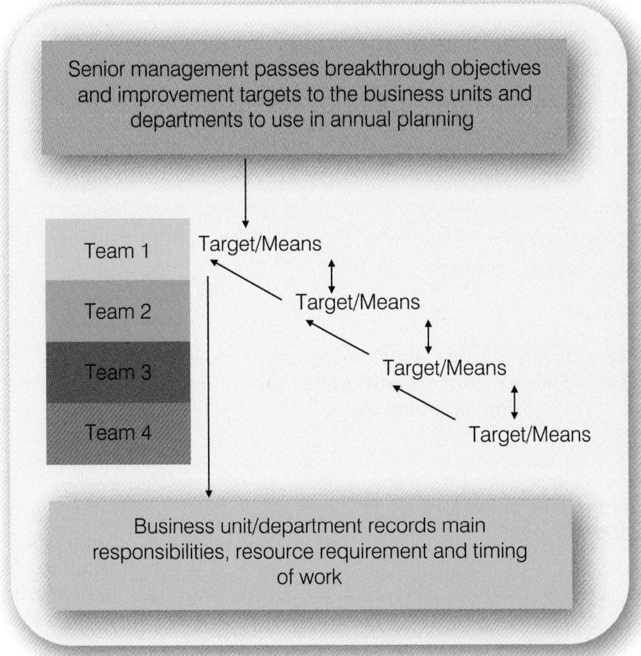

in daily management. The sources of change associated with continuous improvement in process management were noted in Chapter 5 in relation to total quality management (TQM). This approach for managing work is typically based on the PDCA cycle. However, the real driver of change on the operational processes comes not from doing work better, but from working to objectives and targets that are derived from strategy and the medium-term plan. In other words, the operational processes are as much influenced by strategic considerations as they are by the immediate need to satisfy the present customers: for example, an annual objective may be crafted by senior managers to encourage the organization to build a particular unique advantage into operations to combat the activities of an important competitor.

The organizing principle for the management of objectives is that work should be done along the lines of something like PDCA, where the specification of the work being performed is used to monitor the progress of the work, and that if things are not going to plan, then it is possible to intervene to problem-solve the reasons and put things right. If this requires changes in the objectives and the means to achieve them, then the implications have to be understood and acted upon for anyone else working in the organization. This is the management *of* objectives (MoO) and not management *by* **objectives** (MbO).  Objectives should be managed by people to facilitate their work, and should never be used within a context that is cut off from other objectives and means. In the management of objectives it is the transparency and relevancy of objectives to each other, that condition how people work together strategically.

This is a very different approach from MbO, which is an approach that is still used widely in organizations. MbO is an approach that deploys (or cascades) objectives down through the levels of an organization, by sub-dividing them, so that a superior's objectives become the sub-objectives of subordinates, who in turn, pass parts of the sub-objective to their own subordinates, and so on.

Originally it was the clarification of objectives, and the self-management aspects of MbO, that were emphasized; the approach was thought to be a way for harmonizing an individual's goals with strategic

PRINCIPLES IN PRACTICE 10.1

Preparing the ground for implementation

The Japanese take more time and involve more people in the agreement of proposals and plans, so that the implementation of these is quicker and more likely to succeed[14]. This is especially as the people who must carry out the decisions, because they have been involved in making the decisions, understand what is required and what the possible problems will be.

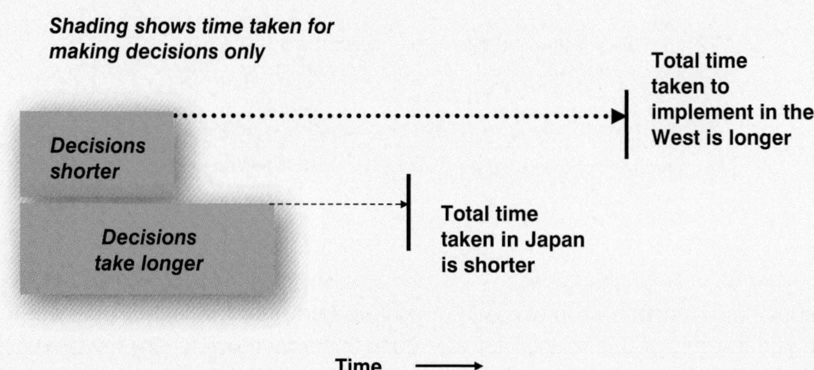

Decisions are conditioned by `nemawashi'–an activity to prepare the ground for a proposal[15]. This involves doing a lot of informal consulting with colleagues (including superiors and subordinates) before there is a formal meeting to agree the proposal. This has the advantage of uncovering unforeseen issues and prevents conflicts from becoming public. Its essence is not directly about agreement as such, but it is about people understanding each others' roles, which makes it easier for everybody to rely and communicate with each other.

Question: Nemawashi may prevent public argument, but could it limit creativity?

objectives.[3] However, it has been used by managers to command and control their subordinates to perform to numerical goals, and to hold them to account for their work. In this way authority is imposed in a hierarchical way through top-down objectives, which have little to do with the implementation of strategic objectives. For these reasons MbO is now largely discredited.

Review

There are two kinds of **strategic review** at a daily management level: (1) a series of **periodic strategic reviews**, held every two or three months to oversee the progress on the annual objectives, and (2) an annually-held **capability review**.

KEY DEBATE 10.1

Is consensus really a form of groupthink?

The idea that people should work together and agree mutually reinforcing objectives is open to question if it leads to narrow organizational agendas and limits the discussion and exploration of alternatives.

Irvine Janis, in research about US policy-making groups, found that senior management was prone to defective strategic decisions, especially in crisis situations, unless precautions are made to avoid 'groupthink'[20]. This happens when people think and behave in similar ways. Groupthink can be a result of an overly dominating leadership associated with a culture of fear. A 'not one of us' syndrome is not good for a dissenter's career. This mentality may even be felt at board level if directors and managers fear they may get reputations for obstructive thinking.

Janis argues that uniformity in group thinking may be good for quick routine decisions, but is detrimental when it pervades a team's deliberations on policy and strategic changes.

Michael Porter, with others, criticize Japanese management, arguing that consensual processes have important adverse consequences for strategic positioning: 'First, the need to obtain so many approvals almost guarantees that bold or distinctive strategies will not be pursued. The chances of making choices and trade-offs that favour one unit or division over another are minimal. Second, once so many have signed off on a decision, it is very difficult to exit unsuccessful product lines or businesses.'[21]

It is also possible that approaches like nemawashi can be used in a conspiratorial way to choose options that are influential, rather than useful, and that a consensus can be agreed in ways that prevent people from being blamed if a decision turns out to be faulty[22].

Question: Can people be trusted?

These are different in character from operational and departmental reviews, which are primarily used by functional management to oversee and address immediate issues. Strategic reviews held at a daily management level are also different from **strategy reviews**, which are conducted to explore the longer-term critical success factors and the cause-and-effect assumptions of the organization's longer-term strategic

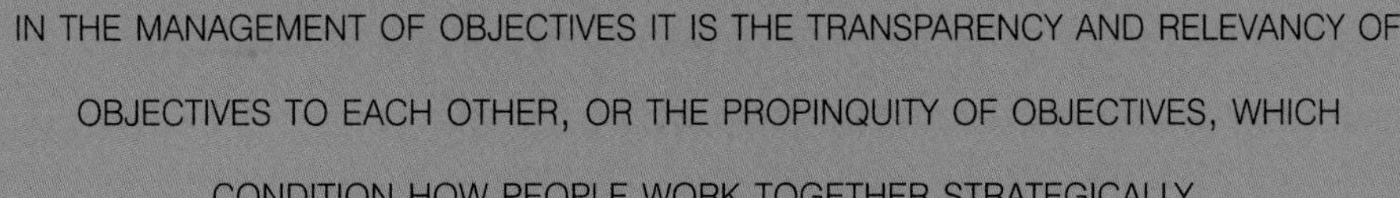

position. Strategic reviews, of course, input into strategy reviews, but their purpose of strategy reviews extends beyond **strategic performance management** to overall strategic control (see Chapter 11).

Strategic review is normally a formal activity that is likely to involve a presentation by a unit's managers to senior managers from outside the part of the organization that is being reviewed. They are held to check progress on the annual strategic objectives; to provide necessary assistance and advice and, if necessary, to commit resources for follow-up action early enough to be sure that the organization's medium-term plan will ultimately be achieved.

For example, Hewlett-Packard's organization-wide planning and review system is based on the following belief: 'The ultimate measure of the success of the planning process is whether the organization achieves its objectives and has the maturity (and early warning mechanisms in place) to take corrective action should progress towards these objectives start to be a concern.'[4]

Periodic strategic reviews aim to consider only the strategic objectives from the perspective of in-progress issues. Capability reviews are a senior level's annual audit of the organization's management capabilities. They consider how the organization's core areas or processes are being managed and has the object of developing good practice (it is sometimes linked to organizational benchmarking; see Chapter 5). The process is usually informed by evidence from the periodic strategic reviews, and from employees and customers, but the focus of attention is on the enablers of performance and good management practice.

The audit takes place towards the end of the planning year and senior managers (and in some organizations, the chairman of the board and non-executives) participate as auditors. This is important as it is the senior level's check on how the organization is doing its work to achieve the organization's purpose. In other words, it is an important vehicle for keeping top management informed about how the organization manages the core areas of the business. The involvement of senior managers is important since this keeps them in touch with the operational realities of the business.

An organization typically uses a performance excellence framework to review the organization's management of its core areas (see Chapter 5). In some organizations, however, the capability review is used

The ultimate measure of the success of the planning process is whether the organization achieves its objectives and has the maturity (and early warning mechanisms in place) to take corrective action should progress towards these objectives start to be a concern.

as a dynamic capability to develop the organization's core competences. Nissan uses a top executive audit to do this, and one of the core competences is how its units manage strategic objectives in daily management (see Case 5.1). Nissan uses its audit in combination with **hoshin kanri** (policy management), which is a strategic management methodology for deploying and managing senior-level cross-functional policies in daily management.

© Photolibrary

Hoshin kanri

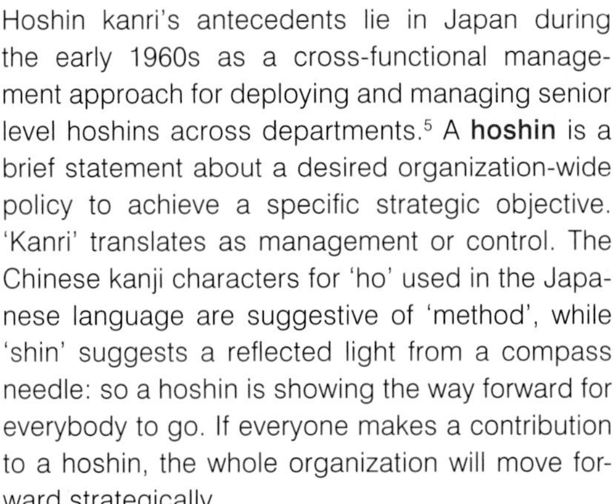

Hoshin kanri's antecedents lie in Japan during the early 1960s as a cross-functional management approach for deploying and managing senior level hoshins across departments.[5] A **hoshin** is a brief statement about a desired organization-wide policy to achieve a specific strategic objective. 'Kanri' translates as management or control. The Chinese kanji characters for 'ho' used in the Japanese language are suggestive of 'method', while 'shin' suggests a reflected light from a compass needle: so a hoshin is showing the way forward for everybody to go. If everyone makes a contribution to a hoshin, the whole organization will move forward strategically.

Hoshin variants are used in many non-Japanese organizations. It typically goes under customized names, such as 'hoshin planning' at Bank of America; 'policy deployment' at Proctor & Gamble; 'policy function deployment' at Mars; and 'strategy into action' at Unilever. While the details vary there is a common set of principles, business methodologies and management philosophies:[6]

- Individual senior executives take responsibility for a hoshin.
- Hoshins are strategic.
- Very few hoshins (less than five).
- The senior level hoshins are translated to take account of the organization's medium-term plan to derive annual hoshins for local levels.
- Senior level managers oversee the periodic strategic reviews of the annual hoshins at the daily management level.
- Participate in and take responsibility for an annual top executive audit (capability review) to evaluate management practices (including hoshin kanri itself).
- PDCA-TQM and kaizen (continuous improvement) are used to facilitate bottom-up management in planning and review of work, where the principle is on agreement and the management of the objective/means.
- Common language of QCDE (scorecard) objectives for use at all organizational levels.

PRINCIPLES IN PRACTICE 10.2

The importance of daily management to strategy

In his book, *Instruction to Deliver,* Michael Barber explains how the UK's Government Delivery Unit worked. Successful strategy is dependent upon managing implementation, and this is likely to be a low key affair[16].

Stubborn persistence, relentless monotony, attention to detail and glorying in the routine are vastly under-estimated in the literature on government and indeed political history. Inevitably the literature focuses on incidents, events and moments of drama, all of which cry out for explanation. Take Andrew Rawnsley's entertaining account of the first Blair term, 'Servants of the People'. It provides numerous insights into how the government worked, but each chapter is built around an incident: the row about social security policy, the Good Friday Agreement, tension between Blair and Brown over the euro and so on. Each chapter is riveting, no doubt, but the overall effect conveys a misleading account of what government is truly like.

... Take a single example: one looks in vain in the index of Rawnsley's book for the national literacy and numeracy strategies which were transforming the performance of primary schools; they were not on his radar because there was no legislation, no row, just steady, persistent implementation.

In the Delivery Unit, a key part of our mission was precisely to develop and prioritize these understated qualities which make so much difference to delivery. The key insight is that well-established routines are as important to the exercise of prime ministerial power and the delivery of results as major decisions on strategy or people; moreover they are precisely what Tony Blair lacked in his first term.

Sometimes I even had to debate this issue with my own staff. Inevitably their attention would be drawn to things that were going wrong and the interventions this required us to make, but the danger came when say of some us shifted from rightly paying attention to these interventions to wrongly thinking that they were the only way we had an impact. Often at staff meetings I would wrench people's attention back to the routines of deliverology – the stocktakes, tracking the data against the trajectory, writing delivery reports, keeping the focus ... without the routine, events cannot be fully understood and, more importantly, results will never be delivered ... Part of the mission of the Delivery Unit was to establish, at least internally, the primacy of order over chaos.

Question: How is daily management important to strategic objectives?

Hoshin kanri is a strategic objective delivery system that is used for a range of organizations, from American hospitals to the army in Turkey. It is perhaps the most comprehensive of delivery systems in present use. However, there are two others that are proving influential in public administration. These are the use of a delivery unit used in central government in the United Kingdom, and a city-based system, originally used for New York, called CompStat.

Delivery units

The responsibilities for achieving government policies in the United Kingdom lie with government departments; this includes the attainment of a number of targets that have featured in the government's election promises. However, during Prime Minister Blair's first term of office the performance had been largely unsatisfactory. In 2001, at the start of Blair's second term of office, a delivery unit was established to oversee government targets. This was in effect the government's strategic performance function.

The unit was charged to oversee 15 targets being managed by government ministers in the health, education, home office, and transport, departments. The unit was kept below 50 staff, and reported directly to the Prime Minister. Its role is to provide a review framework that the Prime Minister can use to progress the work. The unit's contribution to the already existing work in the departments was to organize regular reviews of the targets and delivery reports. The unit also set interim goals for delivery, working with the department concerned to provide delivery maps and plans; the identification of delivery chains; trajectories (to show the progress on targets over time); audits of performance; and the compilation of league tables to show the relative performances on the targets. The unit's concern is not with how government departments should operate or set policy and strategy but with the delivery of strategic objectives.

A key innovation for functionally-based public administration is the unit's concept of a **delivery chain**. This takes a broad view about how policies are implemented and maps out the participants in a chain of cause-and-effect. When, for example, a minister of education makes a promise to improve standards of reading and writing among 11-year olds, a delivery chain shows the connections that must be taken into account to show how the benefit is realized. The thoughts of the 11-year old children are primarily influenced by their teacher, which is the first link in the chain. The teacher is influenced by the school's literacy co-ordinator, who in turn is influenced by the head-teacher; these are the second and third links in the chain. The head-teacher is influenced by the governors and the local authority, who are influenced by the regional director of the National Literacy Strategy, whom in turn answers to the national director of the strategy. He in turn answers to the head of the Standards and Effectiveness Unit, in the Department of Education, who then answers to the Secretary of State.

There are additional chains. Children's reading is also influenced by parents, so there is a shorter chain that can be considered, where parents can be influenced to read more to children at home. Head teachers are strongly influenced by Ofsted inspectors (these perform external audits); this constitutes another potential chain. For the delivery of the target, the key is to do a delivery chain analysis, so that those responsible can think through how best to influence the links, and when the plan is being put into practice, check each link to see it is effective and, if necessary, can be strengthened. In the opinion of the unit's founder director, Michael Barber, if a delivery chain cannot be specified, then nothing will happen.[7]

The direct intervention of a strategic performance management function in the implementation of strategy represents a switch from the specification by elected representatives of goals and missions, to the management of issues, and from measurement of performance, to problem solving. In practice this is likely to mean a move closer to private sector management, although some suggest the involvement of key stakeholders, such as professionals, public service users and citizens, complicates strategic management by requiring action to ensure intra-organizational and inter-organizational co-ordination.[8]

The use of delivery chains suggests it cannot be otherwise. The functionally-based departmentalism of government has to move in the same direction that the large commercial organizations have taken in recent decades, to move from a functionally-organized to a systems view of organizing (see Chapter 9).

CompStat

When Rudolf Giuliani became mayor of New York in 1993, the city was one of the most lawless in America; by the time he left office in 2004, the city had changed to become one of the world's safest. The reason is CompStat, which is short for computer statistics or comparative statistics. It is actually a strategic review system that uses presentations by operational heads and their staffs to discuss patterns (maps and charts are used in the presentations) to provide evidence of what is going on to help the owners of objectives to understand the whole picture. Through brainstorming at the review the result is to try to improve and prevent things before they happen.

The following help make CompStat effective:[9]

- Reliable data are collected preferably on a daily basis, but at least once a week at set times.
- About 20–40 strategic objectives are set to identify and measure the core mission of the agency using the approach.
- Regular review meetings are convened at least once a week to include a floor plan that demonstrates where agency leaders are required to be present at each meeting.
- About ten or more representative performance indicators that the agency wants on its page of the city's website must be submitted.

CompStat is much more than a computer-based information system. What makes it work strategically is a review meeting that is normally held twice a week with senior managers, police precinct commanders and other operational heads, to discuss progress on the city's strategies. The idea is to discern emerging and established crime and quality of life trends, as well as deviations and anomalies, and to make comparisons between the different precincts and commands to promote debate and learning. It serves to help senior managers to understand operations, to evaluate the skills and effectiveness of middle management, and to assist in properly allocating resources for continuous improvement.

Because high ranking decision makers are present, they can commit resources quickly to clear obstacles and avoid delays that are common in highly structured bureaucratic organizations. New York has a number of crime and quality of life strategies, and these are reviewed at the weekly meetings in the light of what is happening in the weekly crime data. Every precinct commander can expect to be called at random to make a presentation about once a month. When this happens the commander's staff are required to be present.

In the view of Giuliani the approach is essentially one that aims to foster a team approach to problem solving; the use of presentations and targets acts as

THE FUNCTIONALLY-BASED DEPARTMENTALISM OF GOVERNMENT HAS TO MOVE IN THE SAME DIRECTION THAT THE LARGE COMMERCIAL ORGANIZATIONS HAVE TAKEN IN RECENT DECADES, TO MOVE FROM A FUNCTIONALLY-ORGANIZED TO A SYSTEMS VIEW OF ORGANIZING.

a motivational and competitive tool that increases accountability. However, he makes it plain that managers must work whole-heartedly with the system or they should face dismissal. It may still be possible for poor performers to try to hide unfavourable statistics, or to manipulate the recording of statistics to hide the true situation (although periodic audits of the system are supposed to pick this up).

Critics have pointed out that CompStat may not be the sole reason for lower crime. National crime had

already started to decline before Giuliani took office and in other major cities crime has fallen over the same period due to an improvement of the economy. There were also other factors peculiar to New York. However, it is indisputable that crime in New York fell faster than elsewhere, and that this has continued since 2001.

New York extended the CompStat idea to other city functions, and many American cities have implemented their own versions of CompStat, which is now more generally known as CitiStat. These cover a range of public services, from education in Philadelphia where it is called SchoolStat, and CitiStat in Baltimore.[10] Robert Behn, of Harvard's Kennedy School of Government, argues these have been largely effective,[11] but he summarizes seven possible errors:[12]

1 No clear purpose.
2 No one has specific responsibilities.
3 Meetings are held irregularly, infrequently, or randomly.
4 No one person is authorized to run the meetings.
5 No dedicated analytic staff.
6 No follow-up.
7 No balance between the brutal and the bland.

Numbers 1 to 6 above are weaknesses that are more generally associated with reviews. An organization's system of strategic review should be a managed activity if it is going to avoid these pitfalls. However, the last point applies particularly to CompStat. In the words of Behn, 'Both NYPD's CompStat and Baltimore's CitiStat are known for being tough and uncompromising with poor performers ... Yet in an over-reaction to ... some jurisdictions and agencies have consciously tried to make their meetings as harmonious as possible. As a result, their meetings have become mostly show-and-tell.'[13] The nature of leadership is important, since senior managers need to both pressure their managers and help them to succeed. The role of leadership, especially in relation to management, is discussed in the following chapter (Chapter 11).

PRINCIPLES IN PRACTICE 10.3

Broken windows theory for the underground

Giuliani's first police commissioner in New York City, William Bratton, had been influenced by broken windows theory.[17] This holds that a seemingly minor matter like broken windows in abandoned buildings lead directly to a more serious deterioration of neighbourhoods. Giuliani argues that the idea is relevant not only to crime but business more generally: leaders should 'sweat the small stuff', because the seemingly less serious things are part of the bigger picture.[18]

AP Photo/Luc Novovitch

Bratton used quality of life issues to help clean up more serious crime. These were small misdemeanours and petty crime, but when they are left unattended, because they seem unimportant, they begin to create a poor environment that begins to encourage more, and often more serious, crime, so that a vicious circle of decline sets in.

Bratton in his previous job as head of transit police in New York had cracked down on fare evasion. It had not seemed worthwhile since the cost in police time was high and the cost of a fare was small. However, many of the people arrested were causing other problems once they got inside the subway system.

When he became Giuliani's police commissioner, he used civil law to enforce existing regulations: 'Time and time again, when cops interrupt someone drinking on the street or a gang of kids drinking on the corner, pat them down, and find a gun or a knife, they have prevented what would have happened two or three hours later when that same person, drunk, pulled out that gun or knife. We prevented the crime before it happened. New York City police would be about prevention …'[19]

Question: Are leaders likely to want to be known for the small stuff?

KEY DEBATE 10.2

Does delegating responsibility help productivity?

Many of the debates about targets and objectives seem to be questions about motivation. This may not, however, be the real issue. For example consider this Japanese view: 'The conventional view, as exemplified by Womack et al.[23], is that productivity and quality will improve when the morale of workers improves, which occurs as a result of delegating authority … productivity and quality will improve because problems will be swiftly addressed or fundamentally solved by workers if the only alternative is a delay in production … high worker morale and an efficient production system automatically guarantee good plan performance …

'[*However*] productivity is something that is planned and managed, and it must not be overlooked that the mechanism for applying relentless daily pressure on all personnel, including line managers, [*is*] such planning and management.'[24]

Question: Is it management or the motivation of people that determines their priorities?

KEY DEBATE 10.3

Do public sector targets really work?

A target is generally associated with short-term objectives and usually refers to tactical or operational objectives. In other words targets are used as milestones to indicate progress in the achievement of a longer-term objective.

John Seddon makes a distinction between 'targets' and 'measures', where the former are essentially arbitrary and express a top-down aspiration, while a measure is used locally by workers to check progress on work: top-down targets belong to scientific management.[25] Things do seem to have got out of control in the United Kingdom. Take this excerpt from Simon Jenkins' award winning book about Government:

> *By Blair's second term, the target culture was near maniacal. The Audit Commission league tables scored [local] councils by how many 'library items were issued per head of the population'. They recorded how many 'nights of respite care were supplied per 1000 of the adult population'. They recorded what percentage of statements on 'special needs children were prepared per six months'. Lest anyone query the answers, private auditors from KPMG were hired to audit the audit. Quangos recruited internal*

By permission of John Seddon, Managing Director, Vanguard, www.systemsthinking.co.uk

John Seddon

and external auditors to mark the Treasury's public auditors. Turnbull, then head of the civil service, was a defender of targets, deriding old guard public administrators as 'knightly professionals left to their own devices'. He felt that doctors, teachers, police chiefs and housing officers have for too long been content with a 'comfort zone' level of service. Targets, said Turnbull, had made public servants 'focus their efforts, requiring them to work more closely with others in the delivery chain'. Yet even he admitted that targets had sometimes proved too top-down, demeaning professional standards, encouraging gaming, undermining trust, distorting priorities.[26]

The impact of top-down targets can have a spring clean effect, bringing urgency to the need to review capacities and capabilities, and the alignment of other goals. It is like moving furniture in a room: the piece you want moved requires you to move other things around, so that finally, the room looks quite different from how it was before. But you wonder in the end, whether you have thought things out.

Deming famously wrote: 'Goals are necessary for you and me, but numerical goals set for other people, without a road map to reach the goal, have effects opposite to the effects sought.'.[27]

Question: What are the perverse effects of setting top-down objectives?

SUMMARY OF PRINCIPLES

1 Good strategic performance management mobilizes an organization-wide effort to achieve four things that are vital to the effective management of strategy implementation: focus, alignment, integration, and review (FAIR).

2 The objectives translated from the needs of the medium-term are of two sorts: a very few vital breakthrough objectives, and more numerous improvement targets. The former may require exploratory thinking and re-working of routines. The latter involve only incremental changes.

3 These objectives drive improvement in daily management. Breakthrough objectives bring an external influence to bear on the management of the internal processes.

4 The management of objectives is more effective than management by objectives.

5 There are two kinds of strategic review at the daily management level: periodic strategic review and an annual capability review.

6 Delivery systems are important to the strategic management of the public sector and these function through the discipline of review and follow-up.

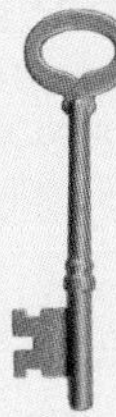

GLOSSARY OF KEY TERMS

Breakthrough objectives strategically-linked cross-functional objectives to which everybody contributes at a daily management level to advance a high priority organization-wide strategic objective. These are normally associated with the management of strategic change to achieve the organization's vision.

Capability review a form of strategic review at the daily management level by senior managers to audit how the core areas of the organization are being managed. For example an audit might assess how the organization is developing and using its core competences.

catchball the agreement of draft plans between affected parties.

Delivery chain a concept in functionally based public administration that takes a broad view of how policies are implemented and maps out the chain of cause-and-effect for the participants concerned.

FAIR strategic performance management mobilizes an organization-wide effort to achieve four main things: focus, alignment, integration, and review.

hoshin a statement of a breakthrough strategic objective and its means.

Hoshin kanri policy management – an organization-wide methodology for the deployment and management of a limited number of senior-level hoshins (strategic objectives and means).

Improvement targets strategically-linked cross-functional objectives that people use to improve continuously performance in daily management. They are normally associated with the management of an organization's mission and the effectiveness of its business model.

Management by Objectives (MbO) the dispersal of objectives through an organization requiring the agreement of superiors and subordinates.

Periodic strategic review formal reviews by senior managers of a unit's performance on its contribution to the organization's strategic objectives, normally to be able to authorize in good time any necessary corrective action (different from strategy review).

strategic performance management a strategically managed system that enables a senior level to execute and manage strategic priorities in daily management.

Strategic performance systems a strategically managed system to link management to strategy.

Strategic reviews these are reviews of strategically-linked performance at a daily management level: they include both periodic strategic reviews and annual capability reviews, and while they feed into strategy reviews (of longer-term strategy) they are different in terms of focus and scope.

Strategy execution the management of implementation at a daily management level.

Strategy review reviews of longer-term purpose, objectives and strategy (different from strategic review).

Target a short-term objective that refers to a tactical or operational outcome.

GUIDED FURTHER READING

A wider interpretation of strategic performance management has been given by de Waal's book. This includes the definition of mission, objectives and strategy and their measurement through KPIs:

de Waal, A. (2007) *Strategic Performance Management: A Managerial and Behavioural Approach,* London: Palgrave.

The classic text on Japanese hoshin kanri is an edited book by Akao and other Japanese writers. It is technical and difficult for non-specialists. An easy introduction is Witcher's article. See below:

Akao, Y. (ed.) (1991) *Hoshin Kanri: Policy Deployment for Successful TQM*, Cambridge, MA: Productivity Press.

Witcher, B. J. (2003) 'Policy management of strategy **(hoshin kanri)**', *Strategic Change* 12:March-April, 83–94.

REVIEW QUESTIONS

1 What is FAIR?

2 Why must objectives be kept to the lowest number possible?

3 What is the difference between breakthrough and improvement objectives?

4 What is the difference between MoO and MbO?

5 How does TQM make objective management easier?

6 What is the difference between a performance excellence framework and a top executive audit approach?

7 How is a delivery chain different from a value chain?

8 Is CompStat too competitive?

SEMINAR AND ASSIGNMENT QUESTIONS

1 Evaluate how a balanced scorecard's strategic objectives can be translated into annual strategically relevant objectives/means. What kind of scorecard can be used in daily management to help FAIR?

2 Put together a team to draw up agendas for a periodic strategic review, a capability review and a strategy review. Make a list of guidelines for managing a review meeting.

3 The use of delivery and review systems to drive progress on social objectives is controversial. One of the problems is that a strategic priority implies ignoring other things that one expects from a universal service. Are 'objectives' really necessary for effective performance management in the public sector and what is the role of 'management'?

CHAPTER REFERENCES

1 Dye, R. (2008) 'How chief strategy officers think about their role: A roundtable', *The McKinsey Quarterly* May, www.mckinseyquarterly.com

2 March, J. G. (1991) 'Exploration and exploitation in organizational learning', *Organization Science* 2(1):71–87.

3 Drucker, P. F. (1955) *The Practice of Management*, London: Heinemann Butterworth; (1954, American edn), New York: Harper & Row; Humble, J. W. (ed.) (1970) *Management by Objectives in Action*, New York: McGraw-Hill.

There are indications that MbO may work differently (and more participatively) in different national cultures, see Hofstede, G. (1980a) 'Motivation, leadership and organization: Do American theories apply abroad?' *Organizational Dynamics,* Summer:42–63.

4 Witcher, B. J. and Butterworth, R. (2000) 'Hoshin kanri at Hewlett Packard', *Journal of General Management* 25(4):70–85.

5 Witcher, B. J. and Butterworth, R. (2001) 'Hoshin kanri: policy management in Japanese-owned UK subsidiaries', *Journal of Management Studies* 38(5):651–74.

6 Witcher, B. J. and Chau, V. S. (2007) 'Balanced scorecard and hoshin kanri: Dynamic

capabilities for managing strategic fit', *Management Decision* 45(3):518–38.

7 Barber, M. (2008) *Instruction to Deliver: Fighting to Transform Britain's Public Services* (revised pbk edn), London: Methuen.

8 Joyce, P. (1999) *Strategic Management for the Public Services,* Buckingham: Open University Press.

9 Giuliani, R. W. with Kurson, K. (2002) *Leadership,* London: Little, Brown.

10 Patusky, C., Shelley, M. and Botwinik, L. (2007) *The Philadelphia SchoolStat Model* (report), IBM Centre for the Business of Government, University of Pennsylvania.

11 Behn, R. (2006) 'The varieties of CitiStat', *Public Administration Review,* May–June:332–40.

12 Behn, R. (2008) 'The seven big errors of PerformanceStat', *Policy Briefs,* John F. Kennedy School of Government, Harvard University, February.

13 Behn (2008) *op cit.,* 6.

14 Monden, Y. (1998) *Toyota Production System: An Integrated Approach to Just-in-Time* (3rd edn), Norcross, Georgia: Engineering and Management Press.

15 Drucker, P. F. (1971) 'What we can learn from Japanese management', *Harvard Business Review,* March–April:11–23.

16 Barber (2008) *op cit.,* pp. 111–12.

17 Wilson, J. Q. and Kelling, G. L. (1982) 'Broken windows', *The Atlantic Monthly* 249(3):29-38.

18 Giuliani (2002) *op cit.*

19 Bratton, W. (with Nobler, P.) (1998) *Turnaround: How America's Top Cop Reversed the Crime Epidemic,* New York: Random House, p. 229.

20 Janis, I. L. (1982) *Groupthink: Psychological Studies of Political Decisions and Fiascos* (revised edn. of *Victims of Groupthink,* 1970), Boston MA: Houghton Mifflin.

21 Porter, M. E., Takeuchi, H. and Sakakibara, M. (2000) *Can Japan Compete?* London: Macmillan, p. 163.

22 Millikin, J. P. and Fu, D. (2003) *The Global Leadership of Carlos Ghosn at Nissan,* teaching note A07-03-0014, Thunderbird, The Garvin School of International Management.

23 Womak, J. P., Jones, D. T. and Roos, D. (1990), *The Machine That Changed the World*, New York: Rawson Associates.

24 Ishida, M. (1997) 'Japan: Beyond the model for lean production'. In Kochan, T. A., Lansbury, R. D. and MacDuffe, J. P. (eds), *After Lean Production*, Ithaca: ILR Press, pp. 45–60.

25 Seddon, J. (2008) *Systems Thinking in the Public Sector: The Failure of the Reform Regime and a Manifesto for a Better Way,* London: Triarchy.

26 Jenkins, S. (2006) *Thatcher & Sons: A Revolution in Three Parts,* London: Allen Lane, p.280.

27 Deming, W. E. (1986) *Out of the Crisis: Quality, Productivity and Competitive Position*, Cambridge: Cambridge University Press.

CASE 10.1 FAIR Hoshin Kanri at Xerox[1]

This case considers how hoshin kanri, in the form of the FAIR framework, was managed at Xerox.

Hoshin kanri (policy management)

Xerox (UK) is the sales, marketing and support subsidiary of Xerox (Limited). It is structured as four business development units based on office document systems, office document products, document production systems and printing systems. It uses a FAIR phase approach for its hoshin kanri (see Exhibit 10.1).

Focus

The American parent, Xerox Corporation, sets the vision, business goals and direction. These are passed to the companies in the group. Vision is a statement, which shows a desired state – 'The Document Company' – and reads 'Xerox will be the leader in the Global Document Market, by providing Document Solutions that enhance Business Productivity.'

EXHIBIT 10.1 The FAIR phases of hoshin kanri at Xerox

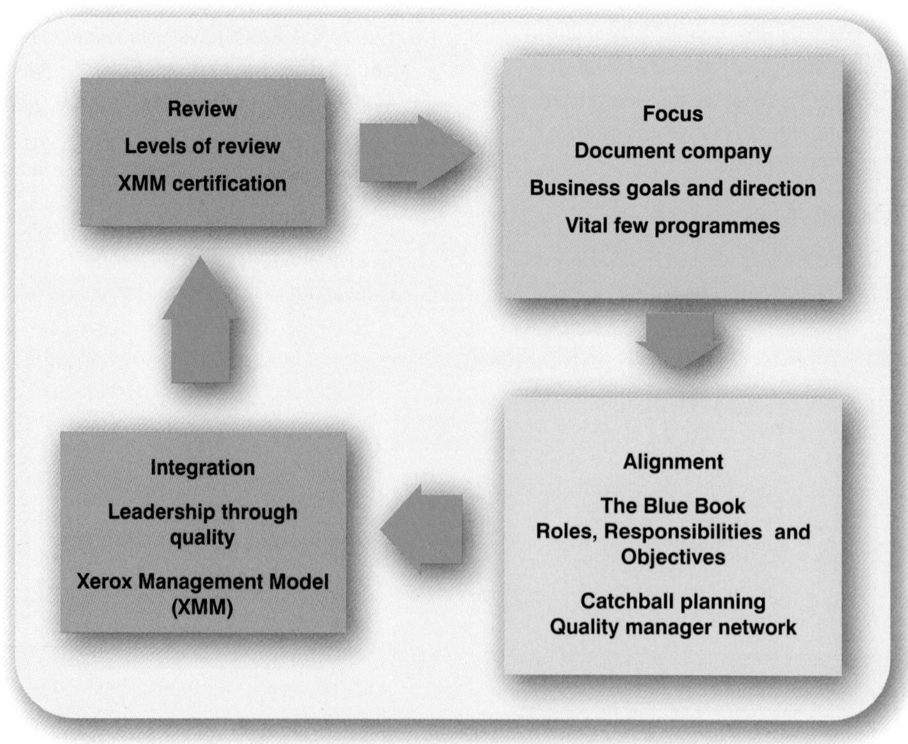

Jeff Greenberg/Alamy

To progress this vision, Xerox uses four types of business goals: customer satisfaction; employee motivation and satisfaction; market share; and return on assets. As 'goals' Xerox sees its purpose as a means to measure progress in the key areas which determine the company's longer-term success, an overall Direction is used to align the goals; for example, for 1997 it was 'Profitable Revenue Growth.' Xerox requires its companies develop 'vital few programmes' (hoshins) which are consistent with the direction.

Xerox (UK) starts to determine its vital few programmes after the board conducts a two-day planning session in July. This meeting produces an outline business plan as well as an outline of the vital few. The business plan is primarily made up of financials, which are worked out in terms of targets and measures of revenue, profit and so on, in collaboration with the business units. The vital few programmes are considered by the organization separately and are developed by central staff working with senior executives to produce more detail with the aim to specific the vital few by year-end for their introduction at Start Year meetings in the business units in January.

An individual senior executive acts as a sponsor for each of the vital few. They are chosen for their potential impact. A lot of this activity is spent in informal discussions between senior directors, with staff putting the information up, rewriting and getting the information into a usable format. The vital few are specified around each of the business goals to ensure they are linked: for example, the customer satisfaction goal was given its own vital few programme, which was documented as 'Only when we can demonstrate our loyalty to our customers can we expect to have their loyalty in return'. This programme aimed to reduce customer dissatisfaction and minimize revenue losses for existing customers. It also called for the introduction of new forms of customer care that would facilitate monitoring and the management of customer contacts during the period customers are with Xerox.

Over the years there is a degree of continuity in the subjects of vital few programmes. The programmes are put together on an annual basis, but they run along a theme that takes perhaps up to five years to implement, with each year being slightly different.

Alignment

The alignment of the vital few programmes at local level in the business units and teams begins with the distribution of documentation known as the Blue Book and the Employee Guide to Policy Deployment. This goes to the unit quality managers in time for the start-up meetings. This 'book' is intended for managers, since they have the responsibility for cascading its information about the vital few programmes to their teams. The 1997 edition listed the details of each programme, sponsor and the scope. It also had a section that covered the key business activities and policies of each of the major business units. There was a section that clarified the role of managers in communicating the programmes. Unit and team managers are expected to produce a local translation of the book, to identify local objectives and for individuals to keep close by in their work.

The Blue Book is translated for every employee as the Employee Guide to Policy Deployment. This is designed as a folder, explaining hoshin kanri and the programmes; it also has a pocket where an individual may attach their Role, Responsibilities and Objectives (RRO). This is a one-page sheet of paper that summarizes an individual's role in contributing to the vital few and a summary of their primary job function (or that of their team). It thus contains those key activities and projects for which an individual is accountable, and the standards, targets and measures which determine the criteria for successful progression and completion of work. All employees are expected to have an RRO, including senior managers and executives. Because the RRO is used for appraisals, it provides a direct link between an individual's performance and the progress of the programmes.

The RROs are updated annually as a part of the deployment process and linked to employee development. Self-managed teams do their own appraisals. Appraisals address the needs of the vital few by ensuring that staff can plan to develop any required new skills. Appraisals are done again towards the end of the year, and a formal review of the individual's development is carried out.

The Start Year presentations go through the Blue Book and Employees Guide, and then they go into detail on the vital few. Basically each unit decides its focus on one or more of the vital few. Managers then take the information away and develop more detail with their own teams. It goes through several strands of deployment. It begins at a large Start Year meeting, and then deploys through line managers through their teams.

Some of the programmes are more relevant to some staff than others. So while some concentrate on one particular programme, others address them all in different ways, depending upon the nature of their work and circumstances. It is difficult to generalize about how the vital few will be taken up and translated. For example:

> *One of the things that we're going to do across the board is customer first training, so everybody will need to know that is there. We are also doing digital skills, which will hit a very small community, so that will be different. It will all go through the various networks that we have got, to get it out to the field. For the individual, say the engineer, they probably won't have much of a clear idea about what is in the document; they will know that 'accelerate skills up' is one of the vital few programmes, they may translate that into say learning about PCs as an individual skills gap. Some of it will be a conceptual translation, which isn't a detailed plan. Others will be – well here is the detailed plan that is part of your job role so go away and implement it. These are all change initiatives so they may evolve over the year.*

It is essential to be realistic about what can be achieved. If there are too many deployed secondary programmes and the cascade is very wide, then things can get quickly out of control and people lose focus. However, if teams are working to total quality management (TQM) then they will have the skills to prioritize so that deployment is manageable. The customer satisfaction management group provides an instance of problem solving priorities. This unit is in charge of the company's total satisfaction guarantee; it also tracks customer satisfaction and is the custodian for customer satisfaction company-wide.

At its Start Year meeting this unit focused on the customer satisfaction and loyalty vital few programme, and worked first on a situation analysis of the present position of the unit's performance. This involved everyone in a series of brainstorming meetings where SWOT analysis was used to determine the unit's existing strengths and weaknesses, opportunities and threats, in relation to a contribution to the programme, and to think up actions. One of these included the use of the voice of the customer in distribution channels; another on how to improve customer retention, and others concerned communications and query resolution. These were assessed for their impact and relation to each other by root cause analysis; actions were then prioritized using Pareto analysis. In this way four actions were selected and each one was ascribed a desired state with a set of means.

The full implications of actions worked out in this way must then be checked with the affected third parties. This sometimes leads to conflict on means but, in the end, units and teams have to agree and prioritize against what is possible with existing budgets. This iterative deployment of plans is a

catchball form of planning. The discussions are not about the correctness of the purpose of the corporate vital few programmes, but centre on the practical issues and how to achieve them. The activity is not a formal process and is influenced by the normal working relations people have in daily management.

Every unit within the company has a quality specialist or manager, and these are co-ordinated through an informal network. This has a pivotal role in that it facilitates deployment by offering advice about how to translate the priorities into local actions. They have an active role at Start Year meetings and informally oversee the progress of vital few programmes through the year. Quality managers do not own the planning process but they are regarded by the centre as the conscience of the organization for the hoshin kanri process. They inspect without people realizing what is happening, and assess understanding at the operational level. They also play an important role in organizing and following up reviews of progress on the vital few.

Integration

The essence of hoshin kanri is that people should work on those activities in their daily work which are vital to strategic success. This is not just about how the vital few are deployed, but it is also about how they are managed day-to-day. It means that daily processes must be managed in such a way as to ensure that they are under control. Thus TQM is fundamental. Called Leadership through Quality, at the heart of TQM at Xerox is the Xerox Quality Policy. This is regarded within the Group as Xerox's Values Statement, which aims to create and maintain a competitive advantage through customer-focused quality.

> *Xerox is a quality company. Quality is the basic business principle for Xerox. Quality means providing our external and internal customers with innovative products and services that fully satisfy their requirements. Quality improvement is the job of every Xerox employee.*

TQM began with a sheep-dip approach when everyone was trained in its ideas. In practice, after the training was done, the ideas were forgotten and people continued in the same way, so that there was a loss of morale and frustration among those who realized TQM could provide the tools to make change happen. It really began to work when managers switched from thinking about the management of quality as such to the quality of the way Xerox manages. A key element was the introduction of the Xerox Management Model (XMM) that clarified and defined the way Xerox manages.

The XMM is a methodology used to deploy Xerox's vision and goals. Introduced in 1994 in a corporate-wide update of TQM, its aim then was to make quality Xerox's general approach to management. It provides a framework for managers to identify the key processes used to manage the business. It is comprised of five categories: leadership, human resource management, business process management, customer and market focus, and information utilization and quality tools (see Exhibit 10.2). Good management practice in all these areas leads to the achievement of its four business goals in the business results part of the model.

In order to achieve the business 'goals', Xerox has to have good leadership across the whole organization to manage people so that they can work effectively with the right processes, with the right information and tools, which are focused on what the customer expects and wants. If the five enablers are managed correctly that should drive out the results. The double arrows in the figure emphasize the need for a continuing dialogue between management and other employees.

Xerox specifies elements of good practice for each of the categories: for example, the elements for Customer and Market Focus are:

- Customer first
- Customer requirements
- Customer database
- Market segment
- Customer communications
- Customer query and complaint management
- Customer satisfaction and loyalty
- Customer relationship management
- Customer commitment

Review

There are three levels of management review. The first two are similar to management meetings anywhere

EXHIBIT 10.2 The Xerox management model

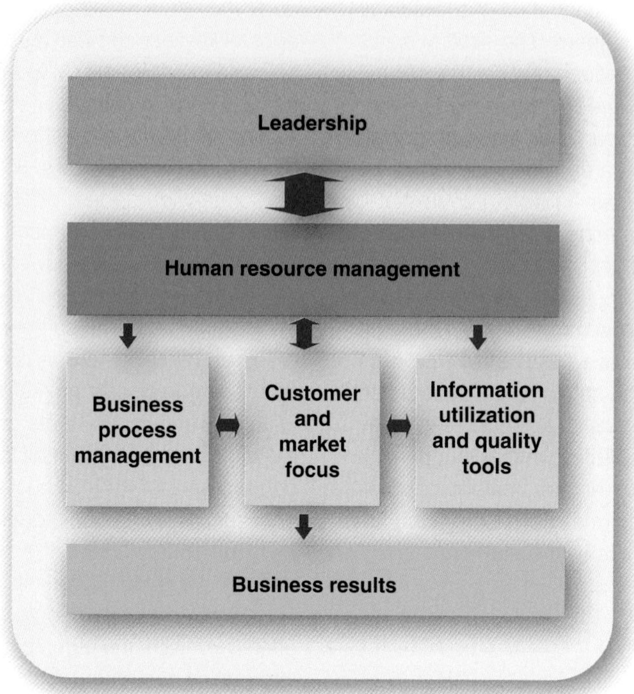

and apply at the business unit and the higher company level. Each business unit uses a management team to conduct a monthly review to sanction short-term action. The quality managers own these to ensure they are carried out and that the right things are reviewed. There is a similar meeting at company level when the managing director and his team (units and network heads) review progress overall. Both these reviews concern general matters and are not solely about the vital few programmes. There is also an operations review and this is entirely centred on the status of the vital few, when senior managers review performance every quarter with each unit's general manager and their staff. The agenda is a standard one that aims to achieve consistency in strategic direction. Unit representatives present current status against plan, and make an assessment of progress of their action plans, so that amendments and additions to local plans can be agreed if necessary.

More generally, progress is reported through the specialist networks, when the company's communications media are used to relay information about best practice and success stories. Through this way the networks, such as the quality managers, play an important learning role in dissembling the lessons from what is happening across the organization. Additionally, Xerox's TQM uses a Deming (PDCA) cycle to manage its business processes, when work is constantly monitored and checked: the aim is to translate the needs of the vital few into process targets that will be monitored and managed daily.

In the final months of the yearly cycle, Xerox conducts an annual audit of its business units, which provides feedback on the overall organizational effectiveness of how people are managing, and provides information to use to change the vital few for the next annual cycle. This activity is called XMM Certification because the model is used as a framework to audit the units. Units self-appraise, but the company uses a senior director and senior line managers from other units to validate appraisals and approve certification. This flags up to the rest of the company that the unit has demonstrated a high level of operational command of the XMM enablers, and has produced good business results. The XMM Certification represents a major event for the unit concerned.

Managing hoshin kanri

Hoshin kanri is organic and varies across the years in its nature and outcomes depending upon how senior management use it to enable the participation of others. For example, the 1996 hoshin kanri programme turned out badly at Xerox (UK) and failed to have an impact. This was a result of too many vital few programmes. Eight had been set for 1996 and these programmes had in turn been split into 24 'critical elements'. These 24 were designed to make the relevance of the vital few clearer to a maximum number of employees, and to help prompt staff to think in a more focused way about how a programme might be carried out. As a result the Blue Book was very complex. It gave: descriptive detail of the XMM; templates for quality tools and deployment procedures; detail of the vital few; and listed the RROs of the major business units. All this meant a document of 35 pages (compared to its equivalent in the previous year of 15 pages).

One of Xerox's quality managers summarized the problems: 'We struggled so much with the vital few. I think with other companies they tend not to do so much with the how. We have objectives where the focus is broader (because of the marketing nature of the work) and so we will give you a few more of the hows, and what you do in support of that is for you to decide. The previous MD could not agree to less than eight and would not countenance two or three. Problem was that by the time you get to 24 critical elements you are beginning to lose focus. My argument is that we do not have hoshin kanri, we have something, which is well recognized and used for communication, but what we actually communicate with – it would be debatable. We introduced elements because we used to have eight vital few programmes but they were then so broad that to try and get anything out of it at an individual level was difficult.'

Many units simply failed to consider the vital few distinctly enough from the things they were doing anyway, and the units designed their programmes more to suit local rather than corporate centre priorities. A new managing director came in who reduced the number to only four vital few programmes, and simplified the documentation, so that a renewed purpose improved results markedly for the following year.

Discussion questions

1 Outline specifically how the four distinct stages of the FAIR hoshin kanri process have been adopted at Xerox.

2 How is the Xerox Management Model similar to, or different from, the European Excellence Model and the Baldrige Criteria?

3 What are the salient lessons from the hoshin kanri experience at Xerox?

Case reference

1 This case is adapted from Witcher, B. J. and Butterworth, R. (1999) 'Hoshin kanri: How Xerox manages', *Long Range Planning* 32(3):323–32.

Chapter 11

LEADERSHIP

Introduction

The prime responsibility for strategic management lies at the top of the organization. The executive and other senior managers must lead the organization so it will achieve its purpose. Effective strategic leadership is the foundation for successfully using the strategic management process.

This chapter considers the role of leadership in relation to strategic management; it covers leadership styles and the status of 'management' in thinking about leadership, and ends with the importance of strategic control to the whole strategic management process.

LEARNING OBJECTIVES

By the end of this chapter you should understand:

- The nature of strategic leadership and 'leadership'.
- Transformational and transactional leadership.
- Leadership tasks and organizational growth.
- The importance of management.
- Strategic levers.
- Strategic control and strategic management.

Business vignette The Nelson Touch: A case of strategic leadership

The British Admiral, Lord Nelson, is still remembered for his defeat of Spanish and French forces at the Battle of Trafalgar (1805). He used his leadership to indoctrinate his subordinate captains, so that once the battle started they would be able to act independently on their own initiative, but in accordance with Nelson's overall strategy to win the battle. Nelson's strategy was original: he needed his ship captains to understand the bigger picture, so they would apply their power where it would have the most effect for defeating the enemy. Once the battle started there would be no chance for the Admiral to direct operations.

Conventionally, sea battles were fought with two lines of ships sailing in parallel lines, firing shots at each other. However, Nelson was facing superior numbers. So he decided to lead his ships in two lines and sail them across and through the enemy's line. This had the disadvantage in the early stages of exposing his ships to heavy fire, which because of the angle of his ships to the enemy, they would not be able to return. His ships split the enemy's line into smaller groups, and overcame their superior numbers by leaving the enemy's forward ships out of the battle altogether, while concentrating his own forces on the smaller numbers further down the enemy's line.

Nelson's Column

Nelson called his style of leadership the 'Nelson Touch'. 'I believe my arrival was most welcome, not only to the Commander of the Fleet, but also to every individual in it; and, when I came to explain to them the "Nelson Touch", it was like an electric shock. Some shed tears, all approved – "It was singular – it was simple"; and, from Admirals downwards, it was repeated ...' Nelson had patiently instilled the idea in his own commanders during tactical discussions in the days before the battle.[1]

Leaders

Consistency and constancy of purpose, objectives and strategies, at every level and part of the organization, require forms of **strategic leadership** that will build and sustain a team effort across the whole organization. Leadership takes different forms for different stages of an organization's development. Even then, leadership styles vary according to the personalities and group dynamics of senior managers, especially of the chief executive. Whatever the form and style, strategic leadership should work to promote organization-wide synergy and harmony.

The popular notion of a leader is of a person who is followed by others. There may be any number of reasons for following, but it is usually because they exercise a power to influence events. In the context of strategic management, a **leader** is one who by influencing others has an ability to take the organization forward to a common purpose. The most powerful people in an organization in this sense are, of course, the executives and other senior managers, who make the most important decisions for moving an organization towards its goals. While the basis for such decisions may emerge and be worked out involving many people throughout the organization, perhaps after conflict and many compromises, it is only the top managers that, in the end, make the decisions for the organization as a whole.

Strategic leadership

However, at every organizational level there are people with leadership qualities and abilities: for

©iStockPhoto.com

example, individuals who lead units, sections, teams, and those who are specialists in important areas of knowledge and competency. Many of these are **strategic leaders** in the sense that they are located in different parts of the organization but they use the strategic management process to help achieve the organization's purpose by influencing and empowering others to create strategic change as necessary. The ability to manage people is central, especially to develop core competences.

Peter Senge, in an influential book about the learning organization, argues for dispersed leadership; this is when it is important to enhance the strategic skills and decision making for managers and employees generally.[2] The word, leader, in Senge's view is not a synonym for senior management, but a more complex concept that applies to anybody in an organization who is able to carry out three roles. The first is as a designer of living systems, or in other words, how a leader conditions working behaviour so that people will say, 'We did it ourselves?' The second is a teacher role, when the leader enables people to self-develop within a space that is a priority for the organization. The third role is to be a steward for the larger purpose of the organization, which a leader uses to bring a depth of meaning to an individual's aspirations. The required skills for strategic leadership involve building shared visions for everybody; this is an ability to bring to the surface and test the mental models people have, or, in other words, the beliefs that people have which underlie their work. Finally, it is also an ability to use systems thinking to see and understand the important organizational inter-dependencies that condition action and relations.

Senge places an emphasis on the reflective nature of good enabling leadership to enhance inter-personal relations. This is present in the work of Goleman and others; they argue that an effective leader must skilfully switch between different leadership styles depending upon the situation they are

PRINCIPLES IN PRACTICE 11.1

No bosses, but plenty of leaders

W. L. Gore & Associates is a privately owned international industrial chemical company. Anyone among its 8000 'associates' can become a leader.

It is a happy company – in polls it is regularly voted one of the best companies to work for. Gary Hamel in his book, *The Future of Management,* uses Gore as a case to illustrate what leadership could be like in the future[32]:

> *Walk around the halls at Gore, or sit in on meetings, and you won't hear anyone use words like 'boss', 'executive', 'manager', or 'vice president'. These terms are so contrary to Gore's egalitarian ideals that they are effectively banned from conversation.*
>
> *Although there are no ranks or titles at Gore, some associates have earned the simple appellation 'leader'. At Gore, senior leaders do not appoint junior leaders. Rather, associates become leaders when their peers judge them to be such. A leader garners influence by demonstrating a capacity to get things done and excelling as a team leader. At Gore, those who make a significant contribution to team success, and do it more than once, attract followers.*
>
> *'We vote with our feet,' says Rich Buckingham, a manufacturing leader in Gore's techno-fabrics group. 'If you call a meeting, and people show up, you're a leader.'*
>
> *Individuals who've been repeatedly asked to serve as 'tribal chiefs' are free to put the word 'leader' on their business card. About 10 per cent of Gore's associates carry such a designation.*

The company explains its approach as a 'Team-Based, Flat Lattice Organization'[33]:

> *How we work at Gore sets us apart. Since Bill Gore founded the company in 1958, Gore has been a team-based, flat lattice organization that fosters personal imitative. There are no traditional organizational charts, no chains of command, nor predetermined channels of communications.*
>
> *Instead, we communicate directly with each other and are accountable to fellow members of our multi-disciplined teams. We encourage hands-on innovation, involving those closest to a project in decision making. Teams organize around opportunities and leaders emerge. This unique kind of corporate structure has proven to be the key significant contributor to associate satisfaction and retention.*
>
> *... How does all this happen? Associates (not employees) are hired for general work areas. With the guidance of their sponsors (not bosses) and a growing understanding of opportunities and team objectives, associates commit to projects that match their skills. All of this takes place in an environment that combines freedom with co-operation and autonomy with synergy.*
>
> *Everyone can quickly earn the credibility to define and drive projects. Sponsors help associates chart a course in the organization that will offer personal fulfilment while maximizing their contribution to the enterprise. Leaders may be appointed, but are defined by 'followership'. More often leaders emerge naturally by demonstrating special knowledge, skill, or experience that advances a business objective.*

Question: How is it possible to manage a latticed network strategically?

> **Men in general judge by their eyes rather than by their hands; because everyone is in a position to watch, few are in a position to come in close touch with you. Everyone sees what you appear to be, few experience what you really are.**

faced with.[3] This ability is (at least in part) dependent upon a leader's **emotional intelligence**, the ability to recognize and understand their own emotions and the emotions of others. The attributes that comprise this quality are:

- Self-awareness (the ability to articulate openly about feelings).
- Self-management (the ability to control and use emotions to good effect).
- Social awareness (the ability to empathize with others).

Executive leadership, however, is by its nature remote in the sense that only a small part of a large organization's staff will have regular contact with top managers. In this case, the appearance of leadership is also important. The political philosopher, Niccolo Machiavelli, writing in the early sixteenth century, observed that 'men in general judge by their eyes rather than by their hands; because everyone is in a position to watch, few are in a position to come in close touch with you. Everyone sees what you appear to be, few experience what you really are.'[4]

The representation of what leaders do, especially in the symbols and artefacts that are associated with them, such as strategic plans, reports, purpose statements, public relations, and so on, can be as important in themselves for credibility, signifying legitimacy, as they are in practical terms to help any strategic decision or action. The management of meaning and the ability of a leader to communicate, and the management of attention and the ability to employ a vision which other people believe in and trust, are ideas present in the writing of Warren Bennis on leadership, especially in his book, *Leaders*.[5]

Mary Evans Picture Library/Alamy

Transformational and transactional leadership

James McGregor Burns, a political scientist, in his book, *Leadership*, distinguishes between **transformational leadership** and **transactional**

leadership.[6] Transformational leadership is charismatic and inspirational in a way that exploits the motives and higher needs of the follower, so that the 'full person of the follower is engaged'. He suggests that the relations between most leaders and followers are transactional, when leaders approach followers to exchange one thing for another, such as jobs for votes, and bargaining is central to most of the relationships between leaders and the groups and parties that follow them.

Burns' ideas have been used to explain the role of leadership in organization management in general (notably in Bass[7]). Transformational leadership aims to associate individual self-interest with the larger vision of the organization, by inspiring people with a sense of collective vision. Good transformational leadership creates excitement and raises enthusiasm for challenges that bring about change. Transactional leadership, on the other hand, is more centred on mission and explicit management systems that clarify expectations and agreements, and which provide constructive feedback about performance. Burns was active in American politics and argued for strong leadership, and he favoured a visionary style of leadership.

Visionary leaders

Visionary leadership is sometimes associated with a personalized form of strategic control that conditions organizational culture: it is based on a dominant leader's vision. One of the most renowned examples is Henry Ford, who had a clear idea about why he founded his car company.

In 1907, four years after the Ford Motor Company was incorporated, he wrote in the company prospectus: 'I will build a car for the great multitude. It will be large enough for the family but small enough for the individual to run and care for. It will be constructed of the best materials, by the best men to be hired, after the simplest designs that modern engineering can devise. But it will be low in price so that no man making a good salary will be unable to own one and enjoy with his family the blessing of hours of pleasure in God's great open spaces.'[8] It would be a few years before this vision produced the Model-T car, and the development of a modern mass production assembly line that made Ford's vision possible.

Sometimes a leader's vision has more to do with values. Richard Branson is never seen wearing a tie and his hair is long; he embodies an unconventionality that is used to colour the Virgin Group's identity. Many of the industries that Virgin has invested in are long-established and the aim of Virgin has been to do things differently, or to challenge the existing rules, to give customers a choice, to be entertaining and 'put a thumb in the eye of complacent incumbents'. The culture is one of 'why not' rather than 'why' – an essence that Branson himself seems to personify and which suggests that Virgin competes very differently from its competitors.

For example, when the Virgin record label was competing with EMI, 'Virgin's studios were more than twice as profitable as those of EMI's, and the reason was not hard to see. At EMI, there was an elaborate system of incentives, with managers setting targets and receiving salaries at the end of the year that reflected how well they had performed against these. At Virgin there was no formal system at all. Yet Virgin was managed more aggressively, and with more concern for the pennies, while at EMI the managers had simply set themselves targets that were low enough to be easily beaten'[9]

A similar form of leadership is **entrepreneurial leadership**, a style that is associated with small and medium-sized businesses. This is characterized by the personality, usually of a single owner-manager,

Jim Forrest/Alamy

Richard Branson

or sometimes of a few collaborating individuals, who impose their view on the business in ways that are characteristically innovative. However, it can also be used to describe an innovative leader, often a visionary one, in a large organization. Both entrepreneurial and visionary leadership have been cited as examples of transformational leadership. Over recent years, these types of leadership have been popularly favoured as the sort of leadership that reflects the pace of change a modern economy requires.

However, if these styles encourage a dominating form of managing, then there are many critics. The Hopper brothers lament the passing of what they call the 'Golden Age of American management', when the chief executive had been a thoughtful listener, who had shared responsibility with the members of his team, and was paid only moderately more than them.[10] Now, they argue, this collegiate style of leadership has given way to the imperial chief executive.

Michael O'Leary, the charismatic chief executive of Ryanair, thinks he can spot the trappings of empire: 'The more successful you are, the more likely you are to lose sight of the things that made you successful ... Someone wrote a book in the States twenty years ago and said the three things you can always use to tell the time when a company turns from being a success to a failure are when they build a headquarters – the glass palace headquarters office – helicopter outside of it, and the chief executive writes a book. So I think as long as we stay away from all those things, we're fine'[11]

Backroom leaders

In research that paired above- and average-performing companies, Bill Collins found that the former group had chief executives who were low-profile and self-effacing. The characteristic of **backroom leaders** is to lead quietly from the backroom, rather than loudly from the front. These leaders do not force change, or even try to motivate people directly, but instead they stress understanding an organization's core values (see Chapter 2), rather than a vision, and work to build up a disciplined culture that sustains results over the long-term.

This does not mean command and control, but it requires that people adhere to a consistent system: '... it gives people freedom and responsibility within the framework of that system ... [*a disciplined culture*] is not just about action. It is about getting disciplined people who engage in disciplined thought and who then take disciplined action.'[12] Leadership is low key and does not require efforts to raise motivation and commitment, particularly if the right thinking people have been put in place.

'Clearly, the good-to-great companies did get incredible commitment and alignment – they artfully managed change – but they never really spend much time thinking about it. It was utterly transparent

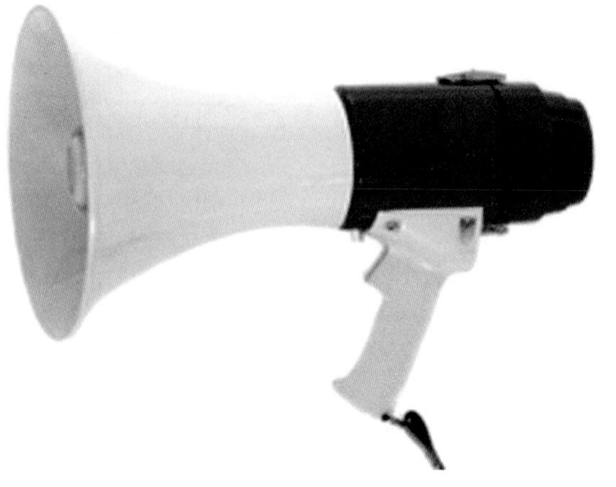

© Kenhurst/Dreamstime.com

WE LEARNED THAT UNDER THE RIGHT CONDITIONS, THE PROBLEMS OF COMMITMENT, ALIGNMENT, MOTIVATION AND CHANGE JUST MELT AWAY. THEY LARGELY TAKE CARE OF THEMSELVES ... CEOS WHO PERSONALLY DISCIPLINE THROUGH SHEER FORCE OF PERSONALITY USUALLY FAIL TO PRODUCE SUSTAINED RESULTS ... [*LEADERSHIP IS A*] QUIET, DELIBERATE PROCESS OF FIGURING OUT WHAT NEEDS TO BE DONE AND SIMPLY DOING IT.

to them. We learned that under the right conditions, the problems of commitment, alignment, motivation and change just melt away. They largely take care of themselves ... CEOs who personally discipline through sheer force of personality usually fail to produce sustained results ... [*leadership is a*] quiet, deliberate process of figuring out what needs to be done and simply doing it'[13]

When it comes down to it, all leaders are likely to claim they 'simply do it'. However, there is an apparent distinction between leadership and strategy as executive leader concerns, and 'management' as the concern of others.

When the British politician John Reid was asked to sort out a dysfunctional government department, the Home Office, he was very clear about his role, and the role of his officials: '... Our system is not fit for purpose. It is inadequate in terms of its scope, it is inadequate in terms of its information technology, leadership, management, systems and processes, ... but he did not consider the Home Office to be irredeemably dysfunctional. It could be managed properly, but it was not his task to do so. While he would provide leadership, strategy and direction, he made it clear that he expected the officials to run it properly'[14]

This divide between strategy and management at root rests with the classical notion that strategy implementation follows formulation (see Chapter 1). The view that leadership is different from management is very strongly represented in the general business and management literature.

Leadership is different from management

Abraham Zaleznik argues that leaders and managers are different things: a leader is proactive and shapes ideas and a manager is focused on processes, teamwork and working within the existing organization.[15] In short, a leader is a change shaper and mover. These ideas are developed by John Kotter, a professor of organizational behaviour and human resource management, who stresses that although leadership and management are different, they complement and need each other.[16] In practical terms a leader has to articulate the organization's vision so that it clarifies and reinforces the values of the organization's people. Everybody, however, ought to be involved in deciding how to achieve the vision so that they have a sense of control. This requires support from leaders through feedback, coaching and role modelling, to help people develop professionally and to enhance their self-esteem through recognizing and rewarding their success. This is important, not just to build people's sense of achievement, but to show them that the organization cares about them.

With these things in place, Kotter argues that work itself becomes intrinsically motivating.[17] For organizations to develop leaders, young employees should be given challenging opportunities by increasing decentralization, and organizational cultures must be developed to institutionalize a leadership-centred culture. Whether or not the qualities associated with leadership can be learned is another matter.

PRINCIPLES IN PRACTICE 11.2

Jack Ma – China's Internet master[34]

Jack Ma, aged 44, is one of China's leading entrepreneurs. He is chairman of Alibaba.com, which is the world's largest on-line trading platform for businesses. For 15 years he has preached the importance of the Internet to convince companies that they should pay to offer their products on Alibaba's website. Alibaba has 36 million registered users worldwide, although the majority, about 29 million, are registered for business that is inside China. It generates revenues of around £220m annually and employs 12 000 people.

Jack Ma

His leadership style has been described by the *Financial Times* as energetic and stubborn. If one of his executives makes a decision he does not like, he says 'I will see if I can tolerate it. And if it's wrong, well, I think it is stupid and change it again.'

Ma wants to be the 'guard' of the group's values and vision, and spends most of his time trying to make sure they are deeply rooted in the minds of each employee. When Mr Ma, a slight gaunt man, birdlike in appearance, tried to sell on-line advertising space on China's nascent Internet in 1994, people viewed him with scepticism and suspicion.

'They would think I was crazy,' he says, gesturing with his bony hands.

In 1995 he established the China Yellow Pages, an on-line directory for Chinese businesses. Alibaba was set up four years later to focus on small businesses, rather than consumers of multinationals. For a fixed payment, Alibaba offers Chinese suppliers a place on its website. Ma believes that small and medium-sized businesses can benefit most from the Internet because it gives them access to buyers they would otherwise only meet at trade shows. With access to a wider pool of customers, it also reduces their dependency on market-dominated clients.

'Companies like Wal-Mart, these big time buyers, killed a lot of SME buyers' says Ma. 'But now most of the SME buyers and sellers started to do business throughout the world because of the Internet. So I think the world has moved. I strongly believe small is beautiful.'

Alibaba has recently facilitated loans in excess of RMB1bn to SMEs that would otherwise struggle in the global recession. The group is optimistic and expects to hire another 4500 in 2009.

'Before this financial crisis, we were helping China's products abroad. Now we are thinking about helping SMEs in other parts of the world. Help them sell across the nations. Help them sell to China,' he says. 'In the next 10 years, we are moving from a pure Chinese exporting centre to a global platform for SMEs to exchange products.'

Question: What is Jack Ma's leadership style?

Warren Bennis observes that there is a profound difference between management and leadership, although both are important. Leading is about influencing people to go in a certain direction, and embark on a certain course of action. Managing is about having responsibility to accomplish the action. In other words, as Bennis has put it: 'Managers are people who do things right and leaders are people who do the right thing'. He contrasts the different activities of both in Table 11.1.

Certainly these things are qualities that are likely to be needed in different quantities for different tasks, and at different times. It is also likely that some individuals will be more disposed in character and experience to favour one set of qualities over another. Of course qualities and individuals complement each other, and we would hope they are present in senior management teams. It is likely that senior managers will proactively spend most of their time on strategic objectives to achieve a vision, and less of it on making interventions to correct performance on the organization's diagnostic objectives (see Chapter 3). These senior managers are more likely to be involved than other managers with these kinds of leadership attributes. However, it is a big jump to suppose that leaders should not manage what they do, or that a manager should not have leadership qualities. The really substantive point is that the management of strategic change is likely to need more leadership qualities than the management of a stable business

TABLE 11.1 The different qualities of leadership and management according to Bennis[18]

Leaders	*Managers*
• Innovate	• Administer
• Develop	• Maintain
• Investigate	• Accepts reality
• Focus on people	• Focus on systems and structures
• Inspire trust	• Rely on control
• Take the long view	• Take a short-range view
• Ask what and why	• Ask how and when
• Eye the horizon	• Eye the bottom-line
• Originate	• Imitate
• Challenge the status quo	• Accept the status quo
• Are their own person	• Are the classic 'good soldier'

KEY DEBATE 11.1

Transformational leadership or managerialism?

Columnist, Stefan Stern, writing in the *Financial Times* in early February, 2008, attacked the idea that management is boring and leadership will take us to the Promised Land, and argued the White House needs a competent manager.[36]

During the Democratic primaries, Senator Hillary Clinton was criticized as a policy and detail-obsessed manager, while Senator Barack Obama was presented as an exciting visionary leader. When criticized that his stirring speeches were long on aspirations but short on specifics, Mr Obama retorted that what his leadership would offer is more important.

Todd Bannor/Alamy

Hillary Clinton and Barack Obama

Clinton argued that the role of the President is not only to provide visionary leadership, but also to control the federal administration downward to ensure that policies are carried out effectively. Clinton has the experience as head of the health-care reform initiative during her husband's first term of office. This involved putting together a detailed and complex plan of reform. However, it created deep dissatisfaction among the relevant stakeholders, whose support was necessary to enact the proposed legislation, and the plans foundered.

Obama argued the job of the President should be focused completely on providing leadership vision, judgement and inspiration. The federal agencies would report to him and he would delegate responsibility to them. He would hold himself aloof, but he would make the agency heads fully accountable for their performance of the public servants in their charge.

Question: Is Stefan Stern right?

model, which is more likely to need the others. These things are not necessary in the person who does the job, as much as they are needed to do a particular task of work.

The role of a leading individual in strategic management is obviously important. It is impossible to dissent when you are looking at a dictator. Dictators may be good for you if they force you to make unpleasant changes that in the long-run will be good for you. Nevertheless, these things are unlikely to work unless this dictator lets you get on and do the work. In the end, strategic management should be an organization-wide function that is intrinsically team-based.

Domain knowledge is important. This involves individuals who have experience and understanding of how the organization works, and what it works on. It may be difficult for leaders who are external appointments. These are generally well-qualified with successful experience at other companies. However it is likely they will have to depend on others in the organization for understanding the content and context of their new organization's work. This is a particular shortcoming if the new appointment has to be able to understand those organization-specific strategic resources that constitute the organization's competitive advantage.

Japan is a special case and stands out from most other countries. Japanese senior managers generally have a high level of domain knowledge and more importance is attached to customer-facing processes and engineering. So there is less reliance on professional management and the financial function. Leadership is less based on individual achievement and more on a sense of a commitment to be part of a greater whole. Traditionally, promotion has depended on the long-term commitment a manager has to the organization, so that one-company work experience is important. There is no equivalent separation in Japan of leadership from management. Leaders expect to manage.

Management as a profession

In the wake of the global financial crisis, the Hopper brothers argue that it is the 'cult of management', or management as a professional discipline, that is responsible for a form of leadership that has been prevalent in western companies since about 1970.[19] The professionalization of management is based on the idea that it is possible to educate and train managers to manage any sort of business without domain knowledge. It was no longer seen as a necessity for leaders to be appointed who had learnt the craft of management as they rose through an organization's ranks. Since the 1970s there has probably been a growing propensity for the board to appoint chief executives from outside and (often) unrelated business. In the view of the Hoppers, the new style of senior manager: 'Sought to control the organization through the medium of the finance department, while delegating the tedious task of

TABLE 11.2 The nature of managerial work

Managers should	*Managers really*
• Plan, organize, co-ordinate, control	• Work at an unrelenting pace, oriented to action and variety, dislike reflection
• Be reflective, systematic, concentrate on strategic rather than routine duties	• Use soft information on many routine duties
• Rely on formal information systems	• Work with verbal media, telephones, meetings, work on 'odds and ends of tangible detail'
• See management as a scientific and professional discipline	• Keep things inside their heads, judgement based on experience and intuition

acquiring and using "domain knowledge" to juniors. The outcome has been managerial incompetence on a scale inconceivable in earlier generations and extending over much of society.'[20]

These are indeed harsh words. Certainly survey data from the United States and the United Kingdom suggest that a majority of middle management lacks confidence in its chief executives.[21] In fact, the nature of managerial work may not be as rational and deliberate as textbooks advise it should be. Henry Mintzberg argues that what managers are expected to do contrasts with what they actually do (see Table 11.2).[22]

According to Mintzberg's research the task of managing is more likely to be about fire-fighting and informal communication, than it is about deliberate planning, writing things down and organization. Mintzberg's work was published over a quarter of a century ago. When he was asked recently if things had changed he thought they had not, except perhaps that the pace of things had increased (and that 'strategy' is in the head); he observed that while everybody is obsessed with management, 'we still barely understand the process'.[23]

It is clear that the nature of leadership and how it relates to the overall management of an organization is conditioned by size and complexity. A useful framework for understanding this is Greiner's growth phrase model.[24]

Leadership, size and growth of organizations

The growth phase model of Greiner suggests that organizations go through five stages of growth and need appropriate strategies to match each (see Figure 11.1).

Each of these stages is brought to an end by a leadership crisis, which is solved by a new form of leadership, until eventually increasing size brings another crisis in leadership. The style of leadership in small organizations is typically informal, personal and entrepreneurial, and growth is achieved through creativity. As the organization grows the original owner-manager becomes overworked and partial, finding it too difficult to manage, so that a crisis of leadership occurs.

This ends as some power is ceded to functional management, when leadership becomes formal and introduces more detailed procedures and standard processes, involving bigger roles for marketing, accounting and finance. Growth is now achieved through directional leadership. Strains appear as senior management's chain of decision making becomes overstretched, and managers at operational and market levels find themselves disconnected from decisions at the centre. This results in a crisis of autonomy about who can effectively make the best decisions.

The solution that arises is a new delegating form of leadership, which decentralizes the organization into separate divisions that take responsibility for their own business strategy. The centre effectively manages by distance: monitoring (typically financial) performance, and by holding periodic reviews. It becomes directly involved only by exception. This form of leadership downplays the potential for economies of scale. A growing group of semi-independent businesses is difficult to control if the organization as a whole wishes to exploit group synergies: this is a crisis of control.

Synergy requires a closer contact with organizational parts. Monitoring is necessary not just of performance, but also of the activities that enable effective performance. It is the enabling activities and processes which benefit most from organizational synergy. Leadership takes on a co-ordinating role, which involves the creation of central support systems and consulting functions, and formal planning. However, with further growth, cross-reporting and the many formal linkages between organizational units become confused, which ends in a red tape crisis.

Greiner's final stage is growth through collaboration, and a style of leadership that is more defused through the parts of the organization. Teams and projects play major parts in forming and developing major decisions, especially cross-functional task teams, which are facilitated by decentralized support functions. Greiner later added a sixth stage to his original model, which was about an internal growth crisis, and which calls for extra-organizational and networked leadership.

Much of the general literature about the management of people suggests that command-and-control forms of leadership have given way over time to more devolved and networked forms of organizing. The latest in this long line is guru Gary Hamel, who advocates a

FIGURE 11.1 Five states of leadership and organizing[24]

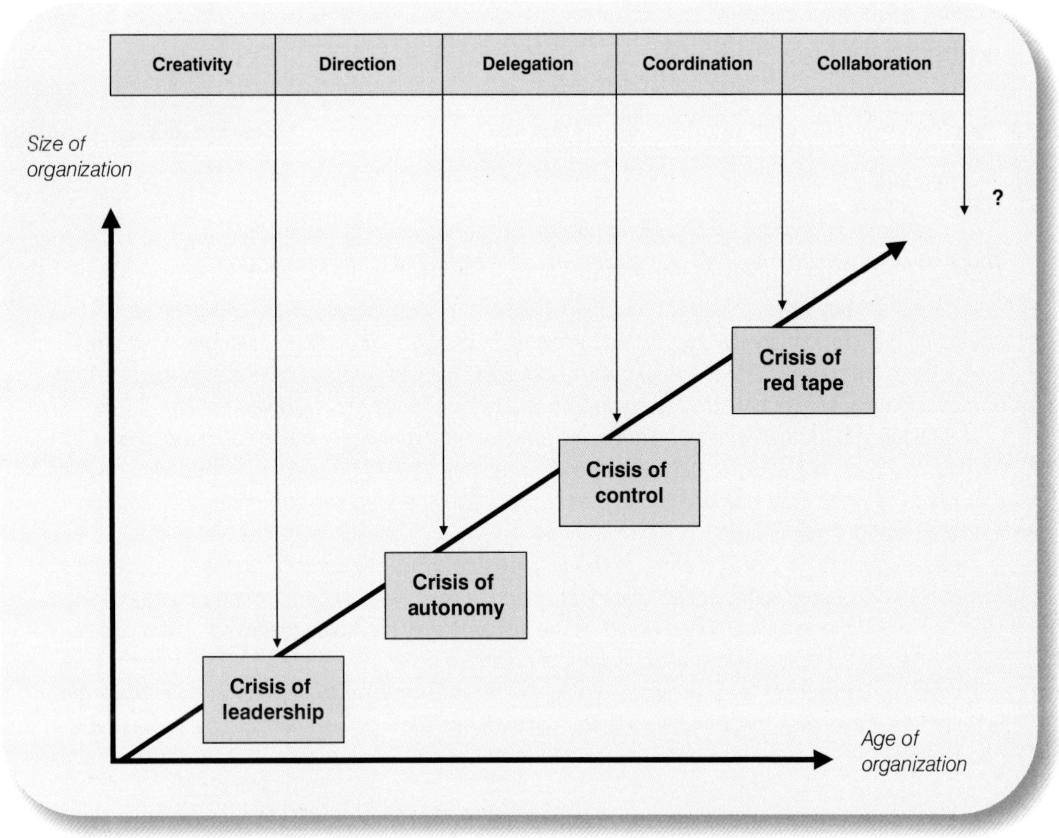

Creativity | Direction | Delegation | Coordination | Collaboration

Size of organization

?

Crisis of red tape

Crisis of control

Crisis of autonomy

Crisis of leadership

Age of organization

latticed and networked style of organization.[25] This is driven by the crisis of the possibilities of the Internet, and the upheaval implied for how people think about information and the community. The boundaries of an organization are often unclear in the modern world. The role for leadership is to stimulate and facilitate staff creativity and innovation. We are back to entrepreneurial leadership, but leadership by employees. To do this effectively, Hamel argues, we need to reinvent management.

The Greiner scheme is, of course, used only as an organizing framework. It is not predictive and its purpose here is only to illustrate how the changing nature of any strategic management task means that the practice of leadership cannot remain static but must evolve to accommodate the different needs for change. Chief executives should adapt their strategic agenda and management style to take account of

PRINCIPLES IN PRACTICE 11.3

Leadership for New York

Rudolph Giuliani was a successful mayor of New York from 1994–2001. In his book, *Leadership,* he introduced his view of leadership[35]:

Leadership does not simply happen. It can be taught, learned, developed. Those who influenced me ... all contributed valuable elements to my philosophy.

There are many ways to lead. Some people like Franklin Roosevelt, inspired with stirring speeches. Others, like Joe DiMaggio, led by example. Winston Churchill and Douglas MacArthur were both exceptionally brave and excellent speakers. Ronald Reagan led through the strength and consistency of his character – people followed him because they believed in him.

Ultimately you'll know what techniques and approaches work best – those you hope to lead will tell you. Much of your ability to get people to do what they have to do is going to depend on what they perceive when they look at you and listen to you. They need to see someone who is stronger than they are, but human too.

Leaders have to control their emotions under pressure. While I was mayor, on the few occasions someone who worked for me used 'panic' to describe their state of being during some crisis in their bailiwick, I made it clear that it would be the last time they'd employ that word ... You can't let yourself be paralyzed by any situation. It's about balance.

I tried to run the city as a business, using business principles to impose accountability on government. Objective, measurable indicators of success allow governments to be accountable, and I relentlessly pursued that idea.

Question: Are the principles for running a major city the same as for running a large commercial business?

circumstances. It should also be remembered that most organizations are everyday affairs, and the people in them are human beings!

In the view of media personality Stephen Fry: 'Anyone who has lived and worked within a large organization, whether it be the BBC, the army, a school or a large hospital, will know that cream and scum alike rise to the top; that blundering, hopeless, blinkered, purblind and ignorant incompetence inform the actions and governance of such places at all times. That bitchery, cattery and rivalry frustrate co-operation, good fellowship and trust.'[26]

Well, it is not always that bad, but the point is we should not expect leadership to be perfect. The thing that is important is that leaders should be open-minded and they have to manage their organizations. For this they need robust information systems for finding out how their strategy is working, and for finding and exploring new ideas about what can work.

Levers of strategic control

Robert Simons argues that leaders need to have systems for gathering information that go beyond goal-oriented activities.[27] For example, ensuring that new stores open on schedule, others that take into account any patterns of unanticipated innovation, such as discovering that branch employees' experiments with the layout of a store have doubled expected sales figures. He points out that control systems must accommodate not just intended strategies, but also strategies that emerge from local experimentation and independent employee initiatives. He maintains that such systems should do four things: 'to signal the domain in which subordinates should search for opportunities, to communicate plans and goals, to monitor the achievement of plans and goals, and to keep informed and inform others of emerging developments.'[28]

Each of these four information-based activities is a control system for sustaining or influencing patterns of behaviour in the organization. In the sense that senior managers can use these to lever the organization into a desired strategic position, they can be called the organization's four **strategic levers**: beliefs systems, boundary systems, diagnostic control systems, and interactive control systems (see Figure 11.2).

Principally, beliefs systems are there to inspire and direct the search for new opportunities; boundary systems set the limits to this opportunity-seeking behaviour; diagnostic systems motivate and monitor current behaviour towards the achievement of the specified goal; and interactive control systems stimulate the organization by provoking newer ideas that emerge. The two levers on the left-hand side of the four quadrants are considered by Simons to be the yang control levers (representing warmth, positivism and light, as positive forces), while the two on the right-hand side are the yin elements (of cold and darkness, which are the negative forces). The yang and yin tensions come from Taoist I-Ching philosophy, and the key thing about them is that they must be in balance.

The two levers, beliefs systems and boundary systems, relate to the framing of strategy and must be in balance with the other two levers, diagnostic control

FIGURE 11.2 The four levers of strategic control[29]

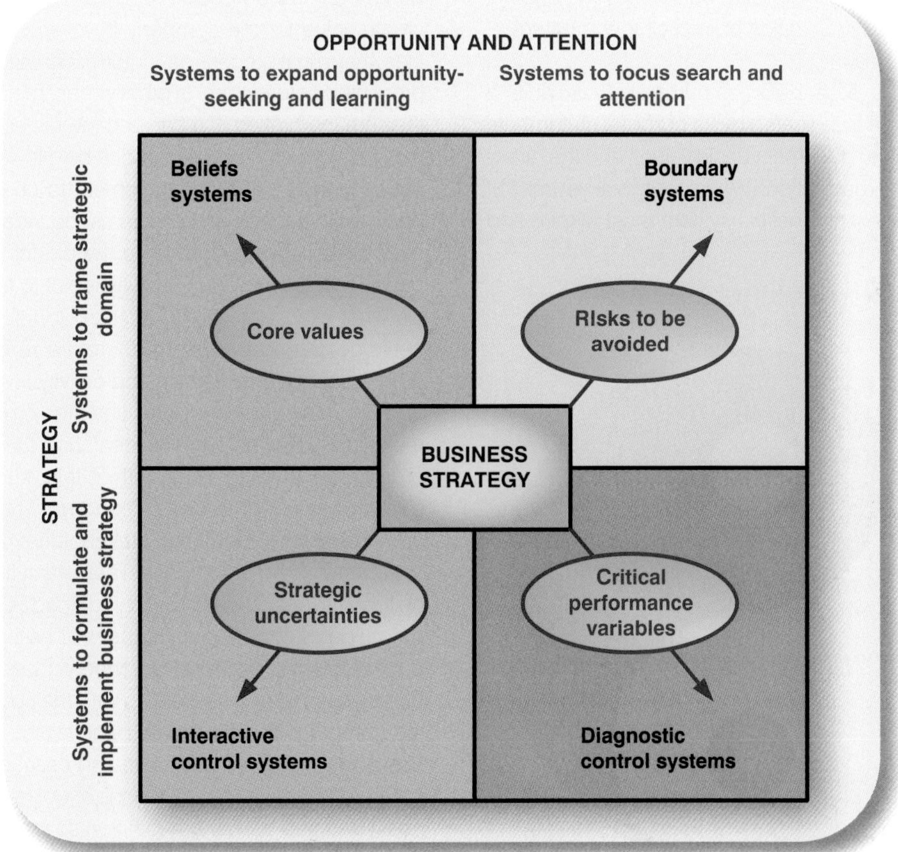

systems and interactive control systems, which relate to the formulation and implementation of strategy. A successful balance will result in the achievement of the organization's strategic goals.

Lever 1: Beliefs systems

Beliefs systems are an explicit set of organizational definitions that senior managers communicate formally, and reinforce systematically, to provide the basic values and direction for the organization. They inspire and help direct staff in the search for new opportunities. The notion of beliefs systems considers the values that are rooted deeply within an organization which underlie the purpose of its existence. This control system is imperative although Simons had originally omitted this from discussion in his earlier work.[30] His change of mind probably reflects contemporary discussion that places a stress on leadership and the importance to it of vision and values. These may be explicitly written into the original articles of the organization or implicit in the nature of the work it does.

Where the organizational purpose is explicit, a beliefs system is indicated by its purpose statements that are used to document basic values and the direction for the organization. Where purpose is implicit and not so clear, the beliefs system must inspire and guide the organization's search for, and discovery of, that purpose; for example, the beliefs system can be used to motivate individuals to find new ways for creating value for the organization. The formal articulation of beliefs systems in purpose statements becomes more important with growth. Whereas in smaller organizations personnel are intuitively clear about the purpose of the organization, this weakens as complexity increases, and there is a need to document beliefs formally. However, beliefs systems are typically too brief and vague to guide implementation on their own and need the second lever of control, boundary systems.

Lever 2: Boundary systems

Boundary systems cover those sets of rules and sanctions that restrict search, and which help clarify those areas of risk that the organization ought to avoid. In other words, they set limits on opportunity-seeking behaviour. As individuals are opportunity seekers who create value for the company by overcoming obstacles, they must process new information and situations presented before them. In other words, metaphorically, they are the brakes of a car, and the faster the car the more effective the brakes need to be. However, as it is impossible for senior management to understand all likely contingencies and problems, boundary systems must be robust enough to be flexible for a range of possible opportunities. One way is not to tell individuals what exactly to do, but instead to tell them what not to do. Boundary systems therefore set the limits of organizational opportunism and activity.

When new situations arise, untested organizational responses may be used to deal with them. Various organizational factors may affect this, such as specific and stringent codes of conduct. These factors are equivalent to dominant stakeholders overlooking the operations of a company. They affect the enforceability of issues. These may include codes of conduct promulgated by a regulator, as well as political and public opinion. Nonetheless, where these codes or factors have strong similarities with the core values of the company, these operate beneficially. The role of senior management is to state and cascade the core values and visions of the organization, analyse business risks and delimit competition so that the work of subordinates can be eased.

These two levers operating together provide the strategic domain of the organization, but in order to sustain resources and organizational strengths, managers must concentrate on positioning the organization to meet the competitive challenges of the marketplace. For this, the other two levers are required.

Lever 3: Diagnostic control systems

Diagnostic control systems are formal systems that are designed to monitor the progress of objectives in the implementation of strategic and related plans. They provide a diagnostic check on how strategy is working. They also motivate, monitor and reward the achievement of specified goals. Diagnostic control systems are designed to serve predictable goal achievement. They are feedback systems which are core to management control. Managers obtain feedback from their subordinates to align the organization's activities with the organizational goals.

There are three principles for managing diagnostic control systems: (1) the ability to measure the outputs of a process; (2) to have predetermined standards against which actual results can be compared; and (3) to be able to correct deviations from these standards. These ensure that managers can control outputs through a careful selection of inputs, and can deal with critical performance variables that represent important dimensions of a given strategy. Critical performance variables take many forms; these are not just financial, but may also include customer satisfaction and quality.

Diagnostic control systems can be devolved to local management. Unlike boundary systems, the freedom is left to the individuals to accomplish the desired ends, as superiors will have already agreed the process specification, and the process team can intervene to take corrective action if performance starts to drift from the original specification. Senior managers will only become involved by exception.

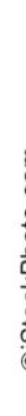

Lever 4: Interactive control systems

Interactive control systems are comprised of formal information systems that managers use to involve themselves regularly and personally in the decision activities of subordinates. Many kinds of interactive control are used, but the important element is the personal participation of senior managers in monthly reviews of progress and action plans that involve other levels in face-to-face meetings. These enable senior managers to try out and introduce new possibilities for change. This activity helps form the agendas for wider debate and includes information gathering from outside routine channels.

This control system brings the organization in line with the changing external environment, since effective managers scan for disruptive changes that signal the need to change organizational structures, capabilities and product technologies. For interactive control systems to function properly, organization-wide involvement is required. When external opportunities and threats are identified, it is important that people across the organization provide input about how organizational capabilities can be changed and brought into play to meet them.

Essentially, there are four distinctive characteristics which form the backbone to interactive control systems: (1) information must be generated by the system and addressed by senior management; (2) operating managers, and other levels of the organization, must review the system frequently; (3) the data generated must be discussed face-to-face in

KEY DEBATE 11.2

What is strategic control?

There is no real consensus about the nature of **strategic control**. One of the early thinkers in business strategy was Robert Anthony.[37] He drew a line between strategic planning, management control, and operations, and argued that strategic control relates only to the control of strategic planning. This form of control is different from management control which is the job of middle management. This level of management implements the strategic plan and provides operational feedback to senior managers who are focused on the longer term and design the strategic plan.

This is the classic control model and it is consistent with the design school of strategy, when implementation follows formulation.

A new model of strategic control is offered by Robert Simons and his four strategic levers.[38] This suggests that control should come before planning.

In an important book, *Strategic Control Systems,* Peter Lorange and others define strategic control as a support system for managers, to help them assess performance against the needs of the longer-term strategy.[39]

Goold and Quinn point out that few companies identify formal and explicit strategic control measures, and build these into their control systems.[40] The confusion of what is really strategic, rather than operational, seems an important problem for organizations. Lorange and his co-authors point to examples where planning and control are organized separately, with little communication between the two functions.

Kaplan and Norton argue that superiors should not control subordinates directly, since strategy-linked action should be controlled by the people who do the work in ways that make its progress visible to all.[41]

Question: Does the word 'control' mean the same thing as 'management'?

meetings at all levels; and (4) the system must be the catalyst for all the action plans of the organization.

Interactive control systems must take into consideration various factors. In technology dependent companies, senior managers must focus on responding to customer needs, as technological advances are so rapid. In companies with complex value chains, accounting-based measures provide opportunities and threats to the company, but where this is simple, they need only focus on input and output measures. In regulated public utilities, for example Simons notes specifically, companies must pay attention to public sentiment, political pressures and emerging regulations and legislation.

The strategic levers are the ways a senior management can control the strategic performance of an organization. Nevertheless, the levers by themselves are de-coupled from the overall strategic management process. We now consider what the overall management framework looks like.

A management framework for strategic management

It is necessary to distinguish between (1) longer-term purpose, objectives and strategy; (2) shorter-term implementation and execution; and (3) the overall strategic control of (1) and (2) (see Figure 11.3).

FIGURE 11.3 POSIES model of strategic management

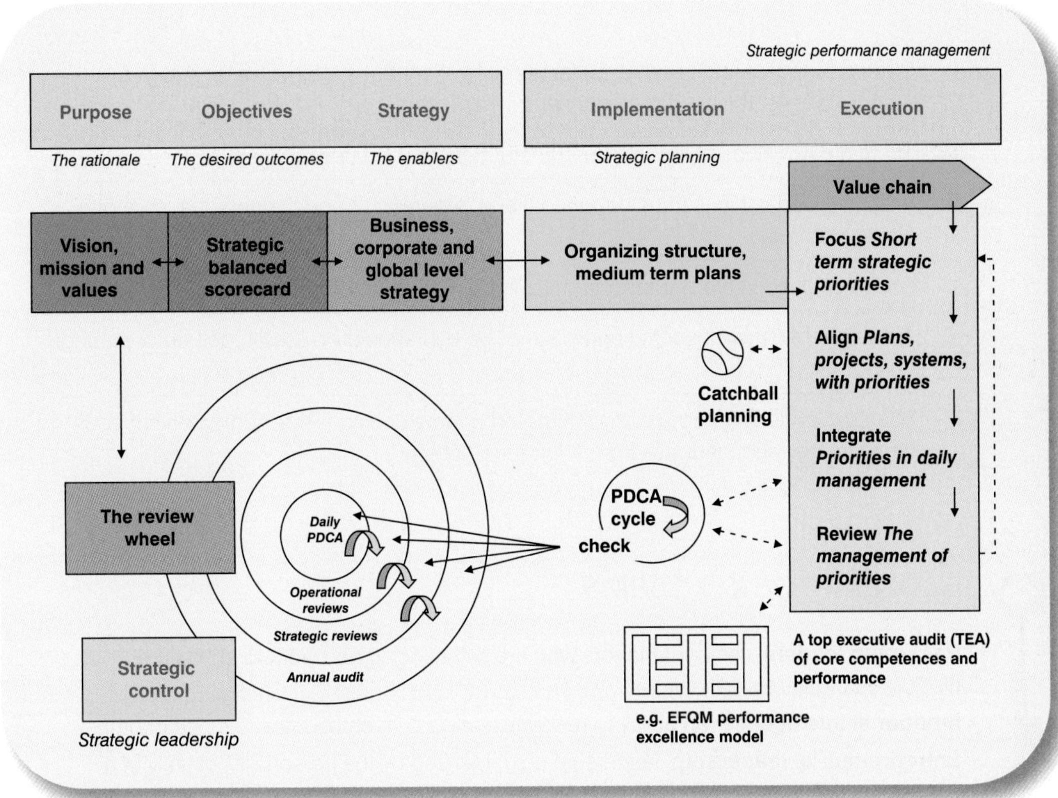

The shaded box in the figure, top left, signifies the longer-term components of strategic management. The shaded box, top right, signifies the shorter-term components. The shaded box, lower left, represents **strategic control**.

Strategic control is the overall control of the effectiveness of strategic management, including both longer and shorter-term components, and is driven by an organization-wide integrated system of review – the **review wheel**. In other words, strategic control is the organization's overall managed system for organizational feedback and learning that informs the senior level's strategic management.

The review wheel turns as an inter-linked system of multi-level review. The overall goal of longer-term strategy is to provide an organizational capability for decisions and actions in the short-term. Put in another way, a strategically organized system gives to people at an operational level an ability to manage their own local decisions. The benefit of their experience is fed back to inform senior managers and to test the viability of the organization's longer-term purpose, objectives and strategy in their strategy reviews. An analysis by the McKinsey Global Institute suggests it is not business opportunities on their own that lead to success, but how they are managed that counts.

'Improved management at Wal-Mart probably played a bigger role in America's productivity miracle of the late 1990s than all the expensive investment in high speed computers and fibre-optic cable by businesses,' observe Baker and Abrahams, reporting on a report of an analysis by the McKinsey Global Institute.[31]

SUMMARY OF PRINCIPLES

1 Strategic leaders are found across an organization, but strategic leadership is a responsibility of the executive and senior managers.

2 There are two kinds of leadership: transformational and transactional.

3 Visionary leadership is transformational and dependent upon the personal style of a single individual.

4 Backroom leadership is transactional and dependent upon a collective discipline.

5 A balance of different control approaches (levers) should be used together for strategic control.

6 Strategic leadership requires an integrated understanding for managing both longer-term strategy and feedback from short-term action.

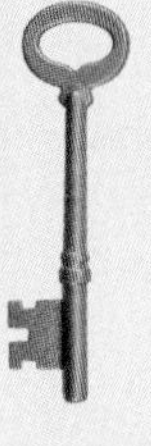

GLOSSARY OF KEY TERMS

Backroom leaders senior managers who are self-effacing and work to build up a disciplined organizational culture.

Emotional intelligence an ability to recognize one's own emotions and those of others.

Entrepreneurial leadership leadership characterized by the personality, usually of a single owner-manager, or sometimes of a few collaborating individuals, who impose their view on the business in ways that are characteristically innovative.

Leader a person who by influencing others has an ability to take the organization forward to a common purpose.

Review wheel an organization-wide integrated system of review.

Strategic control the overall control of the effectiveness of strategic management, including both longer and shorter-term components, which is driven by an organization-wide integrated system of review.

Strategic leaders leaders who are dispersed across the organization, who influence and empower others to participate in strategic management.

strategic leadership the strategic management of the POSIES model as an integrated system of strategic control, that takes into account both long-term and shorter-term components of the model.

Strategic levers four information-based systems that senior managers can use to lever an organization into a desired strategic position.

Transactional leadership centred on mission and explicit management systems, which clarify expectations, agreements, and utilize constructive feedback about performance.

Transformational leadership charismatic leadership which works to associate individual self-interest with the larger vision of the organization by inspiring people with a sense of collective vision.

Visionary leadership a personalized form of strategic control that conditions organizational culture: it is based on a dominant leader's vision.

GUIDED FURTHER READING

Leadership is a subject in its own right and forms an important part of other subjects such as human resource management and organizational behaviour. There are tens of dozens of definitions. The classic text in the context of strategic management is Senge, which has recently been revised:

Senge, P. (2006) *The Fifth Discipline: The Art and Practice of the Learning Organization* (rev. edn), New York: Doubleday.

For an up-to-date historical account of the development of large multi-nations in America and Japan, see the Hopper brothers book. This argues that a change in the nature of business leadership has led to an undesirable form of organizational management, which may be a contributory factor to the world financial crisis.

Hopper, K. and Hopper, W. (2009) *The Puritan Gift; Reclaiming the American Dream Amidst Global Financial Chaos,* London: I. B. Tauris & Co.

REVIEW QUESTIONS

1 What are strategic leaders?

2 Can visionary and backroom leaders also be transformational and transactional leaders?

3 What is emotional intelligence?

4 Do leaders manage?

5 Is professional management necessarily a good thing?

6 What is the relationship of size and growth of organizations to the style of leadership?

7 What is the importance of balance to the four strategic levers?

8 What are the long-term and shorter-term components of strategic management, and what brings them together in an integrated approach to strategic management?

SEMINAR AND ASSIGNMENT QUESTIONS

1 Produce a list of ten leaders, and list them in order of how well-known you think they are. Question why they are so well-known: ask 'why' five times. When you have a deep-rooted reason for their fame, re-do your list. Explain any discrepancies between the before and after lists.

2 For any organization of your choice, explain how Simons' four levers of strategic control can be relevant.

3 Explore websites about well-known scandals and corporate failures. Evaluate these cases to see how 'leadership' could have played a part in their stories. Consider if a well-managed organization can ever fail.

CHAPTER REFERENCES

1 Adkins, R. (2004) *Trafalgar: The Biography of a Battle,* London: Little, Brown.

2 Senge, P. (1990) (2006: rev. edn), *The Fifth Discipline: The Art and Practice of the Learning Organization*, New York: Doubleday.

3 Goleman, D., Boyatzis, R. and McKee, A. (2002) *Primal Leadership: Realizing the Power of Emotional Intelligence,* Boston, MA: Harvard Business School Press.

4 Machiavelli, N. (1950) *The Price and the Discourses,* New York: Random House, p. 165.

5 Bennis, W. and Nanus, B. (1985) *Leaders,* New York: Harper & Row.

6 Burns, J. M. (1978) *Leadership*, New York: Harper & Row.

7 Bass, B. M. (1985) *Leadership and Performance Beyond Expectations*, London: Collier Macmillan.

8 Ford Motor Company (1907) reported in Collins, J. C. and Porras, J. I. (1994) *Built to Last: Successful Habits of Visionary Companies*, New York: Harper Business.

9 Jackson, T. (1995) *Virgin King: Inside Richard Branson's Business Empire* (pbk edn), London: HarperCollins Publishers, p. 295.

10 Hopper, K. and Hopper, W. (2009) *The Puritan Gift; Reclaiming the American Dream Amidst Global Financial Chaos,* London: I. B. Tauris.

11 Quoted in Ruddock, A. (2007) *Michael O'Leary: A Life in Full Flight,* Dublin: Penguin, p. 267.

12 Collins, J. (2001) *Good to Great: Why Some Companies Make the Leap … and Others Don't,* London: HarperCollins, p. 146.

13 Collins (2004) *op cit.,* p. 178.

14 Johnston, P. (2006) 'Reid blasts management failures at Home Office', *Daily Telegraph,* May 24, 1.
15 Zaleznik, A. (1977) 'Managers and leaders: are they different?' *Harvard Business Review* 55(5):74–81.
16 Kotter, J. P. (1990) 'What leaders really do', *Harvard Business Review* (May–June): 68 103–11.
17 Kotter, J. P. (1996) *Leading Change,* Boston: Harvard Business School Press.
18 Bennis, W. (1997) *Why Leaders Can't Lead: The Unconscious Conspiracy*, London: Wiley.
19 Hopper and Hopper (2009), *op cit.*
20 *Ibid*
21 Neilson, G. J., Martin, K. L. and Powers, E. (2008) 'The secrets to successful strategy execution', *Harvard Business Review'* June:61–70; Masters, B. (2008) 'Top managers give chief execs the thumbs down', *Financial Times,* December 10, 18.
22 Mintzberg, H. (1973) *The Nature of Managerial Work,* New York: Harper & Row.
23 de Holan, P. M. and Mintzberg, H. (2004) 'Management as life's essence: 30 years of the "Nature of Managerial Work"', *Strategic Organization* 2(2):205–12.
24 Adapted from Greiner, L. E. (1972) 'Growing organizations', *Harvard Business Review.* 50(4):37–46.
25 Hamel, G. with Breen, B. (2007) *The Future of Management,* Boston: Harvard Business School Press.
26 Fry, S. (1993) *Paperweight,* London: Mandarin.
27 Simons, R. (1995) *Levers of Control: How Managers Use Innovative Control Systems to Drive Strategic Renewal,* Boston: Harvard Business School Press.
28 Simons (1995) *op cit.,* p. 4.
29 Adapted from Simons (1995) *op cit.*, figure 7.2.
30 Simons, R (1990) 'Rethinking the role of systems in controlling strategy', *Harvard Business School: Internal Note* No.9-191-091.
31 Baker, G. and Abrahams, P. (2001) 'Forget IT, it was Wal-Mart behind that US miracle', *Financial Times,* October 17, 15.
32 Hamel (2007) *op cit.*, p.88.
33 Gore & Associates, W. L. (2009) Our culture, *About Gore,* www.gore.com
34 Hile, K. (2009) 'The godfather of small enterprise', *Financial Times,* January 19, 14.
35 Giuliani, R. W. with Kurson, K. (2002) *Leadership,* London: Little, Brown, pp. xii–xiii.
36 Stern, S. (2008) 'White House needs a competent manager', *Financial Times,* February 5.
37 Anthony, R. N. (1965) *Planning and Control Systems: A Framework for Analysis*, Division of Research, Graduate School of Business, Harvard Business School.
38 Simons (1995) *op cit.*
39 Lorange, P., Scott Morton, M. F. and Ghoshal, S. (1986) *Strategic Control Systems,* St. Paul, MN: West Publishing.
40 Goold, M. and Quinn, J. J. (1990) *Strategic Control: Milestones for Long-Term Performance,* London: Hutchinson.
41 Kaplan, R. S. and Norton, D. P. (2001) *The Strategy-Focused Organization: How Balanced Scorecard Companies Thrive in the New Business Environment,* Boston, MA: Harvard Business School Press.

CASE 11.1 The global financial crisis: a question of leadership?

The global financial crisis of 2008 was precipitated by rising interest rates in the sub-prime lending sector of the housing market in the United States. Mortgage lenders had advanced loans to people with bad credit histories and insecure sources of income; many borrowers had bought properties on the expectation that house values would rise to enable them to refinance their mortgages at a profit. Rising interest rates, however, dampened the housing market, and many people found themselves with negative equity and unable to sustain interest payments.

The risk to lenders had been spread by selling loans on as repackaged securities to other banks. However, the scale of the sub-prime market collapse took the financial securities market by surprise, and substantial bank assets were down-valued and written off, to a point where inter-bank lending dwindled to almost nothing (the so-called 'credit crunch').

The 'repackaging' of securities is part of a bigger picture of expanding financial markets stimulated by new sophisticated financial products. This includes securitization, which involves pooling and repackaging cash flow producing assets, like mortgages, into securities for reselling to investors. These assets are derivatives, in the sense that they are financial instruments whose values are derived from something else (such as mortgages). This activity has been encouraged by western governments, which in recent years have relaxed banking restrictions and regulation.

What role did leadership and the strategic management of the financial institutions play in the failure of the banks?

It is not that people did not see the dangers. Stefan Stern, reporting in the *Financial Times,* cites the influential Paul Volcker, an ex-chairman of the American Federal Reserve, speaking in February, 2005: 'Circumstances seem to be as dangerous and intractable as any I can remember, and I can remember quite a lot. What really concerns me is that there should be so little willingness or capacity to do anything about it.'[1]

Stern alleges there has been a turning away from good management. He cites Alfred Chandler's view that the great growth of modern capitalism had been achieved through '... making administrative decisions ... that favoured the long-term stability and growth of their enterprises to those that maximized short-term profits.' He omits Chandler's next sentence, which is more telling: 'For salaried managers the continuing existence of their enterprises was essential to their lifetime careers.'[2] It is some time since top managers, especially in the financial sector, have thought in terms of 'lifetime careers', especially as the tenure of a chief executive is growing ever shorter.

The failures of strategy and risk management suggest that the strategic management of banks has not been as rigorous in overseeing its business models as it might have been. There has been a perfect storm of a strategy-operations disconnect. The traditional model for banking was based on retail business, but a new investment bank model seems to have taken over.

A question was asked in an internal memo at Lehman Brothers, dated just weeks before the collapse of the bank: 'Why did we allow ourselves to be so exposed?'

According to Dick Fuld (in 2005), Lehman's then chief executive, the answer seems to have been: 'I expect everyone at the firm to be a risk manager. All 12 of us [*on the executive committee*] are focused on all parts of the business. It's all about risk management. If it's just me then we're in trouble.'[3]

Stern concludes his article that the banks were: 'Always chasing the next deal, too many businesses neglect the boring but crucial issue of management.' As Tom Stewart, the former *Harvard Business Review* editor and now chief marketing and knowledge officer for consultants Booz & Co, points out, the current financial crisis has its origins in plain bad management.

'It's no accident that Goldman Sachs – which of all the investment banks is the one that appears to value management most – has survived this crisis best,' he says. 'I bet that each of the players and victims in this credit crisis began to smell the rot in their mortgage-derivatives books at about the same time, within weeks, even days of each other. But who managed the crisis – and who just looked for a deal that would save the year?

'... Yes, greed is bad, and stupidity is bad, but bad management is worst of all.'[4]

The Royal Bank of Scotland

In March 2009, the Royal Bank of Scotland (RBS), announced the biggest corporate loss in British history, and the British Government was preparing to underwrite its (rather dodgy) assets to a value of £325 billion (the Government now holds a majority of the bank's shares). Much attention has been focused on the role of Sir Fred Goodwin, the former chief executive. Concerns have been raised about the culture that developed within the bank and the way in which decisions were made.

In 1998, when Sir Fred joined as deputy chief executive, the RBS was a modest Scottish high street bank: by 2008 it was the fifth largest bank in the world by market capitalization. Within three years Sir Fred had masterminded a takeover of the UK's largest retail bank, NatWest. By 2001 he was chief executive and the bank embarked on a series of acquisitions, including leveraged buyouts and had grown so that in 2008 it had lent more than £49.3 billion, more than double its nearest rival. The last high-profile acquisition was the Dutch bank, ABN Amro, in 2007.

The takeover involved a consortium of banks, including Santander of Spain, and the Belgo-Dutch Fortis group. ABN was broken up, with the RBS taking the American operations. Thus the bank had transformed itself over two decades from a provincial niche player, to a diversified global financial services provider. Its alliance with other banks, such as Spain's Bank of Santander, has enabled it to build an awareness of European banking with a minimal capital outlay. However, more recently, Sir Tom McKillop, who was the RBS chairman at the time, has described the investment as worthless.[5] Sir Tom had been chief executive of AstraZeneca, the UK's largest pharmaceutical company, from 1999 until 2005. He is a chemist and had no banking background, until he became chairman of the RBS.

The ABN acquisition at the time met with general acclaim from shareholders; the bank had outmanoeuvred its UK rival Barclays, which had wanted to buy ABN, and there was a feeling that the bank was repeating its success with NatWest.[6] But scepticism started to rise. 'There was a feeling that the bank had a very powerful CEO and the board couldn't stand up to him.'[7]

Sir Fred had put out statements saying that RBS do not do sub-prime, but traders were buying sub-prime assets. It is uncertain to what extent the board really knew what was happening.[8] RBS began buying up about $34 billion of sub-prime assets as US banks were off-loading the mortgages and RBS was unable to sell the assets on as planned.

There is evidence from the UK consumer magazine, *Which?,* that during this time almost half of bank retail customers were unhappy about the interest rates offered on their savings, and that the banks tried to sell them financial products that they did not wish to take on. There were other complaints about long queues in branches, high unauthorized bank charges, small print that is hard to understand, customer call centres located outside the UK, and the closure of local branches. It seems that the banks had become more interested in global growth than in their original core business.

Discussion questions

1. Consider if the global financial crisis owed a lot to bad management at an organizational level.
2. Can effective risk management live within a transformational and visionary organizational culture?
3. How important was leadership style at the Royal Bank of Scotland?

Case references

1. Stern, S. (2008) 'White House needs a competent manager', *Financial Times,* February 4.
2. Chandler, A. D. Jr. (1977) *The Visible Hand: The Managerial Revolution in American Business,* London: Belknap.
3. *Euromoney Magazine* (2005), July, reported in Stern (2009), *op cit.*
4. Sir Tom McKillop, House of Commons minutes of evidence, Treasury Committee, Banking Crisis, February 10, 2009.
5. Winnett, R. and Corrigan, T. (2009) 'RBS was disaster waiting to happen', *Daily Telegraph,* March 23.
6. Burgess, K. (2009) 'Culpability debate at RBS intensifies', *Financial Times*, January 20, 2.
7. Larsen, P. T. (2007) 'Aiming to repeat NatWest purchase trick', *Financial Times,* October 17, 26.
8. Winnet, R. (2009) 'RBS traders hid toxic debt', *Daily Telegraph*, March 23.

This case study was prepared using only publicly available sources of information for the purposes of classroom discussion; it does not intend to illustrate either effective or ineffective handling of a managerial situation.

Glossary

acquisition when one organization buys a controlling interest in another, with the aim of creating a larger entity, or with a view to restructuring the acquired organization to re-sell at a profit.

activity-based view of strategy a view that strategically-relevant (typically cross-functional) activities should be tailored to sustain strategy.

backroom leaders senior managers who are self-effacing and work to build up a disciplined organizational culture.

balanced scorecard (the) a documented set of objectives and measures expressed from the point of view of four key areas of organizational concern.

benchmarking: a comparison of an organization's practices with those of other organizations, in order to identify ideas for improvement and potentially useful practices, and sometimes to compare relative standards of performance.

best-cost differentiation hybrid generic strategy a customer-satisfaction-based strategy that meets expectations on key product and service attributes, while exceeding their expectations on price.

bounded rationality the extent to which making a fully rational decision is limited by complexity, lack of time and absent information.

brand a name or label that incorporates a visual design or image which is associated with a product, service or corporation, to differentiate it from others.

breakthrough objectives strategically-linked cross-functional objectives to which everybody contributes at a daily management level to advance a high priority organization-wide strategic objective. These are normally associated with the management of strategic change to achieve the organization's vision.

BRIC countries the countries Brazil, Russia, India and China, which are fast developing economies.

business ethics the universal morals that an organization works to.

business-level strategy the organization's fundamental strategic choice of what approach to adopt to achieve its competitive advantage from the given options at the business unit level.

business model the clarification of how the organization fundamentally manages its core business activities.

business process a sequence of tasks to deliver a business objective.

business process re-engineering (BPR) the re-designing of business processes.

capability review a form of strategic review at the daily management level, by senior managers to audit how the core areas of the organization are being managed; for example an audit might assess how the organization is developing and using its core competences.

catchball the agreement of draft plans between affected parties.

co-opetition when competing organizations also co-operate with each other.

commoditization the transfer of unsophisticated production and service units from advanced economies to developing countries where the cost of labour is low.

competitive advantage the reasons for an organization's ability to compete effectively with its rivals or potential rivals.

competitive forces the forces (or major impact factors) of the industry that affect the level of competition and management of strategy.

competitive strategy the view of Michael Porter about how competitive advantage is sustainable – this mainly requires close assessment of the impacts of the external environment.

complementarities activities where doing more of them increases the returns to doing other activities.

core capabilities distinctive organizational capabilities that are difficult for a rival to copy.

core competences the organization-specific abilities people have to work together, and use knowledge and learning to manage strategic resources in ways that create competitive advantage.

corporate identity a communicable expression of an organization's purpose.

corporate image an image of an organization held by its stakeholders.

corporate-level strategy a corporate centre's strategic management of a multi-divisional or multi-unit organization.

corporate parenting a corporate centre acts to nurture its dependent businesses to create a unique fit between the corporation's capabilities and the critical success factors of the individual businesses.

corporate social responsibility the view that large (especially international) organizations should fulfil a corporate (and world) citizen role.

corporate synergy a corporate performance that is greater than the sum of its parts.

cost-leadership generic strategy a cost-based strategy that involves having a lead in terms of lower costs per unit produced than the rest of the participants in the industry.

critical success factors (CSFs) the factors that primarily account for an organization's success in achieving its strategic purpose.

cross-functional horizontal management/structure (normally used to work across the functional divisions of an organization).

cultural fit where the organizational culture of an acquisition should be compatible with that of the acquiring company.

cultural web shows the manifestations of an underlying culture (or paradigm).

daily management is work carried out in those parts of the organization that are primarily about short-term operational and functional activity.

deliberate strategy a planned strategy that is designed by senior managers for implementation at other organizational levels.

delivery chain a concept in functionally based public administration that takes a broad view of how policies are implemented and maps out the chain of cause-and-effect for the participants concerned.

diagnostic objectives and measures these monitor the health of the organization to ensure it remains fit for purpose; they indicate whether the organization remains in control and can signal up the unusual events that require attention.

differentiation industry-wide generic strategy a strategy based on having unique, or different, product and service attributes, which other organizations in the industry do not have, and which generates returns that more than offset the costs of differentiation.

disruptive innovation a revolutionary product that replaces existing ways of competing.

diversification when an organization is active in different types of business area.

downscoping a divesture, spin-off, or some other means of eliminating businesses, which are unrelated or are not core to an organization's overall business or mission.

downsizing reduction in the size of a corporate entity.

dynamic capabilities processes that help ensure that the resource configurations of an organization are congruent with the changing external environment.

emergent strategy strategy that is not foreseen by senior management and which arises during the implementation of, and changes, deliberate strategy.

emotional intelligence an ability to recognize one's own emotions and those of others.

entrepreneurial leadership leadership characterized by the personality, usually of a single owner-manager, or sometimes of a few collaborating individuals, who impose their view on the business in ways that are characteristically innovative.

executive the senior level of an organization's management.

exploratory/exploitative learning terms used by March (1991) for the kinds of learning (based on feedback) an organization requires for different modes of change.

external environment: those conditions that influence the external changes in its industry, especially ones that influence the intensity of competition.

FAIR strategic performance management mobilizes an organization-wide effort to achieve four main things: focus, alignment, integration, and review.

forecasting a prediction of future trends and possible outcomes.

focus generic strategy strategy based on a particular part of an industry, such as a market segment or niche; this is based on either low cost or differentiation.

franchising is a contractual relationship between a parent organization (the franchiser) and its partners (franchisees) that specifies the control, sharing, and use of the franchiser's strategic resources.

functional management the management of work involving its division into specialist activities that are normally organized into departments, such as design, purchasing, operations, marketing, finance, human resources, IT, and so on.

General Electric/McKinsey matrix devised for GE by McKinsey, framework for managing a portfolio of corporate businesses, which are grouped according to a market's attractiveness, and the factors that affect the competitive strength of a business.

generic strategy a type of strategy to achieve a competitive advantage that is based either on cost or differentiation.

global-level strategy an organization's strategic management of its operations across multinational borders.

global strategy one of the four strategy approaches for global-level business; it is the use by organizations of a standardized product and service range to exploit markets in different countries.

globalization a phenomenon of changing commonalities and differences associated with a worldwide perception that the world is becoming smaller, similar and more inter-connected.

glocalization a combination of globalization and localization.

governance a non-executive function that ultimately decides purpose, critically appraises and approves a senior management's strategic management, its progress and results.

growth-share matrix the Boston Consulting Group's framework for managing a portfolio of corporate businesses, which are grouped according to their share of a market, and the growth of that market.

horizontal integration the growth of an organization by expanding its operations to offer complementary products and services, or to acquire a competitor with similar products and services.

hoshin a statement of a breakthrough strategic objective and its means.

hoshin kanri policy management – an organization-wide methodology for the deployment and management of a limited number of senior-level hoshins (strategic objectives and means).

hypercompetition a dynamic state of constant disequilibrium and change in the industry.

improvement change is focused on sustaining an existing business model.

improvement targets strategically-linked cross-functional objectives that people use to continuously improve performance in daily management. They are normally associated with the management of an organization's mission and the effectiveness of its business model.

industry life cycle the distinctive stages of the life of an industry's products and services.

inside-out these are influences on thinking about strategy that are primarily driven by internal conditions that are specific to the organization concerned.

international strategy one of the four strategy approaches for global-level business; it is the use by organizations of their strategic resources to exploit markets in different countries.

just-in-time management the management of production so that it responds to the needs of customers as and when the product or service is needed; it involves pulling all the components together, as and when they are needed in the production process.

key performance indicator (KPI) a strategically related incremental objective.

lagged measures (see measures).

lead measures (see measures).

leader a person who by influencing others has an ability to take the organization forward to a common purpose.

lean production a system for ensuring that wastage (or any non-value contributing activity) is eliminated in the production/management process.

leveraged buy-out a group of private investors buys a publicly quoted company in order to take the company private.

logical incrementalism the implementation of a deliberate strategy in small and logical steps.

m-form organization a multi-divisional organization.

Management by Objectives (MbO) the dispersal of objectives through an organization requiring the agreement of superiors and subordinates.

matrix structure units/projects report to more one than one division/unit.

McKinsey 7S framework a framework of seven inter-related variables for managing organizational change.

measures a quantified indicator of an objective: lagged measures are indicators of past performance, and lead measures are indicators of the enablers of future performance.

medium and mid-term plans statements of three to five year objectives (and sometimes with guidelines about means).

merger the agreement of two organizations to integrate their operations as a combined organization under common ownership.

middle management managers placed between the senior/executive and operational levels.

mission a statement of the organization's present main activities.

monitoring keeping a close check on the status and effectiveness of the use of a strategy.

multi-domestic strategy one of the four strategy approaches for global-level business; it is used by organizations to supply different products and services to different markets in different countries.

nemawashi the Japanese equivalent of Western catchball for consensus building.

networks informal groups of individuals, who are typically based in distinct and different parts of, and sometimes external to, the organization.

non-executive directors directors of a board with no involvement in the daily management.

non-profit sectors organizations which are not commercial organizations.

objective a statement of an outcome to be achieved.

organizational culture basic assumptions and beliefs shared by organizational members.

organizational governance direction given to an executive by owners and other stakeholders.

outside-in these are influences on thinking about strategy that are primarily driven by conditions in the external environment.

PDCA an acronym representing the Plan- Do-Check-Act cycle, which is a principle for good process management.

performance excellence models assessment frameworks that are used to audit good practice and performance in the key areas of the business.

performance measurement (management) quantification of purpose, progress, and results, in work (traditionally a human resource concern).

periodic strategic review formal reviews by senior managers of a unit's performance on its contribution to the organization's strategic objectives, normally to be able to authorize in good time any necessary corrective action (different from strategy review).

perspectives different points of view used in the balanced scorecard to specify objectives and measures.

PESTEL a mnemonic framework to understand factors that are Political, Economic, Social, Technological, Environmental, and Legal.

project an organized and finite series of activities that is finite.

purpose the primary and basic reason for the existence of the organization.

quality defined in TQM by customer requirements.

regulation the control of an organization or industry in which an adequate level of competition does not exist, normally by specially established governmental bodies to protect the interest of the public against monopolistic abuse.

related diversification different products and services in distinct business areas, but these are in related markets and/or industries.

resource-based view of strategy the school of strategy that believes competitive advantage is based on strategic resources – those resources that uniquely give an organization its competitive advantage.

review wheel an organization-wide integrated system of review.

satisificing the process of making a satisfactory decision that is sufficient to give a good enough result.

scanning an overview assessment of the external environment.

scenarios the evaluation of critical success factors for varying contexts and their outcomes.

SMART Specific, Measurable, Action-oriented, Realistic, Time-bound, used as criteria to evaluate the quality of objectives.

straddler an organization that competes on both sources of competitive advantage: cost and differentiation.

stakeholders individuals and groups who receive value from an organization.

strategic alliances and partnerships formal and informal associations and collaborations between independent organizations.

strategic architecture blueprint for an organizing framework that conditions how people work.

strategic business units (SBUs) autonomous single businesses within a corporate structure, with perhaps their own business-level generic strategy, distinctive organizational cultures and competencies.

strategic change transformational change that is focused on changing an existing business model.

strategic choices the options open to an organization in deciding on the strategy to adopt to achieve its purpose.

strategic control the overall control of the effectiveness of strategic management, including both longer and shorter-term components, which is driven by an organization-wide integrated system of review.

strategic groups groups of organizations in an industry that share similar competitive characteristics.

strategic intent a very ambitious and seemingly unrealistic long-term organizational goal used by Japanese firms.

strategic leaders leaders who are dispersed across the organization, who influence and empower others to participate in strategic management.

strategic leadership the strategic management of the POSIES model as an integrated system of strategic control, that takes into account both long-term and shorter-term components of the model.

strategic levers four information-based systems that senior managers can use to lever an organization into a desired strategic position.

strategic management the management of an organization's overall purpose, in ways that ensure that the needs and enablers of the present are balanced with those of the future.

strategic map a pictorial assessment of the relative positions of strategic groups, used to assess and predict the possible strategic moves of competitors, and for the identification of strategic space.

strategic move a move of an organization in the direction that better achieves its longer-term strategy.

strategic objective and measures objectives and measures used to progress an organizational long-term vision.

strategic performance management a strategically managed system that enables a senior level to execute and manage strategic priorities in daily management.

strategic performance systems a strategically managed system to link management to strategy.

strategic planning the sequencing of strategic management decisions in advance by an executive or senior management.

strategic platform a basic design or technological system that provides opportunities for the provision of adapted and complementary products and services.

strategic re-structuring when an organization makes fundamental changes to change its set of businesses as a whole.

strategic resources are organizational assets, or attributes, which when combined in ways that are uniquely specific to an organization, constitute its competitive advantage. Strategic resources are not economic resources, because they are valuable only to the organization that uses them and they have no external value.

strategic reviews reviews of strategically-linked performance at a daily management level: they include both periodic strategic reviews and annual capability reviews, and while they feed into strategy reviews (of longer-term strategy) are different in terms of focus and scope.

strategic risk management a systematic and overall approach for managing those external events and trends that could seriously harm an organization's effectiveness for achieving its longer-term purpose.

strategic space a gap identified in the strategic group analysis of potential gain for an organization to move into.

strategizing an activity such as thinking about, formulating and crafting strategy to take account of reality and possibilities.

strategy an overall approach, or a general pattern of behaviour, for achieving an organization's purpose, including its strategic objectives.

strategic execution the management of implementation at a daily management level.

strategy implementation the putting in place of an organization's strategy.

strategy map a document used to think about a scorecard's perspectives, objectives and measures, which explores possible cause-and-effect relationships and the associated CSFs.

strategy review a review of longer-term purpose, objectives and strategy (different from strategic review).

structural break a fundamental and unpredictable event in the general environment, which is likely to require organizations to rethink their purpose and strategy.

structure the organization of effort into a coherent and working entity.

SWOT a mnemonic used to analyse an organization's Strengths, Weaknesses, Opportunities and Threats.

takeover an acquisition that is made when the target organization has not sought the acquiring organization's bid.

target a short-term objective that refers to a tactical or operational outcome.

technology platform a standardized technical system, over which an organization may have property rights, but it can be used by other organizations as a platform to develop their own products and services.

top executive audit (TEA) a senior level business-wide audit of how the organization is managing its strategic priorities.

total quality management (TQM) an organization-wide management philosophy for improving customer specified quality.

trade-off choosing to do one activity that involves a reduced ability to do another activity.

transactional leadership centred on mission and explicit management systems, which clarify expectations, agreements, and utilize constructive feedback about performance.

transformational leadership charismatic leadership which works to associate individual self-interest with the larger vision of the organization by inspiring people with a sense of collective vision.

transnational strategy one of the four strategy approaches for global-level business; it is used by organizations to exploit markets in different countries by using a mixture of multi-domestic and global strategies.

transformational change fundamental change to an organization's business model.

unrelated diversification contrasting products and services in different markets and industries that have little or no similarities.

value the satisfaction and benefits customers receive from buying and using products and services (it can also refer to the value that other stakeholders receive from the organization).

value chain an organization's value creating chain of strategically-relevant resources and activities.

value curve a depiction of how market rivals compete on relative value-creating attributes, such as price, delivery, quality, functional aspects, service and so on.

values the expected collective norms and behaviour of everybody in the organization; this may also include expectations about how people should manage and work together.

vertical integration the growth of an organization by expanding its operations along the distribution chain towards the ultimate customer, and/or along the supply chain towards the primary sources of supply.

vision a view of some desired future state or ideal for the organization.

visionary leadership a personalized form of strategic control that conditions organizational culture: it is based on a dominant leader's vision.

Index